Boricua Pop

SEXUAL CULTURES: New Directions from the Center for
Lesbian and Gay Studies
General Editors: José Esteban Muñoz and Ann Pellegrini

Times Square Red, Times Square Blue
Samuel R. Delany

Private Affairs: *Critical Ventures in the Culture of Social Relations*
Phillip Brian Harper

In Your Face: *9 Sexual Studies*
Mandy Merck

Tropics of Desire: *Interventions from Queer Latino America*
José Quiroga

Murdering Masculinities: *Fantasies of Gender and Violence
in the American Crime Novel*
Greg Forter

Our Monica, Ourselves: *The Clinton Affair and the National Interest*
Edited by Lauren Berlant and Lisa Duggan

Black Gay Man: *Essays*
Robert Reid-Pharr *Foreword by Samuel R. Delany*

Passing: *Identity and Interpretation in Sexuality, Race, and Religion*
Edited by María Carla Sánchez and Linda Schlossberg

The Queerest Art: *Essays on Lesbian and Gay Theater*
Edited by Alisa Solomon and Framji Minwalla

Queer Globalizations: *Citizenship and the Afterlife of Colonialism*
Edited by Arnaldo Cruz-Malavé and Martin F. Manalansan IV

Queer *Latinidad*: *Identity Practices, Discursive Spaces*
Juana María Rodríguez

Love the Sin: *Sexual Regulation and the Limits of Religious Tolerance*
Janet R. Jakobsen and Ann Pellegrini

Manning the Race: *Reforming Black Men in the Jim Crow Era*
Marlon B. Ross

Boricua Pop: *Puerto Ricans and the Latinization of American Culture*
Frances Negrón-Muntaner

Boricua Pop

Puerto Ricans and the Latinization of American Culture

FRANCES NEGRÓN-MUNTANER

New York University Press
New York and London

NEW YORK UNIVERSITY PRESS
New York and London
www.nyupress.org

© 2004 by New York University

Library of Congress Cataloging-in-Publication Data
Negrón-Mutaner, Frances.
Boricua pop : Puerto Ricans and the latinization
of American culture / Frances Negrón-Muntaner.
p. cm. — (Sexual cultures)
Includes bibliographical references and index.
ISBN 0–8147–5817–7 (acid-free paper) —
ISBN 0–8147–5818–5 (pbk. : acid-free paper)
1. Puerto Ricans—United States—Social life and customs.
2. Puerto Ricans—United States—Ethnic identity.
3. Puerto Ricans—United States—Intellectual life. 4. Arts,
Puerto Rican—United States—. 5. Popular culture—United States.
6. United States—Social life and customs. 7. United States—
Civilization—Hispanic influences. 8. United States—Relations—
Puerto Rico. 9. Puerto Rico—Relations—United States.
10. Shame—Social aspects—United States. I. Title. II. Series.
E184.P85N44   2004
305.868'7295073—dc22   2003025217

New York University Press books are printed on acid-free paper,
and their binding materials are chosen for strength and durability.

Manufactured in the United States of America

c 10 9 8 7 6 5 4 3 2 1
p 10 9 8 7 6 5 4 3 2 1

Contents

Acknowledgments   vii

Preface   xi

Part I Founding Spectacles

1   Weighing In Theory: Puerto Ricans and American Culture   3

2   1898: The Trauma of Literature, the Shame of Identity   33

3   Feeling Pretty: *West Side Story* and U.S. Puerto Rican Identity   58

Part II *Boricuas* in the Middle

4   From Puerto Rico with *Trash*:
    Holly Woodlawn's *A Low Life in High Heels*   87

5   The Writing on the Wall:
    The Life and Passion of Jean-Michel Basquiat   115

6   Flagging Madonna: Performing a Puerto Rican–American Erotics   145

Part III *Boricua* Anatomies

7   Rosario's Tongue:
    Rosario Ferré and the Commodification of Island Literature   179

8   Barbie's Hair:
    Selling Out Puerto Rican Identity in the Global Market   206

9   Jennifer's Butt:
    Valorizing the Puerto Rican Racialized Female Body   228

10 Ricky's Hips: The Queerness of Puerto Rican "White" Culture   247

    Postscript: Words from the Grave   273

    Notes   279

    Index   329

    About the Author   337

Acknowledgments

This book would not have been possible in any shape or form without the love and intellectual support of my parents, Ada Muntaner and Mariano Negrón, scholars in their own right. I am especially thankful to my sister, Marianne Mason, now a professor at Georgia Institute of Technology, for her rigorous comments on the manuscript. If she had also not threatened to finish her own dissertation first, I may have taken much longer in completing this book. Many thanks to my *cuñado,* Christopher Triana, for taking time to go on book hunts with me at the University of Miami, where he was a student and I was not.

My infinite gratitude goes to my dissertation committee, Bruce Robbins (chair), Mary Gossy, Pedro Cabán, and Chon Noriega, and to Josephine Diamond, director of the Program of Comparative Literature at Rutgers University. Thank you for your faith in my work and your many words of encouragement as I transformed the dissertation into a book. Special thanks to Bruce, who made me send the manuscript to New York University Press immediately and to series editors José Esteban Muñoz and Ann Pellegrini, who were early champions of the book.

I can probably never thank my friends and fellow travelers José Quiroga, Alberto Sandoval-Sánchez, and Christina Duffy Burnett enough, for their intellectual generosity and affection during the most trying of times. They also persuaded me to accept that I could not devote the rest of my life to revising this manuscript. My family also thanks them dearly.

When I could no longer look at the six inches of paper on my desk, I turned to the writer and editor extraordinaire Celeste Fraser Delgado, whose phenomenal skills made the book a much friendlier entry point into *boricua* pop territory. I am ever grateful.

On occasion I called upon George Chauncey, Steven Huang, Larry LaFountain, and Lybia Rivera with specific queries and they were always gracious and helpful; thank you. My gratitude also goes to Rosario Ferré, who kindly received me in her house and allowed me to interview her and later follow up with even more questions. Thanks to Ela Troyano and Shannon Kelley, both of whom assisted me in locating Holly Woodlawn, and thanks to Holly for her enthusiasm and interest in this project.

Thanks to my editor, Eric Zinner, his editorial assistant Emily Park, and managing editor Despina Papazoglou Gimbel at New York University Press. Only they know what I mean when I state that "their patience is saintly."

My many thanks also go to Yolanda Martínez-San Miguel and Eugenio Frías-Pardo for their energetic support. Eugenio's insistent phone calls asking me if I had already finished the book were some of the many forces of nature that made me finally close this chapter. The only thing that I can say about the support that Maggie de la Cuesta gave me is that I will make it up to her.

Earlier versions of the essays contained in this book appeared in other publications and I would like to acknowledge the journals and editors. "Jennifer's Butt" began as a dare to Chon Noriega, and it was first published in *Aztlán: A Journal of Chicano Studies* 22, no. 2 (fall 1997): 181–94, edited by Noriega. "Barbie's Hair," a continuation of my exploration of Puerto Rican public anatomies, appeared in *Latino/a Popular Culture,* edited by Michelle Habell-

Pallán and Mary Romero. "Feeling Pretty" first saw the light in *Social Text* at Bruce Robbins's suggestion. I also presented versions of "From Puerto Rico with *Trash*" and "Ricky's Hips" at Princeton University and the University of Michigan by invitation of Yolanda Martínez-San Miguel and Tomás Almaguer, respectively. Again, *mil gracias*.

Preface

What do you consider most humane? To spare someone shame.

—Friedrich Nietzsche

"There has never been," wrote the columnist Taki Theodoracopulos in the London-based journal the *Spectator,* "—nor will there ever be—a single positive contribution by a Puerto Rican outside of receiving American welfare and beating the system."[1] Deeply disgusted by the "fat, squat, ugly, dusky, dirty and unbelievably loud" people who disrupted his bagel breakfast during the 1997 National Puerto Rican Day Parade, Taki Tacky—as some Nuyorican intellectuals called him[2]—further declared that "Puerto Rican pride" was an oxymoron, only comparable with that of the city's other "ghastly" community: gays.[3]

Taki is of course mistaken in his historical analysis; Puerto Ricans have been a major force in the creation of significant cultural practices ("positive" or not), including U.S.–born ones such as *salsa,* hip hop, and Nuyorican poetry, and have been prominent participants in important social struggles against racial discrimination, police brutality, and educational segregation. But he is right about one thing: Puerto Ricans make a lot of "noise."

Puerto Ricans constitute less than 3 percent of the U.S. population, but the community's concerns in culture and politics are continuously making headlines. Between 1999 and 2001, President Clinton pardoned a dozen pro-independence political prisoners to a divided response among Puerto Ricans and to the distress of many in Congress.[4] Yet when his wife, Hillary Rodham, objected, still thinking that conservative white voters were worth more than Latinos in her race for the Senate, she felt the political muscle of one million Puerto Ricans—mostly Democrats—in the city of New York. As Congressman José Serrano (D-Bronx) bluntly put it, Puerto Ricans will "make sure that she's not our next senator."[5]

Rodham nearly bombed before she found a way to make up with Puerto Ricans and win the race. But the election results did not have as significant an effect on the representation of Puerto Rican–American relations as the death of David Sanes Rodríguez, a security guard working at a navy facility in the small island of Vieques, who died when two bombs accidentally hit his observation post. Political opportunism aside, the militant cry to get the navy out of *la isla nena* (the "baby island," a term of endearment used by Puerto Ricans to refer to Vieques) became the new political trope on the Big Island and the Big Apple, as well as occasion for an intense display of patriotic exhibitionism, widely indulged in by the news media.[6]

The Vieques scene was just one of many examples that represented Puerto Ricans in a different light on a world stage during the past few years. The Vatican, for instance, beatified native son Carlos Manuel "Charlie" Rodríguez, proving that Puerto Ricans are the *más* saintly; Denise Quiñones won the title of Miss Universe, to confirm that women from the Island are the *más* beautiful; and boxer Félix "Tito" Trinidad knocked out both "golden boy" Oscar de la Hoya and William Joppy to show that Puerto Rican men were the *más* machos.

Most spectacular of all, a constellation of pop stars burst on the global scene, the brightest among them Ricky Martin, Marc Anthony, and Jennifer López. Even if reluctantly at times, these entertainers made their Puerto Rican identity an important part of their star personas and at times conspired to raise the value attributed to *boricuas* in American culture. After decades of being ignored or humiliated by government institutions and the mass media, *boricuas* (the indigenous name many Puerto Ricans call themselves in a nativist gesture to indicate the end of colonial subordination and the beginning of a still politically undefined new era) finally seemed to be blessed by God, civilization, and *Billboard* magazine.

Unlike most empathetic commentators, however, I do not offer this list of *boricua* accomplishments to simply promote pride in place of Taki's disgust. Rather, this book aims to understand *why* and to *what effects* our attempts to value ourselves as Puerto Ricans have so frequently been staged through spectacles to offset shame. In raising shame, I am not arguing that all *boricua* exchange can be explained by this trope, but instead that modern Puerto Rican ethnic and national *identity* has been historically narrated or performed by tropes of shame and displays of pride.

By speaking to—and from—the shame of Puerto Rican identity, I do not mean to invoke the reductive terminology of an "inferiority complex," which assumes that shame is a characteristic of the individual (or the "social" as an amalgam of individuals) and can somehow be treated with therapy. I will instead theorize shame as constitutive of social identities generated by conflict within asymmetrical power relations, not privatized pathologies. For "the forms taken by shame," as Eve Kosofsky Sedgwick argues, "are not distinct 'toxic' parts of an identity that can be excised; they are instead integral to and residual in the processes by which identity itself is formed."[7] In fact, if it were not for the "shame" of being Puerto Rican, there would be no *boricua* identity, at least not as we know it.

The specific ways *boricuas* have been constituted by shame are not, however, the same, nor do they have identical effects. The shame of the privileged tends to be performed as "disgrace-shame," a sense of having done wrong by not living up to their own anticolonial principles and/or being confused with Puerto Ricans of a lower status by others deemed equal or superior.[8] The shame of the *boricua* majority (popular) is associated with what Carl D. Schneider calls "discretion-shame," an affect that "sustains our personal and social ordering of the world" by delimiting sacred spaces that are proscribed to us not only as Puerto Ricans, but as workers, blacks, women, queers, and/or migrants.[9]

Since the Puerto Rican elites represent themselves as normative subjects— white, sovereign, endowed—their strategies to offset shame tend to require simulacrum and denial. As the early-twentieth-century writer Bernardo Vega observed, better-off *boricuas* in New York would try to "pass" as Spaniards while workers "were not afraid of being called 'spiks.' They did not deny their origin."[10] Although not at all times, popular performances are more likely to ebb out in the enjoyment or display of their lacking selves, including transgressive symbolic acts or bodily violence.

These distinctions are of course theoretical, as both forms of shame will often be congealed in the same cultural objects and exhibited by dissimilar subjects. "Elite" subjects on the axis of class, for instance, can be feminine, queer, or racialized, whereas "low" subjects on the axis of race can be highly educated and hence act upon their identities (and interests) in intricate ways. Yet the fact that all Puerto Ricans are constituted as colonial subjects, however differentiated, has resulted in a common and sometimes painfully heightened awareness of being—or potentially being confused with—a spic.

Consequently, *boricua* cultural production is largely made up of the desire to purge, flaunt, deny, destroy, resignify, and transfigure the constitutive shame of being Puerto Rican from our bodies and public selves. Shame, as Sedgwick elaborates, is also a "kind of free radical" that "attaches to and permanently intensifies or alters the meaning of almost anything: a zone of the body, a sensory system, a prohibited or indeed a permitted behavior, another affect such as anger or arousal, a named identity, a script for interpreting other people's behavior toward oneself."[11]

As shame is simultaneously the "affect of indignity, of defeat, of transgression, and of alienation" through which the subject feels "lacking in dignity or worth,"[12] the *boricua* bodies re-membered here give face to shame under multiple guises, depending on the subject's class, racial, gender, sexual, and migratory histories. The book's emphasis on the body is not fortuitous. Shame is not only the affect most associated with the face, but as Susan Miller argues, it is also "invariably linked to a body concern," as pride is constituted by "matters of body investment"—of how we become socially visible as subjects.[13]

Boricua Pop then looks at the most conspicuous of Puerto Ricans—movie stars, artists, and entertainers—to see how these bodies are being shown and showing off. By collecting the detritus of mass culture, the book pieces together the public "biographies" of (professional) cultural performers to show not only the role of shame in constituting *boricua* identity, but also how seeing and being seen contribute to its attenuation or resignification.[14] Each of *Boricua Pop*'s chapters hopes to offer a different gift to this poetics and reconstitutes a "grotesque" (or as Taki might say, a "ghastly") Puerto Rican body brought forth literally (and often literarily) by shame.

In order to account for Puerto Rican performances to offset shame in popular and high culture, *Boricua Pop* opens with three chapters gathered under the heading of "Founding Spectacles." The introductory chapter describes two of the most salient historical junctures by which Puerto Rican identity has been constituted as shameful: the 1898 invasion of Puerto Rico by the United States and mass migration to the mainland. A closing section of chapter 1 explores how the political, symbolic, and economic devaluation experienced by Puerto Ricans as colonial subjects has sought release in political performances as well as mass-mediated spectacles.

Following the introduction are two chapters that analyze how the invasion and mass migration have found a privileged articulation in Island high culture and American popular culture respectively. Chapter 2 discusses how the shame of Puerto Rican identity became the trauma of nation-building literature. Special emphasis is granted to the faux historical chronicle *Seva* (1983), by Luis López Nieves, which narrates that Puerto Ricans in fact—and contrary to historical accounts—did resist the U.S. invasion of the island, and the short story "1898," by Edgardo Sanabria Santaliz, one of the few Island literary texts that acknowledge shame as a constitutive feature of Puerto Rican national identity.

In chapter 3 I will examine the most important cultural product to hail *boricuas* as devalued American "ethnic" subjects, the Broadway show (1957) and film *West Side Story* (1961), directed by Jerome Robbins and Robert Wise. Without denying its long-term effects on representing Puerto Ricans in the United States as racialized others, I propose to review *West Side Story* as a queer film, in which the social and sexual desires of Jewish gay men were performed by means of *boricua* bodies, anticipating the current juncture of cultural Latinization in certain hierarchical terms. In rewinding *West Side Story*, I will also argue that the film succeeded not in excluding Puerto Ricans from "America" but in incorporating *boricuas* to the national imagination in a specific way: superficially black, criminally stylish, and queerly masculine.

Part 2 includes three essays under the heading *"Boricuas* in the Middle." Two of these chapters are about Puerto Ricans who attempted to valorize their black and queer identities in the cultural marketplace at a time when only white performers and artists could fully accomplish this transaction. Specifically, chapter 4 examines the career of Warhol Superstar Holly Woodlawn, the transculturated drag star of the 1970 underground hit *Trash*. Chapter 5 focuses on Jean-Michel Basquiat's short life as the world's most famous Caribbean-American painter and his visual legacy of disarticulated black bodies.

The last chapter of part 2 discusses Madonna's successful commodification of New York Latino cultural practices and her performance of an erotics of transculturation that required racial hierarchies to be globally consumed. In approaching *boricua* practices as a product of transculturation, I am recalling, first, the Cuban anthropologist Fernando Ortiz's definition of transculturation as a process through which a new formation is created as a result of cross-cultural contact,[15] and second, Mary Louise Pratt's narrower definition, which further elaborates on the ways subaltern groups "select and invent from materials transmitted to them by a dominant or metropolitan culture."[16]

Part 3, "*Boricua* Anatomies," highlights how the shame of Puerto Rican identity can lodge itself in specific body parts, even when the bodies displaying it are greatly appreciated cultural commodities showing off pride. In chapter 7, the writer Rosario Ferré gives up the prestige of her native tongue by publishing three novels written originally in English for the globalized literary market. In chapter 8 the question of what kind of hair—"good" or "bad"—*boricua* bodies should exhibit in public is raised by the conflicted reception on the Island and across the mainland to a "fake" *boricua* that also embodies a distinctly American icon—Puerto Rican Barbie.

Chapters 9 and 10 discuss the obsessive attention to the actress Jennifer López's buttocks, widely seen and debated after she starred in the Hollywood film *Selena* (1997), and the entertainer Ricky Martin's "queer" hips as a way to discuss how Puerto Ricans are *differently* racialized in the pop culture marketplace, and how the perception of queerness affects their circulation as commodities. A postscript reconsiders the limits of culture as a political trope centered on the diffusion of national shame.

In making this offering, I am aware of the risk I have taken. Addressing shame is in itself shameful, and likely to stir powerful emotions. Yet studying shame as a socially constituted affect is part of valorizing subaltern groups and recovering that which shame tends to inhibit—interest in the world and enjoyment. Equally important, if contempt has often been the affect of Americans as (white) "nationals" when facing the groups they have devalued, rallying our shame has been an important strategy for social change.

As I write this, I can still, for instance, hear the chants of Act Up, one of the most vital organizations produced by the AIDS crisis during the 1980s, chanting "shame, shame, shame" to those who were indifferent to the epidemic because of the low value attributed to gay men and racialized minorities. An illness that also connoted sexuality, poverty, race, drug use, and the wasting away of the body, AIDS was deemed shameful at multiple levels. But the transfiguration of the bearer's shame into art, political action, and community building saved the lives of many by facing straight on the question of whose shame it was that HIV-positive people were dying.

Always engaged in an effort to—as *West Side Story* would have it—feel pretty, *boricua* bodies are persistently negotiating their shameful constitution, refashioning the looks that aim to humiliate or take joy away from them. At the same time, it is impossible to deny that our most vital cultural production as *boricuas* has sprung not from the denial of shame, but from its acknowledgment into wounds that we can be touched by. While shame, like any self-awareness, is painful, it is no less true that as the affect of reflexivity and self-discovery, it is a precondition to transformation and hope.[17]

Boricua Pop

Part I Founding Spectacles

1 Weighing In Theory

Puerto Ricans and American Culture

We are neither American Me nor American You.
> —ALARMA Manifesto, Los Angeles

Shame is at the core of most cultures' origin myths, and in this sense it is not particular to *boricuas*.[1] Puerto Ricans are also not the only "American" subjects whose identities have been crossed by shame; arguably all other racialized groups and queers are to different effect. Yet unlike African American identity or lesbian identity, for instance, modern Puerto Rican ethno-national identity has been constituted in shame as a result of a transnational history of colonial domination in the Caribbean and the contradictory ways *boricuas* have negotiated with a metropolis at once contemptuous and ostensibly benevolent.

The most patent sign of Puerto Rican specificity is that the high-flying flag of *boricua* pride does not represent a sovereign nation or even the will to found a truly separate nation-state. Regardless of whether they overtly support independence, statehood, or limited sovereignty, the three main parties in Puerto Rico envision different states of cultural autonomy with economic and political ties to the United States. Puerto Ricans, particularly on the Island, tend to style themselves as "nationalists"—unequivocally upholding

3

that Puerto Rico is a nation—without actually desiring to be "nationals" of an independent country. At the same time, a slim majority of the population—approximately 53 percent—also rejects becoming a state of the Union.[2]

For over a century, the majority of Puerto Ricans have in fact pursued a political strategy that avoids becoming fully subjected to any *one* nation. Instead, most seek to partake in the metropolis's wealth and prestige—to "be part of the richest, most powerful country in the world"[3]—while affirming themselves as a *culturally* distinct nation from the United States. *Boricuas* invest in Puerto Rican "culture"—a sign of ethnicity and nationhood—as a different measure of value comparable to but unlike capital and distinctly their "own," not the property of the metropolis.

Puerto Ricans have imagined themselves as national subjects through culture for historical, symbolic, and political reasons. Historically, the "Americanization" campaign waged primarily through the public school system during the first four decades of U.S. rule explicitly made local cultural practices a target of transformation, including the Island vernacular, Spanish. As the political scientist Henry Wells observed, "Far from recognizing the dignity of the Puerto Rican people and the worth of their culture, American Senators and representatives had seemed to be interested only in forcing Puerto Rican school children to learn English."[4] The eagerness with which many *boricuas* spoke about studying English immediately after the invasion indicates, however, that language became an important site of struggle as a *result* of conflict, not as a "natural" desire.

Symbolically, because the overt cultural Americanization project failed yet U.S. political elites and corporate interests continue to dominate core aspects of Puerto Rican life, most view the survival of a different cultural identity as the greatest *political* victory in the face of colonialism. The condensation of much agency through cultural discourse and interventions in music, art, literature, and sports also signifies an unwillingness to contest subordination through terms that are unfavorable to Puerto Ricans and a tendency to participate in joyful social practices. Not coincidentally, the richness of *boricua* cultural production and discourse is, to a great extent, a result of the constraints placed upon Puerto Rican economic and political agency.

Politically, speaking through culture is a strategy for saving face and asserting alternative values. Since sectors of the U.S. political elites have consistently met *boricua* claims for full incorporation as a state with contempt, the emphasis on culture as a "national" resource has been critical in diffusing the shame of U.S.-Puerto Rico relations. Moreover, the repetition of encounters with Americans in which Puerto Ricans were degraded gave way to a sense of being "special,"[5] set apart by suffering and deserving of certain privileges by virtue of having suffered. This "specialness" has been explicitly coded in "cultural" terms and acts as a mask, a symptom of a fracture that also protects the wearers from vulnerability.[6]

An early example of culture as a mask can be found in a message from the insular legislature given to Charles Lindbergh when the pilot landed on the island in 1928. In it, Puerto Ricans demanded "the freedom that you [Americans] enjoy, for which you struggled, which you worship, which we deserve, and you have promised us." The reason to grant such a request is that *boricuas* constitute a "people jealous of their origin and history, inflexible in their personality, and indeclinably defending their liberty and their rights."[7] Within the context of uneven power relations between colonial and metropolitan elites, where other avenues of agency seemed blocked or entailed humiliation, "culture" became the speaking subject of Puerto Rican political discourse.

By dreaming up the nation as primarily a distinct "culture," most Puerto Ricans have purposefully bypassed many of the traditional strategies employed by subordinated groups trying to rid themselves of direct colonial control: appeal to metropolitan public opinion, military insurgency, and infrastructure sabotage. Consequently, modern *boricuas* do not conform to a normative national formation but a "cultural subject," an ethno-nation. In using the term "ethno-nation," I aim to call attention to the ways Puerto Ricans are hailed and imagine themselves as a "people," understood alternately as an "ethnicity" (defined by a specific culture across national-state bound-aries) and a "nationality" (defined in relationship to a specific territory, with full or partial claims to independent sovereignty).[8]

The term "ethno-nation" also incorporates the diaspora in theorizing *boricua* cultural practices and political agency. Puerto Ricans in the United States have been historically constituted as an "American" racialized group, and have often contested this subaltern location as ethnic subjects. From the founding of early working-class organizations such as the Porto Rican Broth-erhood of America (1923) to ASPIRA (1961) and the Young Lords in New York (1967–1968), political objectives in the United States have been articulated in ethno-national terms, with a strong emphasis on "ethnic defense" strate-gies that have consistently valued *boricua* culture as a political resource[9] and generative of nonlegalistic conceptions of citizenship.[10]

Less than a single "culture" in the anthropological sense, what contem-porary *boricuas* often share are common sites of "colonial" shame and re-sources to counter them, no matter how shifting or elusive the investments, memories, aesthetics, and aspirations attached to those sites are. While mod-ern Puerto Rican ethno-national identity is not a simple effect of colonialism (understood to encompass not only political domination but also economic restructuring, interclass conflict, and symbolic violence), as a socially mean-ingful sign, *boricuaness* has been constituted *through* and *from* these con-straints. In other words, *boricuas* do not freely choose to affirm themselves as Puerto Rican or American; they are, as the sociologist Kelvin Santiago-Valles writes, "the effect of a subjection much more profound than themselves."[11]

The ethno-nation hence exceeds the Island's official status as a common-wealth (purposely mistranslated into Spanish as Estado Libre Asociado or ELA, literally a free associated state) and the specific ideology of the party that founded it. Established in 1952 under the Popular Democratic Party led by Luis Muñoz Marín, the ELA allowed the United States to relieve interna-tional pressure to "decolonize" Puerto Rico while still retaining control over the Island. Even though Puerto Rico remains a colony, the ELA provided a higher standard of living for the working class, transferred control of key Island institutions to the local elites, and co-opted many pro-independence supporters to run them.

The ELA also allowed the U.S. political elites to diffuse their own shame as colonial rulers internationally. American officials frequently articulated that they were not only respecting the wishes of the people of Puerto Rico, but shedding the stain of being an "imperial nation" as well. According to the U.S. assistant secretary of state for inter-American affairs, "In view of the importance of 'colonialism' and 'imperialism' in Anti-American propaganda, the Department of State feels that [the Puerto Rican constitution] would have great value as a symbol of the basic freedom enjoyed by Puerto Rico, within the larger framework of the United States."[12] Even as most U.S. decision makers may not have cared about the consequences of U.S. policy on Puerto Ricans, other nationals whom they perceived as equals did, and their judgmental gaze contributed to change.

Likewise, the ELA allowed the pro-*autonomista* and some pro-independence sectors to symbolically flush out their shame as ethno-national subjects and (junior) partners in the colony's enjoyment by *simulating* the founding of a "nation." This nation, however, lacks political sovereignty, its own armed forces, citizenship, currency, a custom system, and power to subscribe to any sort of trade agreement with other countries, but comes complete with a national past, national subjects, a national ruling class, a national culture, and eligibility for Olympic glory and the Miss Universe title. It is the precarious and ambivalent way the nation is imagined and lived—not its intrinsic coherency or common political project—that accounts for the "empirical fact" that Puerto Ricans consistently display "one of the highest indexes of national pride in the world."[13]

The way Puerto Ricans have to date insisted on casting themselves as "national" subjects is, however, itself a strategy of valorization. If in the post–World War II era the Western-style nation-state became the global "norm," the highest aspirations of a colonial people could only be to "have" a nation of its own. Symbolically speaking, the majority of Puerto Ricans would not be an exception in wishing to be "positively" engendered—to possess a *patria*—even if the outcome is that of a queer nation, distinguished by cultural pride and not phallic might,[14] or in the public intellectual Antonio S. Pedreira's terms, a nation "without profound heroic epics, without substantial historical manifestations."[15]

Despite the "rationality" of the commonwealth, a colonial arrangement that has provided higher wages than most Latin American sovereign states, unhindered access to mainland ports, and cultural "independence," being incorporated to the United States as largely consensual colonial subjects has inevitably rendered Puerto Rican national identifications *constitutively* shameful. As the psychologist Silvan Tomkins argues, "the same positive affect which ties the self to the object also ties the self to shame."[16] This ambivalent constitution has even been enshrined in the date chosen to found the ELA, July 25, which simultaneously recalls the U.S. invasion of the Island and the inauguration of the commonwealth.

In this sense, although becoming an independent republic or a state of the Union will not result in the "liberation" of Puerto Ricans from all shameful affects or even colonial domination, cognitively speaking, *boricuas* will be differently constituted *as* ethno-national subjects only if they risk themselves in the pursuit of social desires that may entail death, a "death" that in the context of contemporary politics in Puerto Rico has been defined as either loss of culture (statehood) or loss of access to metropolitan wealth (independence). While negotiating for further economic benefits without demanding political rights and/or showing off cultural pride remain the most essential Puerto Rican identity-affirming practices, *boricuaness* will continue to be reproduced in relation to "American" nationalist and capitalist discourses of what is moral and good, a defining entanglement impossible to undo.

Consensually Queer:
Shame and Purely Puerto Rican "National" Identity

The constitution of Puerto Rican ethno-national identification as shameful, however, did not begin with the founding of the ELA. It did not even start when the United States invaded Puerto Rico on July 25, 1898, during the Spanish-American War, an expansionist project that stretched from the Caribbean to the Philippines. Rather, for broad sectors of the elites—who have historically been the most concerned with constituting Puerto Ricans as national subjects—it is to be located in the last third of the nineteenth century, when Puerto Rico was still a Spanish colony.

The majority of the *criollo* elites during this period frequently acknowledged the shame of their subaltern position under the Spanish regime while seeking self-rule. As a discourse of ambivalent counterhegemony, the elites narrated the shame of their political subordination as a result of the many indignities inflicted on Puerto Ricans by the European metropolis, including slavery, racism, economic hardship, torture, exile, and censorship. Shame also arose in public discourse about Cuba, Spain's most valued colony in the Caribbean, as Puerto Rico was assigned a doubly degraded role ("el papel de segundón") in relation to the larger—and explicitly more desirable—island.[17]

Routinely, political concessions to the "people" of Puerto Rico (which primarily meant the educated, landowning, and merchant sectors) by the Spanish colonial government during this period originated in attempts to redress Cuban grievances, often with a humiliating twist. In 1892, for instance, Spain reduced the Cuban electoral quota—an annual tax that qualified voters—to entice the *autonomistas* to participate in politics. Whereas the amount was also reduced in Puerto Rico, it was still twice as much as the more populous island's quota. Even more distressing, Overseas Minister Antonio Maura Montaner did not have any qualms in explaining the difference by stating that in contrast to the Cubans, Puerto Ricans were "third class citizens" of the Empire, and thus should be content with the improvement.[18]

9

Despite the continuous political and economic humiliation suffered by Puerto Ricans under Spain, when word came that an anticolonial revolution—not simply a riot—had broken out in Cuba in 1895, the mostly reformist *criollos* expressed their full support to the Spanish metropolis, out of fear that the triumph of the Cuban *insurrectos* (rebels) could ruin their own hard-fought autonomist reforms and result in retaliation. It is during this turbulent period, between the reigniting of the Cuban War of Independence and the Spanish-American War, that shame intensified as a key ethno-nationalist trope and affect for sectors of the pro-autonomist Puerto Rican elites. At the precise hour of Cuban "shame" as "traitors" to the Spanish crown, the *autonomistas* seized the moment to finally shine brighter in the eyes of the mother country: "There is but one detail that can establish the difference between the two Antilles," claimed the powerful *criollo* newspaper *La Democracia*, "our eternal meekness; our faithfulness of four centuries. We do not have nor do we care to have the practice, let anyone say what they may against us . . . of seizing the machete and going to the countryside to battle for our rights."[19]

Casting themselves as the reverse of the rebellious *mambises* (Cuban revolutionaries), the usually restrained *criollos* gave their all in a political performance of servility aimed at Madrid, to prove that Puerto Ricans were still the most "loyal" of the Antilleans, hence the most deserving of reforms. Through newspaper commentary, street chatter, and in some cases even fighting in the Spanish military, the *criollos* were bent on "saving" (mother) Spain's honor from the ungrateful Cubans, as a way to protect their interests, provide proof of their honor (manhood), and liberate themselves from the favored island's long shadow: "Puerto Ricans," read a local daily's editorial, "will at last give Cuba a lesson and save Spain from this embarrassment."[20]

While flattering, such spectacle of consensual colonialism would prove Spain's undoing; when the time came to defend the mother country, the "faithful" Puerto Ricans would not get their machetes up. Even though the *criollos* had just won the most favorable political arrangement (the Carta Autonómica) in the history of Spanish colonialism in Puerto Rico only six months earlier, the self-described meek *boricuas*—sympathetically called "insurgents" by the New York press—opted to embarrass the "mother country" by embracing the invaders with open arms.[21]

Influential Puerto Ricans gladly offered to assist the invaders, and many Islanders facilitated the bloodless taking of towns, contributing (by obscuring what happened elsewhere) to the still prevalent myth of the Spanish-Cuban-Filipino-American wars between 1895 and 1904 as a "splendid little war." Peasant and working-class Puerto Ricans also strove to show the newcomers that they were welcome by hoisting the American flag and warmly greeting soldiers en masse. As W. C. Payne, an African American soldier, recalls, "Some of them asked me on sight: 'Are you Porto Rican?' I answered: 'Americano.' They replied, 'Viva Los Americano.' I answered, 'Viva Los Porto Rico Libre,' and they cheered for the United States."[22]

Due to the mother country's humiliating defeat—suitably called "the disaster" in Madrid—Spaniards were among the first to expose the "unbecoming" performance of Puerto Ricans as (former) Spanish subjects. The outrage felt by many Spaniards is colorfully expressed by Julio Cervera Baviera, who wrote, "I have never seen such a servile, ungrateful country. . . . In twenty-four hours, the people of Puerto Rico went from being fervently Spanish to enthusiastically American. . . . They humiliated themselves, giving in to the invader as the slave bows to the powerful lord."[23] While a few observers like Francisco R. de Goénaga understood the response as that of a "suffering country . . . slapped in the face in a thousand different ways, its honor reviled, its generosity disregarded,"[24] most Spaniards on record viewed the Puerto Rican show not as an effect of the shame of *their* ungenerous rule, but as the crass baseness of Puerto Ricans themselves, a characterization that *boricua* nationalists eventually came to share to an ambivalent extent.

Puerto Rico's seemingly baffling response, however, had roots in the growing investment of *boricua* political and economic hopes in American agency during the late nineteenth century. Deep in the bowels of the Puerto Rico section of the Cuban Revolutionary Party located in New York City, for instance, many exiles sought independence from Spain and subsequent annexation to the United States. This position articulated the all too recent memories of state violence during the "terrible year of 1887," when Spanish authorities persecuted, exiled, and even tortured pro-autonomist advocates, and by the economic realities of Puerto Rico as a peninsular colony during this period.

Only a year before the invasion, 60.6 percent of Puerto Rican sugar, as well as almost all of the Island's molasses, was exported to the United States. American corporations also supplied local landowners machinery for planting and harvesting the Island's major crops, coffee and sugar.[25] Moreover, the late nineteenth century marks the beginnings of a diaspora community in New York, diversely composed of merchants, factory and field workers, students, and political activists, whose ambivalent admiration for the United States would inform how other Puerto Ricans saw this "colossus of the north."[26]

Shamelessly optimistic after the invasion, the elites presented Puerto Rican *popular* pliancy as a recommendation for self-rule. Luis Muñoz Rivera, who had been the secretary of state under the Carta Autonómica, told the *New York Tribune* in 1898, "It is my opinion that my country can govern and administer itself, and that is what all *criollos* aspire to. There are very competent sectors to lead and a docile people that seconds them."[27] In spite of these displays of affection and assurances of docility (or more accurately, in part because of what they exposed), the United States Congress denied Puerto Ricans self-government by first imposing a military administration and later a civilian government under direct American control through the Foraker Act of 1900.

The Foraker Act not only robbed the pro-autonomist elites of their aspirations to full local rule, it also signified this sector's loss of power over the representation and political goals of the working classes and the peasantry. Either indifferent to or at times explicitly throwing their lot in with the U.S. colonizers, the Puerto Rican majority pursued their own political strategies to affirm themselves in the new order, including direct peasant retaliation against landowners, militant labor organizing against corporate interests regardless of nationality, and strategic urban violence aimed at those who were perceived to either represent the old regime or oppose the new one. At one rowdy urban gathering in February 1901, for instance, the main leader of the *turbas republicanas,* a San Juan–based pro-American organization, ran through the streets impersonating Luis Muñoz Rivera while dressed as a "loca," a madwoman or transvestite. "The shouts of the paraders were typical," writes the historian Mariano Negrón-Portillo, "'Long live the peoples' [*sic*] rights! 'Down with the despots!' And obviously . . . they also screamed, 'Death to the *'loca.'*"[28]

The new colonial administrators sided with the *turbas* on this matter, and dismissed not only the elites but also all of the Islanders as unmanly and hence not fit for U.S. citizenship. Congressman Henry Teller, a champion of (at least nominal) sovereignty for Cuba, explicitly rejected the proposition that Puerto Ricans become citizens by casting *boricuas* as "queer" Cubans: "I don't like the Puerto Rican; they are not fighters like the Cubans; they were subjugated to Spanish tyranny for hundreds of years without being men enough to oppose it. Such a race is unworthy of American citizenship."[29] In comparing the Puerto Ricans with the Cubans, the American colonial administrators and policy makers—like the Spaniards before them—again found *boricuas* "lacking," reinforcing the larger island's role as one of several fun house mirrors to see Puerto Rican ethno-national identity as queer in the sense of both odd (nonnormative) and effeminate (weak, cowardly).[30]

From the enduring affect of American contempt necessary to pursue colonial economic and political interests, *boricua* agency, be it enthusiasm for the metropolis, demands for self-government, or democratic cravings, invariably came to confirm inferiority, represented in both racial and gendered (or better still, *racially engendered*) terms. Senator Albert J. Beveridge, for instance, justified the colonial project on the Island precisely in those terms, as an American mission to bring about the "disappearance of debased civilizations and decaying races before the higher civilization of the nobler and more virile types of men."[31]

What then made "1898" shameful for the *criollo* elites was not that Puerto Rico was invaded, although this provided a verifiable event that would later be central in narrating Puerto Rican national identity as constituted in shame (see chapter 2). Rather, shame became a key trope and affect due to several unforeseen outcomes that reconstituted Puerto Ricans as ethno-national subjects in terms different from those under the Spanish regime. While the shame of the Island's politics under the Spanish constituted *boricuas* as the victims of a wicked "mother" with whom, however, they shared a common language, culture, and past, in the aftermath of the war, it was *criollo* action—or lack of it—in relation to a potential yet alien "father" that brought about shame.

Prominently, most *criollos* did not only sympathize with the invaders, they also exhibited a spectacular desire to become part of the Union, which was largely perceived as a means to obtain self-rule. This request, however, was brutally dismissed by the U.S. governing elites and public opinion. American contempt made the collaborating *criollos* ashamed instead of angry because they were already invested in the United States and expected great advantages from this association, an expectation that was even evoked during the invasion when General Nelson Miles promised that his troops were in Puerto Rico not to "make war on the people of the country" but to bring "all the advantages and blessings of enlightened civilization."[32]

The humiliation of the *criollos,* however, became constitutive only when, even after American contempt was unequivocal toward Puerto Ricans, far from fighting "honorably" (as "men") for independence as happened in areas of the Philippines, the *criollos* negotiated with, instead of militarily attacking, the United States. This strategy also fed into the metropolis's hardened assumption of the entire population's inferiority, represented through tropes of femininity and infantilization, while it legitimized the Puerto Rican majority's challenges to the *criollos* through "shameless"—that is, purposefully disrespectful—spectacles to upper-class decorum and masculinity.

The *criollos* were then not just humiliated, which assumes that one has suffered a "temporary alteration in status"[33] as a result of external force. They were shamed by this new abject identity as "Porto Ricans" (the newly invented term used in the Treaty of Paris ceding the Island to the United States), which was, importantly, *their* doing. As Aristotle has written, shame is "a kind of pain or uneasiness in respect of misdeeds past, present, or future, which seems to bring dishonour."[34] True to form, it was the loyalist clergy who reminded the locals of their shameful behavior. After Hurricane San Ciriaco devastated parts of the Island in 1899, the clergy interpreted the natural disaster as God's punishment to Puerto Ricans for "selling" their "mother" down the river for little gain.

Consequently, in the aftermath of the war, tropes that address, deny, or convey remorse about Puerto Rican support for the U.S. invasion are at the core of elite nation-building narratives and performances (see chapter 2). Privileged Puerto Ricans, as Kelvin Santiago-Valles has observed, persisted in their efforts to establish that they belonged to a breed which, if not quite the adult/manly colonialist, was at least not as subjected, not as feminized, not as infantilized as most of the Island's transgressive and allegedly backward inhabitants."[35] Whereas the figure for the conquest of the native people by the colonizers in modern Mexican mythology is the raped/whore La Malinche, the shameful subject for the U.S.-Puerto Rican contact is the queer working-class black man who passively allowed the United States to violate the nation.

To ward off the shame of a nationality at once deemed queer, black, and impoverished, and their participation in bringing about this state of affairs, the mostly male, white, affluent intellectual elites elaborated the myth of the *jíbaro*, the nineteenth-century, mountain-dwelling, creolized Euro peasant. "Through him we express our joy, our dispositions, and aspirations," wrote Antonio S. Pedreira, one of Puerto Rico's (still) most influential intellectuals, in the 1930s.[36] Allegedly a direct descendent of the Spaniards, the *jíbaro* was the nationalist symbol of choice for several reasons. Although a transculturated subject, a product of hundreds of years of cultural and "racial" mixture, the *jíbaro* is made up as "white," countering American claims of Puerto Rican racial inferiority. Isolated in the mountains, the *jíbaro* speaks only Spanish, a sign that he is not compromised by American culture.

The *jíbaro* hence symbolically preserved for the elites a separate and unique cultural identity from that of the United States, theoretically free from the shame of complicity. In the social scientist Lillian Guerra's terms, "the elite needed the *jíbaro* in order to remind them of who they truly were— Spanish and Puerto Rican—rather than who their own actions told them they were trying to become—North Americans."[37] The *jíbaro,* and with him the nation, remains intact, authentic, and unchanging despite more than a century of increasing intimacy with the United States. As Pedreira wrote wishfully, "There is a jíbaro *hidden* in every Puerto Rican" (my emphasis).[38]

Of course, not every Puerto Rican. The elite's concept of the *jíbaro* excluded the emerging, and largely nonwhite, working class, which savored previously unavailable political rights under U.S. rule. Unlike the imaginary *jíbaro,* the working class challenged the Island elite in its demand for a decent wage, collaborated openly with Americans to achieve political objectives, and possessed its own intellectual traditions and modes of expression. Some of the working-class leadership even rejected "nationalism" as an ideology. The *jíbaro*—like the elite—hence had to protect himself from "[working-class] encroachment from the urban zones and competition by blacks on the coast."[39]

If nationalist intellectuals invented the *jíbaro* as a symbolic shield against both the colonizers and the unruly masses, a small group of pro-independence activists in the 1930s combated colonial power through a masculinist simulacrum. In contrast to the dominant reformist parties, the Partido Nacionalista, led by the U.S.–educated attorney Pedro Albizu Campos, attempted to address the political and economic crisis of this period by re-engendering Puerto Rican nationalism through military parades and armed attacks against culturally charged targets such as U.S. president Harry Truman and Congress.

Although it would take several more decades for nationalist intellectuals to explicitly equate the shame of ethno-nationality with that of homosexuality (perhaps the most shameful of modern identifications), in a 1935 speech at the University of Puerto Rico, Albizu Campos inverted the meekness argument for self-rule, branding Puerto Rican men sissies—and Puerto Rican women morally "loose"—for failing to fight for an independent nation. Despite Albizu's success in calling attention to colonialism and producing enduring cultural resources for the attenuation of national shame, the crackdown on pro-independence activism that preceded the founding of the ELA and the extension of New Deal–style reforms made political nationalism unappealing for the majority of Puerto Ricans.

Given the failure of hard-line nationalist ideologies and the ELA's ambivalent constitution, pro-independence nationalism would find a privileged refuge in high cultural production, particularly literature. One of the most important intellectuals of the post–World War II period, René Marqués, dismisses equally any military campaign for independence and any bid for statehood. According to Marqués, armed struggle and annexation are both forms of national suicide as the militant nationalists are doomed to defeat and the annexionists, by sacrificing their national identity to that of the colonial power, would convert themselves into the living dead. Rejecting the literal death of an armed struggle for independence and the symbolic death of statehood, Marqués argues for a cultural nationalism born of vigorous literature that can begin to undo the damage of collaboration.

In his infamous 1961 essay "The Docile Puerto Rican," Marqués blames democracy and American-influenced "matriarchy" for the emasculation of *boricua* men and their concomitant inadequacy to perform as national subjects.[40] Taking up the pen as a sword, the writer becomes a national hero and injects virility into the national bloodstream by promoting machismo, or what he calls "a *criollo* version of the fusion and adaptation of two secular concepts, Spanish *honor* and Roman *pater familiae*."[41] By frequently attacking female characters in his own works, Marqués further demonstrates how the writer can cleanse the nation's (menstrual) stain. That a gay man cooked up this recipe of national regeneration is but another queer layer in *boricua* ethno-national identifications.

The docile Puerto Rican, black and queer, would haunt a later generation of avowed nationalists who answered Marqués's call to manliness by denying Puerto Rico's history of ambivalently consensual colonialism. "When we arrived at the university in 1955," writes Juan Angel Silén of what he calls "la generación encojonada" (the generation with balls) in his paradigmatic book *Hacia una visión positiva del puertorriqueño,* "we found an enormous vacuum, which we had to fill with our balls."[42] First published in the early 1970s, this book covers up the long tradition of accommodation to colonial rule by turning the heroic deeds of (even non–Puerto Rican) freedom fighters, from the Taíno chiefs Agueybaná and Guarionex to the anonymous African leaders of various slave rebellions during the eighteenth and nineteenth centuries, into the eternal struggle of Puerto Ricans for independence.

Pride replaced shame for pro-independence supporters and cultural nationalists, who reinvented Puerto Rico's heroic past and projected a "positive" national future. As the members of Silén's generation found work as academics, technocrats, advertisers, and public servants, they spun feel-good stories that would saturate public culture and set the stage for *boricua* identity in ways that elite attempts to attenuate shame never could. Although nationalism has not been successful in canceling the shame of *boricua* identity, one of the most important effects of this strategy has been that Puerto Rican "nationality"—in certain terms—became a *compulsory* social artifact with which both elite culture and popular culture have since had to contend.

Pride and Prejudice: Labor, Migration, and Ethno-National Shame

Spanglish-speaking, residing in the United States, and/or counting on federal aid, the majority of Puerto Ricans do not share the elite's fear of belonging to a queer black nation to the same extent, or in the same terms. Whereas homophobic and misogynist acts or discourses are often deployed as (hopeless) schemes to purge the shame of subaltern masculinities on a daily basis, the Puerto Rican working class and the expelled labor force also tend to be the least racist of *boricuas* and are often wary about nationalist politics.[43] As the majority of Puerto Ricans did not perceive the invasion or its aftermath as a political loss, the shame that would ultimately spur over half the population to proclaim a specifically *boricua* pride came from experience that was largely unacknowledged in Puerto Rico and was only modestly assimilated in the United States: mass migration.

From the 1940s to the 1960s, nearly a million Islanders left for New York and other cities to relieve the Island's economy and serve as an expendable source of labor to the mainland's manufacturing sector.[44] Prior to this displacement, considered the first mass airborne migration in world history and often called the "great migration,"[45] the Island's economy had suffered significant restructuring to serve U.S. corporate interests, most notably a shift from a subsistence economy based on multiple crops like sugarcane, coffee, cattle, and tobacco to primarily sugarcane. As a result, U.S. absentee owners held up to 60 percent of the lucrative sugar industry while most Puerto Ricans became dispossessed laborers without access to land and hence forced to work for wages.[46]

Since sugarcane was seasonal work that continuously incorporated new technologies to increase productivity, unemployment and underemployment became the norm rather than the exception for an increasing number of rural and urban workers after 1898. Artisans and craftsmen were also affected by changes in the economy as American-made manufactured goods flooded the market and forced skilled laborers into factory jobs. Symptomatic of Puerto Rican discontent with economic instability and high rates of exploitation were the numerous strikes that took place on the Island during the 1900–1940 decades.[47]

The Great Depression further weakened the Island economy and the traditional forms of contestation such as the labor movement, effectively suppressing the tobacco industry and lowering wages. In the 1930–1940 period, the per capita income of Puerto Ricans actually declined, from $126 to $120.[48] Although women joined the labor force in greater numbers, particularly in the needlework industry, their work was considered less valuable and hence female labor received even lower wages than male labor.

At the same time that the economically displaced left the Island after the 1940s, U.S. government and corporate investment poured into Puerto Rico. The shift in strategy—from denying self-government reforms to the founding of the ELA, from the extreme exploitation of Puerto Rican labor and resources to the implementation of New Deal–inspired programs and corporate investment—was part of a campaign to "showcase" the Island as an alternative to communist insurgency in the midst of the Cold War.[49] As the sociologist Ramón Grosfoguel and the writer Chloé Georas have written, "in order to use San Juan [as a showcase] without causing major embarrassment to the United States, it would be first necessary to eliminate San Juan's huge shanty towns, . . . improve the conditions of extreme poverty—and conceal Puerto Rico's colonial status."[50] In rethinking U.S. policies, the metropolis's political elites had to acknowledge the shame of colonial exploitation, yet reiterated their contempt in two other ways: first, by "granting" a commonwealth status that they knew to be colonial, and second, by ignoring the effects of Operation Bootstrap on the imported labor force.

Largely disavowed (if inherent) in elite references to pride, the shame of Puerto Rican ethno-national identification in the United States became overtly linked to processes of economic restructuring and stigmatization as a subaltern other—a "spic."[51] Yet it is significant that the low value accorded to Puerto Rican migrants—who were openly described as "redundant" by allies of the Commonwealth project—preceded migration by four decades of colonial discourse and economic policy that benefited American and some "native" elite sectors.[52]

Upon arriving in New York, Puerto Ricans experienced further devaluation. All *boricuas* were collectively racialized as "nonwhite" and assigned a low rank within the city's ethno-racial hierarchy, as signs that read "No Dogs, No Negroes, and No Spanish" so brutally reminded them.[53] A 1948 travel book, *New York Confidential* by Jack Lait and Lee Mortimer, minced no words in describing the new migrants in the following terms: "They are mostly crude farmers, subject to congenital tropical diseases, physically unfitted for the northern climate, unskilled, uneducated, non-English-speaking, and almost impossible to assimilate and condition for healthful and useful existence in an active city of stone and steel."[54]

Boricua ethno-nationality was publicly constituted as shameful due to processes and public discourse that degraded Puerto Ricans as less than "human." Most migrants were "treated as second-class citizens—with disdain, disrespect, discrimination, and dishonesty."[55] They had come to New York to work and largely shared in the expectation that the United States was a land of opportunity for all, yet although many earned more income than on the Island, it came at a high social cost. Even *boricua* strategies to attenuate shame and prevent injury by staying away from "white" neighbors, an avoidance of "seeing" contempt in the face or being the object of physical violence, were scornfully represented as "clannish" behavior by Euro-American middle-class critics.[56]

Equally important to constituting Puerto Ricanness as a shameful identification in the United States is the persistent claim that *boricuas* as a people had nothing to contribute to "America." An early—if ultimately unsuccessful—protest staged by forty community organizations in 1940 was in fact over the publication of a *Scribner's Commentator* article entitled "Welcome Paupers and Crime: Puerto Rico's Shocking Gift to the U.S."[57] The importance of this claim in constituting Puerto Rican ethno-nationality cannot be underestimated. As Frederick Turner has observed, "Shame . . . does not come from a lack of ability to have or possess; it comes from the consciousness of a lack of ability to give."[58]

Despite the determination of most Puerto Ricans to survive in a hostile environment by performing virtually any kind of work, including "jobs of lower status" when they were skilled and criminalized work,[59] New York *boricuas* were publicly held responsible for all the social problems they confronted: structural poverty, lack of education, inability to speak English,

21

housing discrimination, police brutality, and racist violence.[60] The extent to which Puerto Ricans were constituted by shame and calling attention to *boricuas* was in itself shameful can be gleaned from Oscar Lewis's preface to *La Vida*, "I am aware that an intensive study of poverty . . . runs the risk of offending some Puerto Ricans who have dedicated themselves to the elimination of poverty and who are trying to build a positive image of an often maligned minority group."[61]

The extreme forms of discrimination suffered by Puerto Ricans in most cities in the United States were not the product of cultural deficiencies or congenital inferiority, but strategies of exclusion and global economic restructuring. Many Puerto Rican women working in the garment industry, for instance, were deliberately "funneled into industries that were declining."[62] The labor market was racially classified within a strict hierarchy of value, and opportunities were available accordingly. Puerto Ricans also migrated to New York at a time when the city was experiencing a shift from manufacturing to a service economy and higher education and English-language skills were necessary to find employment.

From 1960 to 1980 alone, New York City lost half a million jobs in manufacturing.[63] Similar to Islanders, ties to the United States both devalued and valorized Nuyoricans. Although unlike other Spanish-speaking immigrants, *boricuas* were U.S. citizens since 1917 and hence could arguably access more resources to assure upward mobility, the ability to legally protest working conditions, demand better treatment without fearing deportation, and count on government resources when unemployed actually made many experience a "unique marginalization . . . [that] translates into Puerto Ricans being seen as the least desirable group to employ."[64] Not surprisingly, even this predicament was judged a *boricua* moral lack, a self-inflicted wound. In Linda Chavez's terms, "Citizenship, which should have enhanced Puerto Rican achievement, may actually have hindered it by conferring entitlements, such as welfare, with no concomitant obligations."[65]

As New York's labor market shifted to a service economy, the shame of not being the bearer of appropriate gifts became further entrenched in public discourse. Although unskilled jobs became largely unavailable, participating in the workforce remained, in the social scientist María Milagros López's words, "undaunted in its function as moral arbiter of people's worth."[66] Many Puerto Ricans, who had for decades been defined by work, were now faced with a semipermanent and often indefinite inability to find employment. If before Puerto Ricans had a low value as laborers, now they had none.

While there is some debate regarding whether Puerto Rican men felt "emasculated" by not being able to provide for their families, some *boricuas* viewed public assistance as especially shameful to men. As María Pérez y González wrote, "When a culture requires that men provide economically for their family and be the head of the household, or be shamed, it is particularly difficult to admit the need for government assistance, even though one is entitled to it."[67] The fact that many Puerto Rican women had fewer qualms in demanding assistance, given their assertion that work inside the home was not only work but a valuable investment, articulated alternative values but did not attenuate public shame.[68] In the words of the sociologist Susan Baker, "Rather than receiving recognition and validation for prioritizing family, the education of their children, and indeed of themselves, these women were socially stigmatized as 'unworthy.'"[69]

Figures concerning the number of Puerto Rican families receiving federal aid programs such as Aid to Families with Dependent Children vary from 13.5 percent to 35 percent, depending on the study. Yet although a comparable percentage of African Americans tend to receive aid, and some *boricua* families refuse the assistance, "welfare" came to "symbolize the type of dire poverty one does not easily escape from, compounded by the additional stigma of ineptitude and shame."[70] The link between Puerto Ricans and welfare became so strong in U.S. public discourse that J. Peter Grace, a Reagan appointee, labeled the federal food stamp program "basically a Puerto Rican program."[71] The shame of public assistance hence became yoked not only to specific circumstances—being unable to find work—but to *boricuaness* itself. As a result, it was not only poverty that was allegedly reproduced through welfare, but Puerto Rican ethno-nationality as shameful.

Federal aid and low labor participation, however, were not particular to U.S. Puerto Ricans.[72] In fact, Islanders have higher rates of unemployment and reliance on public assistance than *boricuas* living in the United States, due to the mainland's less vulnerable economy. Since the 1980s in Puerto Rico, "the proportion of persons who do not work or search for work is very high and for males it is the highest in the world."[73] But whereas U.S. policy makers often represent all Puerto Ricans similarly, as poor, lazy, and ungrateful regardless of place of residence, the shame of U.S. *boricuas* met a second, ironic, face: other *boricuas*—from the island.

AmeRícans—to use the poet Tato Laviera's brilliant neologism to name U.S. Puerto Ricans—are viewed by many in Puerto Rico as utterly violated by the United States: debased by the English language, denigrated as a "race" not a nation, and devoid of authentic (Puerto Rican) culture. In focus groups conducted in 1995 by the researcher Nancy Morris, Islanders unanimously derided U.S. *boricuas* for not being "real Puerto Ricans." Instead, they are perceived to be a marginal "subculture of the United States," who "watch cable TV all day" and "don't even know how to speak English well, nor to speak Spanish well."[74]

The contempt aimed at AmeRícans on the Island is motivated by a sense of superiority similar to that of white middle-class sectors in the United States. But it is also a result of colonial shame. Many middle- and upper-class Islanders are ashamed of U.S. *boricuas* not only because they embody a loss of symbolic capital as an exposed racialized minority on the mainland, but also because they appear as most Islanders imagine white Americans see them: black, transculturated, and poor. Puerto Rican "pride" discourses should (again) not be confused with an inherently progressive politics—particularly when nationalists, advertisers, and others try to "put them to work"—but always *embodied-in-difference*, according to social context.

Educated AmeRícans have often responded to this double disdain by articulating a radical pro-independence discourse that posits *boricua* identity in moral terms, as opposite to that of the brutal "Americans."[75] The writer

Marithelma Acosta, for instance, defends the importance of keeping Puerto Rico politically "free" (independent) of the United States as a strategy to preserve a "safe space" where "we do not have to feel ashamed. A country where the phrase 'I am *boricua*' does not elicit a gesture of repugnance from one's interlocutor."[76] Yet given the derision that Nuyoricans have experienced on the Island, the general apathy to independence, and the importance of pride as a valorizing trope in the United States, the most important effect of AmeRícan patriotic discourse has been not to change the Island's status, but to address the shame of Puerto Rican ethno-national identification *on* the mainland.

More generally, U.S. *boricuas* have elaborated a discourse of "positive" images designed to raise the low symbolic capital associated with Puerto Ricans as an American ethno-national group. Working through the shame of joblessness (frequently framed as laziness or idleness), racial subjection, and alleged cultural impurity are popular displays of pride that "presume the saliency of the present and claim rights, needs, entitlements, enjoyment, dignity, and self-valorizations outside the structure of wages."[77] Unlike nation-building literature written for elite readers, beauty pageants, sports competitions, stunts, and street parades provide a carnivalesque redefinition of what is valuable and beautiful. These sites are often infused by popular definitions of Puerto Ricanness, an ethno-national identity that particularly when defined from below is inherently aligned with the "vulnerable members of society."[78]

The best example of popular *boricua* pride is the National Puerto Rican Day Parade, the biggest event of its kind in the United States. It was founded in 1958 as the Puerto Rican Day Parade; organizers changed the event's name in 1995 to attract participants outside New York City. (Significantly, the "national" addition to the parade's title intends to refer to the United States, not Puerto Rico.) In 1996 the parade drew 100,000 participants, three million street spectators, and the highest "Nielsen ratings for any televised program."[79] The epic scale of the parade makes Puerto Ricans the "proudest" people in the United States, a distinction that is intimately linked to the constitutive ambivalence—not "natural" resilience—of *boricua* ethno-nationality.

According to organizers, the parade's objective is to "raise the self-esteem of our people and use their pride to promote economic development, education, cultural improvement and recognition."[80] It also seeks to "create a national consciousness and appreciation of Puerto Rican culture and its contribution to American culture and society."[81] The parade then proposes to offset shame through a spectacle of pride that affirms the joy of *boricua* culture, our gift to the United States—and the world. In breaking the taboo of looking and being looked at that constitutes socially shamed subjects, the parade further affirms that *boricua* culture is valuable enough to make Puerto Ricans kings and queens for a day, fit to be favorably judged by other New Yorkers.[82]

Yet even in popular events bursting with "positive" affect, the spectacle of pride demands what the theorist Judith Butler has called the compulsory performance of identity to the eyes of subjecting others.[83] This repetitious action is not voluntary, but a corollary of flights from shaming (and shameful) forces, often narcissistically centered on the self. While common sense regards pride as the opposite of shame, it is the shame of Puerto Rican ethno-national identity—our political and economic "lacks"—that makes exhibiting our pride—*boricua* culture, a "native" value—intensely joyful. So when the sociologist Angel Quintero asks the question, "should Puerto Ricans be ashamed of identifying 'the national' . . . with sensuality and dancing?"[84] the answer is, of course. Not only because it is deemed deviant by properly engendered nationals, but also—and it could not be otherwise—because it is the queer way that *boricuas* have carved out joy from ethno-national shame.

Pop Pride: Buying *Boricuaness* in the Cultural Marketplace

With neither a nation-state nor a privileged economic position in American society to underscore our value, many Puerto Ricans have relied on consumption and self-commodification as two of several means to attenuate shame, negotiate colonial subjection, and acquire self-worth.[85] In fact, one of the indicators used by social scientists to represent the "rapid strides" made by Puerto Rico in demographic, economic, and social terms during the 1940s was to point to consumer behavior: "Today . . . the Puerto Rican consumer spends more than $400 yearly per capita for imported products; this is several times his total per capita income of twenty years ago."[86] Conversely, one of the ways the New York *boricua* community has been historically reminded of its low status was the inferior quality of services and commodities that many had access to, including rotting lettuce in the neighborhood supermarkets.

The economic instability and extreme forms of labor exploitation that have characterized modern Puerto Rican participation in the labor market, as well as the constant comparison between Puerto Rico and the geographically much larger and wealthier metropolis, have made the ability to consume— purchase commodities—a sign of "value" for Puerto Ricans. As Anna Indych comments, *boricuas* tend to overcompensate for our low social status "by hoarding commodities," a gesture that represents "a general fear of not having—and the common phenomenon of aspiring to a higher class than one's own."[87] Her observation recalls the scholar Tim Edwards's truism that consumer society is not only "desiring society, it is hungry society."[88]

Despite the fact that—or perhaps because—Puerto Rico's per capita income is reportedly lower than that of any state of the Union, Islanders "are more than twice in debt" than the average American, with an accumulated $17 billion balance due, and shop at Plaza Las Américas, one of the "world's highest grossing malls."[89] In this context, "excessive" consumption and the demand to receive "welfare" and other entitlements are ambivalent forms of valorization, claims to enjoy—rather than overtly contest—U.S. colonial domination in Puerto Rico.

Although decried by intellectuals for decades as a "vulgar" affliction of the masses,[90] the capacity of Puerto Ricans to consume "positively" distinguishes *boricuas* from "sovereign" nationals such as Cubans or Dominicans, residents of impoverished nation. The pro-independence commentator Fufi Santori observed as recently as 1993, for instance, that Puerto Ricans may be "a little less than Dominicans and Cubans [politically]," but "we eat better."[91] Precisely because *boricuas* perceive themselves as being outside the most exploited labor markets—those countries that actually manufacture the commodities and grow the food that they purchase—conspicuous consumption is a form of ethno-national distinction.

The use of Puerto Rican culture in advertising is also widely understood as confirming rather than compromising ethno-national identity and worth.[92] As the success of Puerto Rican Barbie implies (see chapter 8), transnational corporations such as Mattel reap impressive profits by selling products to *boricuas* that cater to a sense of national pride and identity. This marketing strategy, which often consists of advertising products as if they were produced solely for Puerto Ricans or with local characteristics, raises the self-appointed value of the *boricua* consumer. Consequently, pride can now be found anywhere (and everywhere) as consensual national symbols like flags or landscapes have been made part of commodities selling beer, cigarettes, and cars through mass media, print ads, t-shirts, hats, beach towels, key chains, boxer trunks, concert props, jewelry, and even hairdos.

In the United States, many Latinos working in advertising also perceive their trade as a "tool for promoting pride in all things Latin" and attention to the Hispanic market as a "public statement of their 'worth.'" Arlene Dávila quotes the founder of Caballero Spanish Media, Cuban-born Eduardo Caballero, as affirming that the main obstacle to the creation of a Spanish-speaking Hispanic market was "a lack of identity, or more exactly people's shame about their identity," during the 1960s and 1970s, the height of civil rights struggles in the United States.[93]

As transnational commodities go native, the most visible *boricua* ones—pop music and movie stars—are going global like never before. If commodities are fundamentally "objects of economic value,"[94] Puerto Ricans are not only able to buy their ethno-national identity but, in effect, to sell it; being *boricua* is valuable enough that (even "white") people want to buy it. Regardless of the stars' willingness or ability to reflect on their contradictory location, *boricua* stars in American pop culture now stand as the most visible paradigm of Puerto Rican value.

Stars lend themselves to discussions of social worth because in being both commodified and being able to sell other commodities, they have a "market value" explicitly gauged by box office receipts and record, art, magazine, poster, and book sales. Stars are also assets to themselves and employers, producers, managers, and advertisers. The fact that Puerto Rican globalized stars had not quite existed in the same way before the present juncture, further offers an opportunity to analyze the conditions under which *boricuas* have been considered susceptible to commodification and examine the relationship between social valorization and other processes.[95] As Arjun Appadurai argues, value "is never an inherent property of objects, but is a judgment made about them by subjects."[96]

Racialized performative laborers in fact have always been aware of the doubleness of commodification processes. Incommensurable criteria for valorizing cultural practices and identities have often been a source of intensified shame rather than enjoyment for Puerto Ricans, as the careers of the Warhol Superstar Holly Woodlawn (chapter 4) and the painter Jean-Michel Basquiat (chapter 5) suggest. Woodlawn was deemed unviable as a commodity beyond narrowly defined niche markets, eventually hindering her creative possibilities. Basquiat was able to spectacularly market his body of work, but this process did not undo his social status as a racialized subject, arguably contributing to his premature death from an overdose at the age of twenty-seven. Basquiat's career scholar Jonathan Flatley's critical question regarding the consequences of being "valued as a person only insofar as you are taken for a thing [commodity]."[97]

As Stuart Hall theorizes, commodification also decontextualizes, supplants, and even crushes popular practices in "the constitutions of a new social order around capital."[98] The emphasis on loss has prompted several cultural critics like Juan Flores to dismiss "consumer ethnicities" in favor of barrio-centered theories of Puerto Rican culture.[99] Although the cultural production of *boricua* communities plays a leading role in scripting the performance of Puerto Rican identity (although it is also not independent of the marketplace), the study of specifically commodified transculture is critical for any understanding of contemporary Puerto Rican ethno-national identifications.

Mass culture has been a significant target of *boricua* political activism in New York City, most notably since the 1940s, when degrading portrayals of Puerto Ricans in the print and television media were normative.[100] More recently, activists like Richie Pérez have argued that "the cumulative exclusion, dehumanization, and discrimination" found in media representions of Puerto Ricans and other racialized peoples have robbed "an entire people of our history, culture, sense of pride, and self-respect."[101] Demands to include Puerto Ricans in mass media as on-camera and behind-the-scenes talent in television programs, movies, advertisements, and the news have been historically deployed as a strategy to gain inclusion and measure social enfranchisement.

Since they are public *boricuas,* the stars' discourse about their place in American society, their identity as Puerto Ricans, and their relation to capital as performative laborers also make available common references to debate these issues in mass culture. As Richard Dyer has argued, stars are "embodiments of social categories in which people are placed and through which they try to make sense of their lives, and indeed through which we make our lives—categories of class, gender, ethnicity, religion, sexual orientation."[102] The Puerto Rican stars discussed here, for instance, articulate different relationships between each of these categories, ranging from critique (Rita Moreno) and despair (Jean-Michel Basquiat) to accommodation (Ricky Martin) and protest (Jennifer López) as well as diverse ways of being *boricua.*

Moreover, widely disseminated Puerto Rican stars often crowd the social field with comforting and pleasurable representations of *boricua* bodies in public spaces, reassuring spectators that they cannot be easily rendered invisible. Given that shameful subjects simultaneously desire to be seen and not be seen by the contemptuous gaze, "star" performances often succeed in becoming the other's object of desire, and in this way attenuate shame and brand *boricua* identity in the United States as enjoyable. However trivial celebrity culture may appear to some, to see and be seen as Puerto Ricans are important forms of agency, for shame "robs a person of normal exhibition-istic capacity and pleasure."[103]

Even though it is true that fans never "own" their idols' success and a star's struggle is rarely represented as other than that of an individual, iden-tification with *boricua* stars by Puerto Ricans is as much a misrecognition of their marginal location as an articulation of a desired insider status.[104] Bathed in the light of *boricua* pop stars, for instance, Islanders can visualize them-selves as flawless sovereign subjects, unhampered by colonial subalterity. Puerto Ricans on the mainland can see themselves as a valuable part of Amer-ican culture, integral to the economic and symbolic exchanges that make up the nation's imagined community. To the extent that stars call attention to the "contributions" of Puerto Ricans and Puerto Rico to the United States, they also make *boricuas* feel valuable—that they too have given to American culture—and hence more socially secure and less ashamed.

Puerto Ricans, of course, began contributing to American culture long be-fore the first *boricua* appeared on MTV and continue to do so with or with-out globalized stars. Yet those contributions have not been acknowledged be-cause American culture is heavily transculturated without its subjects being aware of their own status as transculturated subjects. Through a process of asymmetrical cultural exchange, artists producing for the mass media mar-ket—from the creators of *West Side Story* to style thieves Andy Warhol, Keith Haring, and Madonna (see chapters 4, 5, and 6)—have incorporated Puerto Rican and other subaltern practices while consistently erasing or displacing the source. Some Puerto Ricans have lacked the means to pass on their cul-tural capital on a transnational scale, the record of Puerto Rican culture has in fact often only been accessible beyond its immediate community through mainstream popular culture made famous by white and African American performers or featuring *boricuas* in supporting roles.

It is not until the 2000 census that a conglomerate composed of many eth-nic, national, and ethno-national communities was officially recognized as the United States' most sizeable "ethnic" minority, that "Latinos" were socially recognized so they could be delivered as consumers and voters on a expansive scale. This translation's success is partly fueled by the rise of an optimistic U.S. Latino middle and upper class convinced that "the shame once attached to being Latino in America is disappearing. Upwardly-mobile Latinos have begun to define their ethnicity in a way that is compatible with achieving success in America and not just a milestone along the road to assimilation."[105] Or in the novelist Rosario Ferré's terms, "ethnic diversity has become a fundamental value in the United States."[106]

The "Latin" market, however, extends beyond the United States and is constituted by "Latin America" as a globalized location, underscoring that it is not Puerto Rican identity itself, but "Latinness" that is for sale. Furthermore, even though the market "elevates" some *boricuas* to commodity status, it may do so in ways that also re-racialize and devalue Puerto Ricans. A case in point is Jennifer López (chapter 9), whose insistence on addressing "low" subjects such as her racialized butt has come to embody a way to acknowledge the shame of *boricua* racialized identification in the United States through a belly-down epistemology that upsets "white" notions of beauty and good taste.

In founding this inquiry in transculturation processes and performances to offset shame, it is not my intent to affirm that *boricuas* are simply "Americans," as some Latino cultural producers have proposed with interventions such as the recent PBS series "American Family." Although a book like this may only be possible now, when coming "out" is but a symptom of how culturally "in" some *boricuas* have become,[107] my aim is to recover Puerto Rican cultural practices as resources for all readers, and to underscore the extent to which the "true" history of the United States—and the Caribbean—is that of its many and intricate transculturations.[108] Which is why Puerto Ricanness here does not only (or always) imply an identity or a sign, but a technology to "see" for the eccentric "self" in others and find not necessarily what one is looking for but something that could simultaneously be more thrilling, reassuring, or terrifying: a piece of yourself everywhere.

The Trauma of Literature, the Shame of Identity

The dream reveals the reality, which conception lags behind. That is the horror of life—the terror of art.   —Franz Kafka

A survey conducted in 1998, on the centennial of the Spanish-American War, revealed that only 12 percent of Americans were aware that "Puerto Rico has been part of the United States for the past 100 years."[1] If Americans have chosen to forget how and under what circumstances the United States became an empire—and hence mask the shame of the Republic—the invasion of the Island by U.S. troops on July 25, 1898, is compulsively recalled by Puerto Rican nationalists and pro-independence cultural producers. In the words of the *independentista* playwright Roberto Ramos Perea, the invasion is "the most important date of our history . . . a cut in the face . . . which has marked us forever."[2]

If under the Spanish regime the shame of colonial subordination was largely acknowledged by the *criollos*, the aftermath of the U.S. invasion required its diffusion. Not only were Puerto Ricans dismissed by the new metropolis as "unfit" for self-government since the "nation" was declared black (not Hispanic), a "race" (not a people), and effeminate (not virile), most *boricuas* actively participated in bringing about this new state of affairs and intimately—if contradictorily—invested in its reproduction.

Since even the avowedly nationalist elites continued to negotiate with, rather than militarily confront, the U.S. regime, Puerto Rican national identity became more intensely narrated through tropes of shame. The obligation of each succeeding generation of intellectuals was now to either shamefully cover or shamelessly expose (as "real" men would) the *criollo* nation's queerness, while sidestepping the elite's complicity with the status quo. This futile task, however, has come to define much of the Island's high culture as a "torment of self-consciousness,"[3] a fixation with the self, with who we are as *boricuas*.

Fittingly, the trope that followed the late-nineteenth-century discourse of the "humiliated culture"[4] was dramatically synthesized in one word, "trauma." In his classic survey on Puerto Rican literature, Francisco Manrique Cabrera condensed the impact of the Spanish-American War on twentieth-century *boricuas* as follows: "It was simply a trauma: the violent historical tear consummated against our will, and presented to the dazzled, naive and childish—not to say deluded and empty—Island liberals who confused pretty words with reality."[5] Presenting the *criollos* as abused children, Manrique Cabrera inaccurately asserts that they did not want the invasion and documents a "rape" that never took place.

While many scholars, including myself, have dismissed the assessment of the Spanish-American War as a national "trauma," given that most Puerto Ricans did not perceive it this way, there are powerful signifying reasons why this became the trope employed by sectors of the elite.[6] In speaking from and through trauma, postwar intellectuals identified with the *criollos'* fright at their nearly fatal lack of foresight, and established an *epistemological* continuity with the affect of shame. The experiences of shame and trauma have in common the inability to see and/or contest an overwhelming force that—significantly for the gendered coordinates of *boricua* ethno-nationality—renders us "small," "'takes us' unawares," and leaves an emptiness, a hole.[7]

This *lapsus*—what they could grasp only after the fact—had the effect of traumatizing the mostly male, white, affluent, and educated elites for two basic reasons. First, because it seems that they escaped "unharmed" from the invasion, despite "being had"—losing their now racialized masculinity—to the Americans. Second—and just as important—because in the post–1898 reshuffling of power, the elites lost not only some of their recently acquired political gains and relative economic privilege, but also their ostensible ability to represent and control Puerto Rican subaltern groups, who now brazenly—and successfully—sought to independently perform themselves in the public sphere.

The fact that at the moment of the invasion itself there was *no* "trauma" (bodily wounds or body counts) has further facilitated the cultural elites' ability to represent themselves as a locally hegemonic if colonized group by explaining Puerto Rican history after 1898 as a history of a trauma—theirs. As Laura S. Brown argues, "'Real' trauma is often only that form of trauma in which the dominant group can participate as a victim rather than as the perpetrator or etiologist of the trauma."[8] In claiming a traumatized identity, these sectors have also cultivated the "feeling that they have been set apart and made special"[9] and hence speak from a position of moral authority over the "ignorant"—not nationally traumatized—*boricua* majority.

Trauma has further constituted nationalist literature as a form of testimonial writing, one that requires that a witness to trauma (the writer) guide an initiate (the reader) to a higher truth, and in the process also transform him or her into a witness. Narratives about the "trauma" of 1898 are reproductive as they validate the injured community and create "a mood, an ethos—a group culture."[10] Much of Puerto Rican (high) culture to date, particularly its literature, is then a wounded voice that speaks *through*, not *despite*, colonialism, and repeatedly attempts to narrate the "origin" of modern *boricua* nationality in the encounter with the "other." This "other" (American), significantly, did not annihilate, but allegedly damaged—racialized and feminized, that is—Puerto Ricans in intangible ways that only writers can properly repair. Or in the words of the French critics Gilles Deleuze and Felix Guattari, "the suffering machine . . . never stops creating its own bliss."[11]

The majority's pro-American sentiment at the time of the invasion and contradictory investment in the new metropolis's modernizing project, however, have deprived Puerto Rican nationalist writers of an "authentic" re-sistance narrative, a story that is able to represent the liminal moment when "nation" and "foreigner" confront each other and where the invader is re-pelled, thus founding a heroic national subjectivity. As the Cuban historian Ramiro Guerra y Sánchez writes without a trace of irony, "[A nation] needs to possess a spiritual patrimony of glory and heroism, of epic and legend."[12]

In the chronic absence of great nationalist leaders and revolutionary masses, military might and epic battles, canonical Puerto Rican writers have devoted themselves to at least textually generating a subject capable of build-ing a nation, a "virile people, with a soul of fire, the tenacious courage of the Spartan and the Greek's intractable pride,"[13] as Luis Muñoz Rivera wrote. For if it is "true" that a modern subject will have a "nation" as much as a gen-der,[14] given the questionable possession of the first, masculinity itself is in-dispensable to narrate *boricuas* as viable national subjects.

The literature on and around the invasion and its aftermath hence does more than articulate nostalgia for presumed glory. As the paradigmatic form through which the elites invent their past, literature is not only the trau-matic site from which the "nation" speaks, but also where writers attempt to refashion the shame of a purely Puerto Rican *national* identity, a shame that is not experienced as an addition, but as a constitutive element, a "nexus of production," in the words of Eve Kosofsky Sedgwick.[15] The epic vacuum has been generative as writers attempt to fill the void—the black hole of his-tory—with more redeeming fictions. Accordingly, despite the many avowed differences between the texts discussed in this chapter, these cannot help but show off the (queer) aphorism of elite national identity: "We" (Puerto Rican men) can be seen only through their (American male) eyes, hence, we are al-ways ashamed.

Seva: Seven Days That Shook One World

The impulse to invent a heroic past for *boricuas* has been attempted by many writers, including modernizers of Puerto Rican literature like Luis Lloréns

Torres and René Marqués.[16] As late as 1998, the novelist Olga Nolla published *El castillo de la memoria,* which tells the story of the Spanish conquistador Juan Ponce de León—founder of the capital city and a participant in the extermination wars against the Island's native inhabitants—who finds the Fountain of Youth and lives to be four hundred years old.[17] Despite Ponce de León's genocidal role in the conquest, Nolla morphs him into "the Puerto Rican hero we never had," who "died defending the Hispanic Puerto Rico he had founded."[18]

Although a handful of writers have narrated 1898 in different terms, these texts have been largely marginalized in the canon. A notable example is *La llegada,* "a chronicle with fiction," by the late José Luis González, which stages the invasion as a conflict not between Americans and Spaniards and/or Americans and Puerto Ricans, but between differently racialized *boricuas* from differing classes. *La llegada* has been forgotten, however, in part because it does not fulfill the obligation of nation-building fiction: to racially re-engender the *boricua* subject as heroic.

La llegada relocates the founding shame of Puerto Rican national identity from 1898 to slavery and racism, and provides a more inclusive (if no less mythical) narrative of *boricua* ethno-national identity. González's multivoiced account convincingly offsets the elite's representation of 1898 as a national rape; the Americans in *La llegada,* in fact, do not invade or penetrate, they simply *arrive.* But as a work of fiction the narrative fails thrice by mistaking historical fact for seduction, confusing shame for a voluntary mask, and underestimating the common idiom of shame between privileged and subaltern sectors in narrating their agency in the aftermath of the invasion.

This is why the most revealingly shameful text on 1898 is the work known as *Seva: Historia de la primera invasión norteamericana de la isla de Puerto Rico ocurrida en mayo 1898* (Seva: History of the First North American Invasion of the Island of Puerto Rico in May 1898), by the writer and journalist Luis López Nieves. Despite the dismissal by several historians of *Seva*'s power as a nationalist narrative, it is in engaging with Seva-as-dream that one comes closer to understanding the workings of Puerto Rican elite nationalism as a racially engendered ideological fantasy. As Slavoj Zizek has observed, it is in "the dream that we approached the fantasy-framework which determines our activity, our mode of acting in reality itself."[19]

Originally published in the leftist pro-independence weekly *Claridad* on December 23, 1983, and little known outside Puerto Rico, this text has managed to spectacularly exemplify the shame of elite national identity, not only textually, but also at the level of reception. Tellingly, when José Luis González first heard of *Seva,* he assumed that it was a deliberate attempt to point out the "mythmaking proclivities" of the pro-independence sectors and was later baffled to hear from López Nieves himself that, on the contrary, the story was designed to "strengthen feelings of national pride among Puerto Ricans."[20]

Through photographs, "fake" documents, and several letters addressed to a friend who acts as editor and narrator ("Luis López Nieves"), *Seva* tells the story of professor Víctor Cabañas, who chronicles a groundbreaking "discovery": that U.S. Army General Nelson Miles tried to invade Puerto Rico before July 25, 1898, and was defeated by the people of a small town called Seva. In order to destroy the evidence of his defeat—the general's shame—Miles orders the total destruction of the town. A black boy named Ignacio Martínez, Cabañas uncovers, escapes from the slaughter and hides in the mountains for most of his life. After corroborating his tale in the imperial archives of Spain and the United States, Cabañas finds Martínez, who confirms that he is the sole survivor of the Seva massacre, perpetrated by Miles's army. *Seva*'s hero is, of course, a professor, since the academic figure is part of a long tradition of nationalist discourse in Puerto Rico where, as Juan Gelpí has argued, patriotic teachers personify "examples to overcome passivity and moral lack."[21]

While the text is loaded with inaccuracies that should have been obvious to anyone familiar with Puerto Rican history, the majority of *Seva*'s readers believed the tale to be true. The noted historian Fernando Picó commented that this response was particularly curious, as "The readers of *Claridad* are probably among the Island's most sophisticated and critical; professors, students, academics, left cadres, lawyers, labor leaders, professionals."[22] During the first week of its publication, in fact, *Claridad* sent out press releases to the major media outlets clarifying that *Seva* was a story, but these were systematically ignored. According to Josean Ramos, who chronicled *Seva*'s reception, dozens of people refused to believe that the text was fictional and demanded the formation of investigative bodies for assorted purposes, including finding both Ignacio Martínez and Víctor Cabañas.

The readability and believability of *Seva* were possible partly because of elements both familiar and ingratiating to its *letrado* (educated) audience. Similar to the way many readers of *Claridad* see themselves, *Seva*'s protagonist is a highly literate nationalist hero, pitted against a widely scorned historical figure representing American colonialism, General Nelson Miles. Furthermore, the story referenced the recent events of Cerro Maravilla, in which high-level government officials were implicated in the murder of two young *independentistas* and the subsequent coverup.

Not coincidentally, these killings occurred the same day of the invasion, July 25. Six-month anniversary coverage on the matter appeared in the *Claridad* issue prior to the publication of *Seva,* including articles by the writer Pedro Juan Soto, father of one of the slain young men, critical commentary concerning the ongoing investigation into the possible complicity of Puerto Rico's pro-statehood governor, and coverage of the 1983 U.S. invasion of Grenada.[23] In each of these instances, the U.S. and Puerto Rican mainstream media and government institutions are continuously assailed for their lack of objectivity, at the same time that the people's heroic resistance to colonial aggression is "documented" and highlighted.

Yet the public's insistence that *Seva*'s story was "true," despite disclaimers and factual errors, suggests that more than a narrowly defined political narrative, this text served as a collective dreamwork, a stage for performing *boricua* national identity as one born not in shame or trauma, but in honor and military might (its reverse). In Slavoj Zizek's terms, this was an ideological fantasy that allowed a relatively small community to overlook "the illusion which is structuring our real, effective relationship to reality" through the printed word (a classic Benedict Anderson scenario).[24] As the poet José Manuel Torres Santiago insisted even when the text's status as a work of fiction was revealed, "Seva tells the truth of who we are; the true story of Puerto Rican heroism."[25]

Seva's enchantment, however, was short-lived. Readers heeded modest calls to action, forcing the "author" to publicly affirm that the text was "un cuento" (a story). This revelation made some readers feel cheated, activating a response of resentment and anger toward López Nieves. Josean Ramos tells, for example, of a "veteran nationalist" who refused to accept that Don Ignacio Martínez was a "fictional entity created by Luis López Nieves,"[26] giving way to a classic Freudian diagnosis: "If phantasies become over-luxuriant and over-powerful, the conditions are laid for an onset of neurosis or psychosis."[27] López Nieves's life was in fact threatened for shamelessly "duping" the Island's *independentistas*.

The beleaguered author responded by inviting the incredulous to see what was not evident: "Now we know that we are not docile and impotent."[28] As no revolutionary action took place nor was a more militant independence movement ignited, López Nieves's defense seeks comfort in the fact that although Puerto Rican history does not afford the raw material to build a heroic national narrative, nor have *boricuas* risked their lives in great numbers to assert their political independence, some still *desire the desire* to do so. And in desiring so, *Seva* hopes to demonstrate that Puerto Ricans are not yet fully "Americans"—that is, dead *boricuas*—if invested with (and in) U.S. citizenship.

Contrary, however, to its avowed anticolonial stance, identifying with *Seva*'s narrative (as in Olga Nolla's novel) required a reidentification with Spain, the former reviled—and defeated—empire responsible for slavery and endless counts of humiliation. In the absence of a heroic performance by the *criollos* and distrust of popular forms of defiance, López Nieves calls upon the former colonial masters to *fill in* for the lacking (national) subject through a genre dear to the Spanish literary tradition: the epic. As Ramos narrates, López Nieves had been deep into the study of "the dazzling and marvelous Spanish epic" when he suddenly understood what was the cause of his nostalgia: he longed for a Puerto Rican epic. . . . a few months later, he made a decision: since there was no glorious or compelling epic (at least that he was aware of) that would "move me and fill me with pride, there was only one thing left to do: invent it."[29]

This marvelous invention would allow the national subject to proudly expose himself not as he "is"—colonized, racialized, queer—but as he wishes to be seen—sovereign, white, and virile.

The Spaniards in fact disseminated one of *Seva*'s central plot premises—that the Americans were not able to land the first time around. Once Admiral Sampson pulled back after attacking the San Cristóbal Fort to test its defenses on May 12, 1898, the Spaniards claimed that "a group of *macheteros* wielding knives against the Americans had forced them to re-embark with great loss of life. When I [Spanish soldier Angel Rivero] requested the latest news, an aide to General Macías secretly told me, 'We made them re-embark solely with our bayonets.'"[30] This inaccurate story was circulated for reasons of military strategy, but Puerto Ricans in *Seva* actually do what neither the *criollos* nor the Spanish did in 1898: honorably defend their "mother" to the end.

Identification with the former colonial power is only one of several devices required to narrate a Puerto Rican heroics. Equally important is the fact that *boricua* heroism can be narrated only as a case of mistaken identities, errors, and omissions. Víctor Cabañas's founding clue, for instance, is a supposed error found in a book by Marcelino Canino, *El cantar folklórico de Puerto Rico,* in which a single verse, a stanza plucked from oral history, affirms that a U.S. invasion occurred in May, not July. A second important omission, particularly for the tale's reception, occurred when *Claridad*'s editor, at the petition of the author, suppressed any mention that the text is a story, generating the critical misunderstandings that transformed the text into a memorable dreamwork.

Moreover, the most compelling evidence of *boricua* heroism is the *translated* words of the alleged perpetrator, underscoring that Puerto Rican national identity can be imagined only from elsewhere but inevitably lies in the colonizer's "staining" gaze, outside itself. The words of the killer (General Miles) are, in fact, strangely endowed with higher authority, as if to suggest that it takes a man to know a man. "I must admit that they put up a ferocious battle, organized, heroic, worthy of our independence struggle against the British and at the level of El Cid or Wellington."[31] Miles also confesses that the Seva dwellers' ferocious defense rendered the American troops "completely *impotent*" (my emphasis).[32] Yet precisely if one relies on *Seva's* evidence, Puerto Rican virility and heroism seem like nothing but "un error" imagined far from the site, conveyed through a translation of a fake document written by a dubious protagonist who had obvious reasons to exaggerate and uplift the enemy to justify his actions.

There is also a significant dystopic aspect of the story's intent and reception, which is closer to the structure of trauma and undoes the overt purpose of the text: Puerto Rican national identity is *elsewhere* and can be apprehended only in flight. Cathy Caruth, for instance, observes that "the traumatic event is not experienced as it occurs, it is fully evident only in connection with another place, and in another time."[33] Consistently, discovery in *Seva* is always preceded by travel from San Juan, and the evidence of national resistance is in the libraries of Galicia and Washington, D.C., and on the desks of empire builders. López Nieves also conceived *Seva* from another site represented as traumatic by nationalists: migration. "It was precisely in New York where *Seva* was born seven or eight years ago."[34] And although López Nieves himself only really lives to tell the tale from the United States—having fled—he is ironically crossing out New York, the multilingual and transcultural capital of Nuyoricans who borrow less from the Spanish epic and the imperial archive than from African American poetry and popular culture.

Despite its avowed intent of purging shame from *boricua* identity, *Seva* demonstrates that it is in leaving the site of conflict—rather than heroically resisting—that Puerto Ricans have survived as ethno-national subjects. Not only is Ignacio Martínez's identity as a survivor implicated in having escaped from the place of Miles's massacre, only in the trauma of leaving can one discover the wound, the text itself. *Seva*'s circuitous narrative ends up arguing that Puerto Ricans have historically understood political "freedom" not as an absolute struggle to death—*patria es muerte*—but "a question of a line of escape, or rather, of a simple *way out*"[35] and around overwhelming power.

Emptiness, however, needs a vessel. Accordingly, *Seva* appropriates the voices of African American soldiers and other colonial peoples' dead, to confirm *boricua* heroism. Cabañas's correspondence, for instance, remits us to the "real" letters sent home by American soldiers in the Philippines, Cuba, and Puerto Rico, who wrote to describe their experiences and offer their analysis. Historically, in fact, African American soldiers, whose military achievements were either distorted or ignored, became particularly assiduous letter writers in an effort to "set the record straight" and assert their pride in spite of shameful treatment in the United States. Many of these letters were censored, as they challenged official government versions of events. This was particularly common in sources originating from the Philippines, where massacres and other abuses went unacknowledged by authorities.

Significantly, it is the historical letters sent from the Philippines, not those written by American soldiers stationed in Puerto Rico, that most closely resemble the fictional correspondence in *Seva*. These letters documented the atrocities in the Philippines that, at least symbolically, *Seva* wishes upon Puerto Ricans. Archival letters from soldiers in the Philippines bear striking resemblance to *Seva*'s entry of August 10, 1898, in Nelson Miles's fake diary. In *Seva*: "We took action quickly but the extermination was not easy, although we were almost 4,000 against 721. . . . But now it is necessary to erase all tell-tale signs. The next day, I ordered the execution of all prisoners. We burned and destroyed whatever was left of the town."[36] Also in Miles's diary: "before the execution, one of those little black boys ('niggers') escaped."[37]

According to a February 27 letter written by Captain Elliott of the Kansas Regiment in the Philippines: "Caloocan was supposed to contain seventeen thousand inhabitants. The Twentieth Kansas swept through it, and now Caloocan contains not a living native. . . . The village of Maypaja, where our first fight occurred on the night of the fourth, had five thousand upon top of another."[38] In language similar to Miles's racist characterization of Ignacio Martínez's flight, an anonymous letter from a soldier fighting in the Philippines with the First Regiment, Washington State Volunteers, could be the voice of the "ugliest" American found in *Seva:* "The weather is intensely hot, and we are all tired, dirty, hungry, so we have to kill niggers whenever we have a chance, to get even for all your trouble."[39]

The appropriation of Filipino textuality is a nostalgic borrowing designed to authenticate the symbolic, political, and material losses of the elites, purge Puerto Rican complicity with American rule, and delegitimize *boricua* subaltern histories in the name of a Hispanophilic nationalism. Under the weight of Filipino bodies, López Nieves tries to hide *boricua* national shame, for "Under shame, what must be covered up is not your deed, but yourself."[40] Even though the critic Myrna García Calderón is correct in arguing that *Seva* constitutes an "assault" on canonized history, the resulting story is no less problematic. Even if ultimately *Seva* reinscribes the nation's queerness, as in most nationalist tales, it does so by reversing the alleged effeminacy of *boricuas* (collectively gendered as men) via a narrative of simulated virile warfare.[41]

Seva's politics in fact recall and refashion the colonial texts of 1898, including the infamous *Our Islands and Their People,* written by a (Hispanic) defender of the imperialist project, José de Olivares. An overtly colonial fantasy, the travel narrative claims to commit "the islands and their people to the printed page, for the information and pleasure of the American people."[42] *Seva* is a mirror image of that earlier text, a covert "anticolonial" fantasy compiled through the adventures of Víctor Cabañas for the pleasure of dejected *boricua* nationalists.

Both texts *invent* a place to *take the place* of memory and serve as a stage for fantasies to be constituted and projected onto a more wholesome past-as-future. In *Seva*'s case, the textual corresponds to the fictional town of Seva;

for *Our Islands and Their People,* it is the equally fantastic island of "Porto Rico." The ways that One (nationalist or imperialist) needs an Other (imperialist or colonial) to establish its identity are also instructive. Olivares's narrative demands a docile, friendly Puerto Rican laborer to make his colonial fantasy possible; *Seva* demands dead *boricuas* to enable an anticolonial, living nationalist rhetoric.

Visual Aids: Photography and the Unrepresentable "Black" Subject

Until the publication of *Seva,* no literary product had been able to satisfy the insomniac hunger of so many readers for a counternarrative of *boricua* resistance to the U.S. invasion. Ironically—and contrary to most commentary—I would argue that literary skill was not enough for the text to succeed. In fact, López Nieves deployed two other extraliterary strategies to bolster *Seva's* truth claims: mythic speech and photography.

López Nieves built upon widely believed existing myths linked to photographs to provide an even more satisfying one with a "clarity which is not that of an explanation but that of a statement of fact," as the French critic Roland Barthes has written.[43] This strategy is particularly effective because *Seva's* readers constituted an "isogloss," a "social region where [myth] is spoken."[44] Josean Ramos succinctly summarized the affected demographic as follows: "During that week, there was no other topic of discussion among the intellectual, artistic, pro-*independentista,* and academic sectors."[45] But while the mythically constituted photographs were meant to validate the narrative (and apparently for most readers, they did), these ultimately could not verify the text. Instead, as Susan Sontag has written, the photographs stimulate "inexhaustible invitations to seduction, speculations, and fantasy."[46]

In the original *Seva* text, as published in *Claridad,* the photographs are strategically displayed in an attempt to bolster the narrative's credibility. In embellishing *Seva*-the-happening and creating *Seva*-the-book, the author added images that articulate, at other levels, some of the text's workings, including photographs of the ships *Iowa* and *New York,* the *Gloucester* shooting at Guánica, a fake page of General Miles's diary, a "facsimile" of a letter by Víctor Cabañas, several maps of Puerto Rico (remote and contemporary), and an empty space corresponding to a nonexistent photograph of Ignacio Martínez, the boy hero. The book version of *Seva* unabashedly adds further visual "evidence" even after the contemporary readers of the *Claridad* version exposed the narrative as a work of fiction.

In both versions, the captions tend to anchor and "duplicate" themselves. A portrait of General Nelson Miles carries the caption "General Nelson Miles." The caption of a photograph displaying the *Gloucester* reads "The Gloucester." This mode of captioning suggests a lack of engagement with the photograph, a refusal or inability to "explain," and a parody of the use of photography as a source of authority. There are, however, striking exceptions. In this section, I will consider the first one: a blank (white) rectangle on page 53. The caption reads, "Since Don Ignacio Martínez still fears reprisals from the invading North American forces, he has asked us to not publish his photograph. We have, however, left this space blank, awaiting the day when it will be possible to show the face of the sole survivor of the SEVA MASSACRE."[47]

The blank space is key since it most strongly suggests the inauthenticity of the testimony. Yet the inability to represent the heroic subject invites, in Sontag's terms, excessive speculation. On the one hand, it could be argued that the nationalist writer is perennially mocked by the historical nonexistence of the Puerto Rican nationalist hero. On the other hand, one could claim that the blank space is an invitation for the reader to project her/himself into the void, and democratize the hero. Both explanations may be plausible, but there is an additional detail. The unrepresentable heroic *boricua*—the hole, according to *Seva*—is a "black" man.

That *Seva* cannot *see* Ignacio Martínez is not surprising. As López Nieves explained, his inspiration to write *Seva* came from both his doctoral readings of the Spanish epic and the narratives of maroons. Significantly, both sources are dystopic in representing Puerto Ricans of African descent. The conquer and elimination of the other ("moor"), for instance, is at the heart of the

Spanish epic. In Puerto Rico, unlike Cuba, maroon communities did not exist. Slaves tended to run away, individually, with relatively little success. Remarkably, a failed insurrection tipped off by a fellow slave on July 25, 1821 (the American invasion of Puerto Rico took place the same day, seventy-five years later) resulted in massive persecution of the enslaved population.

Perhaps closer to *Seva*'s fantasy is the experience of dozens of slaves who took part in the pro-independence Lares revolt (1868). Most slave leaders during the nineteenth century, however, were African-born men who harbored dreams of escape and/or taking over the land, killing whites, and declaring a monarchy. As Guillermo Baralt observes, some of these slaves also participated in overtly anti-Spanish acts: "The Beauchamp family took its slaves to Lares and these looted the Spanish stores that were on the way. This was one of the most violent episodes of the Lares uprising."[48]

While in Lares many slaves expressed solidarity with an independence project tied to emancipation, this revolt was anti-Spanish. In assigning a "positive" (nationalist) role to a black character, *Seva* cancels most of the community's anticolonial sentiment during this period, and appropriates a subaltern subjectivity in the name of a political ideology that often insists on a Eurocentric conceptualization of culture that specifically ignores and devalues black practices. The "use" of a black character thus corresponds to mythic speech, to the extent that, as Barthes suggests, "Only speech which is restored is no longer quite that which was stolen: when it was brought back, it was not put exactly in its place. It is this brief act of larceny, this moment taken for a surreptitious faking, which gives mythical speech its benumbed look."[49]

Equally important, *Seva*'s Ignacio Martínez revises the experience of the historical figure Simón Mejil, a master *tonelero* from the British Caribbean islands, upon encountering the Americans. Mejil was the sole resident to meet the invading forces in Guánica; everyone else had abandoned the town. Miles, who was under orders to "flatter the black element," named Mejil the first "boricua" chief of police under the American flag. It must have been a sweet moment for this *tórtolo* (an abject name given to English-speaking blacks from nearby islands in Puerto Rico) who spoke Spanish with a "slight accent,"[50] even if the avowed objective apparently was to "win their [blacks'] support for a pro-annexation plebiscite and, second, through the emigration of black Americans there, solve our racial conflicts."[51]

Seva's blank black man does double duty: first, he legitimizes white nationalist aspirations but has none of his own; readers indeed can never *see* him, he is a ghost. Second, his invisibility allows readers to effortlessly call on a previous myth that the text worked with, and upon, to achieve transparency, even if it was never mentioned. I would argue that the myth and photograph that are projected onto *Seva*'s white, nationalist void are not those of Ignacio Martínez, Simón Mejil, or any of the descendants of enslaved Africans, but that of José Maldonado, alias Aguila Blanca—the White Eagle.

Based on the life of a light-skinned Puerto Rican "bandit," the myth of Aguila Blanca provides the necessary backdrop for the *Seva* narrative to be believed with the potency of "historical" truth. The allusion to Aguila Blanca in fact surfaced in the text's reception: "I think that those who had been moved by the image of Seva—which is nothing but a dramatic summary of our almost century-old struggle—demonstrates that they are the heirs of Aguila Blanca (the man or the myth?), of Hostos, Betances, the artisan, the worker, and the peasant who had to swallow in silence the ignominy of the invasion."[52] This myth is, again, strictly isoglossic, as even one of its most ardent proponents, Juan Manuel Delgado, concedes: "'Aguila Blanca' is not recognized beyond the circle of pro-independence supporters, the small world of academia, and a dozen old people who still remember him."[53] Still, despite the narrow audience it seduces, many nationalist intellectuals have claimed Aguila Blanca as the only *verifiable* Puerto Rican hero of the Spanish-American War.

During the centennial year of 1998, in fact, the *independentista* lawyer José Enrique Ayoroa Santaliz gave a statement to the press in which he insists that several patriots defended Puerto Rico from the American invaders, among them Aguila Blanca.[54] Aguila Blanca's politics, however, are one of the most confusing aspects of the little that is known about his life. In 1898, as part of an effort to clean up his image as a bandit with the American administration, Aguila Blanca managed to persuade the director of the newspaper *El Correo de Puerto Rico* to run his life story. In the picaresque tale, Aguila Blanca describes himself as a "victim of abuses and injustices." Yet, as in many canonical nationalist narratives, Aguila Blanca frequently blames his troubles on black men, "negritos," who incite him to violence or sell him stolen goods, either way landing him in jail.[55]

Ironies abound in the use of this petty bandit as a hero of national resistance, however enticing his excessive masculinity. His name, White Eagle, suggests a twisted coincidence with the coming of empire, since before the invasion he was known as Black Eagle and Blue Eagle. The change of name does not seem accidental. In fact, historians claim that this purported patriot worked as a spy for the Americans. Aguila Blanca was most likely not even in Puerto Rico when Miles arrived, but in New York City.

Even more ironically, the myth of Aguila Blanca's heroism relies on a passage from Olivares's infamous picture book: "The only serious opposition to American rule was manifested by a band of outlaws led by a native known as White Eagle, who operated for a short time during the summer of 1899 on the southwestern part of the Island near Guanica. They had been driven to outlawry by Spanish tyranny, and when the Americans came White Eagle hoisted a flag similar to the emblem of Cuba and proclaimed the Republic of Porto Rico."[56] A photo with a probably erroneous caption[57] supports the passage: "White Eagle's Band of Outlaws" is a long shot of men with undistinguishable features posing in front of generic vegetation taken by an unknown, putatively American, photographer. The group does not seem hostile and few of the "bandits" are armed; certainly they are no match for the invading forces.

In *Seva*, the specter of Aguila Blanca then stands in for the black man in the blank space of national resistance, while the hero called upon to displace the "docile Puerto Rican" is, once again, an error. While the intent is to bolster the national hero, *Seva* returns us to the foundational U.S.–Puerto Rico shameful contact zone, the pathway through which the *boricua* national subject(s) allowed themselves to be feminized by American promises of democratic love. But as Benedict Anderson reminds us, the poverty of nationalist narratives is not an exclusively Puerto Rican lack. All such tales seem to refer to a space of "no there there."[58]

The Living Dead: Visualizing Pain and Other Displaced Matters

If the first remarkable photographic space in *Seva* is empty, the second is deceptively full. Below the book's title, occupying about two-thirds of *Seva*'s book jacket, there is a photograph of what appear to be several dead bodies clothed in white in a trench. The image seems appropriate to the narrative: dead, piled-up soldiers, the alleged victims of the first American attack on Puerto Rico. For the average Puerto Rican or American reader, the cover's photograph will not refer to any known context, nor raise any urgent questions. This nonrecognition speaks to both the American disavowal of its colonial past in Asia and the narrow parameters of *boricua* anticolonial discourse.

The photograph on the cover of *Seva* again recalls dead Filipino soldiers, massacred by American troops sometime between 1898 and 1904. It is an endlessly repeated photograph, found in a wide range of texts, reproduced to remind, excite, and stir sentiments regarding American imperialism. As Vicente Rafael points out, "Photographs of corpses were taken shortly after military encounters by professional photographers working for U.S. newspapers or hired by the U.S. military as well as American soldiers who had cameras. They thus preserve the shock of contact. . . . Unburied, they seem to have no place in the world and so cannot be put out of mind."[59]

In the absence of a picture indexically representing the violence inflicted upon Puerto Ricans by the Americans, the brutality suffered by another colonized people is called upon; the picture of the dead Filipinos becomes the *verification* of the "trauma" described by Manrique Cabrera, the loss of privilege of the white landed *criollos* and their shame in collaborating with empire. In appropriating the Filipino dead, *Seva* fabricates a narration of mutilation; not an image of memory but an image to be memorized, to fill in a pain that has been diffused, displaced, and redrawn—even enjoyed.

The appropriation of this traumatic photograph stresses the refusal of Puerto Rican nationalist myth to die: "Myth," argues Barthes, "is a language which does not want to die: it wrests from the meanings which give it its sustenance an insidious, degraded survival, it provokes in them an artificial reprieve in which it settles comfortably, it turns them into speaking corpses."[60] The need to use this photograph implies that *Seva* is nothing but a fake, a trick played on the dead. Contrary to the avowed intent, the Filipino dead do not confirm *boricua* resistance to the Americans; if anything, they stress how Puerto Ricans, unlike other colonial subjects, refused to give up their life for nationhood, choosing to live instead as *muertos en vida*, the living dead of national imaginings.

Critically, while there are few photographs of the Puerto Rican dead killed by the empire's army, there are many of the hungry, the unclothed, and the impoverished. Emaciated bodies and protruding bellies, the shameful photographs of death by hunger, are there for all to see. These images, however, cannot—do not—verify the "trauma" of 1898 for nationalists. Rather, they suggest that Americans did not bring suffering to Puerto Ricans; that it existed prior to their arrival. Even more poignant, if American political agency and economic policies made hunger more acute in the aftermath of 1898, the nationalist writer finds these deaths "natural" (produced by capitalism) and not useful matters for nation-building fiction. For, of course, the "real" trauma is the displacement of the landowners, not the misery of their workers.

Precisely because there are many memories—and forgetfulness—around 1898 and its aftermath, there is no widely shared traumatic narrative anchored on a single photograph. The only photograph that could be considered paradigmatic, due to its repeated usage in Puerto Rican reflections on the period, is that of *Our Islands and Their People* photographer Townsend holding two babies, one under each arm, with a caption that reads, "Our

Artist in Porto Rico." This photograph, which visualizes Puerto Ricans as children and the imperial project as paternal, is on *Seva*'s book jacket, crossed over by the dead Filipino soldiers.

Yet the representation of the Puerto Rican majority as children is certainly not an American import to the constitution of subaltern *boricuas;* the *criollo* elites and the Spanish also shared it. The fundamental objective of substituting Townsend for the Filipino soldiers is to erase the shameful image of *elite* Puerto Ricans as the dutiful children of Uncle Sam, even if at the cost of killing the humble people of Seva. As the historian Tomás Blanco put it,

> The dilemma is, then: either to take our destiny into our own hands, with serenity and firmness, or submit ourselves like mentally retarded people to a slow agony prolonged by palliatives and orthopedic devices, until we reach the limit of our physical misery and moral subservience, until the total and complete transformation of the island people into a multitude of pariahs, into a herd of coolies. Then, only the dead will be saved.[61]

The use of the photographs of the dead, however, underscores that not even the most sadistic invented scenarios can adequately articulate the specific pains—the shames—of the *boricua* colonial experience, even for the elites. As Sigmund Freud notes in *The Pleasure Principle,* "a wound or injury inflicted simultaneously works as a rule *against* the development of a neurosis."[62] In the emptiness of the imperial archive, in the absence of a photograph or a widely accepted myth, the truth revealed in using the other's picture is that there is no body, no subject of *boricua* nationalist resistance: only simulacra. *Seva* then raises a persistent national doubt urgently brought forth by the blank picture of Ignacio Martínez and the photograph of the Filipino dead: Do we *boricuas* exist? Did we die? Are we alive now?

Seva's overt answer to these questions is deceptively simple: "we" heroically resisted—died as Puerto Rican nationals—and that is why we are alive today. The aporia of this narrative solution is that unlike the traumatic events of the Holocaust and Hiroshima, the invasion is an unbearable event precisely because there are no dead. The *boricua* undead cannot then be buried or put to rest, particularly in symbolic production, giving practically eternal life to nation-building fiction. As Zizek points out, for death to be complete, it must be articulated in both the Real and symbolic realms. Puerto Rican nationalist literature is, in part, an attempt to bridge the gap and keep the national "body" alive long enough for the "people" to awaken to their destiny: exclusive subjection to the *criollo* nation.

What *Seva* aims to unearth—and kill—is shame as a constitutive marker of Puerto Rican national identity. The role of running away from the massacre is assigned to a black boy, who by virtue of his age and race cannot allegedly be ashamed or held accountable for his actions. Rather, his violation is the source of shame for the perpetrator, in an attempt to *transfer* the shame of the elite onto that of the master through a domestic subaltern. Cabañas's disappearance after allegedly trying to dig out the remains of Seva under the Roosevelt Roads military base cannot, however, help but narrate that there is really nothing heroic in the *boricua* character (it is truly a void). Unwillingly—and despite itself—*Seva* ends up telling the truth: elite national resistance is dead and it has survived only in writing.

Giving It Away: The "Faggot" of History

Seva is the most shameful text ever produced in Puerto Rican literature, to the extent that its aim is to refashion the shame of the invasion by covering up the location—symbolic and historical—and to bury it under another colonized group's dead. As a sort of poetic justice, however, one of the few *boricua* texts to openly acknowledge the legacy of 1898 as one of shame appeared a year later. In "1898," a homoerotic story by Edgardo Sanabria Santaliz set in the 1970s, the invasion is a forced—but enjoyable—act of penetration, lubricated by a collective ambition for upward mobility, yearning for transculturation, and ambivalent desire for those who dominate us.[63] The Americans, after all, "entered" Puerto Rico through an open bay.

"1898" tells the story of a young mulatto, Tonilo, who was coerced into getting a tattoo on his buttocks when he was a child by his mother's lover, Bebe (literally "Baby," an infantilized subaltern yet ironically corrosive masculinity), and now seeks to de-skin it. As in most of Sanabria Santaliz's stories, violence and desire are intertwined in the life of a young man.[64] Yet, in contrast to the desexualized allusions to Puerto Ricans as children by prominent intellectuals, here shameful feelings are inextricably tied to bodily pleasure—even if (or precisely because) they are mediated by violence—which in turn constitutes the colonial subject's identity as feminine.

Tonilo's social identity is in fact founded in the act of tattooing, which is immediately equated with homosexual rape, not only from the point of view of the young man, but from the tattoo artist as well, who asks, "Quién fue. Cómo . . . " (Who was it? How?)[65] In his perplexity, the tattoo artist's question underscores that shame arises from "experiences of incongruity"[66] and immediately raises the unresolved mystery of *boricua* national identity after 1898: "I don't understand how was it that you got this [tattoo]," this wounded Puerto Ricanness.[67]

In contrast to *Seva,* from the first line of "1898"'s epigraph ("Y Yahveh puso una señal a Caín" from Genesis) this is overtly a story about shame as an irredeemable fall from which Puerto Ricans (queer black *boricua* ethno-nationals) will never recover: "He was not assured by the tattooist's remedy; the scar would remain. But where could he possibly go without feeling even more *humiliated?*" (my emphasis).[68] By locating the shameful mark in the butt (not in the face, as the playwright Ramos Perea had implied earlier), Sanabria Santaliz also "lowers" national identity to its most shameful place: queer sexuality. The location of shame in Tonilo's buttocks, not his reproductive genitals, explicitly invokes homoeroticism and links shame and trauma to the ambivalent and uneven power plays of seduction, not "straight" virile politics.

The *boricua* relationship to the United States is homoeroticized as a sadomasochistic exchange through the tattoo artist Sailor, who was "hijo de un marino yanqui que llegó en el '98" (the son of a Yankee marine who arrived in 1898).[69] As in *West Side Story* (chapter 3), the reference to military culture in Sailor's name also calls forth a homoerotic world at the heart of heterosexist and masculinist discourse. At the same time, Sailor is a transculturated native, the offspring of an American father and a Puerto Rican mother, whose tattoos consist of a third eye—"un pichón de ojo"—and a whale with a forceful "pool jet" coming out of its top. In both cases, Sailor's body is saturated with signs of homosexual pleasure: a third eye (hole), a whale (phallus), and an open hole that emits water (ejaculation).

Although the story never reveals the image of Tonilo's tattoo, we know that Bebe's consists of "the pointy head of an eagle—you think it should have its wings open under the shirt—. The man perceives your fascination. (Do you like them?)"[70] The question, in plural, denotes a double entendre: Do you like the pectorals? Do you like the tattoos? Do you like the eagle's wings? Bebe's questions represent the *boricua* response to the U.S. invasion as a fascination with strength, and a desire for a social and economic revolution that, however, always entails a risk: rape. Yet rape may be the only way that the victim indulges in repressed desires.

Tonilo's queer shame stirs him to remove his tattoo in a futile effort to purge the demeaning pleasure and found a new social identity. Instead of achieving his goal, the young man relives his earlier experience of helplessness, shame, and pleasure—simultaneously. As Tonilo waits for the tattoo artist to examine him, he is a "maladjusted mannequin lying on a table,"[71] a passive object recalling the man who did it, and the mix of shame and pleasure he evokes: "as if his [Bebe's] image was a needle brought forward with pleasure."[72] Fittingly, when Tonilo attempts to ignore his body's sexual response to the tattooist's hands, allusions to the tattoo artist become orally fixed, culminating in a command, "undress, ordered the lips."[73]

The actions of tattooing *and* later removing the tattoo are represented as painfully enjoyable since each demands the displaying and caressing of the violated buttocks. Hence, while the tattooist examines Tonilo's rear, the young man fixes his eyes on the images that allegedly diminish him as a Puerto Rican black queer (or black queer *boricua*): Catholic iconography,

American popular culture, and compulsory heterosexuality. These oppressive signs only compound Tonilo's struggle with the pleasurable sensations produced by the man's finger upon his back, "the ungovernable tickling and almost perverse feeling that ran through him even in the most disgusting and burning beating that he was getting."[74] Again, the contexts to affirm his masculinity—the tattoo parlor, sex, war—end up by confirming the nationalist writers' fear that Puerto Ricans have been racially re-engendered into submission.

Gender tropes are not, however, the only ones at work in this story. As in *La llegada, Seva,* and "The Docile Puerto Rican" by René Marqués, the paradigmatic subject is a dark-skinned young man. The tattooist, in fact, notices both Tonilo's shame and his color at the same time, when he comments on "the lowered gaze glutinously trembling against the darkness of his skin."[75] As the theorist Silvan Tomkins argues, "when the face blushes, shame is compounded."[76] The rape of 1898, as inscribed in the tattoo on black skin, recalls the *carimbo,* the cattle inscription of slaves. Tonilo is, then, enslaved by his desire for Bebe, and allegorically, by giving up his manhood to the descendants of 1898. Significantly, the procedure to remove the tattoo, "epidermabración," will dislodge his—black—skin, leaving a permanent, lighter scar. It will also "hurt like hell."[77]

The only purification ritual offered by the narrative and consonant with the epigraph is religious, another shameful site of domination and transgressive pleasure. The tattoo artist becomes a priest, the removal of skin, exorcism, where he hopes to experience "an appeasing sense of cleanliness and relief from an insufferable burden."[78] Once the unnamed tattooist completes the de-skinning, Tonilo rises from the table. In a Fanonian moment, the raped one physically and violently attacks the tattoo artist. Yet what seems to motivate this violence is less the shame of rape than his craving for shameful behavior (homosexual penetration), the same desire that led him to follow Bebe into Sailor's shop.

Before striking the tattoo artist, Tonilo calls him "faggot" and adds that after he has finished beating him, the tattoo artist will not have any further strength to carry out his "rapes." Significantly, Tonilo cuts the tattoo artist's "head" in a futile attempt to regain his dignity (signified as masculinity) and eliminate the only witnesses to his undying homoerotic appetites. As in all canonical 1898 narratives, the black subject is represented as a survivor with little dignity, a *muerto en vida,* who gave himself up with the naïveté of a child. The black subject's compulsion can ultimately only lead to death since he desires his oppressor.

Although, unlike *Seva,* "1898" acknowledges rather than denies shame, it is striking that in a literary tradition with relatively few central black characters, the majority of 1898 narratives feature a black male body at their phantasmagoric core. It is no less striking that, regardless of the avowed political ideologies of the writers or the characters, most of the latter lack a body part or tissue. For example, *Seva's* black survivor is missing an ear; Don Martín Cepeda, a man who fought during the Spanish-American War on the Spanish side briefly referenced in Edgardo Rodríguez Juliá's book *Puertorriqueños,* lacks an arm; Sanabria Santaliz's Tonilo desires a piece of his skin removed.[79]

In each case, the narratives either are constructed around experiences that happened during the men's childhood or allude to them with infantile tropes. The black male characters are called upon to represent the shame of the Puerto Rican elites by referencing racist stereotypes of blacks as inherently childlike and lacking in masculinity. Perhaps more important, the persistence of these characters implies that despite their contempt for the low *boricua* others, the nationalist white male elites know themselves to be these maimed black men in the eyes of the colonizer. Puerto Rican nationalist writers hence coalesce around the trope of "the black faggot" (which is already incorporated by lack) as prominent Mexican intellectuals have represented the people of Mexico as "hijos de la chingada" (La Malinche): both delivered the nation to the invaders and both bear the shame and gratitude of ushering their people into modernity.

3 Feeling Pretty

West Side Story and U.S. Puerto Rican Identity

> *For never was a story of more woe*
> *than this of Juliet and her Romeo.*
> —William Shakespeare, *Romeo and Juliet*

> If a time-capsule is about to be buried anywhere, this film ought to be in-
> cluded so that possible future generations can know how an artist of ours
> made our most congenial theatrical form respond to the beauty in our
> time and to the humanity in some of its ugliness.
> —Stanley Kaufman, "The Asphalt Romeo and Juliet"

> The ideas of the past weigh like a nightmare on the brains of the living.
> —Stuart Hall, "Signification, Representation, Ideology"

There are cultural icons that never seem to die no matter how much dirt you
throw on them. And the multi-faced *West Side Story*—Broadway show, Hollywood film, staple of high school drama programs, inspiration for the 2000
Gap campaign featuring "the latest Spring styles and colors of the Khakis and
the Jeans,"[1] and possible remake featuring a "real" Puerto Rican cast—refuses
to bow out after way too many curtain calls. Like the Spanish-American War
for the Island nationalist elites, the 1961 film version of *West Side Story,* directed by Robert Wise and choreographed by Jerome Robbins, can be dubbed
the diaspora's "trauma."

A symptom that *West Side Story* remains a constitutive site for AmeRícan
ethno-national identifications is the fact that although the film is neither the

first nor last portrayal of Puerto Ricans as criminal men and "fiery" women, hardly any *boricua* cultural critic, activist, or screen actor can refrain from stating their own very special relationship to *West Side Story*. References to the film tend to convey a sense of shame or pride in the speaker's ethno-national identity, a desire for valorization, and/or a struggle to articulate an oppositional voice in American culture.

Jennifer López, the highest-paid Latina actress in Hollywood today, recalls that *West Side Story* was her favorite movie as a child. "I saw it over and over. I never noticed that Natalie Wood wasn't really a Puerto Rican girl. I grew up always wanting to play Anita (Rita Moreno's Oscar-winning role), but as I got older, I wanted to be Maria. I went to dance classes every week."[2] For the Bronx-born López, causing the Jets and the Sharks to rumble in *West Side Story* may signify that a *boricua* can indeed be valuable enough to play her own stereotype in a major American motion picture, but for the San Juan–born entertainer Ricky Martin, starring in the infamous musical means contributing to the stereotypes that make him a cultural oxymoron as a middle-class "white" man. Martin has in fact repeatedly rejected the possibility of a starring role in the remake because "It's kicking my culture. And I'm not gonna feed that."[3]

The journalist Blanca Vázquez, whose editorial work in the Center for Puerto Rican Studies publication *Centro* was crucial in fostering critical discourse on Latinos in the media, has also underscored the importance of *West Side Story* in her own identity formation: "And what did the 'real' Puerto Rican, Anita do in the film? She not only was another Latina 'spitfire,' she also sang a song denigrating Puerto Rico and by implication, being Puerto Rican. . . . I remember seeing it and being ashamed."[4] The Island-born cultural critic Alberto Sandoval shares in the shame as the film came to define him after he migrated to the United States: "And how can I forget those who upon my arrival would start tapping flamenco steps and squealing: 'I like to be in America'? As the years passed by I grew accustomed to their actions and reactions to my presence. I would smile and ignore the stereotype of Puerto Ricans that Hollywood promotes."[5]

In contrast to the purported materiality—however discursively produced—of the Spanish-American War and its aftermath, the nearly universal consensus by spectators, critics, and creators of West Side Story is that the film is not in any way "about" Puerto Rican culture, migration, or community life, that ultimately, it refers to "nothing." Even West Side Story's creative collaborators have been consistent in representing the work as non-mimetic. The lyricist Stephen Sondheim, for instance, initially rejected the project on the grounds of his ignorance of Puerto Rican culture and lack of experience with poverty: "I can't do this show. . . . I've never been that poor and I've never even met a Puerto Rican."[6]

Without a touch of irony, Leonard Bernstein also noted the extent to which he researched Puerto Rican culture before writing the score: "We went to a gym in Brooklyn where there were different gangs that a social organization was trying to bring together. I don't know if too much eventually got into West Side Story, but everything does help."[7] The "superficial" way that Puerto Ricans were represented made one of the original West Side Story producers, Cheryl Crawford, insist that "the show explains why the poor in New York, who had once been Jewish, were now Puerto Rican and black. . . . When someone said the piece was a poetic fantasy, not a sociological document, she replied, 'You have to rewrite the whole thing or I won't do it.'"[8] Yet if West Side Story was not intended to be "real," and many boricua spectators insist that it does not accurately represent us as a "people," what accounts for its reality effects? Why is West Side Story a founding site for Puerto Rican–American ethno-national identifications?

The film's durable canonization, I would argue, is not arbitrary on several counts. West Side Story is the earliest—and arguably the only—widely disseminated American mass culture product to construe Puerto Ricans as a specific, and hence different, U.S. ethnic group, ranked in a particular social order, living in a distinct location, yet informed by a uniquely American racialization process. While it is not the only media intervention to represent Puerto Ricans within a legal or sociological discourse (12 Angry Men and The Young Savages, for instance, preceded it), West Side Story remains the most cohesive cultural text to "hail"—and perhaps even more important for a discussion on ethno-national shame, to *see*—Puerto Ricans as a distinctly American ethnic group.

West Side Story is then nothing short of a Puerto Rican *Birth of a Nation* (1915): a blatant, seminal (pun intended), valorized, aestheticized eruption into the (American) national "consciousness." Irresistibly, *Variety* offers a typical *West Side Story* review: "Technically it is superb; use of color is dazzling, camera work often is thrilling, editing fast with dramatic punch, production design catches mood as well as action itself."[9] Or as Stanley Kaufman insists in the *New Republic*, "*West Side Story* has been overburdened with discussion about its comment on our society. It offers no such comment. As a sociological study, it is of no use: in fact, it is somewhat facile. What it does is to utilize certain conditions artistically—a vastly different process."[10]

Indeed, *West Side Story*—unlike the crime-saturated evening news—incorporates Puerto Ricans into the United States through a media product *valued* for its Shakespearean inspiration, aesthetic quality, financial success, and popularity with audiences, a timeless American "classic." This coupling recalls the historian Francisco A. Scarano's observation that "domination is an ambiguous process, a form of creating distance, of othering, and at the same time creating intimacy or bonding."[11] The unanimous regard for the film's quality, which simultaneously shames Puerto Ricans through its racist emplotment and valorizes us by the attachment to an appreciated commodity, continues to seduce audiences into multiple fantasies of incorporation—sexual, social, and (variously) ethno-national.

West Side Story is also not a product of Island high culture but of American popular entertainment, which does not depend on literacy or education to be consumed. If the cinema "homologizes . . . the symbolic gathering of the nation,"[12] the film further demarcates the United States, not Puerto Rico, as the "national" space. In this sense, even if *West Side Story* represents AmeRícans as a subaltern group, the subjects so lowered have more in common with Nuyoricans than the heroic *boricuas* from the Island's nationalist fiction, since they are working-class, not *blanquitos;* English (not Spanish) speaking; urban, not mountain dwelling; racialized, not European; and fully engaged in modernity, even if at a disadvantage.

Equally relevant is the fact that *West Side Story* constitutes Puerto Ricans as criminal (men), and victimized (women)—two gendered sites of shameful identification that nevertheless socially constitutes many *boricuas* in *excess* of ethno-nationality.[13] Educated AmeRícan spectators, who tend to be the most stung by the shame of *West Side Story,* have attempted to offset it by offering a "positive" counterdiscourse, on the "good" side of the law. In doing so they have, however, resorted to the same definitions of justice that criminalize Puerto Ricans and ignore the degree to which *boricua* popular culture reveres outlaws and identifies with alternative codes of honor. *Boricua* popular culture, in fact, often embraces violence by individuals as a means of addressing asymmetrical power relationships. "The right to individually enact coercive reprisals directly, without official institutional mediation," writes Kelvin Santiago-Valles, was "recognized and affirmed among the 'native' laboring classes" during the first five decades of American rule.[14] Similarly, I witnessed in screening *West Side Story* to young Puerto Ricans in the Philadelphia *barrio* during the mid-1990s, that teenagers repeatedly affirmed that the film was not racist, for "that's [gangs, violence, death] how it is."

West Side Story is hence compelling as a founding narrative because it raises both the disgrace-shame of the privileged and the discretion-shame of the majority (see chapter 1). As Blanca Vázquez has observed, what may be the most shameful aspect of *West Side Story* to educated U.S. *boricuas* is not only its racism, but its insinuation that many Puerto Ricans—specifically gendered as women—*want* a part of the American Dream, and that this identification can often be painfully pleasurable. Ultimately, the film's main and long-lasting effect is not that it divides "the Puerto Ricans from the Anglo-Americans, Puerto Rico from the U.S., the West Side from the East Side, the Latino race from the Anglo-Saxon race, the Puerto Rican cultural reality from the Anglo-American one, the poor from the rich," as some critics have claimed.[15] In a queer way, the film incorporates the specter of Puerto Ricans into American culture and provides what no *boricua*-made film has delivered to date: a deceptively simple, widely seen text that dwells on the still constitutive axes of migration, class, gender, race, and sexuality. *West Side Story* has in fact offered U.S. Puerto Ricans a world stage on which to negotiate their ethno-national identity, prophesying the replacement of *boricua* high culture by the mass media as a site of cultural reproduction.

The Puerto Rican "Thing" and the Makeup of Identity

If *West Side Story* has constituted Puerto Rican ethno-nationality as shameful, yet some spectators enjoy it and others decry it, how is the film playing (with) "us," Puerto Ricans and/as "Americans"? From the many ways that spectators complicate and enjoy the subjection of cinema, I will begin by highlighting the "make up" of *West Side Story*—how it visualizes *boricuaness*—by using the queer vernacular methodology of "reading" its performances as do the judges and onlookers at a drag ball. Arguably, one of the pleasures that the film offers *boricua* spectators is how it fails to "get" them as Puerto Ricans.

While little known, the film's origin story provides a valuable entry point. *West Side Story* is based on a 1949 play called *East Side Story*, a love story between a Jewish girl and a Catholic boy frustrated by both families. "As early as January 1949 Robbins had come to Bernstein with a proposal that they make a modern-day version of Romeo and Juliet," wrote Meryle Secrest, "using the conflict between Jews and Catholics during the Easter-Passover celebrations as a contemporary equivalent."[16] After some thought, however, the collaborators Jerome Robbins (choreographer), Leonard Bernstein (composer), and Arthur Laurents (writer) put the project on hold partly because the proposed story line was too similar to Anne Nichols's *Abie's Irish Rose*, the longest-running show on Broadway during the 1920s.[17] "I said it was *Abie's Irish Rose* to music," Laurents commented, "and [Robbins] wouldn't have any part of it."[18]

Read as a national allegory, *Abie's Irish Rose* is about how American "whites" were invented out of a broad spectrum of European ethnicities, immigration histories, and classes. Unlike *Romeo and Juliet,* the final resolution is staged as an integration of Jews and Catholics through marriage and upper-class mobility—a triumph of "whiteness" as a new identity for the children of European immigrants, regardless of their religion. By the end of the play, Abie and Rose, for instance, celebrate a hybrid Christmas with their children, who are fraternal twins. The twins, named Rebecca and Patrick in honor of Abie's mother and Rose's father, respectively, will clearly grow up to be neither Jewish nor Catholic, neither Irish nor European, but "all-American."

At the height of the late 1940s, Bernstein felt that *Abie's* conflict was outdated. World War II had created a new context for Jews in the United States; anti-Semitism was at an all-time low and many first-generation Jews and Irish were integrated as Americans, despite a lingering discomfort. However, the basic premise of "impossible love" based on a socially imposed norm continued to be compelling to Robbins, Bernstein, and Laurents. "We're fired again," wrote Bernstein, "by the Romeo notion; only now we have abandoned the Jewish-Catholic premise as not very fresh, and have come up with what I think is going to be it: two teenage gangs, one the warring Puerto Ricans, the other *'self-styled'* Americans."[19]

According to Bernstein, the new idea emerged spontaneously—and far from the action:

I was at a Beverly Hills pool with Arthur Laurents. I think I was in California scoring *On the Waterfront.* And we were talking ruefully about what a shame that the original *East Side Story* didn't work out. Then, lying next to us on somebody's abandoned chair was a newspaper headline, "GANG FIGHTS." We stared at it and then at each other and realized that *this—* in New York—was it. The Puerto Rican thing had just begun to explode, and we called Jerry, and that's the way *West Side Story*—as opposed to *East Side Story*—was born.[20]

The Puerto Rican "thing" was nothing but the recasting of a colonial migrant community into a distinct and "nationally" recognized ethnic group, now also seemingly available for queer erotic fantasies.

In adapting the play, the film's creators maintained Catholicism as a plot continuity (although the *East Side*'s Italian boy became Polish), but Jewish identity disappeared, a critical displacement since the creators of the film were all Jews. The erasure of Jewish characters, however, did not mean that the questions that have affected Jewish integration into the United States vanished. As Michael Rogin and others have commented, Jews in New York have been productive appropriators of subaltern culture—particularly African American—in an effort to address their own complex process of sometimes shameful transculturation. This process recalls Toni Morrison's comments regarding American literature, "The fabrication of an Africanist persona is reflexive; an extraordinary meditation on the self; a powerful exploration of the fears and desires that reside in the writerly conscious. It is an astonishing revelation of longing, of terror, of perplexity, of shame, of magnanimity."[21]

While blackface was only partially used in the staging of *West Side Story*, the play's music is heavily indebted to jazz and Latin American rhythms, and the casting in both the play and the film could be broadly understood as a minstrel act. In addition, for gay Jewish artists who were working in highly visible venues and in some cases living complex lives as heterosexuals, telling stories close to home through other means was not uncommon throughout their careers. Despite the fact that some have pointed to the surprising ease with which the producers changed one ethnicity for another as a symptom of racism, "passing" and hence substituting ethnicities was part of Jewish (ambivalent) survival strategies in the United States, which, of course, have much in common with (white) queer practices of integration into heterosexist spaces.[22]

The casting of white actors presents a second opportunity to approach *West Side Story* as a transethnic masquerade. Mason Wiley and Damien Bona wrote that the Mirisch brothers, executive producers of *West Side Story*, had "toyed with the idea of casting Elvis Presley as the leader of the American street gang, with his followers played by Fabian, Frankie Avalon, and Paul Anka."[23] No major male stars, however, were actually cast as any of the "white" Jets, although Natalie Wood and George Chakiris were hired to play the two Puerto Rican leads. Predictably, only secondary Shark roles went to Latino actors.

Since Puerto Ricans are a differently racialized people and some are indistinguishable from whites or African Americans (as coded in Hollywood cinema), *boricua* ethnic specificity had to be easily seen and heard. Otherwise, the visual economy separating the Jets from the Sharks—and Maria from Tony—would be lost. To stress the difference between ethnic groups, Puerto Rican characters spoke in a shifting, asinine accent, and the hair of the Jets was dyed unnaturally blond. Not surprisingly, George Chakiris, who played Bernardo, was "brownfaced." Given the history of Hollywood representation of Latino working-class men and Chakiris's own record in the production (he had played the leader of the Jets in the theater) brownface underscored Bernardo's ethnicity; makeup was a clamp used to avoid any ethnic misreading of his "realness."

Ironically, even if designed to make him more authentically *boricua*, Bernardo's brownface and eccentric Spanish pronunciation had the opposite effect and were responsible for what many observers found to be an unconvincing performance (which nevertheless landed him an Oscar). Simultaneously, although Natalie Wood's brunette type was less contested on the basis of appearance, the authenticity of her voice was questioned and even mocked. Not only was Wood's singing voice dubbed, but her "speaking accent helped her earn the Hasty Pudding Club's award for worst actress of the year."[24]

Jerome Robbins had requested Rita Moreno to audition to play Maria in the Broadway show, but once the play was transformed into a Hollywood production, the likelihood that a Puerto Rican actress would be granted the lead role considerably diminished, given the collusion of racism and commerce in film history, and the prevalent taboos on interracial romance. Although Rita Moreno is light-skinned, the union of Tony and Maria could have created anxiety in 1961 (although not in 1941, during the heyday of the "South of the Border" films of the Good Neighbor Policy era). One way to alleviate this anxiety was to allow white audiences to enjoy the interracial seduction by casting actors as Maria and Bernardo whom everyone knew to be white, and making sure that Moreno wore heavier makeup to avoid any confusion with the virginal Wood.

Even though it does not "see" Puerto Ricans, *West Side Story* visualizes a provocative proposition partly informed by the American Jewish experience: that for many immigrants, identity in the United States is, so to speak, a matter of makeup. Due to the instability of the category of "race," ethnics must then be made up with dark powder, bright colored ruffled costumes (women), dark colors (men), accents, and incessant movement. By default, "white" men must be made up of yellows, browns, and light blue, the women, orange. The conspicuous absence of blacks—even Puerto Rican blacks—makes the "epidermal" differences secondary, even an aesthetic affectation.

This "made-up" representation contrasts with the processes of transculturation taking place in New York between Puerto Ricans and their neighbors, and underscores not only why artifice was required to uphold fading differences but also why this could even be a source of enjoyment for *boricua* spectators who wished to retain a distinct cultural identity. As the writer Esmeralda Santiago recalls, New York Puerto Ricans during the 1960s "walked the halls between the Italians and the *morenos*, neither one nor the other, but looking and acting like a combination of both, depending on the texture of their hair, the shade of their skin, their makeup, and the way they walked down the hall."[25] *West Side Story*'s overkill in representing race reveals not the power of racism as an epistemology or the impenetrability of Puerto Rican culture, but how the only way left to disavow transculturation is through color-coding, lest you eat the wrong M & M.

Expectedly—and despite the heavy makeup—the film never entirely succeeds in maintaining the illusion of difference. The dance scene in the gym-
nasium, for instance, succinctly taps into the transcultured core of "American" identifications. The Puerto Ricans "look alike," as do the Anglos; but at
the same time, many Puerto Ricans are indistinguishable from Anglos. The
single exception is Maria, whose name and white costume connote her as a
"virgin," untouched by American culture and uncontaminated by racism.
That the film's arguably "perfect" character is also the most patently "fake"
suggests that the narrative cannot resolve its rips at the seams.

While thematically the film insists that ethnic groups should stick to their
own kind, the gym stages the swan song of anti-miscegenation as white bodies cannot help but perform to Latin-inflected music, even when the dances
are not identically choreographed. As Stuart Hall observes, despite the "in-
authentic" way that blacks are often consumed by the mass media, their incorporation has effected certain shifts that may be lost in a purely thematic
analysis of a cultural text: "Style becomes the subject of discourse, the mas-
tery of writing is displaced by music, and the body itself becomes the canvas
for representation."[26] If not in plot, *West Side Story* is stylishly transcultural
and transethnic.

Ridiculously, as *West Side Story* is staged and restaged, it will become
"more" Puerto Rican, black, queer, and "Latino" at the same time that the
play will continue to raise prickly issues. In the 1980 Broadway revival, a
black actress, Debbie Allen, played Anita and Josie de Guzmán, a light-
skinned Puerto Rican from the Island, was Maria. To her surprise, de Guzmán
was "made up" (as Rita Moreno before her) to look Puerto Rican: "When they
darkened her long silken hair for the part of Maria she revolted at first. 'Oh
my God, I am Puerto Rican—why did they have to darken my hair?' she
thought. They darkened her pale skin too, and after a bit she liked that, wanting to get literally in the skin of Maria."[27]

Yet it is in seducing the audience to look at Maria where *West Side Story*
forces both ethno-national makeups to blush. In the character's most famous
number, "I Feel Pretty," Maria reveals that she feels pretty (visible) only when

Tony, a white man, sees her. In Maria's quest to be seen by only one man, however, *West Side Story* allows other subjects to watch, enjoy, and unsettle his allegedly single authority.

Outing Race: The Queerness of *West Side Story*

The race-centeredness of Puerto Rican cultural critique—a symptom of speaking only from ethno-national shame—has also overlooked the uncanny queerness of *West Side Story,* how it sees *boricuas* not only in makeup but as the objects of homosexual desire.[28] Even when penned by some of its finest gay writers and speaking from queer spaces, contemporary references to the film have to date refused to engage with this differently constituted shameful excess.

Daniel Torres, for instance, refers to *West Side Story* in his novella *Morirás si da una primavera.* The narrator tells the story of an Island gay man cruising a "tomcat" in a New York City bar:

> Same old: a conversation about time or about whatever until the infamous question pops up: WHERE ARE YOU FROM? To which you invariably respond: FROM PUERORICO, I AM PUERORICAN, and then rush to add that you had only been living here for a year and a half, by which you avoid at all costs to be confused with one from the *West Side Story* and company set with the I WANT TO LOVE IN AMERICA, I WANT TO LOVE IN AMERICA thing. Nah, you were not one of those, you are from the island of horror.[29]

In this text, the reference to *West Side Story* tellingly surfaces at the uncomfortable juncture in which a properly nationally engendered Island gay Puerto Rican can suffer ethnic devaluation by being mistaken for a politically "unsophisticated" and transculturated U.S. *boricua.* The narrator succinctly acknowledges the character's subaltern status in relation to "American" white subjects, the re-racialization he has immediately undergone as a Puerto

Rican migrant, and the shame that arises from his inability to control what being *boricua* signifies in the colonial metropolis. The subject can then affirm himself as a "real" Puerto Rican only by rejecting any similarity to those he has indeed become in the eyes of the desired other: a Nuyorican.

The cultural critic Alberto Sandoval has also suggested that *West Side Story* is a rigid text where dichotomies such as sharks/jets, animal/technology, east/west, white/nonwhite constitute the text's main armature. However, if the musical's book requires these oppositions to maintain the illusion of ethno-racial differences, the use of brownface and the ethnic masquerade's makeup construct Puerto Rican identity not as essentially colored but superficially black, criminally stylish, and above all, queerly masculine.

To achieve this singular effect, the film's creators made several queer decisions in selecting and discarding elements from *Romeo and Juliet* for *West Side Story*. The feuding families of Capulets and Montagues, in which people of different ages and genders coexist, are transformed into two all-male, working-class, presumably heterosexual groups. The few women in *West Side Story*, with the key exception of Anybodys, a queer white gang-member wannabe, are mostly enclosed at home or in the workplace. The few times when they venture out without a male companion, as Anita does, hostility and violence threaten them, forcing the character to return indoors. By displacing the nuclear family onto the gang, *West Side Story* relocates "private" conflicts onto the public sphere and refashions them as a struggle over (homo) social space and performance.

In the battle for urban mobility (spatial and economic), however, the conflicts between Jets and Sharks are often superseded by the tension between the gangs and the police. Although it could be argued that the insidious presence of the police may be related to the fact that the force was a constant enemy of New York's gay community during the 1950s, the police, as an institutional body, are akin to the gang, since both are homosocial, hypermasculine, and "rough" worlds. Hence, the interplay of the gang and police is required to engender public space as exclusively masculine territory, even when they are at odds along generational, ethnic, or class lines.

There is, however, a second and perhaps more important reason the Jets and the Sharks ultimately protect each other from the police: the possibility of encountering each other. The "effeminacy" of many dance sequences where Jets and Sharks pretend to fight, one on top of the other, makes space for ritualized same-sex physical contact that would be otherwise impossible in a 1961 Hollywood film. Set to snapping fingers and "boyish" pranks, "race" offers exhilarating tension to the same-sex contact while displacing the possible queer connotations of body movements.

Significantly, one of the queer effects of the film for certain gay spectators is the possibility to live dangerously, to enjoy the surfaces of rough "trade" without any of the perceived risks through performance. The way Puerto Rican men were styled as "masculine" in fact anticipates the 1970s, when the "clone" style of masculinity became widespread and white gay men no longer fashioned themselves in primarily "feminine" terms.[30] At several levels, *West Side Story* is a racialized tale visualized as a musical feast of gay style: a spectacle of desire for working-class, gentile, "rough" ethnic men, as well as a tribute to performative femininity (the "innocent" white star and the spitfire). Consequently, although the context of reception made it inevitable that *boricuas* would be seen as scorned subjects, the most degraded portrayals in *West Side Story* do not correspond to the Puerto Ricans, but to a butch white woman.

Anybodys is a "tomboy" white girl who seeks acceptance and integration into the Jets through her affirmation of whiteness. Like Maria, Anybodys can only conceive of subjectivity in relation to white men. The Jets, however, are a constant reminder of her abject (lesbian) femininity: "I want to fight," announces Anybodys to the gang, only to have a Jet sarcastically respond, "How else is she going to get a guy to touch her?" (The film's gang members could ask themselves this same question in relation to the cinema.) Anita is almost raped when she transgresses white male territory, yet the hostility that Anybodys attracts and projects is unparalleled in the film. The Puerto Ricans are violently racialized but they are socially recognized, even sexually desirable, bodies. All white women, however, are accessories.

A white woman without a proper name, Anybodys, is an open and unde-sirable subject—"anybody"—sitting on the sexual/gender fence. In contrast, the scorn experienced by the female queer who struggles for a place among men is not shared by a second liminal figure, Baby John. Even though the Jets sometimes joke about his lack of enthusiasm for fighting, his name evokes sweetness and innocence, not evacuated subjectivity. Anybodys seeks power by distancing herself from other subaltern (racialized) people and tries to dis-place her gender oppression onto her racial privilege, while Baby John aims to conquer the world through the seduction of popular culture, art, and style.

The bottle-blond, tight-pants-clad, shy, and peaceful member of the Jets is perhaps the most important site of a Jewish gay subjectivity. Baby John is an avid reader of comic books featuring superheroes. This identification can be read as a distinctly Jewish one to the extent that the best-known of all su-perheroes, Superman, was created by Jewish artists. Moreover, Baby John is invested in superheroes as both objects of desire and antidotes to the per-ception of his own body as weak. Significantly, Superman is dark-haired, eth-nically other, and an alien force—like the Puerto Ricans, not the "Anglos." Although the narrative posits Anglo queers as the "good" guys, the desire for the raw sexuality and physical power of Puerto Rican men is what supplies the narrative with energy.

Anybodys is eventually allowed into the all-white male club, at the precise moment when racial confrontation is imminent and death critically undoes the gendered and racially segregated world that the narrative feebly imag-ines. Baby John, however, represents the hope of transethnic queer redemp-tion. Always singled out by Lieutenant Shrank as the possibly most law-abid-ing Jet, Baby John is the first to make a gesture toward the Puerto Ricans. After Tony is killed by Chino, Baby John picks up Maria's mantle from the ground and gently places it on her head. At the film's conclusion, the two bridge subjectivities are the gay man and the virginal ethnic, but neither is what they seem to be.

Suitably, unlike *Romeo and Juliet,* where both lovers are sacrificed to restore peace between the warring families, and *Abie's Irish Rose,* where marriage can be read as an allegory of national reconciliation, in *West Side Story* both Maria and Anita are left without men. In the film, being "ethnic" is more desirable than being married; in fact, heterosexual love itself is repeatedly associated with death: Bernardo dies defending Maria's honor, Riff dies defending Tony (who is sent by Maria to detain the rumble), and Chino will likely rot in jail for his effort to make sure Tony could not marry Maria.

The film's racially engendered sorting is an important departure from traditional Hollywood narratives involving love triangles between racialized characters and whites. In the conventional narrative, the white man conquers the Latino man to win the female racialized object of desire. If a white woman is involved, she will triumph over the Latina, who as a result frequently becomes suicidal. In *West Side Story* the white man does not triumph and the woman of color does not take her life. Actually, Maria achieves agency as a result of losing both her lover and her brother, the two men who controlled her. It is heterosexual coupling, not specifically transethnic desire, that proves lethal for the *West Side Story* characters.

Not coincidentally, all key figures in the making of *West Side Story* had conflicted feelings about their sexuality. The book author Arthur Laurents's work, for instance, was informed by what David Van Leer called the "problem of sexual substitution. . . . Such conglomerate identities come to a head (comically) in Laurents' script for *West Side Story*, in which homoeroticized chorus boys, arbitrarily divided into Polish and Puerto Rican, sing a mix of ballet and Broadway, all under the sign of updated Shakespeare."[31] The choreographer Jerome Robbins's homosexuality was a source of shame to his family and to himself. The shame of his queer identification was so strong that he even became an informant to the House Committee on Un-American Activities (HUAC) for fear that he would be exposed as a homosexual.[32] Like Bernstein, Robbins "wanted to be 'cured' of being gay."[33]

During the 1950s Leonard Bernstein also struggled with his sexuality and according to his biographer, Meryle Secrest, considered his homosexuality "a curse."[34] Bernstein attempted to reconcile to his sexuality—he allegedly thought of himself as "half man, half woman"[35]—through psychoanalysis and was treated by Dr. Sandor Rado, a Hungarian-born psychiatrist, who thought being gay was a "perversion."[36] While he eventually married a Catholic Chilean woman, Felice Montealegre, Bernstein continued to enjoy "slumming with the low life" and indulging in "tall dark, slender, beautiful" men.[37] Bernstein's sexuality was in fact a trope for all the "low" joys of his life: homosexuality, love for the musical theater, and Jewishness, which at times threatened to become major obstacles in developing a successful career.

Biography and thematics are not, however, the only sites to engage with *West Side Story*'s queerness. As noted earlier, the first queer decision is, of course, the text's genre. Musicals have historically been created by gay talent and have been the repository of a broad spectrum of gay cultural strategies, including camp, hyperbole, overstated decor and fashion, crossdressing, quotation, mimicry, gender inversions, put-downs, and bad puns. Even if *West Side Story*'s "poor" setting conspires against certain kinds of campiness, the stylized violence, puns, and other strategies suggest a gay structure of feeling.

Moreover, *West Side Story* is queer—even as a musical. According to Robert Stam and Ella Shohat, "The musical serves up an utopian world of abundance, energy, intensity, transparency, and community, in the everyday social inadequacies of scarcity, exhaustion, dreariness, manipulation, and solitude."[38] Hailed as one of the stage's most sophisticated musicals, *West Side Story* is also a liminal case of both entertainment and utopia, for it does not stage performances "which have the sole (conscious) aim of providing pleasure."[39] Although it is true that "lower class" (scarcity, unemployment) is provided with the utopian solution of abundance and energy, the excess of dynamism and intensity leads not to a utopian community, but to death. All attempts at open communication are mediated by racist discourse, even if queered, and the sole moment when the whole community gathers together, it is to help carry Tony's dead body.

If the count is even—two white men dead, one Puerto Rican dead, one on his way to the electric chair—utopia is beyond the narrative: placed in an undefined time and space, somewhere, sometime. In this sense, the *West Side Story* song within which heterosexuality seems safest is the queerest and voices a transethnic homoerotic utopia: "There's a place for us, somewhere a place for us. . . . There's a time for us, Someday a time for us. . . . Somewhere, we'll find a new way of living. . . . There's a place for us, a time and a place for us. Hold my hand and we're halfway there. Hold my hand and I'll take you there. Someday, somehow, somewhere!"

Skeptics may say that a *boricua* queer reading is possible only now, when so much—and so little—has changed for Puerto Ricans and queers in the United States. Yet even in exemplary cases that affected *boricua* representation in the 1950s, such as that of Salvador Agrón (a Puerto Rican gang member who killed two young white men in 1959 and spent twenty years in prison), homosexuality and ethno-nationality have been historically entwined in our constitution as American subjects. Agrón was considered not only a dangerous gang member, but also a "girlish-looking," "effeminate hoodlum" and "sex deviant" who liked capes and fancy shoes, and flaunted homosexual tendencies in jail.[40]

In a largely inaccessible Andy Warhol film (*Hedy, or The Fourteen Year Old Girl,* 1965), Mario Montez, a full-time postal worker and part-time Factory Superstar (see chapter 4), also provides a queer reading of the film. Montez plays a woman who wakes up from plastic surgery and once she looks at herself in the mirror begins to sing "I Feel Pretty."[41] Montez sees *West Side Story* "as is": artificial, exaggerated, ridiculous, and queer, confirming that even during the 1960s there was an alternative *boricua* reading of the film, one that was not, however, free of shame, but coupled to other social identities in excess of ethno-nationality.

From Rooftop to Bathhouse: Rita Moreno's Queer Career

Discourse around/in *West Side Story* offers one strategy to rewind the tapes of this queerly racialized foundational text. In this section, I would like to follow a different pathway to further own up to *West Side Story*'s shame by critically and joyously examining the career of Rita Moreno, the sole *boricua* principal in the film. While Moreno has been unfairly vilified by Puerto Rican media scholars, her career affords a rare opportunity to revise most of the issues raised by *West Side Story*. Before and after the production, Moreno's career is a case study in passing, stardom, and the transgressive uses of stereotype and parody to create alternative identifications and communities that show off, rather than hide, shame.

According to myth, it all started for the Humacao-born Rosita Alverio when the movie mogul Louis B. Mayer gave the teenager a seven-year contract at Metro-Goldwyn-Mayer.

> Rosita, no Latin spitfire, was perfectly sweet and charming at the meeting. She wanted to look like Elizabeth Taylor, so she carefully dressed and made herself up to look like the famous star, going so far as to use a waist cincher to copy Taylor's figure. To her satisfaction, at the meeting, Mayer observed that she looked like a Latin Liz Taylor.[42]

Mayer's approval of Alverio's crossover looks, however, did not extend to the teenager's moniker: "Mayer felt she needed to change her name. He thought her given name was 'too corny, even for a Spanish spitfire.'"[43]

Before being born again, Alverio debuted as a "delinquent" in *So Young, So Bad* (1950), a black and white production set in New York. After appearing in her first feature, Rosita packed what would become a very versatile suitcase and traveled cross-country with big expectations:

> Like many aspiring actresses, I came to Hollywood wanting nothing more than to be the next Lana Turner, but my education was to be abrupt and painful: the doors of opportunity were only open to me on strict conditions which the studios dictated. . . . Latino contract players were afforded no options in the old studio system; we played the roles we were given no matter how demeaning they might have been.[44]

Recent writings by Latino critics have amply demonstrated the toll of these studio policies on racialized performers, yet a second question often goes unasked and cannot be easily answered: What does it mean that a little Puerto Rican girl, watching movies in New York just after the Depression, identified with Lana Turner, tried to pass as Elizabeth Taylor, and was baptized into Hollywood at the age of seventeen by a Jewish movie producer?

A first clue is provided by Susan Suntree, Moreno's biographer. As Suntree has written, one of Moreno's favorite films as a child was *Imitation of Life* (1934/1959):

> In *Imitation of Life* the protagonist is a woman who hides the fact that she has black African blood and eventually rejects her mother. Rosita was deeply moved by this story and never forgot it. Not only did the mother-daughter conflict in the film touch her, but so did its theme that one could be so ashamed of one's bloodline that one would do almost anything to hide.[45]

The version that the young Rosita watched was Claudette Colbert's, not the more popular one featuring Lana Turner, yet it is a productive coincidence that Turner was one of Moreno's favorite stars and role models during her early career.

What was so special about Lana Turner? According to David Shipman, "Lana Turner has no other identity than that of a film star—and that from a mold, a fabulous creature who moves on screen among beautiful furnishings, and who, off-screen, is primarily noted for a series of love affairs, and marriages. . . . Even her admirers would admit that she couldn't act her way out of a paper bag."[46] Turner's one time assistant, Taylor Pero, agrees: "Image before truth, facade rather than fact, pride over all."[47]

For Moreno, identifying with Turner bestowed a few hours of distance from her life as a child of working-class parents, living in crowded tenements during the Depression. More important, the identification with the star is inevitably implicated in a desire to be looked at and recognized, to exercise the enormous power of seduction on the screen, which at the time was wielded only by white women.

Unlike most *boricua* girls who longed to occupy the space of the (white) star, however, the young Moreno actually gave the starlets of the day a Spanish voice. "She was the Spanish-speaking voice of such well-known performers as Elizabeth Taylor, Margaret O'Brien, Peggy Ann Garner, and Judy Garland."[48] In this work, Moreno "spoke" for/as the stars she could not be, and in speaking through them, rehearsed star fantasies as well as appropriated their voices for Latin audiences, transubstantiating the alleged neutrality of their whiteness and the shame of racialization.

In 1957, after almost two years at MGM, Moreno was "borrowed" by Twentieth Century Fox, where she lived in what she refers to as a "Latin Inferno." In an eleven-year span, she made fourteen films playing "mainly Indian squaws, Mexican dancers, and handmaidens."[49] The press dubbed Moreno not just Rita the Cheetah, but the Chili Pepper and the Puerto Rican Pepper Pot: "The more I played those dusky innocents, the worse I felt inside. Once I was an Indian maiden in *Jivaro* (1954) with Rhonda Fleming. There she was in frills, all pink and blonde and big-breasted. Right next to her, I had an ugly wig on, brown-shoe-polish make-up, and wore a tattered leopard-skin. I felt ugly and stupid and ashamed."[50]

This moment in Moreno's film career registers several key shifts in the representation of Latinos in American cinema. She was first signed during the height of the Good Neighbor Policy, during World War II, when the need to recruit Latin American audiences as allies drove Hollywood to introduce glamorous Latin lovers and exotic beauties on the big screen. By the 1950s, when Moreno's film career peaked, Latinos—and Puerto Ricans in particular—had migrated to urban crime genres. At this juncture, as León Vélez comments, "A character being Hispanic is not just taken for granted, it's often an issue. Usually a social and economic issue."[51]

In Rita Moreno's case, the shame of identity and the gap between talent and casting inspired a reflexive understanding of the actor's craft under racist regimes of representation: "I played all those roles the same way—barefoot with my nostrils flaring. . . . Hoop earrings, off-the-shoulder blouses, teeth gnashing—those were my trademark. The blouse and the earrings would get transferred from studio to studio and it became known as THE RITA MORENO KIT."[52] However painful this typecasting, being barred from Lana Turner–style star roles made Moreno not only a much more versatile actress, but also a discriminating philosopher, a popularizer of media literacy, and a creative risk-taker.

Moreno's critical perspective became an integral part of her star persona as early as 1954, when she was the subject of a *Life* magazine cover story. "Rita Moreno is a 22-year old starlet," reads the copy, "who can sing, dance, and even, to the extent that this ever becomes necessary in Hollywood, act."[53] Trying hard to portray Moreno as a sexpot, the four-photo spread rehearses how an actress should dress to give the impression of "all innocence," "sexy-sophisticated," "half innocent, half wild," and "sexy-wild."

Describing her "half-innocent, half-wild" look, which she also refers to as an "American-girl-type character," Moreno comes close to parodying her former idol, Lana Turner, who was also known as the "sweater girl": "she wears a sweater that is a bit too tight, pearl earrings and necklace and a beauty-mark on her cheek."[54] Yet if Moreno wants to be the all-American girl in a sweater, that is not what she gets to be. Of the low-cut dress, messy hair, sidelong glances, and open mouth of her "sexy-wild" look, readers are told, "Rita claims that she is dismayed that this is the kind of role she is most successful in getting."[55] While the *Life* magazine photo spread represents Moreno's "sexy-wild" image, the interview registers the young actress's resistance to her always already cast type: "But the most engaging talent is her eye for gentle satire, especially in the importance of acting sexy or innocent as the case required, in the casting office."[56]

As is well known, Rita Moreno won a Best Supporting Actress Oscar precisely for her role as the sexy-wild Anita in *West Side Story*. In the estimation of several critics, Moreno was awarded the Oscar for singing the praises of cultural "assimilation," understood as annihilation,[57] and hence affirming that Puerto Ricans were shameless. Although Moreno may have received much less criticism had she played the less interesting, albeit "positive" role of Maria, she rises above the limitations of the social script to show off her talent as an actress, singer, and dancer and paves the way to imagine Puerto Ricans as a valorized part of the United States.

Limited in discussing the specificity of Puerto Rican incorporation into the United States, the infamous "America" sequence in *West Side Story*, for instance, is saturated with "authentic" effects at the level of performance and in the representation of the pains and joys of many immigrant Americans. Furthermore, the level of irony, social critique, and female "excessive" performativity contrasts with most of *West Side Story* in its subtlety and insight. Even if many of us do not agree with what Anita sings, her performance is compelling to Puerto Ricans in large part because she sings to the greatest shame of ethno-national discourse: the desire for incorporation into the American body politic as queerly raced and feminine subjects.

Moreno would recover from *West Side Story*—simultaneously the high and low point of her career—and later win a Grammy for her participation in a recording for the children's television program *The Electric Company* (1972) and a Tony for playing a singer in *The Ritz* (1975), in a role that finally gave bite to her satire of the Latin spitfire. That Rita Moreno would be repeatedly rewarded for her work in dance and music is significant and should come as no surprise. Moreno trained first as a dancer and singer, and the relationship to dance is another way to inquire about how a Latina performer struggled to find a form when speech was denied or constrained, as was her role as Anita in *West Side Story*.

The entertainer's knowledge of the toxic workings of the film industry and use of performance to transfigure Puerto Rican shame fortunately coalesced in the creation of a character named "Googie Gómez." Googie's first public presentation occurred on the set of *West Side Story* in 1961: "Moreno would entertain the cast and crew as Googie Gómez, a Puerto Rican singer who was absolutely untalented, bighearted, and unstoppably ambitious. Googie was always auditioning for truck and bus companies touring the musical *Gypsy*, singing 'Everything's Coming Up Roses' in an extremely exaggerated Spanish accent."[58]

The story goes that Moreno was spotted showing off Googie at a party by the playwright Terence McNally, who promised to write a play that featured the character. The play became *The Ritz* (1975), a cross-identities farce set in a New York City gay bathhouse. According to Moreno, "By playing Googie, I'm thumbing my nose at all those Hollywood writers responsible for lines like 'Yankee peeg, you rape my seester, I keel you!" For Moreno, Googie was a satire of the stereotypical way so many people saw Hispanics but also a reflexive site to refashion Latino stereotypes and critique Hollywood metanarratives, such as the rags-to-riches success stories of stars.[59]

Whereas Lana Turner was white, sophisticated, worked in Broadway theater, and was a big success on stage and screen, Googie is Puerto Rican, vulgar, cartoonish, performs in a bathhouse, and has a jealous boyfriend with a big "knife"; her main success is believing in herself. Mocking the identity that was forced on Moreno, Googie contaminates the naively racist or complacent spectator with his or her own complicity. In exaggerating the most extreme aspects of the stereotype and resignifying it as a clash of worlds and a site for new community formation, Moreno radically refashions the shame of her Hollywood career.

Although the film version of *The Ritz* did not achieve the luster of the play, it is a valuable means of preserving Rita Moreno's performance. Moreno seizes—*echa mano*—the tools fine-tuned in Hollywood to parody how Puerto Ricanness and stardom are constructed for all to see, diss, and cheer. Googie's poignancy is not coincidentally related to Moreno's decades of getting "negative" parts, when the only resource available to the Latina actress was an unequaled passion for being "bad." Parody and comedy are then not only a response to (mis)casting, but also a critique of shaming culture. The "low" world of gays, bathhouses, and anonymous sex provides the required Rabelaisian setting to defeat "fear and all gloomy seriousness."[60] If outside "The Pits," Googie is just another *boricua* woman with a bad hair day, inside the bathhouse she is the undisputed "star" of the show.

Given Moreno's light skin, Googie's accent immediately lets the audience know that the dark hair comes from Puerto Rico, not Italy. Speech—that curse to the Latino actor of the early sound era—now has a critical dimension. Like Caliban, she knows the master's language and curses back, but in a queer—not macho—way. In speaking and singing with a broken English accent, Googie also provides English with new meanings, transforming pain into laughter, and offering a tribute to all crossed/over performers. The double meanings enabled by the gap in "correct" pronunciation are not only the stuff of comedy, they also instill a new cultural competence in the audience.

If gay humor often dwells on word games to subvert established meanings, Puerto Ricans and other bilingual subaltern peoples destabilize English in its alleged neutrality by unsettling the meanings of ordinary words. When Googie claims, for instance, that "My career is no yoke," the (bilingual) listener has several interpretative options available. In the context of a meta-conversation on performance, Latino acting careers are "yokes" to the degree that they are limited by racist convention. But the fact that careers are yokes can also be "lowered," turned into a joke, thus making enjoyment—not money—the ultimate reason to perform.

While the obvious reference to Googie's excessive performance at gay bathhouses makes us think of Jewish singers such as Bette Midler and Barbra Streisand, the most powerful intertext for Googie's "bad" performances in English is, arguably, the greatest *bolero* diva to sing in English, La Lupe. La Lupe's English pronunciation was idiosyncratic and almost unrecognizable, yet her "fílin" exceeds the technique, or better still, it is the technique. In Googie's performative universe, there is a keen intuition that the biggest act in the world is your own life, as La Lupe sang:

> *Dis [sic] is my laif [sic],*
> *And I doun't gif [sic] a dam [sic],*
> *for los emosioun [sic] . . .*
> *Dis [sic] is mee, dis [sic] is mee.*

Through her exaggerated use of gesture, language, makeup, and gowns, Googie is confused with, and doing similar work as, drag queens, a point made repeatedly in the film through its farcical plot. In fact, all heterosexual men in "The Pits" assume that Googie *is* a drag queen. This queerness, of course, is related to the fact that she is imitating stars and mimicking "ethnic spitfires." The setting of the character in a gay bathhouse defamiliarizes Googie's masquerade and makes her constructedness as an "ethnic" subject evident. Otherwise spectators would simply read the character's excessive on-screen behavior as "natural"—for an ethnic. As Googie observes in a conversation with Proclo,

> **Googie:** Look at Katerina Valente, Vikki Carr.
> **Proclo:** But they're real women.
> **Googie:** Oh, noooo . . .
> **Proclo:** They're not?
> **Googie:** Plastic Puerto Ricans.

Googie then artificially claims ethnic "realness" (as a Puerto Rican) at the same time that she parodies *West Side Story*'s Maria by mocking the notion that a (white) man (the "opposite" sex) can make her feel like a real woman by first affirming, "I am the real sing [thing]" and immediately demanding: "Make me feel like a real woman, Chico."

In *The Ritz boricuas* and queers are part of the "laughing people," as the critic Mikhail Bakhtin refers to those at the bottom of social and economic hierarchies. Or in José Esteban Muñoz's terms "*Chusmas* [slaves], like queers, have managed a spoiled identity by disidentifying with shame, making it a source of energy as opposed to an occasion for devaluation."[61] This is why when Googie dramatically begins to sing a *bolero*, "Bésame, bésame mucho," queer Chris "knows" the song and sings along. Eventually the detective also sings, in a utopian moment where excessive sentimentality—a theatrics of love—takes center stage through the *bolero*, that quintessential genre of Latino and/or gay memory and seduction.

There is, however, one fundamental element that Hollywood stars and Googie *do* have in common: stage reality is more satisfying than any other form of reality. In Googie's case—as in that of many shamed subjects—if you cannot become a star in a straight way and for the straight world, you must do it in a "queer" way, creating alternative spaces. Latino actors over the last three decades have protested the narrowing of their opportunities by using the language of positive and negative images and claiming the right to play "American" roles. By "American" roles, they mean white roles, which suggests that from the start, these actors have a fighting chance of racial passing. More radically, what these actors advocate for is the "right" to live on as illusion, to inhabit the fantasies of their childhood, and to represent themselves as fully sovereign subjects, even when no one—including the white stars—achieves this.

Googie goes a step further by being a critical spectator and performing the conditions for a different kind of "star." Unlike other well-known "Latina" performers before her, like Dolores del Rio, Rita Moreno was not an aristocrat. Since early childhood, Moreno's mother saw her daughter's talent as a way to make it out of poverty and hardship. Moreno's constant negotiation and struggle to work within the industry often made her take on work she would rather not, such as the infamous spitfire of yesterday. However, the qualities of the spitfire—passion, determination, and vocalness—if limiting on the screen, are essential to survive a hostile social environment.

Ashamed, Moreno has tried to put some distance between herself and the "spitfire" roles. Yet, had Moreno not had any fire in her, she would have never endured the glaciers of Hollywood executives, casting directors, and infinite offers to repeatedly play the same role, despite her Emmys, the Tony, and the Oscar. The available strategies to Moreno ranged from silence to the occasional prostitute with a heart of gold. But what in the end made Moreno persist, create, and above all, inspire many with the tale was the deep, belly-down, raucous laughter of all who seek to transform worlds not made for us.

Part II *Boricuas* in the Middle

4   From Puerto Rico with *Trash*

Holly Woodlawn's *A Low Life in High Heels*

> *A thief a junkie I've been*
> *committed every known sin.*
> > —Miguel Piñero, "Lower East Side Poem"

> Call me anything, but call me.
> > —Holly Woodlawn, *A Low Life in High Heels*

West Side Story may be the best known but it is not the only cultural artifact to imply that migration had queer effects on *boricuas*. In Island literary narratives and sociological discourse after the 1950s, migration to the United States is often considered a *desgracia*—disgrace in the sense of both a calamity and a fall from grace, a shameful disintegration of one's signifying world. Being the prime destination of the majority of *boricuas*, New York in particular is represented as a terrifying place where women gain agency while men lose their sanity, virility, and role as *paterfamilias*, a place so queer that women become more like men and men more like women, and even writers lose their pen's piercing power.

Complementarily, once U.S. Puerto Ricans (particularly men) began to create a distinct literature, homosexuality became a constitutive trope. Although queerness is often narrated as an obstacle to a dignified (masculine) self, AmeRícan writers also tend to recognize the hopelessness of purging homosexual desire to found a whole ethno-national identity. As Arnaldo Cruz-Malavé has written in relation to a key dramatic text, *Short Eyes*, by Miguel

Piñero, men are either "penetrators" or penetrated, "they are daddies or they are stuff, in a hierarchical chain of abjection."[1] For Nuyoricans, the "big apple" may also be rotten, but in ways that cannot be easily controlled or stabilized, not even in writing.

To dwell in this altered state, I invite you to take a "walk on the wild side" with Holly Woodlawn, a Puerto Rico–born Superstar, cabaret performer, and counterculture icon. The Woodlawn persona, reconstructed here through interviews, her memoir, *A Low Life in High Heels* (1991), and her performance in the Andy Warhol/Paul Morrissey underground hit *Trash* (1970), shows off strategies of valorization and exchange with American culture brought about by migration in a colonial context. Even if canonical Puerto Rican culture is still unable to laugh at what migration has done to (and with) *boricuas,* Woodlawn was already living *la vida fabulosa* (her term) in New York City during the 1960s and 1970s.

From drag shows to the center of New York's Pop Art scene, from the lows of junkie motels to the highs of luxury condos, from Jayuya to Miami and back to *los niuyores,* Woodlawn takes us on a carnivalesque trip where Puerto Rican queers pump new life into urban culture, underground cinema, and the ridiculous theater tradition. This outing, however, should not be confused with tales of gay empowerment, upward mobility, or ethnic success in the normative sense, but as a way to count how many feathers can get ruffled when a queer *boricua* migrant—the "ultimate disgrace"[2]—claims her radical right to beauty and dignity.

A Low Life in High Heels: Making Puerto Ricans Over in the Diaspora

Holly Woodlawn—birth name Harold Santiago Danhakl—was born in Puerto Rico in 1946 and was part of the "big" Island migration to U.S. northeastern and midwestern cities. Harold's mother, Dolores, had been a seamstress, his biological father a transient American soldier of German descent passing through Puerto Rico. Like many other displaced workers who became the "excess" of the Island's industrialization program, Woodlawn's mother left for New York in 1948 without her child, and later sent for him. Two years later, she married Joseph Ajzenberg, a Polish Jew, who adopted Woodlawn. Prefiguring the contemporary Puerto Rican migration to Florida by four decades, the Ajzenberg-Santiago family eventually settled in Miami.

Despite Woodlawn's paradigmatic migration story, in her critically neglected but important autobiography, *A Low Life in High Heels,* Holly represents a queer counterpoint to canonized tales of "becoming" American on a number of axes, including genre/gender, sexuality, race, and language. Unlike the authors of praised narratives of migrant incorporation like *When I Was Puerto Rican,* by Esmeralda Santiago, where overcoming ethnic abjection requires excessive discipline (schooling) and the protection of one's "insides" from transculturation, Woodlawn revels in her lacking location and not only engages in an impressive range of unlawful activities, but implies that the best way to dare shame is not to measure up but to show off one's "*chocha* for the world to see."[3]

The two narratives' divergent styles in performing *boricua* ethno-nationality in the United States are visually evident on the books' covers. *When I Was Puerto Rican* highlights a *jíbarita* (mythical peasant), the girl that was and that Santiago aims to recover by writing. Woodlawn's cover features a "glamour" close-up of herself, fully accessorized and put together by makeup, jewelry, and a good hairdresser. If Santiago gently says, echoing Antonio S. Pedreira, the "real me" (the *jíbara*) is within, Woodlawn vociferously emotes that my inside is male and Puerto Rican; my outside is American and female—or is it the other way around? Uncertain of the answer, Woodlawn simulates the instability of transcultural subjects and implies that all attempts to correct ethnic, racial, or gender shame through linguistic performance are a form of drag—a mask.

Woodlawn's mask, her new face, grows out of the shame of being confronted with the question of whether the teenage Harold is queer. The scene occurs when Woodlawn's father, Joe, finds out that Harold is using the household car without permission to cruise with other queer boys. Woodlawn credits the family conflict with transforming her life forever: "It was the most devastating, traumatic event I had ever endured. . . . I felt so ashamed. . . . My mother began to cry. Queer. The ultimate disgrace. . . . Why couldn't I just drop dead and get this over with before he asked the dreaded question? 'Are you queer?'"[4] Woodlawn's parents' look overtly constituted Harold's queer identity as shameful not only because of their contempt but also because in looking at himself through their eyes, he too found the self lacking.

Consistently, the book's genre (pop biography), subtitle (*The Holly Woodlawn Story*), and co-authorship (with professional writer Jeff Copeland) insist on the necessity of reinvention (and deception) when writing a queerly "successful" migratory tale. Like Andy Warhol, who also "authored" quite a few books he did not write, Woodlawn is interested not so much in writing as an exercise of power or personal expression, but in being written from and about, in valorizing a "low" body by making a spectacle of the dejected self. "In retrospect," recalls Woodlawn about her memoir, "I just wanted people to hear my voice and make people laugh."[5] *A Low Life* in fact suggests that writing is a performance that necessarily sways between subjection in language and the potential dislocation afforded by nonlinguistic gestures like laughter.

Different from Latino writers seeking a mainstream audience, Woodlawn finds particular delight in nonstandard Spanish and tends to use it in the most vulgar of ways for the (low) pleasure of a bilingual reader—and without the courtesy of a glossary. Phrases like "I'm an actress, not a puta" appear repeatedly, drawing an anatomy of queer *boricua* shame across the fissures of wit.[6] While there are some auto-ethnographical moments (e.g., the description of "lechón asado"), idiosyncratic translations and misspellings like "Neuva York" for Nueva York, "Cokie, cokie" for "Coquí, coquí" and "Puta Susia Ase Buena" predominate.[7] In this, Woodlawn offers not a "real" picture of identity but a "grotesque realism," one that articulates "a new kind of popular, convulsive, rebellious beauty . . . the latent beauty of the 'vulgar.'"[8]

Yet even though Woodlawn makes few style concessions to middle-class respectability, she will struggle to become appreciated by dressing up as a fabulous *white* woman. If shame "is like seeing our lives put on stage,"[9] Woodlawn will seek to outperform it by becoming a white female star, or better still, a queer Latin white one. Woodlawn's acting out as a white female is of course not surprising; the conflation of whiteness, beauty, and screen stardom is even yoked in contemporary (high) theory. The philosopher Jean Baudrillard, for instance, writes of "A white face, with the whiteness of signs consecrated to ritualized appearances, no longer subject to some deep law of signification."[10]

Resembling the trash collector that she will one day portray on the screen, Woodlawn will collect her self from fragments of stardom culled from movies, television, and magazines, although the selection of these is far from arbitrary. Given the absence of valorized queer ethnics in public culture, Woodlawn will invoke mostly Hollywood legends like Marilyn Monroe and Kim Novak, Spanish divas like Lola Flores, and notorious crossover successes from Latin America such as Carmen Miranda and María Montez. Even if Woodlawn will also include her mother's *boricua* beauty as an ideal, its value is measured in Hollywood rather than Puerto Rican terms: "She looked just like Ava Gardner."[11]

The assumption that whiteness is the measure of beauty, however, precedes Woodlawn's migration to the United States and is constitutive of Holly's identity. Woodlawn, for instance, affirms that she has never felt ashamed of being *boricua*, but the reason for this is revealing: "I was always told that I didn't look it [Puerto Rican]." While for many U.S. *boricuas* nostalgia for the Island articulates a desire to be free from American-style racism, Woodlawn's longing for Puerto Rico is overtly associated not with U.S. but Puerto Rican racism, with the privilege of being both white and wanted, or more accurately, wanted because of being white. "My grandfather had his own bedroom and I was the only one allowed to nap with him. . . . But then, I was different from all of my cousins as well as other children in town. Due to my German heritage, I was born a natural blond, and with my mother's piercing green eyes, I was a beauty."[12]

If Woodlawn does not generally comment on the relationship between her Puerto Rican ethnicity and racially engendered persona, her dread at the

"Puerto Rican queens" she would meet in New York makes evident an awareness of the low symbolic capital associated with "real" *boricua* queer identity
in the United States, a shame that must be avoided: "The Puerto Rican
queens in New York city were the most vicious. If the snaps didn't do the job,
they'd use a knife. These girls were psychotic. They ran in packs, and I made
sure I stayed clear of their path."[13] This is perhaps *A Low Life*'s most important, if skirted, inconsistency. Although Woodlawn explicitly identifies as a
"Puerto Rican Jew" who is both "man/woman," she refuses to recognize herself in others "like" her. Recently, Woodlawn again puts distance between her
and *boricua* drag queens: "I understand that they were violent as a form of
defense. But I was not a drag queen. I was an actor."[14] Gender, then, is a
marker for a crisis of identity that also builds up elsewhere, along the racial
train tracks.

Drag—and the new identity that it founds—does not then reject racially
engendered roles. Instead, it recognizes how cross-dressing and makeup can
offset gendered ethnicity by offering a way *out* of the queer male body of
color, the "no body" of America. In Woodlawn's words, "I was a fag. A mis-
fit. And I was miserable because I felt like a freak of nature. But when I put
on a dress, fixed my hair, and painted my face, I became a new human
being—and it was then, for the first time in my life, I felt worthwhile."[15]
Symptomatically, even if eliminating her ethnic male self often seems to be
Holly's aim in *A Low Life in High Heels*, when Woodlawn becomes famous, the
victory is ultimately Harold's, the crossed over subject: "I was a Warhol Superstar; a vixen of the underground. Finally, little Harold Ajzenberg was
somebody."[16]

The spectacular success of Woodlawn's strategy—crossing over queer ethnicity—is evident in that even when she affirms her *boricuaness*, this identification is ignored by critics and scholars, and neglected as irrelevant in most
commentary about her work. While Woodlawn repeatedly calls attention to
the fact that she is "very proud of being Puerto Rican,"[17] the publicity for
Holly's memoir stresses her association with Andy Warhol and her transvestism, not her ethno-nationality. As the rocker Lou Reed's famous song "A

Walk on the Wild Side" tells it, "Holly came from Miami, F-L-A, hitchhiked her way across the U.S.A. Plucked her eyebrows on the way, shaved her legs and then he was a she—she says, 'Hey, babe, take a walk on the wild side.'"[18] In a sense, Woodlawn's ethnic passing assures that the name/place of the mother remains concealed, despite the fact that it is the story of erasing the paternal law that is more blatantly alluded to in her work. The mother is, however, hidden not only because she is associated with an abject ethnicity but perhaps most important, because she is the parent who accuses Wood-lawn of "disgracing the family name" by being queer.[19]

Facing shame, Woodlawn will also require a different name to be born again with the denied dignity—ethnically Puerto Rican, racially white, gen-dered female. Harold's new appellation would have to cauterize class, eth-nicity, gender, and sexuality in an effort to erase, intoxicate, and scream him-self into social visibility by leaving a shameful identity hanging in the closet. In various sources, Woodlawn provides more than one, mutually exclusive, explanation of the acquisition of her name. The most circulated one, and the version found in *A Low Life in High Heels* and confirmed by Woodlawn, traces it to the Holly Golightly character created by Truman Capote and played by Audrey Hepburn in the film *Breakfast at Tiffany's,* and New York's patrician Woodlawn Cemetery.

Whereas Woodlawn's name is infantile, religiously gentile, in English, and saturated with references to wealth calculated to distance her from a deval-ued ethno-sexuality, Holly's full name does not even try to pass. Instead, as Woodlawn's racial and gender identification, it performs a conflicted rela-tionship to narratives of upward mobility and social hierarchies, not because Woodlawn does not seek fortune and status, but because she cannot help but laugh at their parameters. Regardless of how one reconstructs the name in writing, it contains high and low values of what is worthy and beautiful, without fully giving in to either side.

On the high end, Hollywood is referenced with its full weight of glamour (whiteness), wealth, and fame. But even in Hollywood, the emphasis is not on the town's hills or gardens, but Hollywood *lawn,* the most common and unglamorous of decorative plants, and furthermore, a plant designed to be walked over. Read as Holly Woodlawn, the name is also ambiguously ironic: "I wanted to be the next Venus de Warhol, and with that thought in mind, it was decided that I, a former housewife, go-go dancer, and Miss Donut of Amsterdam, New York, was to become the heiress to the Woodlawn Cemetery. Hell, it sounded good; I figured anyone with all that granite and marble had to be worth something."[20] Through this operation, Woodlawn does not so much raise her entire "lowliness" to another, higher realm as bring pieces of their "highness" to the lows of queer world-making.

Despite Woodlawn's command performance, she is painfully aware that her birth as a public persona evokes—and even tempts—death. If drag is a way of being reborn as a desirable illusion by burying the parts of an(other) unwanted, unmarketable, racialized, and shameful self, the conflation of dead stars, celebrated authors, grass, and cemeteries unequivocally links gender passing and ethnic masquerade to death. As Judith Butler reminds us in her commentary on Venus Extravaganza, another *boricua* drag queen owing her fame to a white queer filmmaker, "As much as she crosses gender, sexuality, and race performatively. . . . normative femininity and whiteness wields the final power to *re*naturalize Venus's body and cross out that prior crossing, an erasure that is her death."[21]

Transfiguring the dual shame of queer sexuality and ethno-nationality, Woodlawn defaces her former self in body and language only to accept the tremendous risks associated with living as a woman. Woodlawn was, in fact, repeatedly arrested for "female impersonation" (or as a roommate in 1970 put it, "unsuccessful" female impersonation)[22] and as a sex worker, she continuously put her life on the line: "Looking real was very important in my mind, because if there was any question that I was a man in drag, I could be arrested, and worse yet, I could be killed by homo-hating hoodlums!"[23] In a personal interview, Woodlawn narrates an instance when she was almost raped and killed while waiting for a bus dressed in women's clothes.[24] Holly's risky choice—to pass as a (white) woman—poses the question of this strategy's worth in valorizing a racialized subject.

"Glamour is sex and power," says Woodlawn. "I looked prettier that way [in drag]—and it made men look."[25] The risk is perceived as worthy because through the ethno-gender masquerade, Woodlawn refashions the superiority of heterosexuality's "claim on naturalness and originality"[26] and the immutability of abject ethnicity, opening up pathways to the enjoyment of seeing and being seen as a normative subject (a white woman), not a freak (a *boricua* queer). As Woodlawn once yelled at a *National Lampoon* photographer who insisted on photographing her as a man for an assignment, "Natural?! You want natural? Why don't you photograph a chimpanzee beating its breast in the Bronx Zoo?"[27] By claiming the right to a glamorous image, Woodlawn yearns for star status as a means to not only transform her self from anonymous particularity to public and admired abstraction, but also to ambivalently defend the idea that "Puerto Ricans are so beautiful!"[28]

Illusion, however, cannot seduce all the people all the time. If as a peripheral member of the Max's Kansas City crowd, Woodlawn was able to blur class lines and attend the parties of the rich and famous, passing took a fateful turn when a friend of Woodlawn sublet an apartment from Madame Chardonet, a wealthy French diplomat's wife. At a party hosted in the apartment, one of her friends found Mme. Chardonet's bank book, credentials, and passport, which they later doctored so Woodlawn's picture appeared. "Now all I had to do was sashay into the U.N. dressed in a tasteful black Chanel dress with a pink scarf tied in my hair and a French accent to boot."[29] Even though the first time she was able to withdraw $2,000, she was caught in the second attempt. Landing in jail, Woodlawn tried to pass as a woman in order to be placed in the female ward, but upon submitting to mandatory stripping was summarily sent to the male detention center, fittingly known as the "Tombs." In each of these transactions, Woodlawn risked her gendered and racialized life knowingly, unglamorously, and routinely. Yet through a form of poetic justice Woodlawn's deliberate misrepresentation—the symptoms of her shame as a queer *boricua*—led to her discovery as a Warhol Superstar.

The Factory had in fact already taken notice of Holly's passing history when she impersonated Superstar Viva to help a friend "purchase" (steal) a camera by billing it to a Warhol account. On a subsequent occasion, Woodlawn also declared that she was a Warhol Superstar in a magazine interview, a picaresque stunt that caught the Factory's resident film director Paul Morrissey's attention: "I simply had a hunch that here was some kind of 'character' or personality. . . . the combination of lying and larceny only increased my curiosity."[30] Whereas Woodlawn, like *West Side Story*'s Maria, will "feel pretty" only by becoming a distant "star" in overwhelmingly white constellations, she embodied the transcultural subject imperfectly made up by *West Side Story:* Jewish, queer, *and* Puerto Rican.

The Performance of Work and the Work of Performance: Woodlawn's Factory Days

Of all the galaxies where Holly Woodlawn could have shone, none would have been more fitting—and ironic—than Mr. Warhol's *factoría*. If the Factory created an alternative cultural universe for queer and/or racialized performers, once Woodlawn became a laborer in the Warhol cinematic machine, her story resembles that of many other *boricuas* before and after her, who pinned their dreams of financial well-being and social acceptance on good white *patrones*. While complicated by her transvestism, Woodlawn's work history of odd jobs and illegal forms of earning a living is not idiosyncratic, but common to other Puerto Ricans during the 1950–1970 period, who shared "extremely fragmented, erratic, and incomplete linkages" to the labor market.[31]

Even though many critics and collaborators have taken note of the ways the Factory has been represented—"a place that manufactures people, ideas, concepts, films, and even art"[32]—hardly any systematic attention has been turned to the organization of labor inside this seemingly unusual factory, and how its productivity was possible largely because of the radical needs of queers, addicts, and/or racialized groups to culturally valorize themselves. If

Warhol's "greediness" regarding the Factory's underpayment or nonpayment of assistants and the Superstars is often cited as an entertaining anecdote, this was an important business practice that facilitated both exploitation and transculturation.

In looking into the Factory as a site of production, I would like to emphasize that I will be focusing on the Paul Morrissey–Andy Warhol "collaboration" period since it is at this juncture that Woodlawn works in the Factory. As has been amply documented, there are substantial differences between films produced between 1963 and 1968 and those between 1969 and 1972, including the latter's mode of production (larger crews), aesthetics (more conventional yet often improvisational), and ideological slant (more conservative). The films of this second period were tailored to reach larger audiences and attempted—with different degrees of success—to generate income.

Like other labor-intensive industries, the Factory films relied on the least amount of work from the "above-the-line" group, particularly writers, even if Paul Morrissey would often receive a "writer" credit. Despite the Factory's seductive discourse on the uniqueness of the Superstar, the main value of the actors was their capacity to entertain. The lack of camera movement and the barebones outline or script were compensated by the intense labor of the performer, who had to costume him/herself, improvise the dialogue, and create filmable material—in only a few takes. "The unanimous opinion among Warhol's company was that actors should be capable of making up their own lines. 'If an actor can't make up his own lines,' Morrissey declared, "'he's no good.'"[33]

Performers used their voices, bodies, and imaginations to generate memorable characters and hence were, from a creative point of view, doing most of the work. As Woodlawn sums up, "All of the lines I say in *Trash* are mine."[34] In contrast to Rita Moreno (chapter 3), who was called upon to "perform" her ethnicity based on a rigid social script provided by Hollywood or through classical parody (remarkably, Woodlawn starred as Googie Gómez in an off-Broadway production of *The Ritz*) Holly's film career is emblematic of the ways many of the greatest figures of pop art/culture have liberally fed on subaltern culture to keep their work "fresh," encouraging the performer to be "himself"—and to stay in his (or her) place. Or in Woodlawn's words, "We acted like lunatics and he [Warhol] made millions off of it."[35]

Warhol saw the Superstar/Factory exchange as basically fair since "superstars" were people whose talents "are hard to define and almost impossible to market."[36] His comments about drag queens implied both his recognition of the "value" of their cultural work and his low regard for them as people: "I'm not saying [drag] is a good idea, I'm not saying it's not self-defeating and self-destructive, and I'm not saying it's not possibly the single most absurd thing that a man can do with his life. What I'm saying is, it is very hard work."[37]

Unlike mainstream stars during Warhol's time, who were paid large sums of money, his own star stable entailed a return to Hollywood's proprietary era in which actors charged substantially less, were at the mercy of studio heads, and played "stock" roles. Similar to most Hollywood executives, Warhol himself had little creative participation in the productions. The films, however, did require his name to be successfully marketed, suggesting that the artist's signature functioned as a brand rather than representing an artistic vision.

Remarkably, although this branding was a marketing tool and obscures the specific ways that the films were culturally produced, it is still used to identify the work in today's museums. "Since the exact nature of Warhol's assistants has yet to be determined," wrote the preservationist Jon Gartenberg on the occasion of Warhol's 1988 Whitney retrospective, "and since available technical credits are often incomplete, contradictory or unclear, specific attributions for technical or creative assistance have been omitted."[38] The fact that the films were eventually taken out of circulation to avoid lawsuits or claims on residuals (many collaborators were paid only token amounts of $1)[39] underscores that Warhol's main relationship to them was as an entrepreneur and that the actual artists remain unrecognized.

Not coincidentally, Warhol represented the use of disposable labor through the widely used colonialist trope of "family." Like Madonna, Warhol often visualized himself and/or acted as a benign maternal figure ("Mother

Queen"), while the Factory entourage were his "children." Warhol allegedly "felt like a parent bird with an enormous brood of hungry chicks in his nest, as he frequently remarked. 'I have so many mouths to feed.'"[40] In a 1978 interview, Woodlawn herself referred to Warhol as "Daddy Warbucks": "whenever I needed money, I went up to the Factory. . . . And he'd give me a check. They [Superstars] just felt that he would take care of them. I mean, he led them to believe that he would."[41] Warhol preferred to buy food or provide money on the basis of urgent need rather than pay his Superstars a salary. This method of compensation cheapened labor, gave Warhol tremendous control and bargaining power, and underscored the hierarchical bond between producer and Superstar.

The disposability of Puerto Ricans and other subaltern labor became most evident after the 1968 attempt on Warhol's life by the disgruntled lesbian writer Valerie Solanas, when the Factory moved to 33 Union Square West (860 Broadway) and underwent a radical makeover. Warhol instructed the receptionist to stop answering the phone by saying "Factory," and, as Pat Hackett says, the "place became simply 'the office,'"[42] relegating the "old entourage, the bohemians, the stoned strangers who take off their clothes"[43] to the status of relics. To cite Warhol's (or Pat Hackett's) own telling words, "The superstars from the old Factory days didn't come around the new Factory much. Some of them said they didn't feel comfortable with the whiteness of the place."[44] This fade to white was both a downsizing and a cleanup, part of Warhol's "outgrowing"[45] of the old crew. In were the celebrities, the socialites, and the fashion barons. Out were the junkies, drag queens, and ethnics.

Warhol's complex creative and affective relationships to a wide range of off-center subjects earned him the well-known nickname Drella.[46] A combination of Cinderella and Dracula, Drella succinctly synthesizes his double position as a homosexual working-class son of immigrants and a privileged voracious voyeur with a knack for new blood: "I think a lot of the Warhol entourage and how Andy was taking from them, living vicariously through them. Sucking from them what he wanted and then casting their drained souls aside."[47]

The Superstars were, however, willing to perform according to plan because they were recruited among people with radical needs for cultural recognition: "For a while we were casting a lot of drag queens in our movies because real girls we knew couldn't seem to get excited about anything, and the drag queens could get excited about anything."[48] The fact that most performers were also addicts facilitated their engagement: "Andy likes high people: they are animated and uninhibited in front of the camera. They will do anything for fun, and they don't have to be paid. Just give them drinks, drugs, doughnuts, and approval."[49] Equally important, Warhol not only allowed the circulation of drugs and alcohol at the Factory, he himself was a sort of narcotic to many of the Superstars, who felt that performing for Andy—and no one else—would make them famous: "Even though everyone knows that Andy does not move the camera or operate the zoom, his presence inspires the actors. Without Andy, there is no performance, no electricity, no magic."[50]

As emotional drug dealer to the Superstars, Warhol supplied and hooked people on labor with enticing fantasies that provided performers with glamorous reflections of themselves and ephemeral celebrity. Even if Warhol Superstars (unlike the wealthy sitters whose portraits represented a major source of income for the Factory) rarely appeared in their "best light," performing for Andy offered a bang for their buck. Unlike work in the established theater and Hollywood, Factory work promised to deliver the maligned ethnic queer into the public sphere for the least amount of labor, time, and social effort. In Woodlawn's terms, "[*Trash*] seemed like a really good deal. . . . We didn't go to school to be fabulous; we *were* fabulous! Hell, as far as acting was concerned, a stiff vodka martini seemed the best method of all. No discipline, no struggle."[51] Warhol's cinematic enterprise was not successful because it exploited people, but because it exploited "their needs to exploit themselves."[52]

Famous for Fifteen Minutes: Performing *Boricuaness* from *Trash*

At the time that Woodlawn made *Trash,* she perfectly fit the Factory profile. Not only did Holly own a pressing need for cultural valorization, she also had a "big" personality and a drug dependency, was living as a woman, and was turning tricks when things got tough. Because Woodlawn was on the edge financially, the meager amount she received for her work in *Trash* was more than welcome. According to Holly, she was paid "One hundred and twenty-five dollars when I signed the release" for six days of work. "Some salary for a Superstar!"[53] Even though she performed in a second Factory film and other shorts, it was *Trash* that, as Woodlawn ironically put it, "catapulted me to downright stardom."[54]

Trash was arguably one of the Factory's best productions and certainly one of the most lucrative. The film is structured around a series of vignettes featuring frequent Superstar Joe Dallesandro as Joe Smith, a junkie who is the object of every woman's desire but is unable to achieve an erection. Woodlawn plays Holly Santiago, Joe's live-in lover, who wants him to go "straight": stop using drugs, adopt her sister's baby, and live decently. Comically, given his physical disability and chemical needs, Dallesandro spends most of the film fighting women off, and bartering for drugs by flashing his bare body.

Moralistic in intent, the film aims to represent the "trash" of society: junkies, drag queens, double crossers, and sadists. In director Morrissey's words, the "basic idea for the movie is that drug people are trash. There's no difference between a person using drugs and a piece of refuse."[55] As if the message was not clear enough, Joe also looks for "junk," or heroin, and Holly for used "stuff" like abandoned pieces of furniture that she turns into useful objects or income. Allegorically, Woodlawn's character mimics the Factory's own production logic of transforming "social" trash into movie stars.

Initially, Woodlawn was only considered to play a secondary role. But according to Guy Flatley of the *New York Times,* once "Morrissey shoved her in front of a camera giving her no dialogue and just a bare outline of the plot . . . Holly emoted with such astonishing ferocity that her one scene led to another and another and another."[56] While Woodlawn was aware that she was chosen for the part because of her "trashiness" (Holly ironically called it "perfect typecasting"), she accepted the opportunity enthusiastically, hoping that it would make her a bona fide Warhol Superstar. Some of what Woodlawn had to do, however, entailed looking not very glamorous, masturbating with a beer bottle while screaming, "I want welfare" (among other things).

While it is not clear whether this scene was Woodlawn's idea or Morrissey's request, it was to shame Holly for decades to come. "When I was asked to commit sex acts with a bottle," commented Woodlawn, "it didn't dawn on me that I could possibly be embarrassed by this performance in the future. As far as I was concerned, I was doing it for art and to hell with what people thought."[57] To offset the shame of her colored queerness, Woodlawn complied with the director's demands, aimed to please and bought into Warhol's mystique. Yet although many praised her performance (the director George Cukor even tried to nominate Woodlawn for an Oscar as best supporting actress), some reviewers minced no words in describing the film's characters as "utter degenerates."[58]

Notwithstanding the moralization that the film offers regarding so-called low lifes, the fact that in these films the Superstars had substantial creative input in developing the story line allows for engaging with Holly's "Mrs. Santiago" as a site for the representation of widely practiced survival strategies among Puerto Ricans in the diaspora. Despite the social script that subjected *boricua* queers as trash, Woodlawn plays Santiago as a relentless survivor who is actively seeking ways to improve herself not only by "working" the system but by never losing sight of her own nonnegotiable demand for dignity.

From the first frame, "Mrs. Santiago" is unsatisfied with her life. A door of opportunity seems to open when she learns that her sister is pregnant and is not planning to keep the baby. Holly immediately offers to keep the infant and give it a home. In talking to her sister, they develop a plan so Holly has income to raise the baby: "welfare." The plan almost collapses when Holly finds her sister having sex with Joe, but after making up with her boyfriend, she decides to go ahead as planned, and applies for welfare. This time, she must perform the role of the pregnant Mrs. Santiago to assure an interview with the welfare worker, Mr. Michael (Michael Sklar).

On assignment, Mr. Michael visits the apartment and is immediately disgusted by the Smith-Santiago family's abject living conditions. Surprisingly, the welfare worker becomes fixated by Mrs. Santiago's shoes, and offers a truce: he will recommend that the family receive the coveted benefits in exchange for the shoes.

Although Mr. Smith encourages Mrs. Santiago to take the offer, she insists on their value as a unique object—the fact that she would not be able to buy these exact shoes again—and the primacy of her desire: "But I like these shoes." Mrs. Santiago explicitly refuses to comply with the bribe because she feels "entitled" to welfare, a claim that Mr. Michael contemptuously dismisses. "You may be entitled to welfare, but that doesn't mean you'll get it." Indeed. Mrs. Santiago's passionate defense of her valueless shoes culminates in losing the pillow from under her blouse, exposing the scene as a sham, and hence assuring an unfavorable report from the welfare worker.

Unlike middle-class Americans and Puerto Ricans, who represent welfare as a shameful handout from the government that only marks the poor's failure as individuals, Woodlawn speaks from the common experience of having been expelled from the labor force and having to struggle to affirm her worth without being defined by work. "I need welfare," claims Mrs. Santiago. "I deserve it. Shit. My family has a right to be on welfare. I was born on welfare and I'll fucking die on welfare." Furthermore, this scene also invokes a trend ironically described by the social scientist María Milagros López: "Social workers in New York City often refer to some of their clients as having an 'entitlement attitude.' These clients are specifically difficult and demanding and show little appreciation for the social worker's efforts or the grants received."[59] Or as Holly repeatedly challenges Mr. Michael as he tries to buy the shoes: "Aren't we entitled to it?"

"Attitude" in this context refers to a "settled disposition,"[60] through which Woodlawn asserts that not only do pregnant Puerto Rican women need welfare to perform their duties as mothers, but maternal drag queens with two-timing sisters and junkie husbands also *deserve* state support to lead a dignified life. As Woodlawn reminisced, "Paul Morrissey called 'cut' when I refused to give the welfare worker the shoes and asked why wouldn't I give them the shoes. I answered that I didn't give him the shoes because I had dignity. Morrissey said, 'OK' and we moved on."[61]

Through her performance, Woodlawn also articulates another generally noted Puerto Rican "attitude" toward adversity: that regardless of the pain, there is "always something to be enjoyed."[62] Woodlawn, for instance, ironically proposes to Joe, "I want to get back to welfare. Be respectful. Have a nice place." By camping it out, Woodlawn exceeds the moral framework espoused by Morrissey that defines people's value not only in relation to the work they do, but in relation to their sexual identity, ethnicity, and state of chemical dependency. Through *Trash,* Woodlawn's performance reworks normative values and performs *boricua*-specific entitlement "attitudes" with the ridiculous methodology she picked up from working in underground theater and films. In the playwright and actor Charles Ludlam's terms, "if you take the position that you are already going to be ridiculous, they are powerless."[63]

Despite Woodlawn's paradigmatic performance as a Nuyorican woman, *Trash* did not become the ticket to mainstream fame she expected. Woodlawn had undeniably become a celebrity in a queer way and for a queer audience, but not a "legitimate" star. While she would enjoy success and recognition as a result of her starring role, Woodlawn's highest moment of visibility coincided with the awareness that drag had limitations as a strategy to valorize queer *boricuaness:* "I was branded a drag queen (a stigma which has haunted me throughout my life)."[64] "But, God, that's not my ambition, to be a drag queen, I want to be an actor. . . . I want people to say of me, there is a person so gorgeous . . . "[65]

In retrospect, Woodlawn mocks herself when she recalls that upon watching the rushes for *Trash,* Warhol declared that she was going to be a star:

"And to think that I believed that crap. It was as if Zeus had handed down the last thunder bolt and said I was bound for divinity."[66] At the same time, it would be simplistic to "blame" Warhol for the failure of his Superstars to capitalize on their fifteen minutes of fame. As Woodlawn acknowledges, "Obviously, darling, he [Warhol] got the better end of the stick, but that's the breaks, you know? The fact that he was a talented artist and a commercial genius had nothing to do with my financial state. That was my responsibility."[67]

Yet Woodlawn's inability to capitalize on her success was not simply a personal failure. Unlike Warhol, who managed to yoke himself to the (whitely) famous (Marilyn Monroe, Elvis Presley) and gain in value, Woodlawn's value "emanated" from him and could not be reciprocated. If Warhol was able to exploit the shame of his (white) queerness, Woodlawn could not initially curb her appetite for the joys of the moment—sex, shopping, drugs, and fame—that articulated alternative values and allowed her to smooth out the pain of social devaluation. "Drugs made me feel good about myself. . . . All that mattered was being fabulous and looking glamorous."[68]

Equally important, and contrary to stereotypes of Puerto Ricans as lazy, Woodlawn does not reject all forms of work: "I love to work—if I enjoy it!"[69] After the Warhol experience, Woodlawn in fact became a comedic "entertainer," someone who received payment to make people laugh and "turn heads" as a drag performer. According to the actress Tally Brown, Woodlawn "became this beautifully functioned, disciplined creature who gets out and does her 12 shows a week with *total* control."[70] But as Woodlawn remembers, in the aftermath of the Factory days, her manager "tried countless times to get me a record deal, but the American public just wasn't ready for a man who sang in a dress. Little did we know that in eight years, Boy George would change all that"[71]—to a point.

The Unbearable Whiteness of Being:
Puerto Ricans and New York's White Queer Art

Two generations of writing on the avant-garde have clearly sketched out the importance of (white) queer identity as a constitutive element in the works of artists like Kenneth Anger, Jack Smith, and Andy Warhol. Shamefully, *boricuas,* while sometimes recognized as important individual performers, are rarely located within the context of a distinct ethno-national culture that also had an impact on white queer culture. Rather, in historical and critical accounts of the avant-garde and other queer performance spaces, *boricua* gay men often serve as background props of the most entertaining kind, yet I would argue that they were much more than that.

Most writers of this period located the most subversive aspects of queer white male culture under the umbrella of camp, defined as a perspective (or "sensibility") that draws from the incongruity between the normative and the "deviant." Yet critics and artists alike agreed that some of the "campiest" and "wittiest" performers in New York were not white. The *New York Times'* review of *Trash,* for example, notes Holly Woodlawn's performance and how the film differs from prior Warhol fare by the "wit and warmth" of its characters and the more engaging "high camp" style.[72] The reviewer, however, does not link Woodlawn's outstanding performance to her ethnicity or transcultural identity.

Woodlawn was not the only Puerto Rican performer noted for her abilities. One of the most highly regarded actors of both underground film and the ridiculous theater stage was the pioneering *boricua* drag performer Mario Montez. Although Montez himself now rejects all contact regarding his previous life and work, and left little record about how he viewed the relationship between his performance style and Puerto Rican culture,[73] Charles Ludlam recognized that Mario's *boricuaness* was related to his exceptional work: "[Montez] is the first Puerto Rican artist who knew she was Puerto Rican and used it."[74] This perhaps obvious fact begs the question of why *boricua* performers were among "the best," and what made Puerto Rican gay men appealing to even self-described "pasty" white queers.

The historian George Chauncey provides a valuable starting point. During the late 1950s and early 1960s, New York City experienced a massive influx of queer *boricuas,* who "electrified" the local gay sex scene the way working-class Italians had done during the 1920s.[75] Unlike white middle-class gay men, *boricuas* seemed more comfortable with publicly performing and enjoying their sexuality, both as drag queens and trade, and inhabited public space in highly visible ways. An example of how Puerto Rican gay men "captured" the imagination of white queer artists can be found in Charles Ludlam's "fairy tale" titled "Mr. T. or El Pato in the Gilded Summer Palace of Carina-Tatlina."

In the story, a little Catholic (white) boy "found a home in the ghetto at 226 East 4th Street. Here he met Puerto Rican boys who were Catholics like himself. They peed in the hall and made him get down on his knees in front of them and suck on their pee pees."[76] Mr. T. (or El Pato, in *boricua* slang, fag) manages to found a new transculturated place that combined "botanicas, gypsy storefronts and Puerto Rican boys." This space was, according to the text's narrator, popular with neighborhood children because Mr. T. "entered their world and crystallized the Puerto Rican Mystique."[77] That Mr. T. is the articulator of this mystique and not *boricuas* themselves provides a first clue to examine the power asymmetries that structured this cultural exchange and why the transculturation process sparked.

The affinity between white queers and *boricuas* is linked to symbolic strategies, cultural convergences, and historical context. As Ludlam notes, many Puerto Ricans were Catholic and so were several key artists, including Ludlam himself, Smith, and Warhol. Less than a spiritual affinity, Catholicism provided a shared sense of ritual, the importance of costume, and narratives of sin and the sacred that are key to performing queer identifications. In the case of Mario Montez, who was Catholic, it was widely commented that "[he] worried that performing in drag was a sin," a framing that is familiar to all Catholic queers.[78] As Warhol comments regarding (white) Superstar Viva's Catholic upbringing, "when you finally did go out and do all the things you'd never been allowed to do, they thrilled you a lot more."[79]

Apart from drawing on and being drawn from common sources, each community's constitutive relationship to shame required the ample use of the performative arts. If for middle- and upper-class white men "performance" often meant the theater, opera, ballet, and movies, for working-class Puerto Ricans—queer or not—it has meant popular music, dance, and sports. The *boricua* practice that of course proved to be the most mutually enjoyable was drag, since white queer artists validated it as an art form while Puerto Rican performers acquired a legitimizing audience. According to Ludlam, he never tired of writing roles for Mario because he had "dignity."[80] Warhol also tells the story that Montez once got furious with him because "I'd zoomed in and gotten a close-up of his arm with all the thick, dark masculine hair and veins showing, he got very upset and hurt and accused me in a proud Latin way, 'I can see you were trying to bring out the worst in me.'"[81]

White queers and Puerto Ricans shared in social identities constituted in shame by religious and secular discourses, but it was the process of differentiated racialization that played the larger role in bringing both communities together during the 1960s and 1970s. While Puerto Ricans were a racialized ethnic group in the United States, they did not present the same level of tension as African Americans during this turbulent period for white queers in New York. Although it is not clear if the writer Rick Roemer is referring to all ethnic groups or to African Americans in particular, his comment regarding the "opposite" strategies of "minorities" and white queer men is telling of racial anxieties mostly linked to urban blacks: "In contrast to other minority subcultures in our society, which use the very same tools of violence and hatred that the majority culture uses against them in order to combat prejudice and exclusion, gays use camp as a peaceful and humorous way to bolster their insecurities and redefine their perspectives."[82] Woodlawn confirms that

Puerto Ricans may have been more accepted in white queer artistic circles because "black people made whites nervous."[83]

Boricua queer culture, on the other hand, was like "pepper."[84] Since "Spanish" culture was less intertwined with (white) American narratives of national shame regarding race relations in the United States, international and domestic Latinness served as an unthreatening cultural source to indulge in alternative ethnic utopias of queer excess. "White gays found Puerto Ricans attractive because their [whites'] culture was dull and boring," says Woodlawn. "The Puerto Rican drag queens were so much more exciting. They would work a year on their gowns to go to the [drag] balls."[85] The identification and delight in Latin culture included not only references to "kitschy" Nuyorican religious objects sold on the street or the drag balls but also Latin female icons like the Cuban diva extraordinaire La Lupe (who lived in New York) and Hollywood stars such as Lupe Vélez or Carmen Miranda.

María Montez, the Dominican actress whom Mario Montez alludes to in his star persona, was a founding cultural reference for Ludlam and Smith as well. Known as the "Queen of Technicolor," she appeared in films with titles such as *Arabian Nights* (1942) and *Ali Baba and the Forty Thieves* (1943); her appeal to queer culture was that she stubbornly affirmed her right to stardom by flaunting a facile sentimentality and flamboyance that made her the ruler of a luxurious and alternative cultural universe. Significantly, Montez was frequently criticized for her substantial Spanish accent when speaking English. Although there is some debate about whether Montez actually fakes her accent, the fact that she refused to let go of her "flaw" may have fed the Latin stereotype, but also affirmed her as a *different* kind of star, one whose "bad" performance style and enjoyment of glamorous roles were practices of dignity in the context of "straight" dominant culture.

Equally significant, Puerto Rican migrants were quite knowledgeable about the constitutive element of camp, "incongruity." Many had been peasants living in the lush and impoverished Island countryside, and now lived in gray tenement houses in one of the richest cities in the world. Most spoke only Spanish, but had to quickly learn English or Spanglish to get by. In fact, bilingualism itself became a powerful trope to describe the "new" transvestite of the 1960s. As David Bourdon wrote, Mario Montez "exemplified a tacky discount version of the Hollywood dream. . . . His illusion of femininity was as imperfect as his command of English."[86]

The clash of languages further provided Puerto Ricans with additional resources to humorously refer to the incongruities of American life, a practice that remains alive and well in the bilingual drag of contemporary New York–based performers like John Leguizamo and Carmelita Tropicana. The ability of bilingualism to destabilize "straight" meanings was not only deployed by Puerto Rican drag performers. Ludlam was perhaps the most intrigued by the possibilities offered by bilingualism. Not only did Ludlam include characters with names like "Mofonga" (feminization of the word *mofongo,* a dish made out of plantains) and "Chocha Caliente" (hot pussy), he also incorporated Spanish anglicized slang such as "pee pee" (*pipi,* or penis) in his plays.

If white camp's main contribution was that "sex roles are superficial—a matter of style,"[87] U.S. Puerto Rican "campiness" had a wider repertoire that included ethnicity, race, language, and class. In the mouths of *boricua* drag queens in New York, who were constituted by both "white" camp and Puerto Rican irreverent practices such as *jaiba* and *gufeo* (a Caribbean practice of joking, often accompanied by great sarcasm and wit), two great queer traditions of social critique merged, engendering performers like Mario Montez and Holly Woodlawn. As Woodlawn sums up, "Everything that I did as a performer came from Puerto Rican culture: the humor, loudness, melodrama."[88] This was not camp as defined by queer white men, but a kindred sensibility that they clearly saw as a cultural resource, without fully grasping the difference.[89]

The wit of queer Puerto Ricans combined a sense of ethnic and sexual exteriority that was "intellectual" in the sense that it assessed the social as a comedy (from a distance), but it was also "heartfelt," seeking connections to the audience. Smith and Ludlam particularly liked Mario Montez because he was successful in immediately eliciting the sympathy of the audience. This was also Woodlawn's strength and what she explicitly strived for as a performer: "I wanted to look ridiculous, to make people laugh. But I also wanted them to *feel* something for me, to *feel* something for that pitiful girl with no future."[90] Woodlawn's "compassionate" performance and narrative style are intrinsically linked to various social identities constituted in shame, which tend to express solidarity with others who may also be deprived of dignity.[91]

At the same time, while affective and social affinities brought these groups together, uneven power relations have resulted in a situation in which white queer artists are valued for their contributions to "art" (theater, painting, film), while Puerto Ricans and other Latinos involved in these cultural projects are routinely ignored. Regardless of the widely differing politics and relationship to their work of artists like Smith, Warhol, or Ludlam, the representation of Puerto Rican drag queens and junkies as "low" discarded material (from families, communities) was taken for granted.

White queer artists generally perceived *boricua* performers as inexpensive "found objects" that could be useful in the making of art and/or as performing commodities.[92] These artists' individual needs for artistic "expression" tended to objectify subaltern culture, frame it as a low-cost resource, and literally "collect" it. According to David Bourdon, Warhol proceeded to gather the material to do a portfolio of African American transvestites by assigning "a couple of his assistants to cruise the gamier intersections of Greenwich Village late at night to collect outrageously dressed drag queens."[93] The portfolio became *Ladies and Gentlemen*. As Warhol himself summarized, "You're recycling work and you're recycling people, and you're running your business as a by-product of other businesses."[94]

Ludlam agreed with this artistic philosophy: "Our slant [ridiculous theater] was . . . especially focusing on those things held in low esteem by society and revaluing them, giving them new meaning, new worth, by changing their context."[95] Ludlam's "change of context," however, often meant the transformation of discardable people and their culture into "art" by white queer men: "I made stars of bizarre people. I used drag queens off the street as Fire Women in *When Queens Collide* if they had outré wardrobe."[96] Becoming aesthetic curiosities proved to be double-edged for Puerto Rican performers: they wanted to be looked at and seen as "aesthetic outlaws,"[97] but in remaining only "objects" in white queer worlds, they never fully acquired the dignified status or material comfort that they so intensely sought. "Being a Superstar," Woodlawn comments, "was like being a piece of art, and I wanted that status. I needed that stamp of approval. Without it, I was nothing. Not that this so-called status ever paid the bills."[98]

The use of other people as objets d'art also contrasts with the skills of Puerto Rican drag queens who were reputedly formidable recyclers of things—not people. Mario Montez, according to Ludlam, had a "gift for scavenging Lower East Side and SoHo trash heaps. Once, he came in with a bale of sequin material . . . and we used it to make a headdress, which fell apart during a dance, scattering the stage with glitter. It created a set of incredible splendor."[99] In his review of *Trash,* Guy Flatley describes Holly Woodlawn's real-life apartment as just as "topsy-turvy as the pad she shared with Junkie Joe and his downtrodden dog in *Trash*. Rumpled dresses, postcards, magazines, records, bottles, bits of 'found' furniture, Joan Crawford shoes."[100]

Woodlawn and Montez's "garbage" aesthetic is similar but not identical to that of white queer artists. It encodes the shame and violence of multiple subordinations—racial, class, sexual, colonial—while creatively acknowledging and exposing it as their own. As Woodlawn's Mrs. Santiago would say, "Just because people don't like it and they have no need for it doesn't mean it's garbage. I have use for it." Thus, a drawer becomes a crib; a dirty mattress, a bed. In this sense, both performers participated in a Nuyorican kitsch that, as Anna Indych suggests, results in exaggeration, hyperbole, and over-the-top embellishment "not only in the adoption of what is normatively described as 'bad' taste but a spectacular delight in the disdained aesthetic."[101]

Puerto Ricans refashioning themselves from trash and being seen as trash is, moreover, meaningful at another level. During the 1960s and 1970s, the height of the queer avant-garde, it was common to conflate unsanitary conditions or devalued objects with *boricuas*. Poet Pedro Pietri alludes to this state of affairs in his poem "Monday Morning," where an unidentified boss calls out to his Puerto Rican subordinate, "Spic the garbage can / looks like your salary / make it look like / my salary immediately."[102] Suitably, the first action of the Young Lords in New York, a political organization inspired in part by the Black Panthers, was the "Garbage Offensive" of 1969, which "forced the city to attend to the sanitary conditions of the community by building road blockades with the piled-up garbage that was left uncollected in the barrio."[103]

In fact, everything trashy, ugly, or "primitive" seems Puerto Rican to Warhol in his telephone book–size *Diaries*, edited by Pat Hackett. "The building [Neiman-Marcus] had just finished painting the downstairs lobby. They made it Puerto Rican colors and you just hate to walk into it."[104] During a 1980 trip to Miami, Warhol claimed that "New York to Miami is the worst line to go on, everybody's so ugly and Puerto Rican and Cuban and South American, it's just sort of disgusting."[105] At the end, Puerto Ricans stood in as a sign of absolute otherness and barbarity: "A brand-new tree was burning because someone had set fire to the garbage underneath it, and this whole family was sitting on the steps just watching the fire burn—it looked like Puerto Rico—and I just got furious—it looked like Africa."[106]

The casual use of the work of subaltern performers greatly contrasts with the way artists perceived "artistic" appropriations. Although Pop and other avant-garde artists shared cultural codes and had histories of working together, they aggressively avoided the appearance of borrowing—or copying—from each other. This tendency underscores that despite the effect that these cultural producers had on what could be considered "artistic," they still required that "art" and "culture" remain two distinct zones, one high, another low; one centered around the individual, the other diffused around anonymous people. Borrowing from subalterns in general—whether ethnic and/or drag queens and junkies—did not make these artists "less" original, in their own or the critics' eyes. But as Ludlam, the most aware of the avant-garde artists, once wrote, "it's really a cultural prejudice, it's not inherently low."[107]

There was on balance a degree of self-delusion involved in these representations of the other's culture. Since artists and critics had limited contact with their collaborators' communities and ignored larger histories of transculturation, Puerto Ricans became not an important force that informed the new cultural forms produced in the 1960s and 1970s, but one of the tropes through which the avant-garde could represent itself as the coming together of low (culture) and high (art). The failure to critically see Woodlawn and Montez as artists ultimately prevented the inclusion of queer *boricuas* as part of the wandering "low others," to use Susan Sontag's term, who nurtured the city's new high art forms, "evicted from their restricted territories—banned as unseemly, a public nuisance, obscene, or just unprofitable—they increasingly came to infiltrate consciousness as the subject matter of art, acquiring a certain diffuse legitimacy and metaphoric proximity which creates all the more distance."[108]

It is time that Puerto Ricans own their space as one of the key forces that brought about change in contemporary popular and high cultural practices, alongside queer white culture and the objects of their fascination such as comic books, rock and roll, and B Hollywood movies.[109] If for most the edge of culture was popular and queer during the 1960s and 1970s, it was because *boricuas,* while having contributed artists and transforming camp and other practices, were shamefully considered too low a matter.

5   The Writing on the Wall

The Life and Passion of Jean-Michel Basquiat

> *Es difícil ser rey sin corona.*
> (It's hard to be king without a crown.)
> —Shakira

The 1970s and 1980s gave rise to a New York queer-inflected, multiethnic urban culture that spurred new forms in music, the visual arts, and dance. In the words of the curator and art consultant Jeffrey Deitch, it "was an era of greater sexual openness to different cultures, and interchange between races."[1] Fueled to a great extent by racialized communities, this transculturation process was mostly injected into the main cultural bloodstream by white artists like Keith Haring and Madonna (chapter 6). Yet few figures from this—or indeed any—era embody the torment of becoming a commodity as a racialized subject more intensely than the Brooklyn-born son of a Haitian accountant and a Puerto Rican art lover, the painter Jean-Michel Basquiat.

As with hip hop culture in general (to which he had an ambivalent relationship), Basquiat has been primarily studied as an African American artist. Calling him "the most financially successful Black visual artist in history"[2] and the integrator of "African-American culture,"[3] the majority of critics who have to date reflected on Basquiat generally ignore the potential significance of the artist's Caribbean roots for his production and the construction of his star persona. But as Robert Farris Thompson, one of the few critics to engage with Basquiat in all his transcultural complexity, observed, "Wherever Iberian and Anglo-Saxon came together, on the streets of Chelsea, the Bowery, or the Lower East Side, [Basquiat] was ready. When Spanish was the move, everything turned Afro-Caribbean, accent, diction, pacing, intonation."[4]

Given Basquiat's constitutive relation to *boricua* culture and growing importance as a painter, it is even more mystifying that Puerto Rican critics have to date ignored him. This oversight reveals how "black" symbolic practices and artists (with the notable exception of musicians) are often construed as outside the pale of *boricua* culture due to their "low" (raced) identity and notorious "American" tendencies. Losing Basquiat as a vital resource for Puerto Ricans is also the result of a disciplinary trap that keeps scholars looking for (trans)culture in all the foretold places, namely, bilingual literature and lyric-heavy popular music like *salsa* and rap.[5]

Nonetheless, Basquiat—painter, performer, poet, as well as urban myth— is of great significance to a theory of subaltern valorization and *boricua* diaspora culture. Ensnared like few others in the crossing of multiple definitions of what is valuable and moral, Basquiat simultaneously used his paintings as masks to safeguard his dignity as a man of Afro-Caribbean descent in the United States, offered them as gifts through which he hoped to transcend his racialized identity, and displayed them as advertisements to sell himself to white collectors, critics, and consumers. This is why the vernacular methodology of this chapter can only be *the writing on the wall,* for not only does the story start there, the social institutions that offered Basquiat what he wished for also tore him apart, prefiguring the artist's short but intense life.

Labor Repressive: Art, Basquiat, and Capital

Born in Brooklyn in 1960, Basquiat began his race to fame as the graffiti provocateur SAMO, writing public poetry and aphorisms on walls across the power corridors of Manhattan during the late 1970s. If, as the art critic Rene

Ricard suggests, becoming an artist "is an honest way to rise out of the slum, using one's sheer self as the medium, the money earned rather a proof pure and simple of the value of that individual, The Artist,"[6] Basquiat emerged not so much from the ghetto as from the middle-class faith that art could make him free of a devalued racial identity and secure him a safer place in the world.

A collaborative endeavor between Basquiat and his school friend Al Diaz, SAMO anticipated Basquiat's career on various levels. Not only did their tags allude to the "same old racism," these were strategically placed outside art galleries or on the pathways of influential people, even if the writing entailed a critique of greed and white privilege. Like other social identities constituted in shame, SAMO simultaneously hoped to be looked at by the affluent and powerful while affirming other values. Or as SAMO would put it, SAMO@AS AN ALTERNATIVE TO JOE NORMAL AND THE BOURGEOISIE FANTASY."[7]

SAMO's objectives were, however, easier to write down than to execute. Basquiat aspired to become recognized beyond the tag of the "big black artist" within one of the most hostile cultural environments for racialized people: high art. In Greg Tate's unequivocal words, "To this day it [visual arts] remains a bastion of white supremacy, a sconce of the wealthy whose high-walled barricades are matched only by Wall Street and the White House and whose exclusionary practices are enforced 24-7-365."[8] Yet it was Basquiat's fate that he not only received considerable recognition as an artist, but also succeeded at a time when artists could attain major celebrity status and ooze out to popular culture in ways that before were available mostly to Hollywood actors and rock stars.

Being brand Basquiat, of course, came at a high cost. Facing a sharply racialized cultural context that simultaneously valued his work in the marketplace and often humiliated him as a "colored" artist, Basquiat developed modes of accommodation and defiance, including heroin addiction, ambivalent subversion to the mechanics of capital, and nomad behavior that came to define his artistic persona and substantially inform his work. Although art critics have often decried the fact that attention to Basquiat's biography has to date overshadowed his art, both can be seen as performances that used different media toward the same aim: incorporation into the Big White Way of high art. In this sense, Basquiat's "acting out" in life and canvas closely resembles Holly Woodlawn's (chapter 4), creating similar (trans)cultural effects and proposing different logics of valorization that are ambiguously at odds with capital.

As was the case with Woodlawn, one of Basquiat's main objectives in becoming an artist was to become famous. According to the writer Patricia Bosworth, "Basquiat maintained that all he wanted was to be famous. He could learn how to draw later."[9] Fame and money were not, however, ends in themselves, but means through which Basquiat hoped to enjoy the "real luxury goods" denied to most racialized subjects in the United States: respect, recognition, and freedom from want—and shame.[10] One of Basquiat's assistants, John Seed, observed that the artist's Venice, California, apartment possessed "only two pieces of furniture," although the "floor was covered with an amazing array of clutter: art history books, cassette tapes, art supplies."[11]

Consistent with alternative definitions of what is worthy and how to measure value, Basquiat rejected regulated forms of labor. Unlike his idol, Andy Warhol, who dreamed of becoming a machine, or his contemporary Keith Haring, who according to his friend George Condo actually did become one,[12] Basquiat was prolific without being disciplined and indulged in disrespectful behavior when addressing superiors. As his friend the artist Keith Haring recalls, "He [SAMO] bought a canvas at Utrecht's and paint and put all this paint on the canvas and let cars run over it and got the paint all over himself and then got on the subway and went to an appointment at Fiorucci and got paint on EVERYTHING on the way and at Fiorucci he got paint on the rug and couch and rich ladies' furs. He was asked to leave before his appointment."[13] True to SAMO, Basquiat craved attention on his own, nonnormative terms, and dismissed "prevailing definitions of property and propriety."[14]

Complementarily, Basquiat resisted spatial stability, living as a drifter for most of his life. Basquiat's nomadism emerged from, and was evident in, many instances, including his family history as the child of immigrants, his mother's mental illness, and his polymorphous personal relationships. As the biographer Phoebe Hoban noted, Basquiat "couldn't maintain a single emotional bond—whether it was to friends, lovers, or art dealers."[15] Although Basquiat's behavior is often cited as an idiosyncratic feature, the scholar María Milagros López has argued that "affective nomadism" is common among *boricuas* as "temporary jobs, job instability, job migration . . . seem to preclude the possibility of stable, long term commitment."[16]

Basquiat also had a history of running away from home as a teenager, living on the streets (including a time when he slept in a cardboard box), and later wandering like a bum until he was twenty years old. According to Haring, during Basquiat's early years he never had a studio, "but he'd move from one place to another, staying wherever he could stay."[17] Basquiat's forays into the club scene appeared to be initially motivated to "see what my prospects were"[18] in terms of finding a place to crash. These practices of flight were not the result of lacking a home, but articulated a desire to be free from subjecting structures, be they school, family, or capital.

Tellingly, Basquiat's first relationship with a professional art dealer, Annina Nosei, was fraught with difficulties. Since the artist did not have a suitable space to paint, he began to use Nosei's gallery's basement while prospective (white) buyers were let in to see him paint up to three paintings a day in a quasi circus atmosphere. The sight unfavorably impressed the collector Doug Cramer: "He was painting away. He looked like a slave, or very close to it."[19] This was the first time that Basquiat had ample space to work, yet the fact that he was on display as a curiosity transformed painting into "hard labor," immediately changing the artist's relationship to his work. In Warhol's estimation, Basquiat's "early stuff is sort of better, because then he was just painting, and now he has to think about stuff to paint to sell. And how many screaming Negroes can you do? Well, I guess you can do them forever, but . . . "[20]

While Basquiat envisioned commodification as a way out of the racialized body to the extent that it socially valorized him, the requirements of steady output undermined his independence and relationship to painting, making the artist fatally aware of his shameful status as a racialized subject, even under privileged conditions. Whereas Basquiat would not lose faith in art as a means of transcendence until the end of his career, he began to increasingly see himself as a "laborer" who also had to perform for white patrons in order to succeed: "They set it up for me so I'd have to make eight paintings in a week, for the show the next week. . . . I made them in this big warehouse there, Annina, Mazzoli, and Bruno were there. . . . It was like a factory, a sick factory. . . . I hated it."[21]

Basquiat's erratic behavior toward people in positions to assist him was noted as a symptom of individual mental instability, yet his tense relationship with his body as an instrument of labor is common to Puerto Ricans and African Americans, as both groups have experienced different forms of labor coercion, including slavery, colonial subjection, undesirable work, and even the inability to obtain work. Not surprisingly, the historical relationship between low-paid work and devaluation, not only as an individual, but as part of a racialized group, was verbally noted and was evident in many of Basquiat's visual works, including a collaborative painting with Warhol titled *Arm and Hammer* (1984), in which "black" labor is portrayed as the other side of the coin, the unacknowledged foundation of the American economy. A second painting, *Untitled* (*History of Black People*, 1983), portrays slave labor as degrading because it exploits the work of people treated as things; the work also explores how black subjectivity in itself is a humiliating "spectacle"—"el gran espectáculo."

Furthermore, even if Warhol and other key art scene players admitted Basquiat as a star, everyday experiences underscored his precarious relationship to cultural capital and the impossibility of escaping the shame of racialization. "I go on the street," the artist once commented to an interviewer, "wave my hand and they just drive past me. Normally I have to wait for three or four cabs."[22] The fact that this treatment was not confined to the United States further wore Basquiat down. For example, when he was returning from his second show in Modena, the Italian authorities detained Basquiat and his entourage for carrying substantial amounts of money. "They wanted to know where we got the money. We told them Jean-Michel earned it. And it was like, sure, this black guy made a hundred thousand dollars for eight paintings. They didn't believe it for a minute."[23]

Basquiat had varied responses to the fact that fame and a high market value did not valorize him, most of which implicated his body into ritual performances of capital exorcism. To address Nosei's pressure to supply new works, for instance, Basquiat initially created large unfinished paintings so the collectors would take them, and then concentrated on small, layered ones for himself. His girlfriend Suzanne Mallouk also comments that Basquiat refused to sell some of his paintings, writing "'NOT FOR SALE' on them."[24] Later, when the Swiss dealer Bruno Bischofberger began to represent him, Basquiat insisted on being told who each buyer was and insisted on not selling to speculators, while he stashed paintings at a warehouse in Washington Heights.[25]

Simultaneously, Basquiat's inability to fully control the conditions under which he painted sometimes erupted in violence toward his own work, with the goal of subverting its value and preventing its acquisition by the "wrong" (greedy) people. "Sometimes he would complete up to eight paintings a week," wrote Patricia Bosworth. "But he would fly into rages about being pressured to paint; sometimes he slashed his canvases to bits."[26] After Basquiat decided to sever his ties to Nosei, he also made sure to ruin the injurious commodities. Perhaps unintentionally symbolic, Basquiat damaged the new paintings by systematically pouring "a bucket of white paint over the shredded paintings,"[27] destroying not only the goods, but part of himself in the process.

Even if often violent and always performative, from a popular *boricua* logic, Basquiat's actions are not irrational. Rather, they bear a great resemblance to what perplexed American anthropologists have often written about the Puerto Rican laborers' resistance to capital's demands: "their sense of personal dignity seemed to clash often with the requirements of the work discipline."[28] The following anecdote narrated by the writer Jennifer Clement is emblematic:

Suzanne and Jean-Michel have terrible fights because only Suzanne is making money. One day, Jean-Michel says "Fine, I'll get a job." He goes to work as an electrician's assistant at the apartment of a rich, white woman. . . . When Jean-Michel gets back he is furious, clapping his hands together. "That white bitch looked at me as if I was a worker!" he says. Jean-Michel throws Suzanne's dinner in the garbage and does some coke.[29]

As they have done for many racialized artists, drugs smoothed out the crevices between definitions of dignity that are centered on the individual's gifts and socioeconomic forces that render them as interchangeable labor. Narcotics further provided Basquiat a heightened sense of who was friend and who was foe (particularly as many people began to steal money and art) and in giving him distance from his everyday life, preserved the joy of painting.

Basquiat's conflicts with capitalist logic should not be confused with lacking a work ethic or not understanding exchange value. Basquiat wanted his paintings to sell. At the same time, he insisted on being in full control of his creative process, even when he had assistants, and took enormous pride in the fact that the product was his own. In this sense, Basquiat—unlike Warhol-understood art to be "expressive" of a unique individuality, and part of a competition to be the "best" and hence worthy in excess of the product's exchange value. "It was . . . to his despair, that for dealers, collectors, and even his friends, money was the first priority; that the art world was primarily a marketplace that functioned according to the laws of supply and demand."[30] Basquiat never saw his art as strictly a business but as both an "achievement" (labor) and a "gift" (a means to offset the shame of his racialized identity).[31]

This last instance explains why Basquiat was prone to also subvert his own "worth" by showing a purposeful disregard for the workings of art collecting (and collectors themselves), which ultimately afforded him financial stability. As Warhol recalls, "He told me a story about how he'd wanted to buy a pack of cigarettes so he did a drawing and sold it for $.75 and then a week later his gallery called and said they had this drawing of his there and should they buy it for $1,000. Jean Michel thought it was funny."[32] Under all circumstances, Basquiat preferred to literally throw his money "out the window"—he particularly enjoyed giving dollar bills to homeless people—than pay taxes or keep any accounting of his earnings to better direct the accumulation of wealth. In the words of his assistant John Seed, "Once I told him that he needed to make investments, and that he ought to get a stockbroker so that if his career burned out he would have something. He was dumbfounded, and carefully explained that there was absolutely no need for him to plan for the future."[33]

In addition to work rage, drug consumption, and the rejection of labor discipline, Basquiat sought to valorize himself by purchasing what he perceived to be the "best" (and most expensive) available commodities. "He always appreciated expensive things," wrote Jennifer Clement, "as if consuming them would make him valuable."[34] Basquiat was also prone to excessive displays of wealth, such as leaving extravagant tips at restaurants. According to Clement, Basquiat apparently perceived this type of action as akin to "punching someone" who may have looked down on him.[35] Living always for the moment, Basquiat ultimately spent much of his earnings on perishable goods—like himself—friends, drugs, and women.

Basquiat's reluctance to view his own production as merely a commodity greatly contrasts with the confidence of white artists like Madonna and Keith Haring, who amassed fortunes by keeping an eye on their money, getting the right counsel, and wisely investing. They may all have been aware of the contradictions of exchange, but being a high-priced commodity was not as disturbing, since it was commensurate with their value as "white" subjects. Haring and Madonna may have sought to challenge the subalterity of gender, race, and/or sexuality sometimes to a significant extent, but only Basquiat was re-racialized continuously in his attempts to become valuable, even as he reached the snow-covered mountaintop of art legitimacy: Andy Warhol.

Basquiat's brief artistic collaboration with Warhol, which culminated in a joint show in 1985 at the Tony Shafrazi gallery, provides a key example of the tensions between high art, racialization and capital. According to Warhol, the collaboration process itself was fraught with difficulties as Basquiat had frequent paranoid outbursts in which the younger man would accuse the older artist of "using" him.[36] Furthermore—and even more devastating—the show was panned by the critics, who assumed that only Warhol had the ability to artistically influence Basquiat. This appreciation prevailed among most critics even when contemporary artists like Keith Haring agreed that both artists greatly energized each other's work.[37]

The artist angrily responded to interviewers who queried him about the perception that "people attribute your success to the fact that [you] knew how to gain Andy Warhol's attention." "I was the one who helped Andy Warhol paint!" he maintained, to little avail.[38] While in retrospect Basquiat felt that this period corresponded to the "best times" of his life,[39] getting too close to Warhol obviously had (as always) side effects. Since Warhol could not (or would not) protect him from racist remarks, Basquiat opted to break up the friendship, losing much of his larger-than-life celebrity in the process, yet affirming that "I wanted to be a star not a gallery mascot."[40]

Anger was a symptom of a fissure that became more evident with greater success: (white) recognition under racist conditions can take away rather than increase joy. As a result, greater affluence did not change Basquiat's tense relation to labor or space. Basquiat's studios, for instance, were notoriously unkempt and had a transient feel. "Paige stayed overnight with Jean Michel," reports Warhol, "in his dirty smelly loft downtown. How I know it smells is because Chris was there and said (*laughs*) it was like a nigger's loft, that there were crumpled-up hundred-dollar bills in the corner and bad b.o. all over and you step on paintings."[41] Fittingly, as Basquiat's fame grew, so did his drug habit, making work doubly deadly: the more he worked, the more he fed the art market; the more money he made, the more drugs he purchased. Toward the end of his career, under the dealer Vraj Baghoomian, Basquiat was still set up to paint, even when it was clear that he was physically expiring.

Basquiat's acute sense of his status as racialized labor cannot be separated from the specific context of the 1980s, in which art acquired the fluidity of money, collapsing the distinctions between dealer and collector, art and stocks, trading commodities and acquiring unique objects. This novel context made Basquiat a star; he was commodified based upon a significant if sometimes too rapidly produced body of work, almost instantaneously, to feed the frenzy of art speculation. As his friend Rene Ricard has famously commented, "We are no longer collecting art, we are buying individuals. This is no piece by Samo. This is a piece of Samo."[42] The implications were great for Basquiat. Not only was he reduced to the status of a "thing" (a commodity) before he could take ironic distance from it, his high productivity entailed a process of dismemberment, painfully chronicled in most of his paintings.

Awareness of his status as a "thing" arose not only from Basquiat's commodification but also from his racialized sexuality, another conflictive site of pleasure and shame, implicated in asymmetrical power relations. As is well known, Basquiat was reminded of this subaltern status and aimed to transcend it by seeking relationships almost exclusively with white women, especially if they were fighting over him: "He loved to have one woman discover him in bed with another woman."[43] Race, however, did not seem to be the only conflictive aspect of Basquiat's sexuality.

Basquiat had hustled while he lived on the street and often alluded to this part of his life as one he would rather forget.[44] The biographer Phoebe Hoban also suggests that his first significant sexual experience was as the victim of a homosexual rape in Puerto Rico, although, according to his former graffiti partner Al Diaz, Basquiat "enjoyed sex more with men."[45] Precisely because of the traumas of his sexuality, Basquiat used it to seduce patrons, impress people. According to Ricard, "He would take any opportunity to have me see his penis. He used it as an angler bait. . . . He was into sex for power, and then there was his heart. A woman could never really be it for him. The love of his life was Andy."[46] Even when his addiction was ravishing his body, the artist still pursued women, although he bitterly complained that "[girls] can't really see me for who I am." Ironically, Basquiat—who had displayed white women to show the world that he was as valuable as a white man—now resented that white women used him to gain upward mobility for themselves.

Like his commodification, Basquiat's fetishized sexuality was double-edged. According to Jennifer Clement, "a very famous gallery owner in SoHo" chased Basquiat's lover Suzanne around his home, asking her how "big Jean's penis was and if it was true that Jean had herpes."[47] Warhol also made sexual remarks about Basquiat's sexuality on several occasions: "The *New York Times* had a big story on AIDS. The tourist business in Haiti is down to nothing. Probably the tourists were only there secretly for the big cocks. Because Jean Michel is half Haitian and he really does have the biggest one."[48] Ricard's alleged first words to Basquiat upon seeing him naked are equally illustrative: "Not only are you the greatest artist that I have ever seen, you have the most beautiful penis I have ever seen."[49] The persistence of the representation of Basquiat through his penis recalls Fanon's classic observation that "the Negro is eclipsed. He is turned into a penis. He *is* a penis."[50]

The issue is, then, not that Basquiat's "talent had not kept pace with his fame," as Hoban suggests. Rather, once Basquiat gained the critical knowledge that even if the work was deemed valuable, the commodity's worth would never fully extend to the artist who created it, there was little motivation to continue to paint—or even live. If Basquiat's enterprise was, partly, an epistemology of valorization, what killed him as an artist was the knowledge that commodification would never liberate him from racialized shame, even when it could produce handsome profits for himself and others. In the words of the first critic to befriend Basquiat, "To turn one's work into fetish that is almost indistinct from oneself, to overpersonalize and covet one's own work, is professional suicide."[51]

This is why on the 1988 painting *TV Star,* Basquiat boldly declares, "NOTH-ING TO BE GAINED HERE," hence setting himself up for failure in his last attempt to get his "soul" back by participating in a cleansing ceremony performed by shamans in the Ivory Coast.[52] The possibly lifesaving ritual never took place because Basquiat accepted that he no longer had a "soul." As Warhol put it, "when all these dealers heard there was a really talented black artist who would probably die off soon from drugs, then they hurried to buy his things and now I guess they're frustrated because he's staying alive."[53] Basquiat's next step was to bridge the gap between symbolic and physical death, a last attempt to be free. Basquiat's death from an overdose at age twenty-seven is what gave his late work *Riding His Death* such an extraordinary power. At last, physical and symbolic death literally came together on one moving plane.

Owning Up: Basquiat, Haring, and Hip Hyped Utopia

The constraints faced by Basquiat can also be elaborated through a comparison with fellow traveler Keith Haring, a white queer artist from a middle-class background with links to hip hop and a ravenous appetite for black Puerto Rican men and culture. Since both artists were generally perceived as "the most original artists of the new decade,"[54] the Haring-Basquiat counterpoint enables an analysis of the role racialization plays in the making of commercially viable artists. Although Haring was ultimately closer to street culture than Basquiat, his relationship to Puerto Ricans also allows us to further theorize about the comparative "load" of (white) homosexuality and race in the commodification of racialized practices.

Both Basquiat and Haring began their public art careers by writing on public surfaces, a fitting beginning given graffiti's investment in recognition and trademarks. Haring started tagging in the street in 1980 with two images, "dog" and "The Baby." Unhampered by racism, Haring was able to engage in relatively dangerous feats such as drawing on black paper on the subway, "I made these drawings where I saw other people's tags, and I did them so that they would be acknowledged by other graffiti artists."[55] Through wall writing, Haring's initial goal was to earn the respect of other writers "rather than that of the art world, because it was more of a challenge to obtain."[56] Only a (queer) white man could have written this, as Basquiat was all too aware that, "There are no black men in museums."[57]

Practicing graffiti had dramatically different repercussions for Basquiat and Haring on several levels. In terms of personal security, Haring broke the law and risked being caught by drawing along the subway stops, yet once he was arrested, the artist received lenient treatment: "all the cops are wondering what this nerdy white boy could possibly have done."[58] Despite the fact that Basquiat himself was never arrested for his activities, Haring's experience with wall writing greatly contrasts with the fate of other men of color such as the African American wall writer Michael Stewart, who was choked to death under the city's "war on graffiti" policy.

The responses of Basquiat and Haring to Stewart's death are also revealing of the former's most vulnerable social location. Whereas Haring was distraught over Stewart's death, Basquiat became paranoid that he would be "next,"[59] since both men shared the "dreadlocks" look.[60] Basquiat's fear was reportedly so great that he even refused to cooperate with his girlfriend Suzanne Mallouk's legal efforts to learn more about what happened to Stewart. Like Haring, Basquiat was, of course, not oblivious to the bravado of graffiti in affirming masculine identity. But as can be seen in his 1981 blue and white painting depicting two policemen arresting a haloed black man (*Untitled*), he knew that being caught writing graffiti could cost him more than a fun arrest or an awkward photo opportunity.

While Haring has written that his attraction to people of color is based on guilt for "what white people have done to people of color,"[61] it seems that rather than guilt, subaltern male culture provided Haring with a pathway to escape the shame of sexual and gender inadequacies. According to his friend and fellow artist Kenny Scharf, "he thought he wasn't good looking and that he couldn't attract people. He had trouble with his self-image."[62] If Basquiat craved the attention of whites in an attempt to cross out racial devaluation, Haring's attraction to hip hop was one of re-engendering a masculine persona in white-dominated public and domestic spheres.

Haring particularly liked the Puerto Rican "toughs" who, if gay, catered to his fantasies and assured him of his superiority by staying at home and cooking for him, or if straight, allowed him to serve as a "father" or older brother figure. The seduction that seemingly "whole" Latino masculinity had for Haring bears a striking resemblance to the ways the creators of West Side Story represented Puerto Rican male sexuality (chapter 3). Not coincidentally, the producer John "Jellybean" Benítez describes the Fun House, one of the clubs that Haring frequently visited, in precisely those terms: the club "had lots of Latinos, Italians, sort of the eighties West Side Story."[63]

As it did for the creators of West Side Story (chapter 3) and Madonna (chapter 6), African American and Puerto Rican subaltern male culture provided Haring with a surrogate ("real") masculinity, particularly in the context of the hypermacho art establishment that had considered Andy Warhol too "swish" to be one of the boys. In incorporating "men of color" into his work, the queer white boy, as Robert Farris Thompson suggests, "wins" over his "macho" painter predecessors—Pollock, Jules Olitski, Frank Stella: "Haring conquers his rivals, masters their media, in the name of the eroticized fire of New York eighties dance. One more time, in 1988, he deliberately disturbs the optical neatness of his powerful rival with the trace of black bodies in motion."[64]

The two artists incorporated aspects of hip hop culture with dissimilar intent and risks. If as a queer man Haring had to contend with the shame of gay identity and the homophobia of compulsory heterosexual culture, his privileged ethnic identification and de-racializing queerness allowed for the appropriation of graffiti practices in ways that graffiti writers themselves were unable to do and racialized artists like Basquiat were afraid to. According to Jennifer Clement, "Keith was gay and white and could glamorize graffiti in a way that Jean could not."[65] Bill T. Jones, whom Haring painted while Mapplethorpe photographed him for a series of stills, understood the asymmetry of transcultural contact when he insisted that he always be credited as "choreographer" whenever the photograph was displayed. "I said to him 'Keith, these pictures will probably appear everywhere, and your name will always jump out. I want to make sure that every time these pictures are reproduced that my name is there as a choreographer, not just some black dude you painted.'"[66]

Furthermore, although graffiti offered Haring the rewards of masculinity, street respect, and a distinctive edge with the art establishment, Basquiat's loose links to it rendered him a lowly "primitive," rather than a "primitivist" like European painters such as Picasso or Gaugin. Marc Miller, the curator for the Queens Museum, broached the subject with Basquiat in the following terms: "so you're seen as some sort of primal expressionist . . . "[67] Also called "the 'wild child' of contemporary art, who . . . embodies the raw primal energy of the urban jungle,"[68] Basquiat responded to these framings with exasperation: "I don't really consider myself a graffiti artist, you know? And then they have this image of me [as a] wild man, a wild, monkey man, whatever the fuck they thought."[69]

Even though Basquiat would never shed the "primitive" label (and he even ambiguously catered to it by wearing designer suits and going barefoot or wearing African fabrics), one of his first moves to valorize himself was to strike the graffiti association as it had become a stain, a mark that brought his value down as a fine arts ("serious") painter. Unlike Haring, Basquiat had to persistently guard his signature as that of an "individual," a necessary precondition to commodification and recognition as an artist. This partly explains why Basquiat severed his partnership with Al Diaz as soon as he was able to gain legitimacy while "Diaz preferred to keep his graffiti anonymous. Basquiat, on the other hand, was determined to get the recognition he felt he had earned."[70] After the rupture with Diaz, Basquiat immediately proceeded to kill off his community street association by writing "SAMO is dead" where before he had tagged his name.

Basquiat's difficulties in affirming his individuality as a racialized artist are related to the low social value attributed to the culture of subaltern communities and the casting of only white men as eminently sovereign subjects. A clear example of how Haring was simultaneously closer to graffiti as a form and exemplified the workings of the art market as a white subject can be culled from the numerous works that the artist did in collaboration with LA II, a teenage Puerto Rican graffiti writer who "tagged" objects that were later sold and exhibited in galleries, but were often not credited by name. While all the collaborative pieces that Haring created with artists and friends like Kermit Oswald and Herb Ritts are clearly attributed, the question becomes, Why were these works not properly "tagged"?

For supportive "high" art critics and collectors, Haring is an "original" because unlike other painters of his generation, he does not directly refer to other painters' work in his own: "In the eighties, a lot of art is about appropriation—of taking one from that style and two from this style and joining them. Keith isn't about this at all!"[71] Appropriation in this context is understood to mean the borrowing or imitation of another artist's style or the recontextualization of elements of *already* commodified popular culture. As Haring does not overtly "take" from other artists, he is deemed self-generating. Or in David Frankel's terms, "Haring consumed earlier visual forms, but he was less an appropriator than a terrific synthesist."[72]

Much has been said about Haring's inspirations and influences in art history: Christo, Pierre Alechinsky, Jean Dubuffet, and Frank Stella. My objective here, however, is not to explore artistic intertextuality (which is the most appropriate concept to refer to what the art critics call "appropriation"). Rather, I aim to examine the context in which one cultural producer (arguably an "individual") is not considered able to be expropriated *as such*.

In comparing accounts by Haring and LA II about how they first collaborated, I found it significant that although their versions do not differ in any substantial way, each assigns a different weight to the exchange and assumes a dissimilar role. According to Haring,

I was so crazy about LA II's tag that I asked him to collaborate with me. So I invited him to my Broome Street studio and I found pieces of wood and metal shelving and we would draw on them together. . . . One day, one of the works we collaborated on sold for $1,400. When I got the money, I handed LA II half of it—$700.

And LA II's story:

Keith Haring asked me to come to his studio one day. I said, "Can I bring a friend?" because I didn't know him that good, 'cause I was kind of scared and 'cause I was young. . . . There was this metal sheeting at the studio and he said, "If you don't mind, can you write your name on this?" So I wrote my name all over it. Then he did his drawings on it, and he blended my stuff with his stuff, and it looked real nice. He called me a week later and said he had sold that piece for $1,400. He told me to come over and get half of it.[73]

While it is unclear whether Haring's main purpose in the collaboration is to make money, it is evident that the artist was fully aware of his ability to capitalize on the exchange by individualizing the beauty of LA II's street-certified signature with his own. In this transaction, Haring assumes the role of mediator and negotiator with the art world while LA II does not appear to be interested in his creative activity as an economic one and is, in fact, initially afraid of Haring, arguably because he is both white and gay. Although like Haring, Basquiat wrote on walls to gain entry into the high art world, he shares one thing with LA: his horizon of expectations is rooted in the enjoyment of the present. Upon his trip with Haring to Japan to work, LA II comments, "I was so excited. When your parents are on welfare, it's something you would never expect happen."[74] As it was for all other Puerto Rican men in Haring's life, individualized "success" was an alien currency.

Regardless, to the extent that Haring became better known, he came to fully understand the value of the signature and pursue its benefits avidly. Shortly after he met Warhol, for instance, they traded paintings based on the principle of "value for value,"[75] which meant that for Haring to be able to own one Warhol, he had to give Andy many Harings. Paige Powell, an advertising executive for *Interview,* comments, "I was always taking Polaroid photographs, and Keith would just grab some and ask Andy to sign them. Since there were *my* pictures, it really hurt my feelings and it happened *so* many times."[76] The actual picture (use value, record of a lived experience) could not accrue as much value unless it was also a commodified object authorized by the right signature. In this he mimicked the art world's response to LA II.

Several commentators noted that despite early resistance, Haring became increasingly concerned about his commodity status as his career soared. Haring started to follow the auctions in which his work was sold and traded. In one of his journal entries he takes note of the financial effect of his prior collaboration efforts:

> The pieces went for even more than the top estimate, some drawings bringing up to $5,500. This is only good considering that the same drawing in a gallery would cost $3,000 tops. The only piece that went for less than estimated was a piece by LA ROCK [LA II]. It was listed in the catalogue as being by Keith H and LA ROCK, but there were no lines of mine on it. . . . This drawing went for $1,500. That's still OK.[77]

As Baudrillard argues, capital is a code that translates goods into commodities by assigning market value, which erases social forces that determine value in the first place. In this sense, the reason that LA II diminishes Haring's value is not attributed to the market as a purely economic force, but to the knowledge that LA II is not marketable due to the "low" value assigned to his cultural production, class, and ethnicity; like Star Trek's Borg, he is not an "individual." Haring's homosexuality is hence less of an obstacle to self-commodification, and actually, as we will explore in the case of Ricky Martin, further "whitens" the culture of people of color. Through the racist functioning of the market, Haring is able to capitalize on graffiti, but only if he keeps the roots from showing. The tinge of "race" makes the market blush.

Precisely because of the negative load carried by graffiti as a racialized practice, for Haring to successfully valorize "street" culture, he had to take the edge off visually. In drawing breakdancing figures, for instance, the artist began by emptying the form's constitutive violence, for as the rapper KMX Assault says, breakdancing "was a mixture of martial arts and dancing. Basically, you would be competing with another person to see who had the better moves, how could you 'burn' the other guy, humiliate him in a certain way or just be better than him."[78] Haring queers breakdancing and transforms it into a homoerotic utopia, turning rivalry into a celebration of bodily fusion. By queering breakdancing, Haring's drawings and sculptures *also* universalize (whiten) these practices: all the dancers are raceless, painted in primary colors and without any of the features that identify people of color in American society.

Relating to hip hop culture aesthetically, Haring took *West Side Story*'s deferred dream of utopia one step further. In Haring's pictorial universe, black children *can* come from white bodies, as in *Drawings for Fashion Moda at New Museum* (1980). Boundaries constantly collapse and reconfigure as animals and men copulate, Mickey Mouse (*Untitled*, 1982) loses his line definition, and babies evoke the birth of a new culture. The fact that most of Haring's works are titled "untitled" also adds to the illusion of an endless connection between bodies, a brotherhood of (queer) men.

However valuable the approval of graffiti writers might have been to him, Haring eventually came to appreciate market value more. By 1983, after Haring's major Shafrazi show, he began to disassociate from the graffiti scene since it was now considered "passé" and hence an obstacle to his own commodification. In 1986 Haring also stopped doing panel drawings altogether as these began to get stolen for resale, and he decided to open the Pop Shop, a store that would sell Haring-inspired merchandise. Despite his great commercial success, the proliferation of "fake" Harings doomed his Pop Art stores, as if the street took revenge not against Haring the man, but against the concept of the artist itself: Only a fool would tag someone else's signature.

Significantly, Haring's work is thematically and formally closer to hip hop culture than Basquiat's. Yet the latter's work, in its use of language, repetition, and obsession with "colored" visibility, remained closer to hip hop's roots as a culture of dissent. If racialized men were generally absent from or degraded by the culture's main disseminator of images—television—both wall writers and Basquiat made sure that the spectators knew of their bodily and symbolic materiality, of the fact that they were *there,* albeit precariously. Basquiat's art—like graffiti—was a highly coded way to say, "I am somebody," although each practice catered to a different audience and hence was imbued with dissimilar social value.

Moreover, even if Basquiat did not share the class background or cultural objectives of most wall writers, it is not a coincidence that the most famous AmeRícan visual artist in history began his career as a graffiti artist. Through graffiti, Basquiat expressively aligned himself with many urban African American and Puerto Rican young men in their effort to affirm their worth and call attention to the structural precariousness that framed their lives. As the graffiti artist Doze Green suggests, "graf" was a way to communicate rage against exclusion from ownership: "It was like a slap in the face that we don't own anything."[79]

Symptomatically, even when Basquiat stopped writing graffiti, his visual work remained constituted by issues of self-worth and recognition. This is evident in his persistent repetition of copyright symbols, which ambiguously allude to property, authorship, and value.[80] In addition to these affinities, it was also in the non-oral forms of hip hop (writing, breakdancing) that Latinos were mostly recognized as "kings," a royal title that Basquiat would seek all of his life, first as a wall writer ("king of the line") and later as the "greatest" (king of all painters). While *boricuas* were also co-creators of rap music—the only mass-commodified hip hop practice—they did not become stars because Latinos were not considered a large enough market to deliver consumers at a national scale. Ironically in the context of the so-called Latinization of pop music (chapter 10) and Basquiat's current status as the most expensive painter of the 1980s, *boricuas* were dismissed by the rap industry to the tune of "Puerto Ricans don't sell."[81]

The graffiti impulse—like the conditions of his subalterity—never quite abandoned Basquiat, showing up as late as 1987, when the physically ravished artist snuck into Julian Schnabel's show at the Whitney and scribbled "graffiti near Schnabel's paintings."[82] The specific strategies of success and defiance that characterized Haring and Basquiat underscored how uneven the terms of exchange remained, and how ingrained the concepts of "high" and "low" were in the commodification practices of the art world.

Off the Wall:
Shame, *Boricua* Identity, and Basquiat's Transcultural Paintings

If Haring deracialized and celebrated Puerto Rican men to transfigure them into more universally accessible commodities, Basquiat displayed the pain of intercultural exchange in his works, while mostly seeking the company of whites. In critic Thomas McEvilley's estimation, Basquiat's subject matter "relates to the ancient myth of the soul as a deity lost, wandering from its true home, and temporarily imprisoned in a degradingly limited body and an infuriatingly reduced social stature."[83] The different transculturation processes and reception contexts explain why Haring's primary colored (red, yellow, and blue) "breakdancing men" are usually perceived as "happy" (and often erotic) art, while Basquiat's haunting images of disarticulated black male body parts, suffering under the weight of compromised success, hang on far fewer home and museum walls.

While for artists like Warhol, Basquiat can be reduced to so many "screaming Negroes," his work is an extraordinary site of modern transcultural production. Immediately recognizable transcultural features of Basquiat's work include the deployment of various languages (primarily English and Spanish, but also Italian, French, and Latin), artistic traditions (Leonardo da Vinci, Pablo Picasso, Cy Twombly), and "low" culture (comic books, hip hop). Basquiat's painting method itself evokes transculturation in similar terms as the *boricua* garbage aesthetics practiced by the drag performers Woodlawn and Mario Montez, combining collage, multiple textures, photocopies, and found materials on one plane. As the critic Louis Armand has observed, Basquiat, who was always broke during his early years, made some of his early work "on salvaged sheet metal and other materials foraged from trash cans or found abandoned on the sidewalk."[84]

Basquiat's work was also critically influenced by hip hop signifying strategies like "scratchnoise, sampling, freestyle coloring, and bombing the canvas"[85] and diasporic musical forms such as reggae, Afro-Cuban, and jazz, which actively acknowledge the importance of "fusion" and improvisation.[86] Contrary to most critics, who see in Basquiat either a primitive or a primitivist, the artist demonstrates that U.S. culture is not homogeneous, coherent, or "white." In his paintings, assembled from disparate physical and symbolic materials, Basquiat's chaotic synthesis and the world it brings forth resemble the way that Puerto Rican and other migrant Caribbean identities are made up of seemingly opposite elements in the ruins of modern utopias (capitalist or communist).

When exploring the full scope of Basquiat's transcultural production, it is critical to include an unstudied source that textures his visual work: Puerto Rican and Latin American history and culture. If blackness persisted in Basquiat's work as a sign of easily communicable alterity to a white audience, Spanish has the status of a "hidden transcript" that can address *boricuas* and other Latinos in different terms than other (American) subjects. The extensive use of Spanish in asides—often in parentheses—or in seeming throwaways and puns makes Basquiat's paintings a significant canvas for bilingual written expression and an Afro-Latino diasporic cultural competence. Basquiat's Spanish, for instance, referenced a wide range of scenes (cooking, dancing), figures (conquistadors, Puerto Rican politicians like Luis Muñoz Rivera, his "abuelita"), and historical processes such as slavery and colonialism as they were specifically constituted in Latin America.

Basquiat in fact also deployed Spanish outside the canvas to similar ends. As Thompson reports,

One day, in the summer of 1986, a friend (who spoke Spanish) appeared at his door in the company of a rich and famous woman. I was there, and watched them walk around. Suddenly, the woman asked, point-blank, "how much is that painting over there?" Jean-Michel (in a whisper) to his friend: ¿para tí o para ella? (for you or for her?) Meaning: high price for a stranger, low price or even no price for a friend.[87]

Like Basquiat's paintings themselves, Spanish served as a valuable resource: "When he wanted to make a covert point or camouflage a question," adds Thompson, "[Basquiat] switched to Spanish. It was a mask, a very handy mask."[88]

Spanish is a way to both encode Basquiat's outsider status in relation to American culture and inscribe other Puerto Rican and African American structures of feeling regarding dignity and freedom. His extensive use of the "Negro," for instance, can be understood to refer both to a pre–civil rights context, when the devaluation of enslaved Africans and their descendants was sanctioned by law, and to the ambivalent way—as a term of endearment and depreciation—it is used in Puerto Rico. Puerto Rican vernacular terms also make appearances on the canvas, such as the use of the term "gringo" in a painting titled *Gringo Pilot (Anola Gay)* (1981).

In *Natives Carrying Some Guns, Bible, Amorites on Safari,* Basquiat includes a number of thematics, including colonization, slave labor, the Spanish conquest, and religious oppression. Basquiat's use of the word "colonization" is intriguing, as one of the few U.S. subaltern groups to use it are Puerto Ricans, given the Island's enduring colonial relationship to the United States. The name of the Spanish colonizer Hernán Cortez [*sic*] is written three times on the right side of the canvas in a fusion of African and American conquest histories that are, however, discontinuous. Playing with the multiple meanings available to a bilingual reader, "Cortez" becomes "Corte" with a line crossing out the word, and later simply Corte, not crossed out. (In Spanish, *corte* means a cut, but also a "court" of law and the Royal Court.) Furthermore, below the three "cortes," there is a bilingual phrase that reads "I WON'T EVEN

MENTION GOLD (ORO)." Basquiat thus refers to the three forces of Spanish conquest in (Latin) America—capitalism, courts, and church—and their relation to the dispossession of enslaved Africans.

Basquiat's work, like Woodlawn's, creatively sought to deflect, if not erase, the name of the mother, while acknowledging that everything vital came from her. "I'd say my mother gave me all the primary things. The art came from her."[89] Not coincidentally, it was Mrs. Basquiat who handed her son one of his most enduring visual reference points to artistically visualize his self as fragmented—the book *Gray's Anatomy*—after a car hit the artist at age eight. While it is true that, as bell hooks has argued, Basquiat focused all his attention on examining male space, the culture of the mother—if not her particular name—is referenced by the persistent and indispensable acknowledgment of the "mother's" tongue, Spanish.

The juxtaposition of languages and maternal memories further converges on a general faith in art as a practice of alchemy or "voodoo science," a performance that references Caribbean syncretic religious practices and upward mobility. Basquiat attributes his magical qualities to his mother, whom he called a "bruja" (witch), an ambivalent term that nevertheless acknowledges the power of creativity and transformation. In a painting titled *K* (1982), for instance, Basquiat painted a gold crown, and inside the crown he wrote "oro" (gold). Later, Basquiat would reflect on this work, "I was writing gold on all that stuff and I made all this money right afterwards."[90] Detaching words from their context and people from their fixed locations is proposed as a practice that can create value from virtually "nothing" (racialized subjectivity) and nowhere (Puerto Rico, Haiti, Africa), or better still, out of (white) thin canvas.

At the end of his life, once Basquiat could only associate painting with the submission to capital, he wanted to become a writer. Basquiat's writing was nevertheless constituted in the shame of being required to obliterate oneself when pursuing commodified success. In most of Basquiat's paintings words are often purposely crossed out. Basquiat's claim that the practice of crossing out words made people "pay more attention to what I'm saying"[91] is ultimately metaphorically accurate. "The words bothered the collectors. They somewhat equated the work with graffiti, which was carefully obsoleted to a fad by the status quo. Also, the words tended more and more frequently to raise unpleasant issues."[92] A multi-semantic term and visual practice, "crossing out" (and over) as cross-dressing simultaneously connotes death, passing, and migration.

Language is not the only sign to encode Puerto Rican and African diasporic valorization strategies. Although Basquiat himself has stated that the inspiration for the "crown" in his work originated in the *Little Rascals* logo, Basquiat's interest in—if not obsession with—royalty is shared by African Americans and *boricuas* and has common roots: offsetting the shame of racialization and the pain of incommensurable definitions of value by affirming the self in alternative terms. Through his paintings, Basquiat memorialized past kings on wood, glass, canvas, and wall surfaces, and offered portable crowns for ordinary men and even outlaws, hence affording them the dignity denied by racism, regardless of their station in life and relationship to money or the law. In the critic Richard Marshall's terms, "The crown is Basquiat's own trademark as well as a symbol of respect and admiration that he bestows on the figures that populate his work."[93] As with the written word, Basquiat also trusts the power of the crown as amulet, transfiguring socially low subjectivities into royalty.

The simultaneous impulses to be "king," to invent royalty, to honor the dead kings and queens of raced history, and to crown new kings and queens are characteristic of Puerto Rican interventions in popular culture and a feature of the carnival aesthetic. As Ella Shohat and Robert Stam remind us, "Carnival sees social and political life as a perpetual 'crowning and uncrowning' and the permanence of change as a source of hope."[94] Basquiat's painting *Crowns* (1981), for instance, which shows off a landscape of crowned black faces, is significantly also called "peso neto," which in Spanish means "net worth." Basquiat's many paintings that were focused on "cabezas" (heads)—the locus of pride—further articulate a desire to be looked in the face and appreciated as an intellect.

Basquiat also had the insight that culture is a spectator sport: "Jean-Michel loves to see artists as athletes. He thinks it is a wonderful joke."[95] According to some observers, Basquiat even painted like a boxer, with rage and elegance, making himself count by destroying an adversary in an individual way but also representing the race. The selection of boxing as trope is here intimately tied to its role in countering white superiority discourse as the boxing ring (like the canvas) has historically allowed blacks to literally show Negro superiority over whites by the punch of their skill, as Muhammad Ali's famous claim "I am the greatest" encapsulates. Knocking another painter out declares that Basquiat is a world champion, hence defeating the premise that there are "no black men in museums" because there are no good black painters.

The knowledge that artists were like athletes, particularly among subaltern communities, also underscores that both art and sports are strategies of valorization, predicated on the individual's ability to "perform" for a wide (white) audience. This is clear in *Television and Cruelty to Animals* (1983), where a fight between "Popeye" and "The Nazis" is advertised as a "very expensive el gran espectáculo." Basquiat's boxer persona, however, was also a mask. Even if Basquiat indulged in the macho bravado of boxing, he was, "as a black artist in New York," according to the dealer Bruno Bischofberger, "over-sensitive to other artists' comments on his work."[96]

The peril inherent in being valorized as a black king or athlete appears in how Basquiat visualized them: as skulls, deformed, or colorfully transparent, with their internal organs exposed. This mode of representation coincides with Basquiat's star discourse on his own commodification: the process that makes you a black king inevitably defaces you; the white gaze that valorizes will also kill you. As a 1984 painting titled *Zydeco* admonishes, "don't look into the camera," an imperative that recalls the wise *boricua* saying of, *hay miradas que matan* (some looks can kill). This insight may also account for the dystopia of Basquiat's visual work and star persona: he painted his pained insides for all to see while defacing his bodily self in seeking stardom; both were masks in the sense not only of disguise, but "a necessary sign of the actual situation of dis-union."[97]

"Defacing" is actually how Basquiat described his technique in his mid-1980s collaborations with Warhol: "Andy would start most of the paintings. He would start one and put something very recognizable on it, or a product and I would sort of deface it."[98] The pain associated with defacing is clear in a 1983 work, *Untitled (Defacement)*. According to Ricard, it was painted in Haring's old studio in the Cable Building and features two police officers ("c.o.p") beating a haloed yet faceless and bodiless black figure. Scribbled in the top center of the wallboard is a question, "¿DEFAC MENT@?" Basquiat virtually always painted black figures as defaced and objectified—the living dead.

Simultaneously, many of Basquiat's paintings contain aphorisms that can also be read as tragic advertisements, "good money in savages." "False advertisements" actually are plentiful in Basquiat's work, hence underscoring his ambiguous relationship to the market's valorization. Not only does Basquiat's many portraits of famous black men inscribe himself in a valorized pantheon of despair and triumph, there are also ironic promises of "white-washing" (Rinso) soap, "onion gum" that "makes your mouth taste like onion," and "quality meats for the public." In this last case, Basquiat represents himself as one of the pure, high-quality meats—a crowned barbeque chicken—yet also ironically despises that he is for sale as/by swines (whites).

Basquiat's radical need to be valued by the white other recalls Frantz Fanon's observation regarding blacks and Caribbean colonialism: "The goal of his behavior" will be The Other . . . for The Other alone can give him worth."[99] Basquiat's work is, in this sense, traumatized in the same way that Puerto Rican high culture in general is traumatized: it speaks from the open wound and is made possible only through it. Basquiat's images are, as Flatley argues for Warhol, an expression of prosopopoeia, a voice beyond the grave, a "trope that ascribes face, name, or voice to the absent, inanimate, or dead; it means literally to give or create (poeia) a face or person (prosopon), to person-ify. As the medium of face intelligibility and recognition, prosopopoeia is the trope of fame and shame alike."[100]

The shame of Basquiat's art is at least threefold. Many of his subjects were black men, an identity constituted in shame in the United States. These black subjects are often famous, hence publicly giving good face to a racialized and devalued experience that Basquiat knows to also be his own. Their fame, however, was the product not only of their hard work but also of their display and consumption by "the right (white) people." To protect these broken down—if valorized—bodies, a mask-like face topped with a halo often appears, a cover that protects the wearer from the intrusive gaze and protects the sacredness of life and art. A mask that also reflects back, "eyes that stare and peek out from the picture plane . . . from a place that is not our place but in which we are nonetheless thoroughly enmeshed and implicated."[101]

Despite Basquiat's halos, crowns, and masks, art did not save him. In this, Basquiat ultimately inscribes himself in a long line of dead kings like Jesus and John the Baptist (patron saint of derelicts) who have worn the crown of thorns in life, only to be fully appreciated after death. Once Basquiat died, his value in fact went up as his work became rare and his place as the "big black painter" was vacated. People who owned pieces of Basquiat came out to capitalize without having to deal with Basquiat the man, who had been so problematic. "If he had done tattoos," Larry Gagosian has stated, "they would have been amputating themselves."[102] Basquiat's father's, Gerard, oversaw the process of cataloguing and locating his son's inventory and settled on an uptown dealer with no prior ties to his son. Several lawsuits followed from, and to, the Basquiat estate.

The legal rush was a snapshot of Basquiat's realization of what he had become: a rare, exotic, commodified object to be continuously exchanged and appreciated, perhaps ending on someone's wall like the head of a hunted lion. Significantly, although Basquiat commands the highest prices of any 1980s painter, critics do not concede defeat, underscoring how the art world still is hesitant to fully own (up) to him. The dealer Richard Polsky, for instance, has written, "it's not clear whether his work will survive the test of time. Many museums own Basquiat paintings, but it's odd how one rarely sees his work on display when their permanent collections are exhibiting. It's as if the museums are hedging their bets."[103] But if Basquiat's transcultural work continues to inexplicably appreciate, it is in part because his experience has become more recognizable, valued, and indispensable not only for *boricuas* and African Americans, but also for everyone living in conflicted cultural contexts.

The King is dead, long live the King.

6 Flagging Madonna

Performing a Puerto Rican–American Erotics

Imagine for a second that you are Madonna. . . . Imagine, that there are theory books about you, and that you are the main theme of dissertations and academic essays. Imagine that feminists discuss whether you are a heroine or a demon.

—Madonna

This world is white no longer, and it will never be white again.

—James Baldwin

We make our absence palpable.

—ALARMA manifesto

Before Puerto Ricans became "individually" wrapped cultural products, the record of U.S. urban *boricua* cultures was often widely accessible only through mainstream performances that consistently ended up erasing or displacing the source. Without the means to record, disseminate, and pass on Puerto Rican cultural capital on a "national" scale, the hunger to consume and show off *boricuaness* was often fed by white stars who seduced us with their attention and polarized us by their expropriation. And during the 1980s through the 1990s, it was the prophetically named Madonna Louise Veronica Ciccone—a.k.a. Madonna—who came to most successfully commodify *boricua* cultural practices for all to see—if not touch.

On a global scale[1] Madonna embodied the freedom, in/morality, and material "excess" of (white) America. She has been labeled "the most famous woman alive," who has "imprinted, one way or another, not only a generation but the world."[2] Madonna's framing as a paradigm of Americanness is, however, gainfully ironic. Not only was the Italian American entertainer raised Catholic, any attempt to engage with her as a cultural site immediately points to the various racialized communities whose practices flavored Madonna's distinct "American" persona, and to the ways these subaltern groups sought identifications and connections with/through the pop icon. Express yourself, indeed.

As the Madonna enthusiast Camille Paglia narrates, "It all started in 1984, when Madonna exploded onto MTV with brazen, insolent, in-your-face American street style, which she had taken from urban blacks, Hispanics and her own middle-class but turbulent and charismatic Italian-American family."[3] Whereas the adoption of subaltern ethnic and queer styles has been noted as an example of her capacity for "reinvention," I would argue that these cultures allowed Madonna to do much more than simply distinguish her in the cluttered marketplace.

Equally important, Latino and African American masculinities allowed Madonna (like Haring, chapter 5) to represent herself with the same power as "men" in brokering transcultural commodification processes. Perhaps the most obvious gesture deployed by Madonna to signify this strategy was her notorious crotch-grabbing tick, which referenced the most successful queer black entertainer of her time—Michael Jackson—and a theatrics of an excessive black masculinity that dramatically reinscribed her as a powerful white woman, even if she was overtly blurring gender and racial boundaries.

At the same time, if like other white celebrities before her Madonna successfully mined the commercially untapped reserves of Latino creativity, she also envisioned an erotics of transculturation denied by dominant nationalism in Puerto Rico and racist ideologies in the United States. As the first white pop star to make *boricuas* the overt object of her affections, Madonna also produced a queer juncture for Puerto Rican representation in popular culture, especially because the other transnational stages of *boricuaness,* such as *salsa,* sports, and hip hop, often ignored and denigrated queers and women. Inadvertently, Madonna even sparked the first post-1952 skirmish in what has now become a full-fledged war of the flags over the (national) soul of Puerto Ricans.

Madonna's status as the last century's American transcultural domina-trix—medium, performer, and financial powerhouse—would be difficult to imagine without *boricuas*. Yet, in exploring Madonna's relationship to AmeRícan cultural practices, I am less interested in pointing out the many *boricuas* (such as the record producer John "Jellybean" Benítez) who have in-fluenced Madonna professionally or personally than in responding to her own call to "use" her—for "our" own sub(alternative) purposes.[4]

Food for Thought: Madonna's Queer Latin Hunger

Arriving in New York City in 1978, Madonna quickly came to see *boricuas* and other Latinos as raw sources of sexual and cultural energy to be enjoyed, plundered, and eventually drawn from to reproduce. As Madonna an-nounced to a Puerto Rico concert audience in 1993, when she left Michigan for the Big Apple, there were two things that she didn't know anything about: Puerto Ricans and avocados.[5] Once she had Puerto Ricans, the story goes, she had no further need for avocados.[6] Applying the popular maxim that what does not kill you makes you stronger, Madonna accordingly de-veloped what her friend the actress Debi Mazar called "a taste for, you know, Latin boys."

The tropes of food and garbage are as recurrent as they are rich in ironies, for Madonna has arguably eaten, digested, and defecated (on) Latino culture on multiple occasions over her long career, and has been called trash on many more. In addition, food is one of the most persistent ways Madonna's public life, loves, and career have been narrated. "She was lean. She had a nice edge to her muscles. She was hungry. Great appetite," says Gay Delang, one of her early dance teachers.[7]

Responding to an interviewer who hinted that the singer hardly ate, Madonna exclaimed with exasperation, "I have flesh. You can grab me any-where and you'll find flesh, so that's absurd."[8] On the set of *Evita*, Madonna turns philosophical, summarizing the challenges of the acting life by com-paring herself to a piece of meat: "You wonder if you're pretty enough or good enough or thin or attractive enough and you inevitably feel like a slab of beef. Rare, medium, or well done. It doesn't matter as long as people want to eat you."[9]

To eat and be eaten is in fact at the core of Madonna's star persona and it is a fruitful point of departure for examining her relationship to Puerto Ricans—and *boricua* fascination with her. The Madonna public text unaffectedly defines the social as a dog-eat-dog world (capitalist), affirms sexuality as the locus of female power (eating all others), and confirms that "whiteness" is ultimately dark at heart (culture as a cannibal feast). In this sense, Madonna's extravagant concerts and performances can be appreciated as *spectacles* of the banquet of life, in which she proudly displays all that she has eaten—and had to conquer—to get to where she is. Furthermore, Madonna's legendary reinventions of popular culture are not only ways to re-engender her power, but classic examples of the transculturated grotesque body, which in its promiscuity and zest for life is "never finished, never completed; it is continually built, created. . . . the body swallows the world and is itself swallowed by the world."[10]

Through Madonna, food tropes also attest to the transubstantiation of subaltern practices into deracialized and triumphant commodity culture (produce). Yet, although abundance has always been part of Madonna's public persona, this show of force is not a victory of the "people," in the philosopher Mikhail Bakhtin's sense. While Madonna's feast is not "private," the victory is ultimately *privatized* in the white star. Despite the many references to subaltern "peoples" in Madonna's performances, the representation of a world in which the style of queers and ethnic groups prevails over white heteronormalcy is ultimately the triumph of Madonna, the effective (or ruthless, depending on the vantage point) female entrepreneur, who defeats, co-opts, and/or seduces weaker subjects to get the better of capital, the ultimate consumption machine.

Even though for conservative political actors Madonna personifies a debased form of culture (pop) and femininity (whore),[11] her body is connoted as grotesque to a great extent because queer and colored men supply "exaggeration, hyperbolism, excessiveness"[12] to her otherwise own "normal" (white heterosexual) subjectivity, one that is called upon as needed. If as Barbara O'Dair argues, Madonna's early identification with musical genres such as disco created a problem of legitimacy—as it located her within subaltern racial and queer contexts—the aspiring entertainer's instinct fit her (white) imperial ambitions.[13]

Madonna's sources and/or performances may have been appalling to some social sectors—including some feminist communities—but it has been precisely the ability of performers to enable new articulations of race, gender, and class that has transformed only a few pop stars into long-lasting cultural icons. Unlike earlier white stars like Elvis, however, Madonna did not need to camouflage her cultural sources, but rather flaunted her borrowings for all of us to see (and purchase) fragments of ourselves. This strategy was particularly seductive for Latinos and queers during this period, as these groups still had fewer options than African Americans in the entertainment marketplace.

More important—and fueling Madonna's contradictory pop legacy—she not only contributed to valorizing female white subjectivity and the "lowness" of femininity, but also profitably relocated herself to the *center* of transethnic queer America, hence racially re-engendering the relationship between white women and subaltern cultures in hierarchical terms. Madonna may have been queen of the low—"freakish, marginal, abject"— for the moral minority,[14] but for the queers and/or Latinos who worshipped her, she was a rich white lady from the Midwest who lived in Manhattan and cared about them. And one of several graphic ways to visualize the complexity of this S/M relationship is through *Sex*.

Man-Donna: A (Very) White Woman on Top

Published in 1992 and wrapped in Mylar, Madonna's book *Sex* sold 500,000 copies within weeks. Time-Warner released fewer copies than announced to increase demand, simulating the urgency of an orgasmic peak. Historically,

Madonna's *Sex* is partly indebted to two Andy Warhol portfolios: *Ladies and Gentlemen* (1975), featuring African American transvestites, and *Sex Parts* (1978), displaying male genitals in different states of stimulation. Still, *Sex* is not a compilation of erotic images—in fact, that is its lesser contribution—but an epistemological manifesto through which Madonna claims, "I love my pussy, it is the complete summation of my life. . . . My pussy is the temple of learning."[15] Which, of course, begs the question of what does one ultimately "learn" at Madonna's temple? That this seemingly "liberated" epistemology *requires* the subordination of different *others* to affirm—and hence valorize—the (white female) *self.*

Consistently, many of Madonna's hits are anthems celebrating transethnic nonnormative sexuality in which she is, literally, the (only) white woman on top and is calling the shots with imperative phrases. As Madonna (may have) written in *Sex* (as Dita), "Give it up. Do as I say. Give it up and let me have my way. I'll give you love."[16] The extent to which Madonna is visually overinvested in her own (vanilla) sex as majority whip prompted bell hooks to compare her to a "plantation overseer": "Mirroring the role of a plantation overseer in a slave-based economy, Madonna surveys the landscape of sexual hedonism, her 'gay' freedom, her territory of the other, her jungle."[17]

Tactically, *Sex* exposes Madonna to the "darkness" of S/M, working-class roughs, multiethnic queers, African Americans, and Puerto Ricans to underscore the entertainer's whiteness, which the spectator is ultimately asked to admire and protect—even against his or her own nonnormative urges. That whiteness is an indispensable construct for the commodification of subaltern sexualities is evident in the book's careful construction of "blondness," even if being blond is a lot of work, requiring specific lighting strategies, makeup, and bleach. According to Madonna, "being blond has some incredible sort of sexual connotation. Men really respond to it."[18] Blond hair is, in fact, the other part of Madonna's "feminine" anatomy that is highlighted to frame the display of the (other) grotesque bodies and establish a "natural" order that narrates itself through colonial tropes. In Madonna's own words, her "blond ambition" was nothing short of "conquering the world," even if she still gets "nostalgic for a time in my life before I was an empire."[19]

Blondness is not the only strategy needed to guarantee Madonna's whiteness. Equally important are the dearth of other white women, particularly blonds, and the representation of the singer as the only "feminine" light-skinned body in the entire book. Madonna may conjure a world resistant to dominant heterosexist norms, but she is still the undisputed Queen. Equating blondness-whiteness-stardom and value is, of course, not an invention of *Sex*, but it is a fundamental element in constituting Madonna's star persona and her relationship to subaltern communities. As John Simon has observed regarding Madonna's backup singers and dancers, "The women are carefully chosen to be ethnic and less attractive than she is; the men, likewise, are mostly ethnics and, it would seem, homosexuals. This leaves her both an equal-opportunity employer and unequaled in pulchritude and power."[20]

To be surrounded by other whites "like her" would render Madonna *relatively* white and hence less powerful, beautiful, and valuable. hooks's plantation trope is then also significant, since if Madonna's "pussy" arguably serves as a bridge to represent and connect differently sexed multiethnic people, and to a lesser extent white heterosexual women, she can self-represent only by demonstrating the inherent lowliness of other sexualities, often through colonial tropes and discourses such as animalization, infantilization (arrested ethno-cultural development), and overendowed sexuality.

A key example can be found in *Sex*'s middle section. On page 41, a naked Madonna is kissing a young, light-skinned man with brown curly hair. Opposite this page, Madonna narrates a story of how the sixteen-year-old boy—explicitly labeled a "Puerto Rican"—seduced her: "I was so turned on; it was probably the most erotic sex I ever had." Yet the story's twist—"he gave me crabs"—could not be more consistent with colonial clichés, even if Madonna claims that "Everything you see and read is fantasy, a dream, pretend."[21]

The predictability of this ending prompted the writer Pat Califia to ask, not without exasperation, "How can a hairless, virgin boy give somebody

crabs? Where the hell did *he* get them?"[22] The answer, however, is deceptively simple. Despite their allure, *Sex* seems to say, the spics are immacu-
lately filthy, sick even before birth, although not—as the urban crime films
of the 1960s implied—deadly. In this, Madonna is not only Andy Warhol's
heir but the legitimately queer successor of *West Side Story,* as she renders
boricuas desirable yet dirty, vulnerable but fun, beautiful if ultimately expendable. The only tweak is that with Madonna, the medium—her body—is
the message.

Curiously, this Puerto Rican teenager is almost as "white" as Madonna
(unlike the book's "lesbians," for instance), but he is a child, someone the
star can lead and mentor in *ars erotica,* as she announces early on in *Sex:* "I'll
teach you how to fuck."[23] The trope of the racialized queer as a child will get
replayed with a vengeance in the vanity documentary *Truth or Dare,* but it is
this "tender" portrait of miscegenation, which could be titled "Madonna and
child," that sums up the ways most of the singer's exchanges with Latino
men have been staged and narrated in popular culture.

Madonna, of course, frequently self-represents as a phallic mother who
gives, in exchange for submission, a familiar—and familial—structure for
modern neocolonial peoples living under the rule of "law" of a wealthy metropolitan state. As Madonna says of the mothering she provided her "emotional cripple" dancers of the Blond Ambition tour, "I could show them
things and be a mother to them. . . . Assuage my guilt for having so much
money by taking them shopping at Chanel and buying them everything
their hearts desired."[24]

Post-screening debates around *Truth or Dare* imply that the construction
of Madonna as a mother figure may be her own doing, not that of her
dancers. Maternal instinct, for instance, did not apply when "children"
protest. This was evident in the lawsuit brought by several Blond Ambition
dancers, including Oliver Crumes, Gabriel Trupin, and Kevin Stea, all of
whom appeared in *Truth or Dare.* In the lawsuit, the dancers allege that
"Madonna's director promised he would cut anything out of the film they
wanted but later rebuffed their pleas to remove scenes, including some that

exposed Trupin's homosexuality."[25] Madonna's apparent response was, "Get over it," since *Truth or Dare* audiences would allegedly come out in large numbers only if they could watch shameful revelations. Once the film became financially successful, none of the participants received any compensation or residuals.

Not coincidentally, one of the nouns most frequently used by collaborators to describe Madonna (as it was for Warhol, chapter 4) is "vampire." The record on this is extensive. According to Camille Barbone, Madonna's first manager, "She soaks up what she can and drains you in every way and then goes on to her next victim."[26] Justin Bond, a New York cabaret and drag performer who performed at Madonna's second wedding, had this to say about the boss: "Rufus Wainwright said in *The New York Times* that Madonna is a great big machine that sucks people's souls. . . . That's because she hasn't got a soul herself. She's like a vampire: most powerful after the kill."[27] In Madonna's own words, "You take what you can and then move on."[28] While feminist writers have pointed to the misogynist roots of this trope, the fact that both men and women of all backgrounds find it appropriate underlines its ability to represent multiple subaltern relationships to Madonna.

Furthermore, despite the possibly clichéd depiction of Madonna as soulless, this trope is relevant to a theory of valorization. Madonna, for instance, has claimed that "if being black is synonymous with having a soul, then, yes, I feel that I am [black]."[29] Madonna also credits "soul" music as her main influence.[30] But as Frantz Fanon wrote, the "black soul" is a "white man's artifact."[31] Soul is what "white" cultures feel *they* lost in becoming and relating to each other as commodities (things), engaging in violent acts that resulted in the devaluation of others (slavery, colonialism), and ruling as masters and mistresses of the material universe.

Although the concept of "soul" is heavily indebted to Western religious epistemology, the colonized of the new world appropriated this term in their struggle for freedom, not only in producing religious discourse, but in building communities and creating transcultural forms. The currency of "soul" as a trope can still be appreciated in the *salsero* Willie Colón's description of his collaboration with David Byrne on the album *Rei Momo* (1989). For Colón, the danger in intercultural work for Latinos is precisely the possibility of "willingly giving up their juice to some pale, spastic, soulless hack."[32]

Madonna understood—and acritically accepted—the relationship between art and commerce; she even shamelessly flaunted her status as a gendered commodity in songs and music videos like *Material Girl,* clearly acknowledging that female sexuality is the most powerful tool available to white women in their self-marketing processes. As Madonna observes, "Every time anyone reviews anything I do I'm mistaken for a prostitute."[33] Not surprisingly, most of Madonna's popular bibliography rarely mentions her wealth—as if one should take for granted that sex has been effectively exchanged for money.

In contrast to its effect on the painter Jean-Michel Basquiat (chapter 5), "whoring"—which as slavery implies the forced sale of not only one's body but the "soul"—does not destroy Madonna's career. As the daughter of white immigrants, Madonna subscribes to a strong work ethic that defines hard work not as a shameful activity linked to forced labor, but a redeeming practice through which European ethno-nationals become privileged American whites. Fittingly, at the beginning of Madonna's career, she often implied that she "came from a lower-income family" to render her rise to stardom even more dramatic and all-"American."[34] It was in part Madonna's ability to spectacularly play the capitalist game with queer style that made many fans invest in Madonna because she was living proof that the system had (finally) started to work for women, racialized groups, and sexual minorities.

Beauties and the Beast: Madonna's (Quasi)-Foundational Romance

Madonna's indulgence in all things Latino—"even when naming her pets Madonna demonstrates her Latin fever: her dog's name is Chiquita"[35]—gave new twists to old tropes by casting *boricuas* as oversexed low others there for the taking. "I don't know *what* drew us [Madonna and Haring] to these exotic clubs—like the Fun House or Paradise Garage," the singer told an interviewer. "Obviously, it was the sexuality and animal-like magnetism of those people getting up and dancing with such abandon. They were all so beautiful!"[36] As the only queer white megastar to thrive beyond the turbulent 1980s, Madonna came to infuse new life into the episodic foundational romance[37] between "American" and Latino culture most successfully played out before the cameras by Lucille Ball and the "original" Ricky Ricardo (Desi Arnaz). Yet unlike the on-camera Lucy, Madonna staged an elaborate (white) female-centered erotics of transculturation in which the "I" doing the "loving" was hers and no one else's.

In romancing Latinos in this specific way, Madonna made *boricua* men—queer and straight—desirable to an unprecedented degree in (and through) mass culture, but mostly below her "boy toy" belt or behind her back as queer chorus boys. Association with gay men of multiple ethnicities contributed dance movements, fashion, and style to Madonna's act as well as a solid fan base whose tastes often dictated music trends in discos and clubs. Complementarily, heterosexual men provided an imaginary of overendowed primitiveness—hence a scandalous sexuality—that economically signified Madonna's own sexuality as transgressive and "liberated" from repressive ethno-sexual codes. Undoubtedly, if as Camille Paglia observes, "Madonna has taught young women to be fully female and sexual while still exercising control over their lives," this power was often represented in relation to racialized men.[38]

Madonna's appeal to queers and/or Latinos, however, is not only that of the whip, although domination was indeed one of the main pleasures offered by the entertainer. Puerto Rican Madonna fans greatly enjoyed the fragmented spectacle of their cultural production grandly staged and incorporated by one of the most successful white performers of the day. This is not surprising, as both ethnic and gay fans alike have learned to "append their meanings to available images and channels"[39] and seek worth at the bosom of white transcultural icons that by "eating" us as part of their own process of valorization, transfigure and disseminate "pieces" of ourselves for global consumption.

Although Madonna categorically affirms her heterosexuality—a precondition to commodify queer cultural practices—she has often linked her desire for power, boundless sexuality, and glamour to queers. In fact, within Madonna's narrative of becoming, it is queerness that serves the same function Toni Morrison attributes to the Africanist persona in much of American foundational literature—an indispensable means of "self-discovery."[40] As has been recounted many times in the popular literature, Madonna's "liberation" from white middle-class suburban Catholicism began in the Detroit gay discos that her college dance teacher Christopher Flynn introduced her to in the 1970s.[41] Flynn was one of the first adults to see "star quality" in Madonna; it was in his queer gaze that she recognized herself as "beautiful": "Well, no one had ever said that to me before. He told me I was special."[42]

The entertainer also valorized her queer fan base through her commitment to raising funds and awareness around issues of importance to the gay community, particularly AIDS. Stating that AIDS was "the greatest tragedy of the twentieth century,"[43] Madonna used her concerts to promote safe sex, remember the dead, and affirm the living. By virtue of incorporating queer elements in her songs, music videos, and tours, Madonna also created physical and virtual spaces for queers to encounter themselves not only as spectators but as a community. Madonna's desire for gay men was even cinematically consummated when she played Abbie, a woman who ends up having a child with her gay roommate Robert, played by Rupert Everett in *The Next Best Thing* (2000).

In socially recognizing gays and staging queer culture, Madonna fulfills what Dorian Carey, one of the gay men featured in *Paris Is Burning,* described as "the longing to realize the dream of autonomous stellar individualism."[44] Or in the more colorful prose of Miami resident and Peruvian novelist Jaime Bayly,

my dear Madonna, who appears on stage with an incredible desire to tell the world I am like this, a whore with a lot of class, a very rich-millionaire-screwer-who-fucks-anybody-she-wants-whore, and who also has a weakness for gorgeous fags, and me too Madonna, that's why I like you so much, because, as you say, you are a woman with a gay man's soul. I love you, madonna, dominating bitch, cocksucker, and don't let any of those stupid people criticize you or lower your spirits.[45]

Equally important, Madonna's nod created the illusion of insider status for Latinos of all sexualities in U.S. culture. As Thomas K. Nakayama and Lisa N. Peñaloza found, Latinos tended to respond to Madonna texts in a way that underscored their specific cultural literacy, the fact that they were the ones who could provide "insight into what is 'really' going on in Madonna's video."[46] Furthermore, being recognized by Madonna linked subaltern fans to her considerable wealth and made the group feel literally appreciated. As a Latino fan in Miami put it, "She's like King Midas. . . . Everything she touches is gold."[47] Ultimately, it was not *West Side Story*'s Tony who made many *boricuas* really feel pretty, but the Material Girl herself, another queer Italian American.

Akin to *West Side Story*'s queer outlaw poetics, Madonna used the stage as a form of defiance, and even had run-ins with the law for making a spectacle out of her sexual self. (Madonna's appeal as a "lawless" icon was particularly exploited in *Truth or Dare* when Canadian police threatened to shut down her show on charges of obscenity.) In addition to challenging legally codified conservative mores, Madonna's irreverent allusions to Catholic icons and narratives also found a second stage to spectacularly represent the shamed queer subject and consolidate common ground between fans and star. As Michael Musto longingly—if ironically—writes, "we imagine we're sitting *with* her in the arena . . . even if any real attempt to get near our lady of the poses would have a bouncer dragging us out by the neck as she sang 'keep people together' with her usual twisted sense of irony."[48]

Madonna succeeds in bonding (with) the audience as she not only draws attention to the inconsistencies of Catholicism (the entertainer even prays before each public appearance) but also brings the mighty homophobic and misogynist authorities to the lowness of sex, laughs at their hypocritical morality, and relishes their contradictory appeal, confirming that the only real pleasures are always sinful.[49] Catholicism also provided raw material for style, as crucifixes became fashion statements and convent clothing sexually alluring, hence queering religious authority and its symbols of supposed celibacy. Similar to the pan-Caribbean icon La Lupe, Madonna also performed what many dared not do but shamefully desired to: masturbate, engage in orgies, and place "fun" over productivity.

Yet although Madonna's attention to queers in general has been central in cultivating her (gay) Latino fan base, it has been her reputed ("real") relationship to heterosexual Latinos that makes her today's Lucy. "Latin men were put on this earth to charm women," according to Madonna. "And torture them!"[50] It is in fact now humorous to recall that the Spanish (now "Latino") actor Antonio Banderas made his American cinema debut in Madonna's film *Truth or Dare* as the singer hopelessly chased him at a party hosted by the director Pedro Almodóvar.

U.S. media coverage of Madonna's ethnic taste was significantly different from coverage in the Latino press. Despite Madonna's consistent self-representation as a caring mother(fucker) of Latin men, in the *boricua* press, Madonna's love for Puerto Rican men was not judged, but enjoyed. An article in the celebrity rag *Vea* emphasized this sexual connection in Madonna's 1993 visit to Puerto Rico with a three-quarter-inch title that read, "Her First Romance Was with a Puerto Rican."[51] According to the tabloid journalist Dora Pizzi Campos, every time Madonna mentioned her attraction to Puerto Ricans during an Island performance, the audience "desbordaba en histeria."[52] If Madonna had a fetish, Island *boricuas* were rather pleased with that fact, which would inevitably verify the *boricua* male's irresistible virility. While many African American commentators tended to "read" Madonna's appropriations of black signifiers politically, Puerto Ricans seemed happy where Madonna had put them: in the realm of (her) erotic fantasy.

In the U.S. press, Madonna's Latin sex life was reported differently; the focus was on the alleged fact that the men were young (or even underage) and were of an "inferior" class/race. According to Mark Kamins, for example,

Madonna sometimes brought "destitute" boys home to her luxurious apartment on the Upper West Side: "She ran a Puerto Rican stud farm up there."[53] The main reason to pick on these young men was not, according to the critics, their erotic appeal but their vulnerability: "These were just banji boys, downtown kids," says Johnny Dynell. "Madonna was smart."[54] This mythic erotic interest could have culminated in a classic case of a Latin/American foundational romance in which "star-crossed lovers who represent particular regions, races, parties, and economic interests" come together,[55] yet in Madonna's mating with Carlos León, she explicitly backed out of this possibility.

While León is not a *boricua,* the fact that he does not conform to notions of Cuban American respectability and success (he is working-class and was raised in New York City) casts him as a spic. According to interviews in the popular press, León "scribbled graffiti" and "got into a lot of fights" growing up,[56] eventually becoming a personal trainer, hence underscoring Latinos' lowliness as a people who must rely on their bodies (not "brains") to make a living. The casting of León as fundamentally "dark meat" in fact constantly came up; one of the most frequently asked questions hurled at him was whether he was paid for his "stud services," a claim that he denies.[57] Madonna's biographer, however, cites a friend of León stating that the singer actually did pay him "a few million dollars, homes in Los Angeles and New York and $100,000 a year till Lourdes was eighteen,"[58] emphasizing the business nature of the transaction and León's limited contribution to the end product.

The press's incredulousness about Madonna's choice for the father of her firstborn also recalled commentary about her desire for *boricua* working-class young men and her ultimate privileged status as a white woman. Rush Limbaugh, for instance, advised Madonna that when she wanted another child, she should "do what you did. . . . Take a walk in the park, stake out some gang member-type guy . . . pay . . . and bed him."[59] As far as this conservative commentator was concerned, Lourdes is the daughter of a whore and a spic. *Latina* magazine, however, chastised Madonna for leaving León "after he gave her the pretty Latino genes to create daughter Lourdes Maria Ciccone Leon."[60] There may be some truth to that and the reason is obvious.

When seeking marriage rather than sexual partners, Madonna has courted men like Sean Penn and John Kennedy, Jr., who could valorize and provide her with new advancement opportunities. Madonna (as public persona) has made it clear that she views sex and marriage as tools of upward mobility: "And they fucked me to advance their careers, too. Let's face it. It has worked both ways."[61] But, of course, each game has different rules and expectations. The match between León and Madonna, for instance, enacted a mutually pleasurable *transcultural erotics* (cultural difference as a sexual resource), but as a *marriage* it did not offer "fair" compensation, for León cannot match Madonna's status. While Madonna would spend the next five years undoing the idea that she was a "whore," León's disappearance from the public drama confirmed the spic as an enjoyable good-for-nothing father. In fact, the latest news on León, under the headline of "Lourdes' Dad Busted for Pot," is that he was "caught smoking a joint by undercover cops in the middle of a 'buy and bust' operation. . . . After spending the night behind bars, León was arraigned Monday on a misdemeanor charge. Represented by a Legal Aid lawyer, he pleaded guilty."[62] Madonna again announces the "change of epochs and the renewal of culture"[63]—but cannot consummate her message.

Not on the Rag: Madonna's Puerto Rican Flag "Incident"

The contradictory social and sexual fantasies afforded by Madonna bound the entertainer to thousands of *boricua* fans for at least a decade. It was, however, Madonna's bodily smear of the Puerto Rican flag—the ultimate symbolic act of a transnational erotics—that highlighted how Madonna's text has also served a *boricua* subaltern politics, particularly in the Island context.[64]

Although I have highlighted how Madonna's engagement with Puerto Ricans in the United States has tended to accentuate the latter's subordinate position, her virtual encounter with Puerto Rico's political, cultural, and religious elites reinscribed the singer as a queer low-other, much in the way that U.S. conservatives have portrayed Madonna domestically. If according to the Island's power brokers Madonna went against the "ethical and moral values of Puerto Rican society,"[65] it was ultimately not because she was an American per se (the president of the Institute of Puerto Rican Culture went as far as to say that Madonna had *no* culture) but because she came to represent the queerness and "vulgarity" of popular cultural practices, a threatening spectacle for the insular national imagination.

The year was 1993. The pro-statehood governor Dr. Pedro Rosselló had won the local elections a year earlier, and had promised to hold a plebiscite to determine Puerto Rico's political status. Even though the commonwealth option was eventually the winner in the consultation by a relatively narrow margin, the fact that for the first time in history the pro-statehood camp had a fighting chance at winning a status consultation made the context particularly tense for some. The level of media and popular attention showered on Madonna, in fact, prompted some commentators to state that her concert was a "conspiracy" against the plebiscite, a plot to distract attention from the truly "political" arena.[66]

Madonna's "Girlie Tour" arrived in Puerto Rico on October 26, approximately two weeks before the plebiscite. Expectation about Madonna's concert—in contrast to the plebiscite—was feverish, as hundreds of fans opted to camp outside the Juan Ramón Loubriel Stadium a day before the concert to assure entry. As a gay Madonna fan, fully equipped with bleach-blond hair and winning smile, put it, "Anything to see her."[67] The show sold eight thousand $125 tickets in one day, in a country that allegedly has only 50 percent of the per capita income of Mississippi, the poorest state of the Union.

The disparity between local salaries and Madonna's take made some local performers, such as the satirist Awilda Carbia, incensed at the public's valorization of the "foreign" star: "I am angry that someone from outside the Island can charge so much for their show and people just pay it without complaining. But if a local person charged the same amount, nobody would accept it."[68] While Madonna made millions in Puerto Rico, however, it was the nationalist and religious sectors that symbolically capitalized the most on her visit, this time in the slippery currency of nationalist symbolic assets.

Although over twenty-five thousand people braved steep prices and interminable waits, many fans who made it into the stadium did not even get to see the show, as the promoter Larry Stein oversold tickets and mayhem ensued. The lack of appropriate security, the chaos, and the frustration were such that some attendants described the experience of getting to their seats as one of the "scariest" of their lives.[69] In addition, ticket holders had to pass hundreds of fundamentalists chanting outside the stadium for the concert goers' souls.

The Evangelical leader Jorge Rashke's beef with Madonna was that the singer represented "pornography, sadomasochism, lesbianism, and sex outside marriage," neatly alluding to all the reasons most of Madonna's fans like her, and to the communities that she has successfully incorporated into her spectacle.[70] Despite the fact that fans paid no attention to the protesters, just after they settled down or had to make do with their off-center seats, Madonna expressed herself without justifying her love and a nationalist emergency ensued.

According to the local media, a security guard gave Madonna a Puerto Rican flag during the concert. The emblem was apparently meant as a token of affection from a female fan, a detail of some consequence. Despite the fact that the majority of the concert goers could not physically see what happened on stage—and some even claim that this incident never took place (more on this intriguing version later)—Madonna reportedly put the emblem in between her legs while dressed in U.S. army fatigues and singing the celebratory anthem "Holiday."

The testimony of people who attended the concert suggests that the reaction at the stadium was subdued. A *San Juan Star* reporter wrote afterwards that "Even a controversial moment when she rubbed her body top to bottom with a small Puerto Rican flag did not seem to dampen her fans' enthusiasm."[71] The majority of Madonna fans appeared to have either enjoyed or dismissed the moment of transgression. After all, Madonna spoke Spanish to them, told them how her first lover was *boricua,* and how familiar the Island was to her.[72] She also "customized" her song "La Isla Bonita" to a *merengue* beat in order to connect with the local audience.[73]

The on-site fans, however, were literally shamed when indignation became the "correct" response to Madonna, putting people's national loyalties to the test. While the religious right's antics actually generated preconcert publicity for Madonna of the queerest kind, the nationalist aftermath was much more successful in canceling the pleasure of Madonna's spectacle for her fans. Once the news reached the local newspapers, your position regarding Madonna's handling of the *monoestrellada* implicated you within Puerto Rico's lethal culture wars. To enjoy or even defend Madonna's action made you antipatriotic scum doubly shamed by being symbolically attacked by a woman and identified with an American.

Senator Enrique Rodríguez Negrón called Madonna's performance an affront to the "moral and ethical values" of Puerto Rican society.[74] Pro-independence representative David Noriega chastised Madonna by calling her "vulgar and insensible" and quickly introduced legislation condemning the act.[75] The masculinist ethos of the patriots' response, regardless of political party affiliation, suggested that the Island elites no longer accepted that Puerto Rico could be "preciosa . . . sin bandera," a country without a flag, or perhaps more appropriately, lacking a phallic signifier of national sovereignty, which "will one day fly on top of cyclopean castles, erect and resurrected."[76]

In this sense, the journalist Maria Judith Luciano's characterization of the legislative resolution condemning Madonna is exceptionally revealing: "The measure expresses the repudiation of the legislative Body to Mrs. Madonna Louise Veronica Ciccone."[77] Ironically, Puerto Rican patriarchal values became hardened to protect *la nación* from queer desecration, understood as feminine and foreign. Critically, Madonna "lowered" the Puerto Rican nation not only by wearing the flag on her genitals[78] but by calling attention to the nation's own marginal subjects, who are, not coincidentally, the same ones as in the United States.

Largely overlooked was the fact that not all Puerto Ricans were "offended," hence partly contesting the hegemony of elite narratives of shame. The *Vea* writer Dora Pizzi Campos says that many concert goers left the stadium "jumping for joy";[79] the journalist Gino Ponti insisted that at the Puerto Rico police headquarters, only half of the officers were indignant.[80] More than one young man agreed with the university student Daniel Guzmán when he stated that "By passing the flag through her private parts, Madonna might actually be expressing that she is making love with the Puerto Rican people."[81]

But the outraged carried the torch with major sponsorship from the local mass media. In the journalist Ivonne García's key testimony in Island and mainland newspapers, Madonna's act could only elicit a response within the nationalist idiom of pride: "What I cannot forgive and will never forget was when she pulled the Puerto Rican flag, the symbol of my country, and used it like a rag to clean her private parts."[82] And in the U.S. daily *Newsday*, "People's sense of pride in the symbol for Puerto Rico was really offended."[83]

The nationalist sectors hence immediately rose up in arms, getting in bed with (and on top of) the religious right, and proving that evangelist Rashke's admonition regarding Madonna's debased nature was ultimately true. Actually, the religious right had already figured that its cause had many things in common with nationalism; one of the banners it used in the demonstration quoted (albeit out of context) the nineteenth-century pro-independence patriot Eugenio María de Hostos: "Let us live morally since that is what is needed."[84] Luis Lugardo, the coordinator for the Frente Unido pro Mejoramiento de los Medios de Comunicación, also stated that this crusade was particularly pertinent to "our sister countries that share our language and culture," as these should also "say no to sexual disorder, no to immorality, no to pornography, no to obscenity, no to Madonna's show."[85]

The most blatant manipulation of the situation for nationalist symbolic gain, however, came from the newspaper columnist Juan Manuel García Passalacqua when he proposed that the three local political parties "denounce the singer's action and that the Justice Department present a formal complaint against her."[86] The objective of the legal action would be to give the courts "the opportunity to point out the cultural norms of Puerto Rico are different from those of the United States."[87] Significantly, the "cultural norms" García Passalacqua alludes to include nothing less than the First Amendment, since the political commentator underscored that while the "Supreme Court of the United States determined that burning the U.S. flag is an act of free expression," a local court would likely rule that such desecrations cannot be visited upon the Puerto Rican emblem.[88] Interestingly, Madonna, as a *San Juan Star* editorial jokingly put it, "is covered . . . by Puerto Rico's own obscenity law, which exempts artists."[89]

Arguably, Madonna's handling of the flag indeed triggered a crisis, understood as an opportunity to "rework ideological and cultural alignments . . . precisely because they are the events by and in which a relevant public will (or will not) be reconstituted."[90] But the round was lost for queers. Even in nuanced approaches to Madonna's transgression, most Puerto Rican intellectuals ignored the irony of *boricuas* arguing, in part, about their own transculturated practices as if they were foreign. It was only in the response of postfeminist writers like Madeline Román[91] or pro-statehood public intellectuals like Luis Dávila Colón that Madonna's performance raises the question of whether the "national" itself is exclusive of subaltern groups such as blacks, women, youth, queers, and transvestites.

Dávila Colón, in fact, uses the incident as a masquerade to critique nationalist ideologies when he cites a "cocolo's" take on the situation: "Look mister, I don't know why there's such a fuss because the lone star flag has never flown so beautifully. Better in between Madonna's legs than on Macho Camacho's ass."[92] Yet precisely what enticed the alleged *cocolo*—who most likely did not exist, hence recycling the black Puerto Rican male as emptiness—is what repelled the anti-Madonna crowd. As a sign of *boricua* hypermasculinity, the boxer Macho Camacho may sit on the flag, but he is symbolically fighting for the nation—giving face to shame in a virile way. Madonna, on the other hand, is not only lowering the nation to erotic play, she is also facilitating a queer fantasy in which gay and autonomous female sexuality is coded as foreign.

Madonna's erotic use of the flag, probably intended as a heterosexual display of desire, instead drew Puerto Rican nationalists into a lesbian panic. So, when House representative David Noriega says that Madonna's acts "have no parallel in Puerto Rican history," he is surely ignoring other instances of colonial violence, and accentuating the display of "vulgarity"—a code word for popular culture—on a *boricua* national stage.[93] How else could Madonna's erotic handling of the flag—and not political subalternity, capitalist exploitation, slavery, and discrimination in the metropolis—be the worst "infamy" ever to befall Puerto Ricans?

Ironically, in making love to the flag, Madonna made graphic the "masturbations" that Puerto Ricans daily engage with their national banner in a collective quest for valorization. If Madonna was legally accused of violating Article XXXI of the Rules for the Use of the Flag, which states that "no person can mutilate, soil, profane, step on, insult or look down upon the flag of the Commonwealth of Puerto Rico verbally or by acts,"[94] *boricuas* violate most other articles every day, including those that mandate that it must be displayed to the left of the American flag (VIII), that it cannot be placed on any part of a vehicle (IX), be used for decorative purposes (XV), touch land or water (XX), be sewn or woven into handkerchiefs or pillows, nor can it be printed on napkins, boxes, nor any object that is discardable (XXV), and most dramatically, that according to article XXXII, the flag cannot be used for any commercial purpose, as part of a dress or uniform, nor can it be printed in any way for profit. While *boricua* women have always sewn the flags that stand in for the "motherland," these are ideally designed for men in combat, not bleach blonds wearing camouflage. Yet Madonna's handling of the flag while dressed in U.S. army uniform offered at least two alternative—and not mutually exclusive—performances to represent *boricua* engagement with American culture. In twirling the flag, Madonna suggests that instead of being "penetrated" by U.S. culture, as nationalists tend to think (chapters 1 and 2), *boricuas* are instead continuously rubbing themselves against American bodies in a complex process of feminine self-gratification. Also, if Madonna is able to use the flag as a flattened dildo, Puerto Rican nationhood is a simulacrum that can be used at will by any desiring subject, whether *boricua* or not. Or to put it another way, in Madonna's lowly white crotch, it's easy to lose one's patriotic head.

The flag's miraculous appearance at Madonna's concert is not, however, the first or the last queer moment in the flag's history, which reads as an abridged tragicomedy of errors, pointing to the ambivalences of *boricua* constructions of ethno-nationality. In fact, there is no other artifact in contemporary history that better tracks the multiple movements of Puerto Rico's political journeys than the flag, and Madonna's handling of the rag echoed the flag wars that later became a way of producing national consensus, and suppressing dissent.

If This Flag Could Talk: The Queer History of the *Boricua* Flag

Like Madonna, the contemporary Puerto Rican flag was reportedly first dreamed up in New York, and it is universally accepted that the emblem's adoption took place at Chimney Corner Hall in New York City on December 22, 1895. According to Ovidio Dávila, fifty-nine Puerto Ricans, mostly upper-class and from the pro-annexation wing of the Cuban Revolutionary Party's Puerto Rico Section, presented a small model, made by the daughter of one of the members, for the whopping (at the time) sum of $1.60.[95] The flag's status as a commodity was immediate.

As if already feeling the dread of a people who love the flag but refuse to do the work of building the nation-state, the nineteenth-century pro-independence advocate Ramón Emeterio Betances allegedly wrote that the important thing was to achieve independence and then any "rag can serve as the flag."[96] The Puerto Rico Section of the Cuban Revolutionary Party, however, opted for this flag over other possibilities, such as the one created after the anti-Spanish 1868 Lares insurrection, apparently to distance the struggle from previous experiences of defeat and to affirm ties to the Cubans who had offered to assist Puerto Ricans achieve their independence.

Appropriately, there are different versions regarding its legitimate "father" or inventor; the paternity of the flag is as uncertain as the virility of the nation it designates. The most circulated flag origin story is that of Antonio Vélez, a well-off young man who allegedly was the first to literally "see" the flag:

> One June 11, in the beginning of the 1890s, while he worked in his room, he felt the need to rest his eyes by fixing them on the Cuban flag that he had hanging on the wall of his New York apartment. When he looked away, as a consequence of a strange daltonism, his mind inverted the colors of the Cuban flag: red became blue and blue red.[97]

Perhaps the reason this and not some other version has "stuck" is that like all narratives of Puerto Rican national virility, the flag is the product of an "inverted" hallucination in New York, a mirage mediated by a Cuban (phallic) symbol.

The Puerto Rican flag, which had not been the creation of the people in the heat of organized struggle, went into relative obscurity until Governor E. Mont Reilly (1921–1923) declared war on it by calling the banner a "dirty" and "worn out" rag.[98] In the 1930s the Nationalist Party leader Pedro Albizu Campos sought to ingrain a sense of patriotic pride in national symbols, including the flag, as a strategy to provide a heroic national history. The flag's eventual association with anticolonial cultural and political activities transformed it into a sign of *boricuaness* and the American colonial administrations outlawed it.

The extent to which the Puerto Rican flag had been associated with subversion of the colonial state and U.S. sovereignty made it a useful symbol for nationalist struggle throughout the rest of the century. As unrest and perse-cution of Puerto Rican nationalists intensified, by October 30, 1950, the date of the Nationalist Jayuya insurrection, "The mere owning of the Puerto Rican flag came to be considered a crime."[99] Possessing a flag then became evidence of disloyalty to the United States, and the Nationalist Party specifically sought the association between war and the flag when in 1954 four Puerto Ricans who attacked Congress carried the banner. In reaction, pro-American Puerto Ricans and the colonial government reportedly used the flag to hu-miliate political prisoners like Albizu Campos, by using it to mop the court floors.[100]

This radically nationalist period did not last long, as the first symbolic act of the Commonwealth government, founded in 1952, was the adoption of the persecuted flag as an official emblem of the new colonial arrangement. It was during this juncture that the flag suffered some pigment shifts as the light blue and red became almost identical to the hues of the U.S. flag. Whereas Albizu dreaded this as a form of co-optation, the flag's adoption by the government and its display at public functions slowly destigmatized its use and transformed it into a state-sponsored consensual symbol. Yet it also made the flag available to more Puerto Ricans for a wider range of purposes, including erotic ones.

The now widespread display of the flag as synonymous with Puerto Rican pride—not any specifically political project—began after 1952 as businesses and other social actors like athletes used it for promotion and advertising purposes. The process of commodification of the flag, which had accelerated after the radical 1970s, began to reach a peak in the early 1990s, when flag mania reached all social sectors. The hundredth anniversary of the flag, cel-ebrated in 1995 under a pro-statehood administration, exemplified the flag's ubiquitous presence, but also suggested that despite superficially consistent displays of allegiance to the flag, the question of the star's final resting place was still a deeply divisive issue.

For the pro-independence sectors (who cried when Eduardo Morales Coll, president of the Ateneo Puertorriqueño, raised the flag for the first time since

1898 to commemorate its hundredth anniversary and decided to let it fly alone in defiance of the law), the star should remain alone. The lone star, as Tomás Blanco wrote, is the sign of "aspiraciones emancipadoras"[101] with the "orienting" function of the polar star. For those seeking *criollo* statehood, roughly half of the population, the star belongs on the American flag and their struggle is, as Ricky Martin's ode to soccer, "Cup of Life," put it, "for one star" (chapter 10).

In the United States, Puerto Ricans have mainly deployed the flag as a sign to claim a distinct ethnicity and call attention to the value of *boricua* culture. The Puerto Rican Day Parade of New York, held yearly since 1958, is the stage for the display of thousands of flags every year as marchers walk along Fifth Avenue, a site of white wealth and power. As in other performances of ethno-nationhood, the display of the flag and the parade itself are closely linked to narratives to offset shame as *boricuas* are invited to celebrate "our culture with pride" and the "self esteem of being a Puerto Rican in the United States."[102] The enjoyment of the marchers is, not coincidentally, intimately linked to the proscribed space that they are temporarily occupying.

The conflation between the commodified flag and the ethno-national body has become entrenched in New York. In 1999 the Puerto Rican community rallied against NBC when in a *Seinfeld* episode one of the show's characters accidentally burned a Puerto Rican flag. The protesters won an apology and the promise that the episode would not be rebroadcast in the future.[103] Ironically, the use of the flag as part of the show suggested that the Puerto Rican flag had become sufficiently recognizable to serve as a major narrative thread in the highest-rated show of the time. The value of the flag also received similarly ambivalent confirmation as a commodity when two years later a boxer opposing ex-champ Felix "Tito" Trinidad—in full knowledge of the flag's importance to Puerto Ricans—took it from Trinidad's hands and stomped on it as a way to promote the multimillion-dollar fight.

Beyond strictly partisan lines, the flag marks Puerto Rico as *boricua* territory, and the bearers of the rag as Puerto Rican ethno-national subjects. This explains why all political parties supported resolution 1601 condemning Madonna's "lascivious" use of the flag, and no public figure dared to say he or she was not offended by the incident. Yet perhaps the most telling irony of Madonna's flag incident has escaped all critics: as in *Seva*, there is no visual evidence of the outrage. No image shows Madonna putting the flag between her legs: "the photojournalists had access to the show when the first song was almost done and were expelled from the Juan Ramón Loubriel Stadium as soon as the fourth song was over. So there is no visual evidence of what really happened when Madonna had the Puerto Rican flag in her hands."[104]

The on-site reporter for *Vea* magazine insists that the only thing she saw was that a security guard gave Madonna a flag after receiving it from a fan: "What some people saw was that she unfolded it [the flag], showed it to the audience, then took it in her right hand, tried to put it away in her pocket and when she could not put it away, she gave it back to the guard."[105] In the taped material I personally acquired documenting the show, it is impossible to tell what Madonna did with the flag. But as a *San Juan Star* editorial put it after Madonna visited Puerto Rico, "Goodbye, Madonna. *Adios. Ciao,* baby. You're history."[106]

Like a Virgin: Madonna's Born-Again Whitening

If queers and ethnics offered inexpensive materials from which to create an appealing product during the 1980s and early 1990s, Madonna made a u-turn during the late 1990s. True to form, the entertainer was born again after her daughter Lourdes came forth in 1998. "That's the year the Material Girl found God or gods, as evident on her multi-mystical *Ray of Light* album."[107] Madonna allegedly underwent a significant transformation after Lourdes, named for a French town in which a fourteen-year-old girl saw visions of the Virgin Mary: "With the birth of her daughter came an 'enlightened' Madonna, who explored her spirituality with the same fervor that she once explored—and flaunted—her sexuality."[108]

This "enlightenment" became evident in a major shift in musical inspiration, public image, and interests, including the study of the kabala and non-Western culture. "She's into a daily dose of yoga, for one."[109] To critics who claimed that this was just another phase, Madonna responded, "I'd rather think that I'm slowly revealing myself, my true nature. . . . It feels to me like I'm just getting closer to the core of who I really am."[110] The woman who once cannibalized dark flesh when she had nothing better to eat, and who served as public culture's "grotesque" had finally "grown up."[111] As with the original Madonna, childbirth did not lead to the lower stratum but instead elevated her to *ideal* womanhood—a (white) mother.

Curiously, Madonna was pregnant with Lourdes while on the set of *Evita* (1997), arguably the singer's best leading screen role and the delayed realization of a number of her Latin fantasies, including finally sharing the spotlight with the Spanish actor Antonio Banderas, and reaching a broad audience via a movie musical, a thrill "rarely found . . . since the days of *West Side Story*."[112] Madonna secured the role of Eva Perón amidst great controversy among Argentineans—who felt that a "whore" named Madonna could not play a "saint" named Evita—and over the reservations of the film's director and producer. Predictably, the only Argentineans willing to openly express their support for the embattled actress were young women and gay men challenging the classic Catholic dichotomy by screaming "Eva Madonna" outside the actress's hotel window.

Madonna identified with Eva, and once more slipped under the skins of "Latins" for success. But if Madonna passionately deployed a seductive affinity discourse to justify her right to play an Argentinean, her so-called private diaries published in *Vanity Fair* suggest that the singer's gaze toward Latin America remains surprisingly similar to Andy Warhol's distressed look at a Latinized Central Park (chapter 4). Complaining that she could not leave the hotel in this "godforsaken" country without stirring a major commotion, Madonna (presumably) writes, "just because I'm stuck in an uncivilized country doesn't mean I can't have a little fun. I was determined to go sight-seeing."[113] Unlike Warhol, however, Madonna is not afraid of the natives and is well assured that her value as a white American star will protect her from any possible aggression. Responding to her manager's concerns regarding death threats against the star, Madonna rejoins, "He doesn't understand that all Latinos exaggerate and are all over the top."[114]

The singer won a Golden Globe for her portrayal of Eva Perón and the film showed that Madonna's screen career was not yet totally over after several disasters such as *Body of Evidence*. Yet *Evita* actually spelled the beginning of the end. "I'm tired of being her," wrote Madonna in her diary.[115] Eva Perón might have been the role "Madonna was born to play,"[116] but either Madonna had already sucked all she could from Latin culture, or she no longer needed a patron saint. Madonna's subsequent two transformations came to suggest that, in hindsight, the identification with Latino culture's vitality and the sins of the past were as recoupable as high fashion.

Madonna's next station as mother, in fact, seemed to require that her spirit find another trans-ethno-national body to occupy. In 1998 Madonna turned Asian in a relatively brief transition period in which she combined Indian and Japanese motifs with Latino images, as seen in the *Rolling Stone* cover article aptly titled "Indian Summer." The feature contains six pictures highlighting Madonna in (East) Indian costume, but consistent with the phase's transitional nature, the article includes an image of Madonna bathed by the (white) "light" of a hydrant's water ejaculation, surrounded by mostly dark-skinned black and Puerto Rican matrons, drag queens, moms, kids, voguers, and studs.

Again, as in *Sex* and *Truth or Dare,* Madonna's whiteness connotes superiority through rarity (she's the only one), although this time the valorized currency is not the power of sexuality but the power *over* materiality, including the body. In this new scene, one of the last Latin studs to populate a Madonna spread waves a Puerto Rican flag toward her, reinscribing the singer's centrality as transcultural medium—the vehicle through which American mass culture peeps at *boricuas*. Yet by now Madonna had embarked on a journey to transcend onto another, spiritual (white) side in Asian costume and gesture, leaving the (low) Latin others to the hopeless physicality of sex and food.

The most recent chapter in Madonna's transformation coincided with her departure from the United States. Madonna decided to sell her Miami home and move to London, where she eventually married the British film director Guy Ritchie. Madonna's wedding, which took place in a Scottish castle, suggested the ways the Madonna "empire" was now interested in representing her public persona. In Susie Bright's terms, "She's done a lot of formal PR to downplay her 'wild' past, to stress what a puritanical Midwesterner she is at heart."[117] This refashioning would also include her daughter by Cuban American Carlos León.

Despite León's claim that his child is "very Latina,"[118] Lourdes, one of the world's most famous Latin children, is now being schooled in British ways, lest her heritage choose to rear its *cafre* head later on, especially now that Madonna thinks that the "British are more intelligent than Americans."[119] Madonna, the epitome of unrestrained—hence shameful—sexual energy and interethnic eroticism, is now sporting new manners and taking classes to "correct" her English so she speaks like a Brit. At the same time, if Lourdes is simultaneously high (wealthy) and low (Latina), Madonna's son with Guy Ritchie, Rocco, consummates a foundational romance between America and Britain, stage and the movies, new money and old money, and "completes" Madonna's body in Bakhtin's sense of it becoming an "impenetrable façade."[120] Unlike her former self, who required a constant supply of bodies to nurture her and connect through multiple cultural orifices, Madonna is now Mrs. Ritchie—as she proudly wears on jackets and T-shirts—the mother of two, and the singer of an album blandly called *Music*.

Ridiculously, it is Madonna who is now ashamed. In an effort to distance herself from the formerly desirable objects, Madonna is channeling significant resources to spit out "the bad-tasting food" of racialized flesh.[121] "Now, her image is polished—not trashy. Her clothes tease without screaming and are by Versace, Dolce & Gabbana, Oscar de la Renta and Gianfranco Ferré."[122] In her latest concert tour, "Drowned" (2001), she does not even perform any material recorded before 1998. The "Express Yourself" set was particularly telling: Madonna rode an electric pony, spoke with a southern accent, and wore cowboy attire.

Despite the "soulless" performance, generally devoid of American subaltern cultural references (one reviewer commented that it simply looked like "work"),[123] the tour was still successful, selling out and rousing some of her traditional fan base groups. Many (white) gay men dressed in "retro British punk," including kilts, and one local station, WHYI-FM (Y-100), gave away some free tickets to the male contestant who could best imitate Madonna— bustier and all. In Florida, tickets went for as much as $1,000 apiece and for the many Latinos who attended, Madonna was simply the "awesomest."

Impressively, less than twenty years after Madonna's first successful single and despite her many transfigurations of shame, she has managed to verify that sex is colored, spirituality is Asian, and being high-"class" is white, whiter than AngloAmerican, bloody British. "I did my sexual rebellion thing," complains Madonna. "I've been naked in every state and country. . . . I've dated the NBA. I mean, there's nothing more!"[124] Madonna hence journeyed through black and queer continents alike to, as Toni Morrison suggests, move "from discipline and punishment to disciplining and punishing; from social ostracism to social rank."[125] Untouched by such contact, Madonna rose like a virgin—and a princess. According to Michael Musto, the British are delighted that Madonna lives in London, where she is perceived as the new "Princess Diana."[126]

In her desire for Caribbean culture, Madonna, who embodies the "past and the future, the obsolete and the youthful, the old truth and the new truth,"[127] helped to create the conditions for her own demise as a prime transcultural medium, since "white" culture and markets have opened up to Latino agency, even if within limited parameters. Diva Jennifer López, for instance, had no problem in dissing Madonna's acting by asking her to not "spit on my craft,"[128] and it is hard to imagine that anyone but a Latina would have played Evita today. In fact, the Mexican actress Salma Hayek edged Madonna out of the competition to play Frida Kahlo in the 2002 biopic about the famous painter.[129] And of course, you can now even buy your own first-class Frida Kahlo stamp by going to your nearest U.S. post office. *Gracias,* Madonna, for being swept away.

Part III   *Boricua* Anatomies

7 Rosario's Tongue

Rosario Ferré and the
Commodification of Island Literature

> Let us acquire the language of Webster and Dickens without losing the language of Roque Barcia and Galdós. We occupy a privileged position at the intersecting point between two hemispheres. Let's take advantage of it!
> —Luis Muñoz Rivera, 1898

> While Puerto Rico continues to be, as it is, a colony of a metropolitan power that speaks a different tongue, the language dilemma will never have a definitive solution. —René Marqués, 1972

> En los Estados Unidos, me alegra poder decir que estamos dejando atrás antiguos temores. —President George W. Bush, presidential address (delivered on Spanish radio), 2001

During the 1990s, Puerto Rican agency in mass culture became more noticeable. Yet, despite "foreignly" induced debates such as the Madonna "incident" or perceived subaltern assaults on upper-class taste such as Island-style hip hop, Puerto Rican high culture still seemed "safe" from the corrupting forces of commodified transculturation. Until the national organ most invested in separating what can be culturally tasted, swallowed, and digested— the "native" tongue—took on a life of its own in the reconstitution of an elite *boricua* body.

In 1991 pro-commonwealth governor Rafael Hernández Colón revived the bogeyman of linguistic impurity by proposing a bill that would make Spanish the Island's *only* official language. Ironically flanked by the Puerto

Rican and American flags during the signing ceremony, Hernández Colón gave his all in a symbolic "coming out" performance in which making Spanish the official language was a way to "define ourselves in front of our fellow American citizens and to the world."[1] Backing up the law was Senator Severo Colberg, who declared that opposition to this legislation was not only "anti–Puerto Rican" but *"antinatural"*—resorting, not coincidentally, to the same term that is usually deployed to condemn sodomy.[2] However unnatural or anti–Puerto Rican English might seem to some, the Official Spanish Law proved unpopular among Puerto Ricans, who, depending on the poll, supported it by less than 22 percent to at most 31 percent of the population.[3]

Nevertheless, a handful of conservative Republican U.S. congressmen contemptuously decried the legislation as a snub of "America," and declared that the legislation was "a referendum unto itself."[4] Eager to convince an unresponsive Congress that Puerto Ricans are loyal citizens willing to master (or be mastered by) English should statehood ever be granted and just as eager to reassure the Island electorate that "extreme" nationalist elements would not threaten the Island's bond with the United States, Hernández Colón's successor, pro-statehood governor Dr. Pedro Rosselló, pledged during his election campaign to restore "official" status to both languages.

Speaking about language to define national boundaries was not peculiar to the Island during this period. In the United States the spectacular demographic growth of the "Latino" population in the 1990s, which according to the 2000 census finally became the United States' most numerous transethno-national aggregate, gave rise early in the decade to a political backlash. Bilingual education and the use of Spanish in the workplace came under attack, and the English First lobby stepped up its efforts to impose English as the official language across the country. By the close of the decade, however, major corporations and political parties changed their xenophobic tune to a market-driven mambo, a shift most audible in the actual use of mambo music in the Gap jeans ad campaign of 1999.

Only ten years after Hernández Colón sought to underscore the essential difference between Spanish-speaking Puerto Ricans and English-speaking

Americans, President George W. Bush gave the first bilingual radio address in the history of the U.S. presidency on May 5, 2001, as part of a Cinco de Mayo celebration at the White House. Although the president's address was meant to flatter Mexican Americans into Republican action and consolidate U.S.-Mexico relations, and many Latinos viewed Bush's two-step as opportunistic, but its symbolic weight was not lost on the adversaries of Spanish-speaking America.[5] The English First advocate Jim Boulet, for instance, stated that Bush's address put a "White House imprimatur on a culture of mandatory multilingualism."[6] Speaking in Spanish, the Texas-raised conservative president, however, may have heralded the beginning of a new era in which it was no longer true that "only homosexuality was less tolerated than bilingualism" in the United States.[7]

Caught in the crossfire of a culture war waged over the use of the Spanish language in Puerto Rico as a sign of "nationalist" specificity *and* in the United States as a symbol of Latino "ethnic" enfranchisement, was Rosario Ferré, the "grande dame" of Puerto Rican letters.[8] The daughter of a foundational marriage between a businessman from Ponce who became governor in 1968 and an heiress to an *hacendado* family, Ferré has cultivated the commentary column, essay, novel, short story, poetry, biography, and children's genres with equal enthusiasm—and almost exclusively in Spanish. She is one of the Island's few literary celebrities, but it was the author's English-first publication of her novels *The House on the Lagoon* (1995), *Eccentric Neighborhoods* (1999), and *Flight of the Swan* (2001) that have made Ferré one of the few Puerto Rican writers on the bookshelf all over the Spanish- and English-reading world.

In raising her cultural stock by writing in English, the formerly esteemed patrician bottomed out with linguistic nationalists. Hurling insults in the language of Cervantes, critics have accused Ferré of writing in English to sell more books and to become better known (which she does not refute), but they also have charged with betrayal of the motherland (which she does deny). Even more galling, the nationalists find her literary work in English overly accessible, simplistic, and facile. The intensity (to say nothing of the sarcasm) of these critiques misses—or perhaps recoils from—the full impact of Ferré's gesture.

The Tongue of Treason: Ferré and National Literature

Approvingly labeled "subversive" by literary critics for most of her career, Ferré burst onto the Puerto Rican high culture scene during the seventies as the editor of *Zona de carga y descarga* (1972–1975), a journal that was crucial for the modernization of Island literary production in terms of both "technique" and themes. With a daring that often scandalized her peers, Ferré's work critically explored the classist, racist, and sexist underpinnings of elite Puerto Rico and went where few writers had gone before: the very organ of white female sexuality. In representing the shame and pleasures of white women, Ferré's early production implicates an entire world. As Deleuze and Guattari suggest in relation to Kafka's work, "[the] most erotic desires bring about a fully political and social investment."[9]

In excess of her strictly literary achievements, however, it was arguably Ferré's early rejection of her father's pro-statehood political ideology that consolidated her cultural capital within an intellectual community for which the upholding of "nationalist" ideologies was—and still is—a requirement for membership. As Ferré herself acknowledges, "The pro-*independentista* reputation that was created when I began to write . . . I think it was a projection. People read me and interpreted my writings in a certain way, and this is why the books of that period were so successful."[10] The fact that Ferré's flirting with nationalist positions resulted in the rejection of her own class further enhanced the writer's prestige with the Puerto Rican nationalist left: from "the point of view of friends and family . . . Rosario Ferré became a traitor."[11]

La lengua's ability to stir such strong political passions is not arbitrary. As I have argued elsewhere,[12] as expectations of home rule withered away after the U.S. invasion and imposition of an authoritarian colonial government (which, like Spain, manipulated language policy to suit its own needs), a broad coalition of interest groups, including intellectuals, seized upon their "Hispanic" heritage and Spanish language to symbolically encase their opposition to the English-speaking "Anglos" who became major obstacles to their political project. Linguistic desertion hence brings shame not only to one's self, but also to the nation. As Ferré has pointed out, "Spanish is used to define not what is Puerto Rican, but what is patriotic. If you do not write or speak Spanish, you are a traitor."[13]

While an increasing number of Island-born and -raised intellectuals are writing their work in English to communicate with monolingual colleagues in the United States, reach a wider audience, and/or imagine Puerto Rican concerns as part of a transnational dialogue, before Ferré's conversion, creating literary works in the language of the current metropolis had been virtually unheard of except by *boricuas* raised in the United States. In writer Magali García Ramis's succinct summary, "the identity of our cultural product up to now is totally fused with Spanish."[14]

This is the case because *boricua* Island literature in Spanish has long compensated for the absence of a sovereign state by performing the role of a "national constitution."[15] Puerto Rican writers (including critics and essayists) imagine themselves as virtual heads of state and protectors of the nation's integrity against foreign "penetration" and domestic contamination—at least on paper. By recasting the role of the Puerto Rican writer not as textual nation builder but as transnational commodity producer, Ferré's work also enables subaltern subjects—particularly women and/or Latinos—to imagine themselves as powerful insiders within the U.S. public sphere.

In this context Ferré represents a significant rupture, as she is a bilingual member of the literary elite—the sector most heavily invested in preserving its considerable power as protector of the cultural patrimony—writing in both English and Spanish, for readers of either language, and with a specific political agenda of integration into selected U.S. public spheres (media, academic institutions, cultural marketplace). Contrary to the vast majority of

Island writers, Ferré's writing not only textually affirms but also enacts the continuously derided idea that the United States is a relevant cultural context for Puerto Rican culture. As Ferré snaps, "I defend my language, Spanish, but yes, I am anti-Spain. What has Spain done for us lately?"[16]

In opening this Pandora's box, Ferré knowingly gave a new twist to the century-old drama about the relationship between literature and Puerto Rican ethno-nationality. A transvestite of the tongue, Ferré exposes the linguistic cross (dressing) and cultural impurity of the *boricua* ethno-nation and relishes in this eminently "low" pleasure. By forking her tongue, Ferré turned *la lengua*—which in Spanish can refer to either language or the tongue—into a drag epistemology that shamelessly proposed the marriage of transculture and commerce to valorize Puerto Rican elite literary production. The "lazy organ," as Fanon inaccurately called it, became the slippery instrument for making out what Ferré does with the padre (father) tongue, and what many flicking the mother *lengua* do unto her.

Without Hair on the Tongue: The Critical Backlash

The conversion of a reformed bourgeois Island intellectual who had served the nationalist cause so well into the messenger of a commodified literary practice in English unsettled feminist writers, nationalist polemicists, and academics alike. Ferré provoked Island literary critics not only because she called attention to *boricua* literature written in English, a textual body that Islanders have widely ignored due to its perceived low value as the product of English-speaking working-class writers, but also because Ferré was "one of their own."[17] Identification with "foreign" literature, however, began early in Ferré's life. According to the writer, she learned to read English at age seven by "sneaking into my father's library,"[18] and once gleefully declared, "I always wanted to be Virginia Woolf."[19] But it was not until she affirmed that *boricua* writing was not a matter of language—"I am not any tongue"[20]—that her Anglophilia came under attack.

In what some critics saw as coming full circle in the Shakespearean drama of her public life, Ferré not only held her *lengua* to tell her father's story as the coauthor of his memoirs, *Memorias de Ponce*,[21] but turned her formerly "feminine" tongue into a phallic signifier, "a magic peduncle with which one reached out to touch one's neighborhood. One groped around with it to examine a face, tweak a nose, or poke into someone's eyes and ear."[22] *La lengua* was no longer the affective link to one's *patria*—neither the organ that renders subaltern feminine identity socially intelligible, nor the sound that makes "newborn babies suck faster at the [mother's] breast"[23]—but the aggressive instrument with which the female transvestite subject can dart and lick its way into global visibility.

Originally published in *The New York Times*, "Puerto Rico, USA," a by now infamous manifesto on cultural hybridity (whose terms she has since partially retracted),[24] Ferré offered a rationale for Puerto Rican cultural and political incorporation into the United States under statehood and as "Latinos"—in English. Ferré affirmed that "As a Puerto Rican writer, I constantly face the problem of identity. When I travel to the States I feel as Latina as Chita Rivera. But in Latin America, I feel more American than John Wayne. To be Puerto Rican is to be hybrid. Our two halves are inseparable; we cannot give up either without feeling maimed."[25]

Fellow writers like Ana Lydia Vega were appalled at the gendered language, selection of figures, and public commitment to statehood contained in Ferré's text. In a harsh critique of Ferré that was published in the Island's most important Spanish-language daily, Vega wrote, "I hope that my dear Pandora, she who once slapped the hypocritical face of society with the explosive truth of her papers, had not sold out to the one who now disseminates the false stereotypes challenged by her own books."[26]

Although Vega is compelling in pointing out the crude duality of Ferré's tropes, her dismissal of Ferré's argument for Puerto Rican transculturation as a mere "personal affectation" is equally problematic.[27] Not only are there over three million English-speaking Puerto Ricans in the United States, many of whom consider themselves part of the *boricua* ethno-nation, the Island it-self is increasingly the home of different Caribbean ethnic groups who move to Puerto Rico precisely for its liminal "Americanness."

Vega, however, was not alone in upholding the Islanders' cultural whole-someness. In her "Carta abierta a una estadista híbrida," the critic Liliana Cotto agrees that "there is no such hybridity" and quickly moves on to point out the most threatening aspect of Ferré's shamelessness, why she should feel guilty for her transgression.[28] The core issue is not that Ferré writes a *dis-paratado* phallic English but *who* gets to read it: "Ferré's writings display bias and inaccuracies in the presentation of the facts and their interpretations. This failure is serious because it misinforms the reading public of the Puerto Rican press, intellectuals, the political sectors in Washington and the Latin American cultural elite that read the *New York Times*."[29] In other words, Ferré can think that she is John Wayne all she wants as long as John Wayne him-self does not read about it.

The fear that English-speaking *boricuas* or their writings in English can in-fluence public opinion or send the shameful messages that Puerto Ricans "desire" to be part of the United States, identify as Americans, and/or are bilingual did not, of course, begin with Ferré, even if she moved the debate up to the front page. An informative precedent can be found in Pedro López-Adorno's 1991 prologue to a significant anthology of Puerto Rican poets in New York, in which the critic "defends" Nuyorican writers against their most conservative detractors, yet recommends that they learn Spanish to dissuade Americans from thinking that Puerto Ricans "in exile" write only in English: "Nuyorican poets . . . need to understand the incomplete and hence danger-ous image of our personality as a people and of our collective culture both in Puerto Rico and the United States that this ideology can project to the world."[30] López-Adorno himself aims to correct this "misperception" by translating all English texts into Spanish for his book.

What increasingly seems to get lost in translation—in this case from the United States to the Island—is that culture cannot be theorized as transpar-ently contained or locked inside language.[31] It is the way subaltern people deploy language for their own survival according to context that makes it constitutive of a specific cultural formation. Yet the panic over unpoliced transculturation and the perceived loss of political control that will follow is so intense for some, that it is deemed preferable for Island children not to speak or receive an education at all than to be transculturated. As René Marqués puts it, "It's better for the little one to be mute than to stutter the essence of his spirit."[32] The underlying premise is that only certain educated elites can be trusted with knowledge of more than one language, which is exactly what the nationalist Salvador Tió claims when he affirms that "in trying to incorporate another tongue we encounter two obstacles that can be perfectly mastered only by exceptional individuals: stuttering and vacillation."[33]

The rallying cry of "one history, one culture, one language, and one race"[34] ultimately has less to do with saving Puerto Ricans from becoming stuttering Americans than it does with masking struggles among classes in Puerto Rico. Authoritarian writings by prominent language nationalists subsume the interests of all Puerto Ricans under the language issue, glossing over the violence of slavery and conquest by stating that the Spanish (phallic) *lengua* "entered" black women in Puerto Rico through loving caresses,[35] and declaring that those who (dare) not speak Spanish "well" should be taught—and "if they don't want to learn, let them explode."[36] Shamefully, it is not unusual to read Puerto Rican linguistic nationalists defend their cause by referring to the equally "legitimate" right of the American racist elites to aggressively police language use in the United States and to curtail minority language rights, including those of Spanish-speaking Latinos.[37]

Just as remarkably, many who champion policies that would limit the use of English in the private sector or curtail its teaching in the public schools are themselves bilingual and send "their own children to private schools where English is the medium of instruction."[38] English is thus recognized as an essential element in reproducing class distinction and assuring upward mobility—a "choice" made by concerned parents in "private"—but is rejected as a public policy since it legitimizes what linguistic nationalists deny: the border "state" of Puerto Rican culture on—and beyond—the Island.

The seizing of language as a sword by sectors of the elite does not diminish the majority's investment in English as a valorizing resource. Despite the growth and acceptance of multiple nationalist cultural ideologies in Puerto Rico over the last decade, recent newspaper polls revealed that a whopping 83 percent of Puerto Ricans "believe English and Spanish should be kept as the official languages of the Island."[39] An attempt to protect language and cultural rights in the local constitution was also rejected by the electorate through a direct consultation in 1993. On both occasions, *boricuas* articulated a desire to retain the English language as a public symbol because it politically signifies that Puerto Rico is part of the United States, and because on a practical level, a command of standard English enhances employment and educational opportunities *on* the Island.[40]

The language plebiscite and public opinion polls underscore one of the paradoxes of language nationalism throughout the last century: the majority of Islanders use Spanish as the undisputed vernacular but support bilingualism as the "ideal" state of affairs; by contrast, many among the educated sectors are bilingual but promote monolingualism as a "barrier"—the ultimate cultural condom—to prevent political incorporation.[41] At stake is not language practice itself but the very boundaries of the Puerto Rican ethnonation and the determination of who speaks for the ethno-nation, under what terms, and to what effects, in the context of increasingly diverse and even divergent Puerto Rican communities.

In this sense, I would argue that despite giving lip service to decolonizing rhetoric, "Spanish Only" discourse *contributes* to the preservation of colonial status in the post-1952 period. If using the vernacular in the public schools is a victory for minority language rights in relation to the United States, the fact that lower-income students attending public schools are less likely to be bilingual indicates that monolingualism is actually a symptom of lack of access to educational resources, rather than a patriotic choice. Furthermore, by refusing to use English for "public" purposes, (bilingual) Puerto Rican nationalist intellectuals have also shunned the intense exchange across "national" contexts that has been pivotal in bringing about decolonization and civil rights victories throughout the world during the twentieth century.

Although opaqueness is often a useful strategy for the subaltern, its (ab)use by the elites has severely narrowed the field of Puerto Rican agency. By defining "culture" as the nation's highest priority and investing substantial resources in legislating the use of Spanish, already the undisputed vernacular, the language nationalists have evaded the Island's thorniest political, economic, and social issues. Keeping the focus on the language matter has perpetuated Puerto Rico's colonial subordinate position, furthering the interests of both native elites and colonial rulers—two groups who more often than not understand each other perfectly.

Giving Up *la lengua:*
The House on the Lagoon and the Cannibalized Text

Ferré's decision to write fiction in English seems to have taken many by surprise, but her earlier essays about translation, a number of poems originally written in English,[42] and the controversial translation of her first novel, *Maldito amor* (1986)—published in English as *Sweet Diamond Dust* (1988)— had already made explicit the author's considerable interest in addressing "Americans" in different terms from Islanders at least since the mid-1980s. "Translation, for Ferré, is an opportunity to rewrite the original for a distinct targeted audience," says the biographer Suzanne Hintz, appropriately using advertising lingo, "and it is also a challenge to present thematic concerns of a Latin American, Puerto Rican novel to an Anglo reader who does not understand the cultural and social background of the original text."[43]

First published in 1986, *Maldito amor* (literally, damned—or cursed—love) proposed a feminist rewriting of Puerto Rican nation-building narratives in which "whiteness" is revealed to be a textual sham: the effect not of lacking a true "national" hero, but of crossing out the mulatto "father's" face. Appropriately, the novel's title refers to a *danza* by the mulatto composer Juan

Morel Campos, and through it, to Puerto Rico's complex transculturation process and the upper class that insists on denying it. Narrated by a family cast composed of former slaves, landowners, writers, and upwardly mobile professionals as a series of cross(ed) racial love affairs, "Maldito Amor" (music, lyrics, novel, and failed foundational romance) serves as a trope for the differently experienced dislocations brought about by the American colonial regime.

The "official" voice of the novel belongs to Don Hermenegildo Martínez, an attorney and novelist who in allegorical fashion represents the patriar-chal, capitalist, and nationalist values of the ruined *hacendado* class and its nostalgia for the Spanish past, before 1898: "Today everything has changed. Far from being a Paradise, our town has become an enormous funnel through which flows the terrifying swirl of sugar that the Ejemplo sugarmill vomits day and night to North America."[44] Like the displaced elite that at-tempts to save face through heroic fantasies like that presented in *Seva* (chap-ter 2), Hermenegildo's tale overlooks racial mixture and interclass conflict in order to nationalize (that is, whiten) the Puerto Rican body politic under the *hacendado* descendants' leadership.

While the enlightened white matriarch Doña Laura's desire (in the form of a living "will") ultimately structures the entire narrative, it is sabotaged by her mulatta nurse and daughter-in-law, Gloria Camprubí, who in refusing the older woman's will, challenges the gender, racial, and class order that constrains subaltern agency. Substantially informed by José Luis González's essay *El país de los cuatro pisos* (although it strikes a different chord), *Maldito amor* became an isoglossic scandal at the moment of publication precisely be-cause the young working-class mulatta Gloria Camprubí defiantly talks back to nationalist discourses as exemplified by canonical writers.

With Gloria Camprubí, Ferré attempts to democratize the *gran familia* from within its entrails and help to give birth to a feminist *nación soñada*, once Gloria brings down not only the Big House, but all the myths upon which Don Hermenegildo attempts to construct his foundational literary corpus, the basis of the desired nation. If the dichotomy of genres (linguistic registers) strengthens the already established oppositions of gender and race (white/heterosexual/wealthy/male versus white and mulatta/heterosexual/ cross-class/female) and Gloria embodies the persistent binaries that structure Ferré's universe (saint and whore, nurse and arsonist), by avoiding closure, *Maldito amor* skillfully disallows most reductive readings.

In her translation of *Maldito amor,* however, the writer makes a number of choices that make this work one of transition from Ferré-as-feminist-nation-alist-writer to Ferré-as-Latina-commodity-producer. Whereas *Maldito amor* aims to shake the Island elites into recognition of their racist nationalist project, and warns of its dead impossibility, *Sweet Diamond Dust* transforms the tale into a non-confrontational history lesson for mainland Americans while seductively whispering into their ears that the Island's upper classes have a History and a Culture—with capital letters—just like they do.

Although Ferré has claimed that the text needed to be toned down so as not to offend Nuyoricans (a jarring proposition, since Puerto Ricans in the United States are quite aware of American racism), she instead reenacts the traditional elites' anxiety of always putting the best (white) cheek forward. In this way, the shame that informs Ferré's earlier work—*criollo* racism, class oppression, and gender subalterity—is rearticulated as the blushing shame of racialization when facing a "real" white (American) audience. This is an even more visible formula in the manufacturing of *The House on the Lagoon,* for in shame, as Tomkins suggests, "I wish to look and be looked at, but I also do not wish to."[45]

In extracting *Sweet Diamond Dust* from *Maldito amor,* Ferré uses two basic skills: addition and subtraction. Most of the additions to the new text, which is longer than the "original," include pseudo-folkloric references ("under Spanish rule every Guamaneño had . . . a polished stone idol"), cultural references familiar to American audiences ("Philadelphia Cream Cheese"), as well as enhanced details regarding historical events like the American invasion of Puerto Rico and the gothic "cruelty" (or "black legend") of Spanish rule disseminated in the United States through the late-nineteenth-century yellow press. The added passages have the effect of both providing "background" information and representing U.S.-Puerto Rican relationships harmoniously, for this is a *danza* of a very different kind.

Embodying the classic specter of the "traduttore, tradittore," Ferré hopes to diffuse the shame of colonial rule and the unruliness of the "native" subject by minimizing racial differences between Americans and Puerto Ricans, neutering sexual language, morphing pro-*independentista* characters into statehooders, and melting Americans away as nondescript "northerners." The most evident sign that there is, indeed, (an)other reader in mind occurs in the ideological orientation of Doña Laura, who in criticizing the Puerto Rican bourgeoisie is now *also* burdened with the need to redeem the Americans, "all young and handsome, engineers, architects, doctors, energetic entrepreneurs who believed they could transform the world and bring us the blessings of progress."[46]

English will not, then, be the only thing in common between *Sweet Diamond Dust* and *The House on the Lagoon,* and perhaps not even the most important. *The House on the Lagoon* cannibalizes the author's earlier texts in an effort to present a sort of summa of Ferré's work to a "fresh" (previously untargeted) audience. And I use the term "cannibalize" purposefully, as this rewriting constitutes a destructive act, a dismembering and withdrawal from an ideologically bound community, so that Ferré can serve herself and her Island to a bigger tribe of transnational consumers.

"Cannibalization" also remits the reader to the irony of *The House on the Lagoon*'s status as the most cohesive "Caliban" text of modern Island letters, the greatly delayed literary "talking back" in the language of the "new" (if century-old) colonizer. Ferré is fully aware of writing as "a cannibalistic activity, and speaking your neighbor's language is a way of becoming him."[47] Yet in addressing the colonial master, Ferré does not curse; she is not Caliban but Ariel, the self-appointed intellectual go-between, dictating history lessons in the service of Prospero-Capital, those "first-rate American publishers" open to disseminating "Latina" literature to the world.[48]

The House on the Lagoon tells the tale of Isabel Monfort's quest for individuality by writing a novel based on the history of her family. Her authoritarian husband, Quintín Mendizabal, infuriatingly corrects Monfort's version of family history until their marriage dissolves violently. Through this writing and rewriting of family history, Ferré attempts to reproduce the multi-voiced structure of *Maldito amor,* but ultimately *The House on the Lagoon* does little to challenge exclusionary metanarratives or give voice to a plurality of social subjects.

Whereas *Maldito amor* is narrated by five incommensurable storytellers, speaking from different perspectives along the axes of race, gender, and class, *The House on the Lagoon* reduces the social field to two voices: a white woman and a white man, supported by a "colored" chorus. In this allegory for Puerto Rican history in the life and times of a bourgeois family, Ferré breaks down some of her most complex and previously elaborated insights and plot lines, and brick by brick lays down an essentialist dichotomy between history (masculine/conservative) and literature (feminine/liberating).

In general, Ferré opts for both homogenization and eccentricity to render "minority" culture digestible and appetizing to a non–Puerto Rican audience. She stirs in age-old conventions present in both Spanish and Island literature, and pilfers from her own previous texts. Examples of these modes of address include tautological sentences ("one could see a tiger-eyed guaragao, the nearly extinct local eagle)"[49] and the recitation of historical information such as the granting of U.S. citizenship in 1917 or the events leading to the Ponce Massacre of 1948. *The House on the Lagoon* also draws on conventions of the picaresque (Buenaventura Mendizabal emerges as a picturesque smuggler), Latin American romance novels (Buenaventura is "six feet tall, tan-skinned and dark-haired, and had eyes so blue they made you want to sail out to sea every time you looked at them"),[50] and romanticism (nature is represented as exuberant and wild, filled with "exotic wildlife and strange botanical specimens").[51]

For her transcultural experiment, Ferré received a nomination for the National Book Award, despite its dismissal by Island critics. Lola Aponte Ramos ranked the writer's dexterity in the father tongue as "elementary school English" and as a "shaky attempt . . . by someone who writes in a tongue that is not yielding to her."[52] Critics degrade Ferré's English tongue in its desire to be readable without nationalist elite cultural competence as her greatest pitfall. Yet I would argue that the most problematic transmutation in terms of a critique of ethno-national subalterity occurs in the racial re-engendering of the narrative, not in the diluted *lengua.*

In contrast to *Maldito amor,* where racial purity is exposed as an *effect* of representation, in *The House on the Lagoon, criollo* whiteness is an uncontested identity that requires a fetishized blackness for ratification. This is evident when the housekeeper Petra decides to take one of her clan's babies (Carmelina Avilés) into the master's house. On one occasion, Quintín's sisters Patria and Libertad play with the baby until they become bored and decide to paint her white: "When Carmelina saw the little white ghost staring back at her in the mirror, she let out a terrified wail and Petra came running out from the kitchen."[53] But not only do white girls need black dolls to play with, in *The House on the Lagoon* white women writers also require black alter egos to help them convince American readers who would otherwise be suspicious of their alleged whiteness. Isabel in fact devotes considerable energy to assuring the reader that her husband's ancestors are (really) perfectly white Spaniards, just as hers are, even if she is olive-skinned: "When he fell in love with me, this wasn't a problem, since my lineage was clean."[54]

The House on the Lagoon is a differently "whitewashed" text from the writer's earlier works, even if whiteness is a central trope for both. Whereas in all of Ferré's work there is a tendency to exoticize, eroticize, or allegorize black and mulatto characters, the representation of a repressive whiteness was a textual strategy to underscore the shame of white female sexuality. Now it is a way to continuously assure the reader of the irrefutable whiteness of the female characters, whose anatomies are constituted by "cream-puff shoulders,"[55] "coconut-custard breasts,"[56] "a long swan's neck,"[57] and skin as "smooth as ivory,"[58] "tightly packed vanilla ice cream,"[59] "satin-white,"[60] and "milk-white."[61]

Ferré does not deny racial diversity on the Island; instead, in the image of the mythic American South, she presents two fairly impermeable Puerto

Ricos: one poor, black, and exotic; the other rich, white, and eccentric. This, in a move very different from her earlier work, represents the value of racial purity as a social fact, not a construct. By plotting Puerto Rican ethno-nationality through the subjectivity of *white* women and their fundamental and foundational conflict with Puerto Rican *white* men, Ferré cancels out asymmetrical power relations between Puerto Ricans and Americans and reinscribes the supreme value of whiteness over racialized subjects.[62]

Fittingly, the character Isabel understands her own pro-independence sympathies as a *trope* for her subordination as a *white upper-class* woman, not as a racialized or even colonized subject. When Quintín, for instance, asks Isabel to destroy her manuscript in exchange for a new will that will not disinherit Willie, his illegitimate mulatto son, Isabel claims, "My novel is about personal freedom, Quintín, not about political freedom. It's about my independence from you."[63] The book's concern with gender, rather than colonial, conflict is graphically depicted by the cover illustration: a papaya being sliced by a sharp knife. The steely knife (of the Puerto Rican patriarch?) slices through the sweet tropical fruit whose name is also a slang term for female genitals among neighboring islanders, Cubans.

But if gender is paramount in *The House on the Lagoon,* the generative symbolic power of mulattoness is still at work, though the trope undergoes an important transfiguration. In the texts aimed at Spanish-speaking readers, Ferré denotes the Island's transculturation through the trope of race—through the shame of "white" Puerto Rican ethno-nationality; in the works written for American comsumption, race is subsumed by "ethnicity," with white Puerto Ricans giving (good) face for all of us.

The "mulatta" trope for the racial synthesis of the Puerto Rican nation gives way to a "Latina," now the product of an ethnic "white" bilingual fusion between Island and mainland. As Doña Laura puts it in *Sweet Diamond Dust,* "In her [Gloria's] body, or if you prefer in her cunt, both races, both languages, English and Spanish grew into one soul, into one wordweed of 'love.'"[64] Ferré's current discourse on cultural "hybridity" is not foreign to her previous work, but it does entail an alter/native re-elaboration in which race becomes ethnicity, mulattos turn into light-skinned (white) Latinos, and fe-male defiance is deflected into flirtation.

By writing so, Ferré does not simply displace the mulatta heroine, whose skin once represented the racial mixture of Puerto Rican culture and whose reproductive capacity made her the brave new mother of a more inclusive nation. Rather, Ferré herself takes the mulatta's place. "Like other Latino au-thors," writes Ferré, "I hope to broaden and enlarge the conscience of our readers into something different, into a 'new' concept of what it means to be American—from the north and from the south."[65] In other words, Ferré is no longer interested in exposing white female sexuality at the service of Puerto Rican nationhood; now she is flashing the white female as Puerto Rican na-tionhood in the interest of an American trans-ethno-nation, sponsored by U.S. capital.[66]

Ferré's exhibitionism is not idiosyncratic; she lays out the crux of the mat-ter increasingly facing Puerto Rican cultural producers everywhere: being licked by the father tongue offers a queer pleasure of previously unimagined celebrity. As Ferré writes, once "the first line of defenses [is] overcome, we thrust even deeper and with more daring into the other's territory. The amorous wrestling of the tongues is a prelude to the vehement struggle in which our bodies will later be engaged."[67] Trading tongues is a form of tran-scultural foreplay. Reinventing herself not as a Puerto Rican but as a Latina—which implies a duality—Ferré transfigures the shame of "nationality" into that of femininity (as does Holly Woodlawn, chapter 4). She imagines herself as a new bridge between Island and mainland, male and female: "it is through us, after all, that the human race arrives on this earth from 'cosmic space'; [women] often have a greater ability to build bridges between cul-tures."[68] Ferré hence affirms an epistemology that represents women as the most viable transvestite subject, since "women are able to look at things not from an either/or perspective. But from an all-around stance."[69]

Celebrity and commodity status are not the only two reasons Ferré is will-ing to lose the national prestige of her feminine *lengua* to gain the transves-tite value of her ethnic tongue. More politically definitive than Isabel's exotic nationalist identification is the reason she gives for writing her own novel in English: to partake of "modernity," one of the few political projects that most Puerto Ricans have actively supported.

If the nationalist Isabel trying to found a female identity in writing can be read as the "old" Rosario, Quintín provides a glimpse of the "new" Ferré. Compare Ferré's conflation of language and modernity in a newspaper article, "As a Puerto Rican and an American, I believe that our future as a community is inseparable from our culture and language, but I'm also passionately committed to the modern world. That's why I'm going to support statehood in the next plebiscite"[70] with Quintín's argument that "English had made it possible for Puerto Ricans to be a part of the modern world, whereas Cuba, the Dominican Republic, and Haiti were still in the Middle Ages."[71] In fact, despite the gender and political squabbling, the unsympathetic Quintín and the heroine Isabel ultimately share one thing: their faith in English as a beacon of modernity.

Being modern has been a continuous concern for Ferré since her *Zona* days and her incursion into English could be seen as the logical conclusion of desiring to be a globally known writer. As Ferré is likely aware that Quintín can be dismissed as a racist conservative, she condenses the costs and consequences of turning your back on modernity through the story of Bernabé, the housekeeper Petra's grandfather.

Bernabé is a native of Angola, a Bantu speaker who is brought to work on a Guayama plantation in the late nineteenth century. Ferré emphasizes that the most difficult thing for Bernabé to accept was not hard labor but that "he was forbidden to speak Bantu,"[72] for one's "tongue was so deeply ingrained, more so than one's religion or tribal pride; it was like a root that went into one's body and no one knew exactly where it ended. It was attached to one's throat, to one's neck, to one's stomach, even to one's heart."[73] To liberate himself from this pain, Bernabé organizes a rebellion of *bozales* (not Spanish-speaking *criollos*) by communicating in Bantu with only African-born slaves, but a combination of bad luck and lack of support derails the effort.

As the rebellion's leader, Bernabé is singled out for special punishment in the public square, underscoring *la lengua*'s status as a national phallic signifier: his tongue is sliced off. Less than a story about the evils of slavery, however, this is a cautionary tale against using the mother tongue for frontal attack. Bernabé, in fact, literally lost his tongue because he was not of the modern world; he was motivated by the belief that the news of his freedom had not yet arrived: "Five years after his arrival there was a false rumor that Spain had granted freedom to the slaves in its colonies but that the news was being kept from distant towns like Guayama, which were cut off from the rest of the world."[74] Through English and in the name of modernity, Ferré recovers Bernabé's story, to caution the bilingual Puerto Rican reader that it is preferable to give up the national tongue (virility) than be chopped off from modernity, especially when the news we cannot hear in the mother tongue—that the value of Latinos has gone up in America—is good.

To write in English is, then, to promote the project of modernity: individual rights, equality, rule of law—and freedom to consume in a market economy. This appreciation is not peculiar to Ferré and is shared by most of Puerto Rico's middle and upper class, regardless of narrowly political identifications. If Ferré's textuality is a failed foundational romance on all national axes (whites do not mix with blacks, marriages between Americans and Puerto Ricans do not last, good matches end up in flames), the novel is also an unflattering portrait of the centuries-old contradictions of the Puerto Rican elites, "wishing for independence and at the same time dreaming about our island being part of the modern world."[75] Given the failure of the modernization project in Puerto Rico, "dreaming" is actually the precise term.

Ana Lydia Vega mocked Ferré's representation of Puerto Rican ethno-national identity as "a sort of monster with two heads and two souls" (una especie de monstruo de dos cabezas y dos almas). Yet Vega sees no irony in the fact that at least half of Puerto Rico's population supports a bicephalous political status—two flags, two anthems, two languages. It is even enshrined in the Commonwealth's constitution, which states that "We consider as determining factors in our life our citizenship of the United States . . . [and] the coexistence in Puerto Rico of the two great cultures of the American Hemisphere."[76] The "monster" of the Puerto Rican ethno-nation, however, cannot simply be criticized and cast out. For what national body is not monstrous?

I for one agree that Ferré's work *is* monstrous, to the extent that it is not "organic." Ferré's texts are often assembled from previously published material, objectified as a commodity and "frozen" by what she herself describes as the coldness of English. Yet this series of *injertos,* these monstrous texts, show a deceptively smooth face—the perfectly designed covers of the commercial publishing industry—with tucks under the skin to mask the many scars of plastic surgery. In rejecting the organic and the "natural," which in Puerto Rico is understood as the "national" and in the United States is understood as the racialized subject, Ferré, like Holly Woodlawn, is transfiguring her shameful location through the (modernly) imagined right of self-invention—even if only to show off its limits.

Speaking in Tongues: De-Insularizing Puerto Rican Literature

Despite a centuries-old literary tradition in Spanish, it is the "monstrous" writing in English, not only by Ferré but also by other Puerto Rican writers living in the United States, that has finally propelled Island literature out of its solitary confinement and bestowed value on ethno-national literary production as a cultural resource and as a commodity. Ferré confirms that it is often in the imperial center—due to subaltern struggle—that the margins will gain a modest degree of value.

The reason cited most often to explain this valorization phenomenon is that English is the world's lingua franca, the language of the globe's most "powerful" nation, and the preferred tongue of business and technology, including in Puerto Rico itself, as evidenced by the outcry of the business sector over the Official Spanish Law of 1991. In the words of an Island-based marketing firm president, the law needed to be overturned simply because "Culturally speaking we're Latin. But we get paid in English."[77] Discourse about English by a broad range of social groups, in fact, tends to represent this language as possessing the same properties as commodities themselves: abstract, unmarked, and universal.

Yet English is seen as a vehicle off the Island not only because it allows Puerto Rican writers to reach English-speaking readers, but because it helps reach the Spanish-speaking outside Puerto Rico as well. Despite the fact that there are more native Spanish than English-language speakers (346 and 330 million respectively) worldwide,[78] most prominent Puerto Rican writers are barely known outside the Island or academic settings. Different from other Spanish-language literary traditions such as the Mexican, Cuban, or Argentinean, a lack of publishing infrastructure and distribution, the narrowness of literary themes linked to the national "trauma," and contempt for Puerto Rico's "mongrel" political and cultural state of affairs have condemned most Puerto Rican writers to over one hundred years of literary solitude. As Ferré argues, "we have been inhabiting a cultural no-man's land."[79] In fact, it is this "shameful" reality—the pariah status of Puerto Rican culture in Latin America and Spain due to its perceived "hybridity" and its inaccessibility to monolingual readers in the United States—that Rosario Ferré aims to queerly refashion.

The English tongue offers a way in—and out—by facilitating distribution and tapping into metropolitan interest about Puerto Ricans. Regardless of American political ambivalence toward the Island's incorporation as a state of the Union, the fact that Puerto Rico is a territory of the United States and that so many *boricuas* live on the mainland makes the metropolis an important market for Puerto Rican literature. This discovery should not be surprising; most postcolonial and Caribbean literatures are predominantly consumed and legitimized in the current or former metropolis's capitals, as the careers of the Nobel Prize–winning Caribbean authors Derek Walcott and V. S. Naipaul, living in the United States and London respectively, attest. This colonial algebra is even noted by the Cuban writer Roberto Fernández Retamar in his book *Calibán,* when he writes that "We only read with true respect anticolonial authors who are *disseminated from the metropolis*" (my emphasis).[80]

If this metropolitan appeal underscores the colonial notion that English is "superior" to Spanish, Ferré's relative commercial success in *both* languages also implies that under the current conditions a bilingual Puerto Rican writer can not only multiply the spaces of subaltern agency beyond the stronghold of nationalist intellectuals, but can even call attention to *boricua* literature in Spanish—she can de-insularize.[81]

For the critic Juan Duchesne Winter, "An active Spanish-language bilingual population is much more capable of positioning Spanish favorably in multiple contexts. This state of affairs will continue under any political status."[82] Not coincidentally, Ferré has described her desire to write in English as a way to reach not only American readers, but also Spanish-speaking ones, particularly those residing in the old metropolis—and prestigious literary center—Spain.[83] English, long believed to be the vehicle for "assimilation" and loss of social prestige by Island intellectuals, is redefined as a way to accrue cultural capital, valorize Puerto Rican literary production (in any language), and significantly expand its readership.

Figures can come in handy here. Ferré's books in English—and their "translations" into Spanish (and I will return to this shortly)—have largely sold according to theory. An example of this is the fact that the translation of *Eccentric Neighborhoods* (Vecindarios eccéntricos) was the second biggest selling book in Puerto Rico in 1999.[84] According to Ferré, *The House on the Lagoon* sold eight thousand copies in the first few months on the shelves in the United States, and due to this interest, it also sold fifty thousand copies in its first Spanish run.[85] To place this in perspective, in the United States, a book needs to sell at least four times this number of copies to be considered a mainstream bestseller, yet in Puerto Rico a popular book is one that sells five hundred copies over a period of many years, not weeks.[86]

But bulk is only part of this story. In Ferré's defense of bilingualism as a resource, she has also challenged the elitist notion of the primacy of the "original" by arguing,

They [both editions] are both original because I don't identify with one over the other. With my two last books, for instance, the one written in English was released first for practical reasons since it could enter the international market. If it was published as a translation from or to English, then it would not receive the same kind of critical attention nor appear in the mass media.[87]

Ferré hence distances her production from any aspiration to "cultural authenticity"[88]—which has too often meant the products deemed so by the Island dominant intellectual sectors—and sides with the popular propensity to enjoy the mass-produced, artificial, and transculturated, even if her textuality denies these same subjects. In this transaction, literature "originally" written in Spanish stands to lose its (high) status (if low market value).

To dismiss Ferré's literature in English by claiming that it is of poor quality—which always comes too close to poor taste—misses the significance of the work as a minor, even microbial, literature with the potential to influence and reach a broad readership. In fact, for critics like Deleuze and Guattari, lack of "talent" is characteristic of minor literature: "Indeed, scarcity of talent is in fact beneficial and allows the conception of something other than a literature of masters; what each author says individually already constitutes a common action, and what he or she says or does is necessarily political, even if others aren't in agreement."[89]

Ferré has then hit on a "winning" combination: while the "low" literary quality of the texts facilitates circulation outside nationalist circles and the academic cocoon, these books are also read by segments of the Puerto Rican literary elite who dislike the product but feel compelled to consume—buy into—it due to their particular professional "deformation" as intellectuals. As the anthropologist Mary Louise Pratt has written, "Autoethnographic texts are typically heterogeneous on the reception. . . . usually addressed both to metropolitan readers and to literate sectors of the speaker's own social group, and bound to be received very differently by each.[90] From the point of view of reception, Ferré can, then, have her cake and eat it too.

If this recipe may be distasteful in San Juan, where objects confirming the insider status of Puerto Ricanness are everywhere, in the United States, where Puerto Ricans still occupy a precarious position within public culture, Ferré's novels are ambivalent confirmations of worth. Commodification—decontextualized, abstract, and not relational—provides a surface upon which some Latinos can read themselves into the public sphere. In this sense, the commodification process is simultaneously exoticizing (for Euro-American readers), empowering (for educated U.S. Latinos), and dislocating (for the Island elites). The *Miami Herald* reviewer Fabiola Santiago asks rhetorically of *Flight of the Swan,* the author's most recent English novel, "Who doesn't search for the essence of what it means to be Puerto Rican in every piece by Rosario Ferré?"[91]

By Ferré's own admission, her English production is more belabored than her Spanish, yet it is significantly more accessible than her earlier erudite and baroque prose, broadening her readership not only due to the use of English but also because of her mode of textual production. The condescension that has plagued Ferré is linked to the assumption that the literary text is the work of the solitary artist, whose sole purpose is to express herself in a satisfying way for the elite consumer, without minding the marketplace or making a living from her work.

Taking her cues from pop culture and popular valorization, Ferré engineered her crossover as a popular singer or actor might, with the assistance of editors, publicists, and market research. In Anglicizing the Puerto Rican tongue, Ferré proposes a sticky seduction that entices readers with stereotypes worthy of a Univisión *telenovela* in exchange for sales that will signal to the publishing world and the culture industry that Puerto Rican writers are viable commodities in the marketplace and that *boricua* consumers are worthy of American political and cultural attention.

That is why Rosario Ferré is more easily dismissed than engaged with, even if all these choices place the queer potential of her novels under house arrest. She makes English tell stories in unnatural ways, crafting ridiculously lush universes set off against the "pasty normals"[92] of the American cultural context, much as the Hollywood B-movie diva María Montez did in her "sarong" sagas. As Frances Aparicio has argued in the context of Latino writers in the United States, Ferré's handling of literary English, however awkward, opens "new possibilities for metaphors, imagery, syntax, and rhythms that the Spanish subtexts provide literary English."[93] Ferré's prose further forces English to "bear the burden"[94] of dislocated colonial memories for the unsuspecting reader, and allows them to consider alternative—if compromised—scenarios of Puerto Rican–American valorization. Ferré proposes, with all the phallic power of English, a foundational marriage between transculture and commerce that represents the United States as both female (Nuyorican) and male (white). "The tongue," writes Ferré, "becomes a piece of our *corazón* that we introduce into the beloved's mouth. We exchange hearts, we taste him or her, and he or she tastes us."[95] In this sexualized exchange, which for Ferré is a transaction, the Puerto Rican female elite subject seeks valorization through trading *la lengua*—the most valuable bargaining chip of her privileged ethno-national location—for the English tongue, the vehicle to an enfranchised position in the United States, which as such is already more valuable. To questions about why she chose to write in English, Ferré responds, "I 'did it' in English and Spanish, and will go on doing so because I believe in freedom of speech."[96]

For all its seductive charms, Ferré's strategy has failed its avowed project in at least three ways. First, Ferré is routinely unable to defend bilingualism or narrate transcultural processes without first establishing racially engendered dichotomies that unabashedly accentuate imperial values over subaltern ones. In "Words from the Womb," for instance, Ferré suggests that "Spanish is for me 'la lengua escrita'; English is the 'written word.' . . . 'The written word' has Milton, Shakespeare and the King James version of the Bible standing behind it, swords drawn. Spanish, 'the written tongue,' doesn't have to be taken so seriously; there's more room for *bachata* and *relajo,* for word play."[97] Ferré's juxtaposition reveals a perplexing disregard for the work of writers like Salman Rushdie and Toni Morrison who have successfully—

and even brilliantly—made English express their own relationship to power and dominant culture, to say nothing of humor and verbal innovation.

Second, her strategy has not displaced shame as constitutive of Puerto Rican ethno-national identifications; she has only complicated it. Like the beauty queens, boxers, and pop stars out to promote Puerto Rican pride, Ferré has dedicated her entire literary corpus to lifting the country's collective self-esteem. "Ultimately, I have tried to do one fundamental thing: give Puerto Ricans back their self-respect."[98] And although Ferré locates the shame of Puerto Rican ethno-nationality not in the invasion but in the rise of the sugar plantation that dispossessed the people from the land and turned them into disposable labor ("People lost the land. . . . They had nothing"),[99] her revisions of Puerto Rican history and her English language production only offer devalued subjects the opportunity to represent themselves as commodities and measure themselves in relation to the capitalist marketplace that simultaneously exalts their power as consumers and denies their agency as laborers.

Lastly, whereas Ferré's novels are relatively valued commodities, they are still sold as Puerto Rican and/or Latino "ethno-national" products, fully bathed in subalterity and upholding ethnic differences as niche markets. Ironically, in most of Ferré's work from the early 1970s through the late 1980s, the writer explicitly links the *blanquita's* shame to her objectification as a commodity with a specific exchange value depending on her age, looks, skills, racial pedigree, and class position in the trading game of prestige and capital accumulation between upper-class white men. Ferré even declared that" to be a writer . . . [to] play with the imagination . . . is a subversive task, it is neither dignifying nor lucrative."[100] Today, however, only as a valorized commodity (a "thing") does Ferré foresee the possibility of becoming part of the modern world, giving new life to the famous dictum that Puerto Rico is the corpse of a society that has not yet been born. In *dos lenguas*.

8 Barbie's Hair

Selling Out Puerto Rican Identity in the Global Market

> [Toys] cannot bear witness to any autonomous separate existence, but rather are a silent signifying dialogue between them and their nation.
>
> —Walter Benjamin

> Era una chica plástica de esas que veo por ahí . . .
>
> —Rubén Blades, "Plástico"

> Vikki Carr, Katerina Valente. . . . They're not women. Plastic Puerto Ricans! —Rita Moreno as Googie Gómez in *The Ritz*

This essay is dedicated to my mother.

A year before the life-size Puerto Rican "Ken" doll—Ricky Martin—jolted a jaded Grammy Awards audience to their feet with Latin pop, Puerto Ricans from both the Island and the United States were tearing their hair out over the impact of another "plastic" globalized commodity bearing the sign of *boricuaness:* the Puerto Rican Barbie. Mattel seemed genuinely surprised at the unforeseen entanglement. After all, the company had already manufactured dozens of dolls representing countries from the world over without any complaints, including such close cousins in the ethnic and colonial divide as Hispanic Barbie, American Indian Barbie, and Hawaiian Barbie.[1] As with many other objects of *boricua* wrath or affection, however, this Puerto Rican doll is unique, if only because it comes with anticipated political baggage. No assembly required.

The notorious "PR" Barbie was introduced to eager Island consumers with some fanfare at a ceremony held in the capital city of San Juan in February 1997. The first doll, in what many saw as a biased political performance, was presented to Irma Margarita, the wife of Pedro Rosselló, the pro-statehood governor who at the time was investing considerable energy to obtain binding congressional legislation on the Island's political status for the second time.[2] The convergence of capital's gaze at Island consumers and a congressional wink toward a process of formal decolonization, which some feared favored statehood as the "final solution," prompted an anxious response, particularly on the mainland: "This toy can be seen as something of a pro-statehood move, and certainly a tricky issue when it comes to the question of our identity," stated Concordia University professor Víctor Rodríguez, with apparent seriousness.[3]

Rodríguez's take was, however, far from universal, and instead became part of one of the most intense debates on Puerto Ricans, ethnicity, and pop culture since *West Side Story* (chapter 3).[4] Many U.S.-based *boricuas*, who already live in a state of the Union but still consider themselves Puerto Ricans, feared Barbie as a Trojan horse of identity destruction; in contrast, Island nationalist intellectuals and consumers, who often denounce the eroding effects of Americanization on Puerto Rican culture, gleefully embraced the doll and their right to enjoy it. Evidently, both communities wrapped a different narrative around the plastic and made the Barbie a desirable playmate to engage in the increasingly high-stakes game called Puerto Rican "identity."

Barbie is one of the most globalized toys in history—"every second, somewhere in the world, two Barbies are sold"[5]—as well as the most transnational of American icons. Barbie play constitutes a privileged site to convey discontent and to negotiate conflicts in (and with) the United States, particularly around processes of racialization, ethnicity, and gender. Indeed, one of the aspects that made this contest exceptional is that it took place on the pages of mainstream American and Puerto Rican newspapers, rather than in the usually more rarefied halls of academia and organizational newsletters. Furthermore, the Barbie skirmish reiterated for all to see that cultural rearticulations of Puerto Rican national identifications are increasingly sponsored by American-made and/or -distributed commodities, even when they feature "fake" Puerto Ricans.

The few weeks that public intellectuals and academics debated the dangers and charms of the Puerto Rican Barbie can also be revisited as a virtual play-therapy session through which each community used Barbie to tease out its location regarding its subaltern status, both avowed (by most U.S. Puerto Ricans) and disavowed (by most Islanders), on the uneven playing fields of (national) cultures, albeit with different resources and from varying capital(s). Although both groups used the tools of globalization to tell their story, Islanders engaged in a game of make-believe under the slogan of "we are Barbie," while U.S. Puerto Ricans focused on the violence and pain of asymmetrical intercultural exchange. AmeRícans positioned themselves as "masters" of another game—the political domain—and pointed out that Barbie was an inappropriate plaything for Puerto Ricans. Angelo Falcón, director of the New York–based Puerto Rican Policy Institute, defended this oppositional stance in urgent terms: "Over here, there's a real question of how we're presented because the negative stereotypes hit us hard."[6]

That one of the most public disputes among Puerto Ricans in recent years took place over a toy rather than more stately matters stresses that "play" allowed specific subjects and groups to "model and experiment with personhood, [and] different contexts in which we may be selves"[7] without the risk associated with binding political action—precisely what Governor Rosselló was after in seeking a congressionally sanctioned plebiscite to determine Puerto Rico's ultimate status. Play became politics as a way to negotiate inclusion—and/or autonomy—within several national imaginaries, not coincidentally through a feminized object that all aimed to control, but whose ultimate meaning no one could quite pin down.

The striking divergence between pro- and anti-Barbie camps quickly became evident in the field of vision itself, as highly educated and hence arguably good observers could not agree on what the doll actually looked like. The writer Aurora Levins Morales, who is of Puerto Rican and Jewish descent, was raised in Puerto Rico's countryside and New York City, and currently resides in California, claimed that the Puerto Rican Barbie was "an Anglicized image of what we're supposed to be like."[8] On the other side of the Dream

House, though, light-skinned, Island-based, and pro–associated republic advocate Juan Manuel García Passalacqua saw quite the opposite, a doll that resembles who "we are" as Puerto Ricans: "mulatto complexion . . . almond eyes . . . thick nose . . . plump lips . . . raven hair."[9] As in most lengthy conversations about Barbie, through which "one usually learns more about the speaker than about the doll,"[10] a distinct pattern emerged from the fray. Those who identified as Island Puerto Ricans saw the doll as a *wavy-haired mulatta*. The majority of U.S. Puerto Ricans disagreed: the doll was *straight-haired* and *white*.

The most documented exception to the U.S. trend—Puerto Ricans in Florida—poignantly establishes, however, that less than a dichotomy between Puerto Rico and the United States, at issue is the real and perceived power of different Puerto Rican communities to invent, control, and deploy their cultural specificity in hostile or auspicious contexts. Many Puerto Ricans in Florida, who in the last decade have migrated directly from the Island and/or come from upwardly mobile backgrounds, tend to view themselves as either part of a Hispanic cultural majority in Miami or the dominant Hispanic group in Orlando, and are less likely to mobilize against disenfranchisement if couched in racialized terms. Although inter-Latino conflicts exist—particularly with the more influential Cuban Americans—Florida Ricans live in environments where bilingualism is an appreciable commodity and where they can enjoy a significant presence in local politics and the media. In fact, Florida is currently the home of many prominent and well-off Puerto Ricans, including the singers Ricky Martin and Chayanne, the television personality Maria Celeste Arrarás, the *merenguera* Olga Tañón, former Miami mayor Maurice Ferré, the newspaper publisher Alberto Ibargüen, and even the astrologer Walter Mercado.

Feeling excluded from the imaginary created by the Puerto Rican Barbie, U.S. Puerto Ricans outside Florida (and to some extent Washington, D.C.) refused to play with it in the way that it was intended and proceeded to "remove the sting," to quote Walter Benjamin,[11] by validating their own brand of (neo) Puerto Rican experience, using the weapons stored up by decades of civil rights struggle in the United States. That so many men felt compelled to play with the Barbie as a way to publicly express themselves politically also recalls what the cultural critic José Quiroga has argued in relation to the increasing popularity of gay dolls.[12] As in the situation of gay men who long to caress their own brand of queer plastic, for some Puerto Ricans who faced Barbie glaring from its box at Toys R' Us, "childhood is not necessarily something that is looked back on with affection. They remind the subject of all those dolls that were never given and never received, all those prohibitions."[13] The irony of this strategy, however, is not only that they were aiming all their guns at only one of the "enemies"—Mattel—but also that the U.S.-based intelligentsia hurled at Puerto Rican Barbie the one charge that Islanders had traditionally—and painfully—thrown at them: inauthenticity. As a *Miami Herald* journalist put it, "Le imputan [a Barbie] que su 'puertorriqueñidad' no es genuina" (They claim that Barbie's Puerto Ricanness is not "genuine").[14] And this had hairy consequences.

Raising Hair: Barbie's Locks and *Boricua* Identifications

The cultural knowledge that Barbies are "essentially" white, despite their outward appearance, constitutes the first clue to the seemingly untenable color blindness. As Erica Rand has observed, "Although some 'ethnic' dolls now get the name Barbie, a 'nonethnic' Barbie still occupies the center stage."[15] Most consumers seem to be able to accept an ethnic Barbie doll as both culturally specific and "white" at heart, since the ur-Barbie is unarguably light-skinned, blond, and blue-eyed.

The lingering impression that the Puerto Rican Barbie was essentially white and that its "mulattoness" was a deceiving masquerade was reinforced by the box's ethnic "origin" story for Puerto Ricans: "My country was discovered in 1493 by Christopher Columbus who claimed it for Spain." In mentioning only that the Island was discovered by Columbus, Mattel and its *boricua* allies connote that all Puerto Ricans are fundamentally Europeans and push the influence of Natives and Africans to the back of the bus.

210

If Puerto Ricans in the United States have historically visualized themselves as "of color" in the struggle for enfranchisement, then the Barbie could
be authentic only if it were "brown." Due to the preeminence of racialization
processes in the reproduction, regulation, and management of U.S. minorities, and the shame associated with these identifications, Puerto Rican struggles on the mainland over representation historically tend to demand "realistic" depictions (epidermal and demographic) as a measure of democratic inclusion. Significantly, Puerto Rican Barbie's perceived skin color was not the
doll's most controversial physical aspect for *boricuas* in the United States, particularly women. While in Puerto Rico and Florida the doll's "racial" makeup
was deemed acceptable, representative, and even beautiful, much of the U.S.
discussion focused on a specific Barbie feature: its hair, or more specifically,
the doll's hair *texture,* not color (black) or length (long).

Lourdes Pérez, a Puerto Rican Chicago-based, San Juan–raised interior decorator, was horrified at what she saw: "I don't care that she's white. Puerto Ricans come in all colors. . . . But when I saw that hair, I thought 'Dios mío'
('my God'), we just passed on a terrible legacy to the next generation."[16] Despite exasperated responses from some Puerto Rico–based (white) men
("[t]his woman is saying that the prevalent lack of respect, the lawlessness,
drugs, driving conditions, domestic and child abuse aren't as terrible a legacy
as a straight-haired Barbie")[17] the charges stuck. The journalist Louis Aguilar,
who wrote several stories on the topic as a sort of expert witness, confirmed
that Lourdes's response was not isolated: "For some Puerto Rican women
who have spent countless hours ironing the curl out of their hair before
going to the office or school, it's Barbie's hair that makes them cringe."[18]

Playing with the doll's hair is reportedly the most popular activity that
children engage in with Barbie, and the grown-up argument over the doll's
locks raged on for weeks in print and on the Internet. Hair became, as the anthropologist Patrick Olivelle has theorized, a "condensed symbol": "so powerful that it encapsulates all the diverse aspects of the symbolized, which
under normal circumstances would require separate symbolic expressions."[19]
That the dead weight of Puerto Rican identity fell on Barbie's weave, however,

should not be surprising on at least three counts. The ways hair is coiffured are universally used to signify cultural identity, social status, age, and gender. Across many cultures and historical periods, hair is also linked to the power of women to destroy, kill, and seduce, hence its care and representation are not trivial matters. Most important in this case, the Barbie's Puerto Rican roots could only really show up in its intractable hair.

In Puerto Rico, unlike the United States, a person's "race" is not solely dictated by a single African ancestor. "Color and features," writes the appropriately surnamed Tomás Blanco, "count more than blood."[20] Whereas one drop of "black" blood makes you African American in the United States, one of "white" can have the reverse effect on the Island, where a person does not need to claim exclusively European lineage to access the benefits of whiteness.

A clear example of how racism, however, informs self-identification within parameters that are different from American ones can be observed from the outcome of the 2000 census: a whopping 80.5 percent of Puerto Ricans considered themselves white, while only 8 percent identified as black.[21] The greater value attributed to white blood in the Puerto Rican scheme allows for a larger number of "mixed-race" people to qualify as *blancos,* yet this does not diminish the fact that Puerto Ricans of African descent are socially encouraged to seek upward mobility by flushing out the shaming "black" blood in each subsequent generation, as the infamous—yet largely accepted—slogan "mejorar la raza" (improve the race) implies. Given the possibility of *becoming* white—which is denied in the United States—"racial" identification (and attribution) in Puerto Rico is partly determined by a combination of phenotypical factors, including thickness of lips, skin tone, broadness of nose, eye color, cheekbones, and—most important—hair texture, which is physically coterminous with the skin and hence often symbolizes the entire body's "race."

The lavish attention given to "black hair" in Puerto Rican racializing discourse—it has considerably more (mostly demeaning) names than any other corporeal matter—prompted the anthropologist Sidney Mintz to claim that

"Puerto Rican cultural standards for racial identity appear to place the most weight on hair type, less on skin color."[22] Yet it is not so much that hair is more important than color, but that once hair is called upon to stand up for (the) race, it is not necessary to also mention the skin's hue. The mulatta poet Julia de Burgos, for example, identifies hair first in defining blackness in her well-known poem "Ay ay ay de la grifa negra" (Ay, ay, ay of the kinky-haired black woman) (not the *negra grifa*),[23] while in Francisco Arriví's play *Sirena,* the mulatta character Cambucha describes herself as "Pasúa, hocicúa y bembúa" (kinky-haired, snout-nosed, and thick-lipped), not dark-skinned.[24] Luis Palés Matos's foundational opera magna celebrating Caribbean syncretism and black (mythic) sensuality could then only be aptly titled *Tuntún de pasa y grifería—tuntún* of kinky and mulatto hair.[25]

Despite the deceiving laxness (from a U.S. standpoint) in determining race among Puerto Ricans, the emphasis on hair remits to biologically based understandings of difference that are shared with Americans. The anthropologist Franz Boas, who once testified in a 1914 case in which a white man sued for divorce on the grounds that his wife was not really white, argues for both sides when he claims that "You can tell by a microscopic examination of a cross section of hair to what race that person belongs."[26] In fact, because it can be altered or hidden, hair is the object of much scrutiny in liminal social situations involving *boricuas,* particularly if background information is not self-evident or forthcoming. As the social commentator Renzo Sereno bluntly phrased it, "Hair texture—whether it's good or bad—can decide an interracial marriage."[27]

The researcher Isabelo Zenón Cruz confirms the crucial role of hair when in his fundamental book *Narciso descubre su trasero,* he recalls a "test" through which "whites" can detect whether someone is a *grifo* (racially mixed) or simply an "olive-skinned" white, by placing him in front of a fan to see if the hair follows the wind: "If the hair stays put, he will stay outside the privileged group."[28] The sociologist Eduardo Seda Bonilla also found that in a field study in which he used photographs featuring people with hats, the fact that the subjects could not see hair "disturbed the interviewees, as 'type' of hair represents a relevant indicator to classify [race]."[29] Hair is, undoubtedly, the thin wavy line that separates the "authentic" whites from the deceptive upwardly mobile mulattos.

Suitably, although U.S. Puerto Ricans repudiated Barbie's straight hair, these discriminating—and discriminated against—consumers were not demanding that the doll have "bad" hair, as if a "black" *boricua* could not be representative of all Puerto Ricans. Ironically, an Afro-Boricua Barbie, particularly one who wears contemporary clothes, could not have looked much different from Black (African American) Barbie, thus undermining the notion of essential differences between both groups, and any modest racial capital that light-skinned Puerto Ricans may wish to claim in the colonial metropolis.

Due to the many cultural convergences between Puerto Ricans and African Americans in cities such as New York, a dark-skinned Puerto Rican Barbie could have ended up legitimizing the poet Willie Perdomo's motto that an Afro-Rican is just a black man—or woman—with an accent.[30] As a skeptical Víctor Rodríguez affirmed, "to introduce a doll . . . that looks like it has no *trace* of African ancestry, to a group of young Puerto Rican females who are at a crucial age in the formation of their identity, this becomes a very serious issue" (my emphasis).[31] Hence, what U.S. critics were after was the "correct" ethnic representational formula that could prevent Puerto Ricans from being confused with *either* African Americans or Anglos, safeguarding culture as the speaking subject of *boricua* politics. In this, they converged—perhaps inadvertently—with the Island elites, who would likely agree that it's tough to play at being *boricua* with the "wrong" kind of hair.

Considering that Puerto Rican ethnic identity in the United States has often been produced within discourses of racialization, the mainland's response to the Barbie's hair evokes a social distress over losing control of an important—and already invested in—identity marker. The fears of cultural consumption and political dissolution triggered by Puerto Rico becoming the fifty-first state of the Union—and Puerto Ricans morphing into "Americans"—were hence curled around tropes of de-ethnification such as "straight hair." The organizing assumption was that the Barbie's hair could only have been straight if it had been "straightened," a shameful act of self-hatred or conformity that would also be judged by American whites derisively. Critics highlighted wavy hair to protect the specificity of the group against changes already taking place in the United States, such as language dominance (to English), territorial residence, intermarriage, and hyphenated children. Ultimately, pulling the Barbie's hair back was a way to manage anxieties about the further transculturation of future Puerto Rican generations, for as Walter Benjamin has written, "toys are a site of conflict, less of the child with the adult than of the adult with the child."[32]

The fears of giving up your hair (to Mattel) also recall the importance that many cultures assign to the custody of hair. In Africa, for instance, only trusted friends and relatives may touch or have access to your hair, since "in the hands of the enemy, it could become an ingredient in the production of a dangerous charm or 'medicine' that would injure the owner."[33] The relationship between hair and potential harm is not confined to actual people's hair, but also to hair found in sculptures, which the Barbie arguably is. Puerto Rican popular sayings further stress the importance of keeping hair in its proper place—*cuídate los pelos*—and of getting rid of it if you need to defend yourself: *sin pelos en la lengua*. To allow the Puerto Rican Barbie to have the wrong hair and to put it into the wrong hands can be quite dangerous to a group: it signifies social submission, can bring about shame, and even lead to (cultural) death—the "terrible legacy" alluded to by the Chicago decorator. But as some observers noticed (though they preferred to stay at least a hair away), one community's bristly nightmare was another's synthetic fantasy.

Playing with Your Self: Why So Many Islanders Loved Barbie

Barbie was a reliable—if frustrating—toy claimed by U.S. *boricuas* to imagine Puerto Ricans as a distinct ethnic group, to make demands on American public culture as a politically disenfranchised minority, and to seek dignified valorization in the marketplace. The doll's wild success with Islanders (by

215

December 31, 1997, one Carolina store alone had sold over five thousand dolls)[34] asserts, however, that the Puerto Rican Barbie was the *perfect* doll for many to play with their national "selves" in Puerto Rico. In playing with Barbie, these consumers not only "enjoyed" themselves, but also enacted the material and symbolic conditions that make their (constrained) identity play intelligible.

Tellingly, although Island intellectuals and institutions often make use of cultural differences as part of a struggle to expand or protect local political control within a disavowed colonial context, the Puerto Rican Barbie was not perceived as threatening to the main pillars of national identity as defined by the official cultural institutions and the most conservatively nationalist intellectual sectors: Spanish language (Barbie does not speak), symbols such as *el jíbaro* (which it is), and sports sovereignty (which does not apply). While it is a rampantly "commercial" product made by an American multinational (as opposed to the "purely" folkloric art dear to the Island nationalist intelligentsia), the Puerto Rican Barbie is more consistent with dominant discourses of *puertorriqueñidad* on the Island than many "real" Puerto Rican–produced art forms that have undergone different degrees of commodification, such as *salsa* or hip hop. In this sense, the Puerto Rican Barbie is the consummate "nationalist" elite product bred by the contradictions of the commonwealth: a modern packaging (plastic) of a premodern essence (rural Puerto Rico) for postmodern nationalists (colonial survivors).

The emphasis on Barbie's hair and the attack on Mattel as a symbol of corporate whiteness in the United States did facilitate a dialogue on racialization processes, but overlooked Puerto Rican agency in the doll's production as a symbolic good (or evil). As has been noted with a mixture of scorn and disbelief, the Institute of Puerto Rican Culture, the official voice of government-sanctioned *boricuaness* created by the commonwealth, was the corporation's chief advisor in designing the doll's accessories and writing the box's copy (which, ironically, contains several mistakes and typos).

Most notably, these critics did not engage with the significant fact that the doll was fashioned as a *jíbara*—the now mythical nineteenth-century, mountain-dwelling, white Spanish creolized peasant—with all that this implies within elite narratives of Puerto Ricanness. U.S. critics did not address how Island-bred *jibarismo* excludes them as much as—and perhaps more than— Mattel with its dreadlocked Hispanic Barbie and the broad-nosed Quinceañera Teresa. This critical slip can be partly attributed to the acceptance and reworkings of the *jíbaro* myth in the United States, including Rafael Hernández's New York–born ode to the *jíbaro*, "Lamento Borincano," and the popularity of this icon to rally the virtual tribe in multiple contexts, including Internet sites such as jíbaro.com ("el lugar Boricua más jíbaro del Interné"). In hindsight, Mattel's contribution was relatively minimal, albeit practically indestructible: it commercialized the already officialized *jíbaro* myth by casting it in plastic and giving it worldwide commodity status.

The pro-statehood administration also seemed to have supported the doll, underlining the success of *jibarista* (national) discourse among all ideological sectors. Although the local state apparatus continues to lose strength as the chief regulator of local social, economic, and political conflicts, the hold of *jibarismo* is, in fact, so strong that statehooders refer to their brand of federalism as *estadidad jíbara,* a specifically Puerto Rican "way" of becoming a state of the Union, and the supporters of commonwealth still use a silhouetted *jíbaro* as a beacon, even when their party's economic policies were largely responsible for the obliteration of the peasants' way of life. The obviousness of why Barbie had to be a *jíbara*—and not a "Return Nuyorican Barbie" or a "Sugarcane Babe Barbie"—begins to untangle the question of who belongs— and who calls the shots—in *jíbaro* country.

From the nineteenth century, the mostly male, white, affluent intellectual elites have been elaborating the myth of the *jíbaro* as the repository of the Puerto Rican people's true (white) soul. "The rich spiritual content," writes Luis Zayas, "is the Hispanic soul's legacy."[35] As Francisco Scarano argues, early-nineteenth-century identification with the *jíbaros* by the "liberal" elites can be reasonably interpreted as a progressive gesture to include the peasants in (but exclude slaves of African descent from) a proto-national project in the face of a retrograde colonial regime.[36] After the Spanish-American War, however, this investment became increasingly problematic as a sign of democratic inclusion. Despite the fact that the term *jíbaro* was generally used to refer to a (mixed) racial category in several regions of the Americas (a usage not unknown in Puerto Rico), this knowledge was conveniently disregarded as living peasants became (white) paper icons in the hands of nationalist writers.

The *jíbaro* was the symbol of choice for a wide range of reasons, including the peasants' alleged "whiteness" as the presumed (pure) descendants of the Spanish. The insistence on the peasants' uncorrupted Europeanness suggests that the *jíbaro* became the "great white hope" for the elites in defending a separate and unique national identity from the United States.[37] The more Puerto Ricans resembled Americans (in this *boricuas* share some terrain with Canadians), the more imperative it was for cultural discourse to create and police distance. We may often "look" American, but Puerto Ricanness comes from the soul, not the body; it can only be heartfelt. Or collected.

Investing in the *jíbaros'* whiteness served (and continues to serve) at least two political impulses. On the one hand, it affirms that Puerto Ricans share a (European) culture that is as civilized as that of the new colonial ruler, who branded us racially inferior. On the other, it allowed the elites to ward off uncomfortable associations with the emerging working class, whose differently racialized members, despite increased capitalist exploitation, were savoring previously unavailable political rights and challenging their subordinate class status at the moment in which Pedreira wrote.[38]

Conveniently, twentieth-century elites called upon the *jíbaros'* specter to serve their spiritual and political needs at a time when peasants themselves were undergoing a rapid process of proletarianization. The vanishing *jíbaro* became the emblem of another time, in which the currently displaced elites faced less subaltern competition for control over bodies and resources. The *jíbaros'* intimate relationship to the land is also crucial to this formulation, as not only did the soil literally change hands during this period (from Spanish and *criollo hacendados* to American corporations), but also Puerto Rico was reduced to being a property of the United States: it legally belongs to, but is not part of, the metropolis. By exalting the *jíbaro*, the elites aimed to symboli-cally repossess the land and regain its hegemony. The main irony of this identification, particularly for future generations, is that the elites fashioned national identity as a simulacrum—technically dead but symbolically alive, like a doll.

Although never a static discourse, *jibarismo* has been primarily concerned with the *jíbaro*, not the *jíbara*. In the words of Arlene Dávila, "An African con-tribution to the *jíbaro* is never acknowledged or emphasized, as neither is a female gender identity."[39] The (male) engendering of the national myth is, of course, not surprising, particularly when control over the *jíbaras* was taken for granted by men of all classes and the female proletarian represented dou-bly transgressive possibilities. As was not lost on most observers, women took advantage of American-sponsored modernity in ways that challenged social and reproductive structures, including labor, politics, and the patriarchal family. After 1898 *jíbaras* joined the workforce and then the unions in sub-stantial numbers, sought divorces, used birth control, publicly challenged male authority, and gladly incorporated technology into their lives. If the *jíbaro* constituted a space/time of longing for the old labor regime, the *jíbara's* proper place could only be safely evoked as passively below the belt.

Expectedly, elite discourse about *jíbaras* tends to highlight their seduc-tiveness, even amid the squalor. According to the poet Virgilio Dávila, the *jíbara* is anemic and sad, "like a squalid flower of wasted spring" and her dress is "a rag that hardly covers a virginal body."[40] The sociologist Salvador Brau describes the peasant woman who inspired him to write one of the first soci-ological texts on the *jíbara* as "a poor woman, indolent and sensual."[41] The writer Abelardo Díaz Alfaro also contributes his pity when he says that *jíbaras* are "Women wasted by maternity and excessive labor."[42] Yet, in welding the Barbie and the mythical *jíbara*, the contemporary elites modernized and let go of the crudest discourses of female subordination. In doing so, the mainly male elite found global recognition through a feminine icon that, like them, lives in a sanitized world of glamour and autonomy (commonwealth) in which men ("Americans") are just one more accessory.

Given the meager, but fairly consistent, discourse on *jíbaras* and the hegemony of the male *jíbaro* myth, the Puerto Rican Barbie has rewritten parts of the *jibarista* script for generations to come, awarding it even more currency. If early *jibarista* discourse was concerned with the *jíbaro*'s grave sociological, political, and economic problems, the Puerto Rican Barbie is fantastically free from want and openly transnational. Furthermore, it is American-financed and Malaysian-made, and it's definitely not going back to picking coffee. The doll's main concern is for you to "like the special white dress I am wearing. It is very typical of a dress I might wear to a festival or party." The use of the *jíbara* as a spectacle, however, is not new. As Guerra has compellingly argued, the *jíbara*'s imagined "natural inclination toward promiscuity made her fair game for these intellectuals to put her body on display for their own amusement and to invade her gynecology for the sake of the public interest."[43] In fact, the back of the box is clear about the intent of urging the Barbie to put on a *jíbara* show: "Tourism is a very significant part of our economy. . . . Today, people from all over the world come to enjoy our beautiful country, delicious food and friendly people. I hope you can come and visit us soon."

The Puerto Rican Barbie's divorce from the realm of agricultural want is particularly signified by its accessories: a disproportionately large hairbrush, a pair of high heels, earrings, a ring, and, above all, its "magnificently simple but gorgeous local folkloric dress."[44] The dress worn by the Barbie was criticized by some Puerto Ricans as forcing women to be "stuck in the feminine stereotype of the nineteenth century,"[45] but no one questioned its contribution to whitening Barbie or its status as a tradition invented from above. A Mattel spokeswoman defended it by affirming that "Barbie's dress is a traditional costume not meant to offend, and not meant to depict the clothes of today's women."[46] Still, the doll's elaborate costume does not conform to any dress worn by a peasant in the visual record. In an essay criticizing a 1953 competition to reward the best entry depicting a Puerto Rican "regional dress," the writer Nilita Vientós Gastón categorically denied its existence and chastised those who seek this form of national validation by labeling it "a product of fantasy, an invention. . . . I assume that in time it will become a costume."[47] Indeed, the dress definitely makes the Barbie a plastic *jíbara*, in the slang implication of the term: superficial, fake, and materialistic.

Barbie's dress is also an important part of the elaboration of a post-mortem *jíbaro* myth as it incorporates a wide array of influences and patriarchal nationalist desires. For instance, the dress is low-cut (quite rare before the 1940s but emphasizing the *jíbara's* femininity) and has five pieces of *encaje,* a very expensive material that only wealthy women could purchase during the first part of the century. By using *encaje,* the dress is fit to signify the Barbie as a "country" girl, but imagines it with the same affluence of the *hacendada,* the landowner or his wife. The extensive use of the *encaje* also brings the Barbie closer to Spain, as folkloric Spanish costumes usually exhibit large quantities of this fabric, including in the Mattel versions of Spanish Barbie. Furthermore, the dress's finery and elaborateness connote access to the city, not the mythic isolation of the countryside. The general acceptance of the doll's dress spells yet another victory for the elites by avoiding questions about the "authenticity" of the *jíbaro* myth and affirming that "culture" is not a struggle over representation or participation, but a collection of essential accessories. Once more, corporate America and "national" Puerto Rican colonial institutions see eye to eye: It's the dress that makes the *jíbara.*

The fact that Puerto Rican Barbie is a "collectible" doll further reinforces its colonial cast as well as certain *jíbara* imagined characteristics. In Mattel's universe, to be a "collectible" is to live as a folkloric object with limited agency (i.e., accessories). The doll's transformation into an aesthetic commodity also takes *jibarista* discourse further than even Pedreira intended when he wrote, "Beyond his economic anguish, we will highlight his human worth, his beautiful representative quality."[48] Puerto Rican Barbie confirms the *jíbara* as the symbol of a Puerto Rican essence, not a historically specific subjectivity engendered by colonial relations and economic exploitation. Unlike other black and white Barbies, but similar to most other Latin American ones, the Puerto Rican Barbie does not achieve anything but being itself, eternally and tirelessly "national," hence stressing what many consider the greatest *boricua* political victory against colonialism. In culminating the *jíbaro* myth as an aesthetic commodity, Mattel rejects the economy of lack associated with the *jíbaro,* and actualizes an orgy of plenty in which the consumer in need of national affirmation is "free" to buy himself or herself some pleasure—and own it (if not own up to it).

This pleasure is further enhanced by the fact that the doll is perceived as a light-skinned mulatta, a departure from most historical accounts of the *jíbara,* who is often represented as sickly pale. Puerto Rican Barbie is, however, the kind of mulatta "que no mueve el pie" (that doesn't tap its foot) when it hears the drum, but instead dances the *seis chorreao* wearing a bleached-white virginal dress. The passion for the whitewashed mulatta among the middle-class elites, however, should not be confused with the questioning of racism as an ideology of exclusion. As Tomás Blanco remarks without a trace of irony, the mulatta "seems to have aesthetic value or erotic interest for Puerto Rican (white) men."[49] Not coincidentally, the embracing of a mulatto aesthetics comes at a time when the upper class—more "American" and "modern" than ever—wish to distinguish themselves from (other) Americans by establishing that they are not racists. In fact, the educated elites, as Seda Bonilla has written, tend to produce the most inclusive democratic public discourse, while continuing to exhibit segregationist behavior in their familial lives, with the possible exception of (out-of-wedlock) sexuality.[50]

Simultaneously, the Puerto Rican Barbie established several lines of continuity with certain *jíbaro* texts, as the doll is sexually desirable and eager to do the work of the nation.[51] The fact that the Barbie is gendered feminine also wards off associations with threatening mulatto sexuality (urban, male, and possibly homosexual). While never vulnerable within Mattel's gripping narrative, the Puerto Rican Barbie can be imagined as the seductive body—*sabrosamente femenina*-dreamed most forcefully by the twentieth-century poet Lloréns Torres. The Barbie fuses the passive (yet sensual) *jíbara* with the social climbing hot mulatta, transforming it into the ultimate user-friendly object of national excitement and interracial desires, queerly recalling the doll's historical predecessor, the post–World War II German novelty toy for men, Lilli.[52] In the elite's collaboration with Mattel, you could say that they had their way with the Barbie thrice: as a *gringa,* as a *jíbara,* and as a mulatta. Not surprisingly, many indignities projected onto the *jíbara* have been forced upon Barbie dolls by their (ab)users with a vengeance. Both bodies have been known to suffer the erotic urges (hard-ons, breast fondling), paranoia, racist rage, misogyny, amputated limbs, and decapitations by their owners—with a pasted-on smile. Ironically, if as Lillian Guerra suggests, the elites have historically perceived the *jíbaros'* alleged passivity as a "deep reservoir of nationalism,"[53] the Puerto Rican Barbie is the most anticolonial object ever invented.

Furthermore, whereas Barbie's corporate "parents" do not encourage consumers to imagine it as a mother, some nationalist intellectuals were able to transfigure the doll into a reproductive vessel—of *jibarismo.* The political analyst Juan Manuel García Passalacqua, in fact, specifically praised the doll because it would help Puerto Ricans "explain ourselves, as we are, to all Americans."[54] In becoming a *jíbara* commodity, the Puerto Rican Barbie is unable to physically give birth to the *jíbarito* of tomorrow, but does reproduce its myth to new generations. Characteristically for the Island's elites, although the Puerto Rican Barbie is doing their symbolic work, it is mostly benefiting American capital and the colonial status quo. Although the persistence of the "jíbaro" is often understood as the survival of an oppressed culture, in the context of contemporary Puerto Rico, its primacy over other possibilities most accurately registers actors of the domestic elite's still substantial investment in policing the boundaries of "national" culture.

Traído por los pelos: Selling Out Puerto Ricanness

A Puerto Rican Barbie dressed as a *jíbara,* however, would not have been enough to draw thousands of *adults* to Island stores. To sell Puerto Ricanness out, the *jíbara* had to stand in the "right" political pose; it needed to affirm hegemonic ideas about Puerto Rico's (central) place in the world, not only local racial hierarchies. Luckily, Mattel was again able to capitalize on the winning formula. By including the Puerto Rican Barbie as part of the "Dolls of the World" series, Mattel recognized Islanders' need to be appreciated as a distinct Spanish (only) speaking, white, Latin American nation, with merely bureaucratic ties to the United States, and without a sizable diaspora, political colonial status, or financial interdependence. Ironically, the series' main objective is to introduce "children in the United States to other cultures,"[55] as if there were not already three million Puerto Ricans in the United States and the Puerto Rican doll was not based on the "Hispanic" one. In this, the elite's culturalist strategy of difference coalesced with Mattel's marketing department to shamefully deny U.S. Puerto Ricans their market worth. But as we know, the Barbie aims to please—for a profit.

Mattel has always been aware of its Latin market, not only because one of its plants is located in Mexico, but also because it was born in a state that is home to millions of Latinos: California. As early as 1968, the company came out with "Spanish Talker," a Barbie with a Mexican accent. The first "Hispanic Barbie," launched in 1980, was dressed in a pseudo-Spanish costume called "fiesta-style."[56] Ironically, the Barbies' colorful wardrobe and risqué pose have been partially attributed to the dress codes of working-class Hispanics: "Whatever the fashion, the California version will be more extreme . . . much more colorful. . . . Clothes tend to fit more tightly than is considered proper elsewhere, and to expose more flesh."[57] No wonder Ken Handler, the son of two of Barbie's "inventors" and the reason the doll's male companion's name is Ken, calls Barbie a "bimba," not a bimbo.[58]

In 1996, a year before the introduction of the Puerto Rican Barbie, Latin America had been experiencing a higher rate of growth (47 percent) than the United States (32 percent), consolidating itself as the doll's third largest market.[59] Puerto Rico's four million consumers do not constitute in themselves a substantial market; there are almost as many *boricuas* in the United States. Islanders, however, have the highest per capita number of Barbies in Latin America, the context in which Mattel and most of the Island's elites locate Puerto Rico. A whopping 72 percent of Puerto Rican children own at least one Barbie, as compared to the second highest, Chile, with 49 percent. Eight-year-old Amanda from Bayamón alone owns forty-three Barbies, but the Puerto Rican Barbie reigns "supreme in her collection."[60] The difference in Barbie penetration can be linked to closer economic and cultural ties to the United States, a higher per capita income than most Latin American nations (at twenty dollars, Barbie is considered an expensive children's toy), and higher consumption rates.

Since the changes Mattel makes to each doll are minimal—pure genius from a Warholian ethos—the company is able to change hair color, pigmentation, and costume and appeal to dozens of markets in their best (white) light, which tends to be appealing to the country's most affluent sectors. Puerto Rican Barbie may be a globalized product, but it is ably designed to cash in on the needs of many to deny the shame of their ethno-national location, affirm their national pride, and prominently take their place in the "family" of nations. In many parts of the world, and notoriously in Puerto Rico, advertising a product as if it was native or with native characteristics can spell impressive profits, even if changes to the product are nil.[61] A disgruntled Nuyorican consumer, Andrés Quiñones, criticized the doll precisely on those grounds: "what Mattel did was to make her nose bigger and darken her eyes. Now they want to sell us the same old doll as if it were 'Puerto Rican.'"[62]

Even though Andrés was not impressed, Mattel managed to do what Bacardí, Budweiser, and Winston have already achieved on the Island: sell Puerto Ricans an "American" product while affirming Puerto Rico's unassimilable difference and specificity (nationality) in sameness (capital). True to form, Mattel's boxed history makes it clear that the Island is separate and different from the United States, in every exoticizing way, including culinary traditions (*plátanos, arroz con gandules*) and wildlife (*coquí*). The doll was a triumph for Island elites: corporate America gave them what reality denies them—a purely plastic Puerto Rican identity—and they enjoyed it without financial or political risk. Unlike other, more impoverished markets, the Puerto Rican consumer is proud to verify his worth in the commodity form, even if he does not financially benefit. This is consistent with Anna Indych's observation that Puerto Ricans have a cultural tendency to "embrace the imported, the plastic, the mass-produced, and the industrial" in constructing identities still deemed "authentic."[63] Purchasing also highlights how hegemonic identity constructs—even if culled from elite culture-are today manufactured for mass consumption and largely understood as accessories: Island map T-shirt, Vieques souvenir, and CD car flag.

The tendency to construct identity as an accessory, however, points to the increasing complexity of the current cultural terrain for Puerto Ricans. The same year that the Puerto Rican Barbie was introduced to the world, a second *boricua* doll made an entrance fit for a queen. In *Latina* magazine's words, "Now there's more to complain about with the debut of a Puerto Rican doll named Carlos: If Barbie wants to date this plastic *papi*, she can forget about it. He's gay. Carlos is the boyfriend of Billy."[64] While *Latina*'s complaint suggests a lack of imagination, it also fails to take into account to what extent playing with Barbie, Ken, and G.I. Joe is always already a queer experience for most. Although this debate lasted less than the Barbie's and was not performed for the *New York Times*, Carlos's existence makes it difficult to see the Puerto Rican Barbie straight. As *Latina*'s campy prose summed it up, "the *fashionistas* outraged over Barbie's clichéd vestido *criollo* should find solace. At least he's not wearing a straw hat."[65]

Queerly, the same year that the Puerto Rican Barbie came out, it occurred to the Island-based drag performer Vanessa Fox to refashion the Puerto Rican Barbie's wardrobe to her own as a strategy to raise money for charity. After the introduction of Fox's personalized Puerto Rican Barbie, she was able to raise hundreds of dollars to purchase dolls for disadvantaged girls and boys: "In other words, with one Barbie we have made many children happy."[66] With Fox, the Puerto Rican Barbie brought about a miraculous state of affairs, akin to the biblical miracle of the loaves and fishes. Fox not only managed to make more children happy and created value for a doll that has not experienced any appreciation among Barbie collectors, but also transfigured her own queer shame by offering the community a gift. Mattel may have made the doll for corporate profit, but it has ultimately been *boricuas* who have infused it with alternative values and made it theirs.

Barbie's Aryan origins and "white" corporate parents, however, limit its capacity to articulate a decolonizing politics, even as it raises the "value" of the Puerto Rican consumer. Yet, when Mattel put Puerto Rican Barbie within our mature reach, it forced us to relive our childhoods as colonial survivors, racialized migrants, and/or queer kids, and enact our frustrations toward whoever made us feel subordinate, ugly, and vulnerable. As a middle-class child living in a San Juan suburb, I do not remember ever giving much thought to my Barbie, Ken, and G.I. Joe. I do vividly recall, however, the day when, looking for a gift, I stopped along the Barbie aisle in a Miami toy store, and could not believe my wondering eyes, hurt in so many battles for dignity. The big, corny white and pink letters spelling PUERTO RICAN BARBIE drew me in, for they seemed to confirm what as a child I always knew, but as a migrant adult, had been denied: Barbie has always been Puerto Rican. Even as I delighted in the recognition of this archaic and secret code, I was mostly savoring the bittersweet constraints of my own political agency.

9 Jennifer's Butt

Valorizing the Puerto Rican Racialized Female Body

> True wealth and abundance are not on the highest or on the medium
> level, but only in the lower stratum.
>
> —Mikhail Bakhtin, *Rabelais and His World*

I went to see the Hollywood-financed film *Selena* (1997) in a half-empty suburban theater with about a dozen other solemn, mostly Puerto Rican families dressed up in their Sunday best, parents scolding *los niños* in a low voice,
telling them to eat their popcorn, sit down, and shut up. The sight was unusual, even extraordinary, since one rarely sees Philadelphia-bred *boricuas*
outside a few segregated neighborhoods, much less in the bizarrely named
middle-class suburb of Andorra. Once the movie began, unsure about what
mystical forces had dragged me to that cushioned seat on a Sunday after-
noon, I began to wonder why *los otros puertorriqueños* had also trekked so far
from the streets of *el norte*, where people are more likely to follow La India,
Olga Tañón, and Thalía than Selena, and bootleg video copies of the film can
be easily obtained from your neighborhood corner store at a cost of only nine
dollars.

There is the possibility that we—like so many others—were swept away by
an intense necrophilia, momentarily followed by spasms of melancholia and
sadness for the loss of a young life, a frequent occurrence in inner-city
Latino-America. Selena's exceptionality, however, was that unlike most

Latino youths who get killed after a drug deal has gone sour or a bullet surprisingly arrives with their name on it, she has passed on to sainthood, not only for dying young, but for passing on the way to another, better place, the seamless plot known as the American Dream.

Yet even for those of us who no longer believed in a dream that slipped away faster than welfare reform was enacted, the movie spared us any psychic anxiety, hence assuring our enjoyment. On the one hand, the film affirms that with hard work, talent, and a strong family, "we" Latinos can make it too. On the other, the possible trepidation over not belonging to an ambitious close-knit clan, procreating ordinary kids, or lacking the strength to push ourselves harder is pacified by how Selena died: *los ricos también lloran.*

Twenty minutes into *Selena,* however, a queer sense of dread began to overtake me. Like Quintanilla's big bus, the mimetic pact that generally binds spectator and biopic inexplicably broke down. Regardless of how hard I tried, I did not see Selena. I either saw Jennifer López and Selena, phantasmagorically juxtaposed as if on a glass surface, or *simplemente* Jennifer. This mystifying state of mind seemed to have occurred not only to Selena's parents and producers while filming the reenactment of the Houston Astrodome concert, but to the slain singer's fans as well. "When I came into the stadium, the fans started screaming," recalls López. "They were saying 'Selena!' But they were saying 'Jennifer,' too."[1]

This Holy Ghost effect was not, of course, an accident. Mark Sánchez, makeup artist for both performers, takes the credit for altering López's features to match Selena's: "Jennifer has a wider, flatter nose than Selena, almost like a boxer's. I had to contour Jennifer's to make it look narrower and larger. . . . As the makeup progressed, I was taken aback, and had to stop what I was doing. It was almost as if I had Selena in my makeup chair again."[2] Despite Sánchez's efforts, however, "Jennifer" continued to ring louder in my ears than Selena. From the heavens above me, I heard voices ordering my removal to the lower depths of cultural criticism, away from the pie-in-the-sky myth of the American Dream, and into the flesh of unjustly denied discursive pleasures. Possessed, I began to write deliriously in the darkness.

Rear Endings: Jennifer Is the Medium

In contrast to most U.S.-born Puerto Rican actresses of the last five decades, Jennifer López has been able to play on the hyphen and come out *al otro lado*. Although she embodies ideal *boricua* beauty (which Rosie Pérez seemingly "failed" to do)—that is, neither too dark nor too light—the Puerto Rican label does not seem to stick to her in the mainstream media. A *People* magazine column, for instance, referred to her as "being of Puerto Rican . . . *descent*."[3] In a handful of other newspapers and magazine articles, she is simply a New York "native" and/or raised in the Bronx.

While the "Bronx" is a loud enough cue for those in the know, it certainly does not ring the same bell in Texas—or perhaps it does for some. Ironically, the only time during the *Selena* prerelease hype that López unequivocally became a *puertorriqueña* was when some Mexican Americans protested her being cast as a Chicana: "While many of her fans of Mexican descent anxiously awaited the opening of the movie, some are angry that a Puerto Rican was cast as Selena."[4] Constantly quizzed by the media on the disapproval that met her being cast for the part, López shot back that she was well suited to play Selena because they shared an ethnic identity beyond their "national" origins. "I don't think the actress who played her had to be Mexican-American because Selena was," López said. "Selena and I are both Latinas and both had the common experience of growing up Latina in this country. This was good enough."[5]

At this juncture, López's argument was fundamentally strategic. Given the current political economy of representation for Latinos in mass media, Puerto Ricans, with less institutional clout, general population, and numbers on Hollywood's home turf, identifying as a "Latina" expands *boricua* agency and accrues additional value. Even if Latinos arguably do not constitute a cultural formation that has erased or completely displaced ethno-nationalist investments, it is undeniable that while not "real," this construct matters.

Selena's career, for instance, is a good case study. In order to go beyond the *Tejano* niche market, the singer expanded her repertoire to include

Caribbean, South American, and pan–Latin American genres such as *boleros,* and later went on to record in English, incorporating New York Caribbean influences. In this marketing and audience-building trajectory, Selena went from being a *Tejana* (a territorialized "regional" identity) to being a Latina (a national "ethnic minority"); "Latino" here refers less to a cultural identity than to a specifically American national currency for economic and political deal making, a technology to demand and deliver emotions, votes, markets, and resources on the same level—and hopefully at an even steeper price—as other racialized minorities. It is also an appeal for ethno-national valorization, a way for diverse groups who are similarly racialized to pool their resources.

Suitably, the epic scale of *Selena*'s casting call has been compared to that of *Gone with the Wind.* The ironies (and flawless logic) of such a comparison aside, much was at stake in the making of *Selena.* No interested parties— Warner Brothers, the Quintanillas, or the Mexican American producer and director—were going to risk blowing the movie's possibilities of becoming the "official" celluloid story on Selena, the biggest Latino movie hit since *La Bamba,* and a moneymaker that could finally (and once and for all) prove that the now largest racialized group in "America" will pay to see "themselves" on the big screen. The bottom line was that, as the most valorized Latina actress in Hollywood at the time, López was picked so she could deliver in the language every backer understood best: *dinero, mucho dinero.* That she had dance and vocal training probably helped in her casting, but at issue was whether Latinos had indeed become so much part of America that we joyously craved such exploitation.

In the long run, the controversy on López's casting did not go any deeper than ethnic *dimes y diretes,* and many who were disgruntled by the choice later admitted that "once we saw the trailers, we were happy."[6] But for López, the film's prerelease debate signaled the start, not the end, of nationally broadcast transcultural hostilities. Feeling overly exposed in performing Selena's desired yet deadly role, López sought refuge in a pan-Latino (and African) site of identification to protect herself in alternative terms and to major effect: "Saying a Puerto Rican couldn't play Selena, a Texas girl, is taking it a bit far. Selena looked like me. She was dark and she was, well, *curvy*."[7]

López's close identification with Selena was based not only on their parallel "crossover" ambitions or on politically and commercially expedient definitions of Latinoness, but on a common experience of having a similar build, a body generally considered shameful by American standards of beauty and propriety. In the words of the journalist Barbara Renaud-González,

> With her simple clothes and cinnamon skin, [Selena] looked exactly like the people. . . . She showed us just how beautiful we could be and she did it without dying her hair Fanta orange or wearing those oppressive blue contacts that make so many of us look like fallen angels—she was the gorgeous *chola morena* who never forgot her pueblo and we feel under her protection.[8]

This pious site of identification between fan and star was also not lost on the director, Gregory Nava, who had a significant part in casting López: "If you're raised in this country, since childhood, you're given this image of beauty. And if you're *pocha*—Mexican American—it is not you. So you're made to feel bad about the way you look or the way your body is, having big hips or whatever, from when you're a kid."[9] López could not have agreed more: "when I was younger I had a bit of a complex about it [my body]."[10]

Academic discourse on "Latino" cultural practices tends to be managed by "serious" concepts such as class, language, religion, and family—the stuff of sociology and political activism. Yet it was precisely the body, particularly the curves (or, in less poetic *boricua* street language, *el culo*), that proved to be the most compelling way López and others found to speak about how Latinas are constituted as racialized subjects, what kind of (low) cultural capital is associated with these bodies, and how the body can materialize as a site of pleasure, even if it is produced by shaming discourses not under our control. As

López recounted to consciousness-raising effect, "In my movies, I've always had costume people looking at me a little weary and immediately fitting me out with things to hide my bottom. I know it. They didn't say, but I know it. With this film, it was different."[11]

Even if "race" was hardly mentioned in this debate over curves and buttocks, for any Caribbean interlocutor, a reference to this part of the human anatomy is often a way of speaking about Africa in(side) America. Not coincidentally, the major work on racism by a Puerto Rican author, Isabelo Zenón Cruz, is titled *Narciso descubre su trasero* (Narcissus discovers his rear end). And despite the fact that Selena was Chicana, an ethnicity not associated in the Caribbean popular imagination with big butts, her measurements, which according to her seamstress actually match Jennifer's,[12] characterized her as not specifically Mexican American but "Latina," and hence more easily embraced as one of our own.

Butt Nation: Toward an Epistemology of the Rear

Marketing *Selena* to Latino audiences required that the cast, director, and producers be available to the Spanish-speaking media, which mostly cater to recent and older immigrants. This inevitably created the context for each key player to show their fluency in Spanish, and hence their "realness" in relation to their respective national cultures.

During a special episode of *Cristina,* a popular Univisión talk show, the audience had a chance to discern whether these "Latinos" were "one of us" (Puerto Ricans or Mexicans), secondhand copies (Nuyoricans or Chicanos), or downright impostors (Americanos). The actor Jon Seda (also of Puerto Rican "descent") could only begin his sentences in Spanish and then quickly had to switch to English; the producer Moctesuma Esparza spoke *bien mejicano;* Jennifer López's Spanish was classic Nuyorican. She spoke a second-generation, Bronx-inflected Spanish, with its distinctive twang, occasional English vocabulary, and syntax *en español.*

Whatever the qualms any Puerto Rican language purist entertained while López spoke Spanish, these must have quickly withered away when the main question of the night finally arrived. As in other talk shows during the promotion of *Selena,* there came a moment during the interview when *the* question had to be posed to Jennifer López: "¿Todo eso es tuyo?" (Is that body for real?) In other words, is that big butt yours or is it prosthetic? The query is considered fair game when directed at many Hollywood actresses' faces and breasts. López smiled as if she had been waiting a very long time for this question. She stood up, gave a 360-degree turn, patted her butt, and triumphantly sat down: "Todo es mío." It's all mine. But, as the Puerto Rican rapper Lisa M. warns the inexperienced suitor or *ligón,* "No invente, papito / que no va' a tocar" (Don't even think you're going to have a piece of this!).

López's compulsion to speak about her own butt in interview after interview—before and after the movie's release—constituted a keen awareness of her historical role as the next big bottom in Puerto Rican culture, our great avenger of Anglo analphobia, and embodiment of a subaltern way of acknowledging, not denying, the shame of *boricua* identity in the United States. As López said, "Selena could be who she was and, as for me, for once, I could be proud of my big bottom."[13] In the context of American popular magazines and entertainment sections of daily newspapers, López's affirmation of her body read as a defense of another sensuality and alter/native standards of beauty, but I would argue that it was much more.

As just and noble as the claim of diversifying the concept of beauty may be, I would take López's praise of the butt further and propose it as a way of popularizing an "attitude" in relation to hegemonic culture. As Freud argues, an invitation to view or (visually) caress the rear end expresses "defiance or defiant scorn, and this is in reality an act of tenderness that has been overtaken by repression."[14] The Russian philosopher Mikhail Bakhtin concurs that showing ass is a sign of getting even: "The rump is the 'back of the face,' the 'face turned inside out.' The grotesque gesture of displaying the buttocks is still used in our day."[15]

If the shame lies in the face, López's display was (at least) a triple sign of symbolic warfare: "showing ass" as a sign of pride, "kiss my ass" as a form of revenge against a hostile cultural gaze, and "I'm going to kick *your* ass" to offset the economic exploitation implicated in racism. In López's case, this third rear victory is now dramatically evident in her current status as one of Hollywood's highest-paid actresses—Latina or not. No wonder she says, "I have a curvaceous Latin body. . . . I like to accentuate that."[16] So would I—all the way to the bank.

Constantly speaking about big rumps in the American media is also a way to "lower" the discussion away from the value granted to celebritydo(o)m and the upper stratum of breasts, (straight) noses, (blond) hair, and (white) faces. Despite López's relative victory and the Latino community's growing demographics, the big Latin rear is far from sitting easy. Dominant culture still obsessively prohibits its display and punishes transgressors. During one of Selena's last music videos, for example, included in a sixty-minute tape titled *Selena Remembered* (1996), produced by Abraham Quintanilla and José Behar of EMI Latino, she sings her number three hit single "No me queda más" in a tight white sequined dress. In the documentary, the actual music video is intercut with its making, including some "spontaneous" sequences of the production process.

The viewer can see an awkward Selena walking under archways wearing what seems to be a white, see-through veil—or better still, tail—cascading from her waist. A few minutes after the enigmatic garment makes its entrance, Selena speaks to the camera in a candid moment between takes, while several attendants undo her dress's hem. The mystery of the tail is revealed: "This is what happens when you gain weight before a video." Selena breaks down laughing and one might fancy her making fun of people who think a big butt is something to hide. Unfortunately, that was probably not the case.

According to the journalist María Celeste Arrarás (but denied by Abraham Quintanilla), had Selena lived the dream, she would have done so with a surgically intervened body. Selena had then already been caught in the crossover fire. As her success increasingly placed her on a mainstream—white—stage, Selena's shame about her body mounted.

> She started watching her diet and keeping herself looking svelte. . . . She drank gallons of water with lemon juice and she herself would massage her thighs in a circular pattern believing this could help her to combat cellulite. She also saw herself as having a more than abundant derriere, not realizing that her voluptuousness was one of the characteristics her fans most adored about her.[17]

Indeed.

Arrarás adds that sometime after September 1994, Selena actually did have liposuction surgery. The spanking gaze of puritan culture seemed to be breaking the singer down. Her growing attachment to the doctor thought to have performed the alleged surgery, Ricardo Martínez, also proved to be doubly treacherous. It represented not only Selena's shameful flight from her voluptuous body, but also a turning point in her relationship with her fan club president and confidant Yolanda Saldívar: "Yolanda was not at all happy that her friend was coming to depend more on Martínez and less on her. She was quite perceptive and immediately knew that she was losing control of the situation."[18] While it is impossible to speculate whether Selena's destiny would have been different had she not met the doctor, narratively speaking, the suspected operation was a fateful turning point.

Perhaps Jennifer López is aware of the perils of this story, and as a talisman against death is compelled to repeat a litany of complaints aimed at American anti-butt attitudes. She loudly and publicly complains that costume fitters and producers suspiciously look at her behind and mentally rehearse different ways to hide it. "All the other movies I've done [besides *Selena*], it always seemed like they're trying to hide it or they think I look fat. Or I'm not in the American tradition of beauty."[19] If shame may be aroused "by the visibility of a disvalued or an undesirable quality,"[20] López immediately acknowledged her compulsion to talk about her butt as "some kind of defense,"[21] a punch thrown at the shaming gaze even before being attacked. Yet given all the bad blood about this state of affairs, it seems fitting to ask, why is a big butt so upsetting to so many American gatekeepers?

A big *culo* upsets hegemonic (white) notions of beauty and good taste because it is a sign of the dark, incomprehensible excess of "Latino" and other African diaspora cultures. Excess of food (unrestrained), excess of shitting (dirty), and excess of sex (heathen) are its three vital signs. A big Latin butt is an open air invitation to pleasures construed as illicit by WASP ideologies, heteronormativity, and the medical establishment through the three deadly vectors of miscegenation, sodomy, and a high-fat diet. Unlike breasts, which are functional, big bottoms have no morals, no symbolic family function, and no use in reproduction. Or in the feminist Simone de Beauvoir's classic terms, "the buttocks are that part of the body with fewest nerves, where the flesh seems an aimless fact."[22]

Of course, feminists and antiracism activists will complain that the worship of the bottom is but another way of enslaving women to their bodies and linking Latinos to stereotypes of hypersexuality. In addition, there are *puertorriqueñas chumbas* (flat reared) who are victimized by their lack, and other erotogenic zones that should not be subsumed and ignored under the weight of the big butt. But what makes the ass attractive as a defensive strategy is that nobody can quite take a behind seriously, and even when its deployment is meant to be insulting or political, its aim is to lower the dialogue enough to enjoy ourselves.

Like the camel hump, a Puerto Rican big butt also suggests that bodies are made of something else besides language even when we can only speak about them discursively, and the gap between the materiality of speech and flesh can never be totally bridged. The Island-based writer Magali García Ramis, for instance, agrees that Puerto Rican "identity" is based not on political positions or our exaggerated love for the *monoestrellada* flag, but in the amount of excess fat we consume: "a *tun tún* of grease and fried food runs through our *boricua* veins, it joins us, it makes us one, it brings us together as siblings over politics and politicians, cults and religions, *salsa* and rock, matriarchy and patriarchy."[23] In other words, the rear end is where our Puerto Ricanness is stored, but never safely: we all know that lard melts under fire.

Still, while starch and grease may bind some of us, López, who grew up in the Bronx, has likely seen the effects of too much *arroz y habichuelas* on her fundamental commodity and has found a distinctively American way of putting a stop to its overflowing traffic: "Unlike the real Selena, who joked that she kept her curvy shape by eating pepperoni pizza, Lopez watches her diet and works out four times a week."[24] And moderation is not unwarranted.

Times have changed since the golden years of Puerto Rico's most notorious big butt, the dancer and singer Iris Chacón. Ambiguity about the "rightness" of a woman being able to build a career on such a "low" attribute as her bottom has even invaded one of the most celebratory genres of rump worship: *salsa*. In a song titled "Talento de televisión," a parody of Iris Chacón's rise to stardom due to the unanimous acceptance of her having a fabulous butt, Willie Colón—do I dare write Culón—attempts to trivialize La Chacón's achievements by moralizing against her strategy: "No tiene talento pero es muy buena moza" (She has no talent, but looks good). This assessment is premised on several high/low dichotomies that include television as the site for unsophisticated pleasures, the *trasero* or rear end as a sign of vulgar taste, and a heterosexual universe where men have "great sympathy for her splendor" and women "antipathy because / she used her body and not her merit to climb up."[25]

Yet even Willie has to concede that in the realm of television or indeed any spectacle (including cinema), "talent" and "seduction" are difficult dichotomies to uphold, and that *un buen cuerpo* (a good-looking body) is not only *otra cosa* (something else) but also a *razón poderosa* (powerful reason) for making it in the movies. Furthermore, it is also doubtful that talent is not needed to become a legend on the basis of your accumulated fatty tissue. How many big rear ends become songs, novels, popular wisdom, and the paradigm for a whole country's wet dreams and cultural representation? I say that it takes at least some "talent"—perhaps the well-administered seductive arts—to make the talented (Willie himself included) pay attention to such a thing as your humble little rump.

The privileged location of the Puerto Rican butt as an epistemological resource in fact registers the ambivalent triumph of nonwhite aesthetics upon *boricua* cultural production, even among the educated elites. Writers mulatto and white, queer and straight unanimously hail the butt, as can be appreciated in Edgardo Rodríguez Juliá's essays in *Una noche con Iris Chacón* and Luis Rafael Sánchez's well-known novel *La guaracha del Macho Camacho*, with its queer refrain of "Life is a fabulous thing / regardless if you're on top or at the bottom."[26] In both cases, sexuality is the discursive flow where the butt acquires its meaning and raison d'être. This framing is, however, limiting. Even in Puerto Rico, references to the buttocks have many other uses. For example, when a social situation turns chaotic or out of control, we say that it became an *arroz con culo* (rice and butt) or that *se formó un culo* (it became a butt). If we are *groseros* with our mothers or helplessly ask what to do about any displaced object, we will be smilingly told to stick (blank) in our ass.

In the diaspora, the sexual epistemology of the butt gets even more complicated. Gay men may carry the bottom's fetishism to bed as a nostalgia for Condado cruisings; nationalistic lesbians use their *culómetros* to distinguish the *boricuas* from other too-close-to-call ethnicities; and many Puerto Rican women, who have and admire their Chacón bodies for their power over men and circumstances, roar as they are subjected to the everyday indignities of being told that they are fat, should get on a diet or sign up for the gym. Migrant life, with its characteristic economic and emotional instability, ultimately becomes a struggle to avoid ending up with *el culo al aire* (our butts exposed).

Enter Jennifer López

Enter Jennifer López playing Selena and now the Puerto Rican diaspora has a big *culo* to call our own, ending a long stretch of second-class citizenship in both the United States and Puerto Rico. Which does not mean that we have forgotten La Chacón. The myth of La Chacón lives on, especially in the Latino drag repertoire, but it is no secret that younger generations are growing up without anyone to fill her *tanga*. I was in fact astonished to confirm that eighteen-year-old college students at the University of Puerto Rico do not know who Iris is. Perhaps no one can really replace La Chacón, a queen for a different era.

And certainly not López, who is a "serious" actress and will not be seen flipping her rear end on weekend nights in a cheesy television show—although that's how she started, as a "Fly Girl." More to Willie Colón's liking, López is not on television, but on the big screen; her claim to fame is through playing a "modern-day saint in Spandex."[27] Jennifer's butt then commands respect in its own right. A gay journalist and friend based in Miami confirmed my flickering appreciation—only based on images and a fifteen-second brush on Miami Beach's Lincoln Road—with the following eyewitness account: "I saw Jennifer at a party with her [first] husband, and I could not help but to stare at her butt. Her dress was so tight you needed a can opener to get it out. She looked glorious."

Albeit in racially engendered terms, for U.S. *boricuas,* the big rear end acts as an identification site for Latinas to reclaim their beauty, a "compensatory fantasy"[28] for a whole community, and a demand that "we" big butts will not "be excluded from publicity because of our bodies," as Jonathan Flatley has written in a queer context.[29] Insisting on writing or talking about big butts is ultimately a response to the shame of being ignored, thought of as ugly, treated as low, yet surviving—even thriving—through a belly-down epistemology that acknowledges that our beauty is often linked to those shameful identifications. The pain alluded to by Selena's operation and López's narcissism (in the Freudian sense) can be resignified not as an "ícono de la inclinación erótica del varón puertorriqueño" (icon of the erotic inclinations of the Puerto Rican male)[30] or as an exotic (racist) entertainment for (white) American men, but as an inscription of a different sexual and cultural economy in *gringolandia.*

Through Jennifer, the rear end can also become a more ample (popular) trope for Puerto Rican ethno-national belonging, as one of the last bastions of Island specificity is redefined, and more elitist criteria such as language and place of birth are relocated. López's popularity among *boricuas*—including Islanders—also underscores that our intimate relationship with "American" culture and capital is also a domestic affair that constitutes us as Puerto Ricans. Unlike La Chacón, Jennifer's butt reaches our *boricua* living rooms through Blockbuster Video, financed by Hollywood or Sony, speaking English, and playing a *Tejana, Italiana,* or just plain *Americana.*

In writing Selena's story to reach a mass audience, the director Gregory Nava defended his choice to sidestep the circumstances around the singer's death by saying that the film is about "celebrating the American dream."[31] After canonizing Selena, the Mexican philologist Ilán Stavans optimistically concluded that sooner or later "gringos will make room for Latino extroversion and sentimentality."[32] Removed from the prophets' words and the chimeras of upward mobility, I can only claim to have joyously watched Jennifer's quintessential *boricua* butt splashed on a suburban (white) screen, and humbly offer my testimony.

Thank you, Saint Selena, for allowing us the grace to see it.

Postscript: Kissing Jennifer's (Lashed) Butt

Arguably, the landmarks following Selena Quintanilla's death in 1995 gave birth to a new sense of optimism, possibility, and self-worth for a significant number of Latinos. The publisher of *People* magazine, for example, had a taste of this formerly repressed cultural appetite of over 30 million Latinos with $190 billion in purchasing power when in twenty-four hours, the publication's special issue dedicated to Selena sold close to one million copies, more than any other collector's edition, including Jackie O's. The gazes of capital and the yearnings for cultural citizenship among Latinos locked into a long kiss of possibility as each partner finally saw eye to eye and "boomed" into the current Latin juncture.

Having made a mark in popular music, Selena made an especially strong impact among her Latino peers in the entertainment business, who catered to a loyal fan base in need of cultural products that immortalized the singer. Eager and confident Latino theater producers responded with cries of *Selena Vive!* and *Selena Forever* (the musical), while Hollywood executives took risks on Latin talent, washed-up careers were revived, and crossover dreams came true for (light) brown actresses.

A diligent evangelist, López preached the new gospel of Latina pride with (stereo)typical *boricua* passion. (That López's mother's name is Guadalupe may have been prophetic.) In fulfilling her mission, López not only provided Selena's fans with a vehicle for joyful mourning—her own body—she also led a crusade to make her earthly self the obligatory subject of discourse on the new dialogue of race and ethnicity brought about by altered demographics. Among the many who felt called upon to assist her—myself included—the mood was jovial, flagrantly confident, and wildly Dionysian.[33] Despite the Catholic overtones of Selena's popular canonization, the atmosphere was closer to a revival Pentecostalist gathering singing along to the beat of a thunderous *pandereta:* "¡tengo un gozo en mi alma y en mi corazón!" (I am joyous in my soul and heart!)

During her first utopic reign—so far there are three distinct periods—endless articles praised López's curves. Between 1997 and 1998 it seemed that the endless chatter from the bottom up had won the war on white waif America. For the average consumer of magazines and trivia, there was no doubt that the butt was, to recall Leonard Bernstein, finally feeling pretty. But most important, the press seemed to eagerly announce that the big Latin rump was here to stay, sitting on its rightful throne, fully aware of its erotic potential, political clout, and commodity status. Unfortunately for the faithful, the battle over the value of racialized bodies is never over. A backlash ensued.

Although López's image became a staple in mainstream as well as niche market publications and her value continued to ring up, her critically panned debut as a singer of hip hop-inflected pop and *salsa,* her romantic links to the rapper Sean "Puff Daddy" Combs, and the increasingly frequent outbursts of diva attitude met a surge of particularly virulent hostility. In chat rooms, television shows, gossip columns, and cartoons, López was no longer the working-class girl who made good, but the swarthy bitch who made trouble.

The diva pose itself—exhibitionist, narcissistic, and theatrical—can be partly understood as a symptom of López's growing racialized celebrity status. In approaching this backlash, however, I am not interested in assessing whether López is undeserving of criticism (the well-publicized rampage questioning other actresses' talent certainly made her no friends, especially among Latinas); rather, I want to explore the specific ways that antagonistic commentary derived from prior successful battles around bodily racialization was effectively waged against her.

The bearer of "the world's most popular butt"[34] was, in less than a year, forced to abdicate the crown by peers and commoners alike. Even the World Boxing Association named Salma Hayek their queen, over Jennifer. López became one of the easiest moving targets for cheap laughs as well as anxieties about working-class "loud" sexuality and specifically Latino visibility. In a nationally broadcast program, the African American comedian Chris Rock, for instance, joked that López needed two limos: one for herself and another one for her butt.[35] Animated cartoons depicted her as a human rump with arms and legs. Marky-Mark Wahlberg claimed that López gave him a private showing of her behind after she disappointed him by wearing too much clothing on their joint presentation of the 1999 MTV awards.

On the day that newsstands publicized her alleged decision to insure her body for millions of dollars, Internet chat rooms exploded with anti-López babble: "Her body shouldn't be insured for even a penny, her butt is as big as a house," wrote one. "I know that Mariah Carey received best artist of the decade. A big butt can only take you so far!" And the final blow: "That girl has been fuked [sic] by so many men; she probably slept her way to her position!"

The butt's luminous moment slowly faded (back) to black; López's big *culo* was, as so many suspected, the sign of her lowliness as a racialized Latina. To punctuate his disdain, an angry Internet user, for instance, simply called López "the poor man's Catherine Zeta-Jones." López's victory in bringing about a nationwide discussion on "butts" as a way to address the entertainment industry's racism and valorize Latina bodies in the public sphere seemed to become her personal defeat as well.

Precisely because her back end became a required and often a central concern for journalists and other mass media observers, the disproportionate attention to her body began to overshadow any of López's other possible achievements or abilities. Jennifer no longer had the best, the biggest, or the baddest butt in the world; the butt had her. Commenting on articles that describe her as a "large woman," López gave in with uncharacteristic humility: "I don't take it as an insult, because they're identifying as a real person. If that helps other people's self esteem, good! It helps mine too!"[36]

López was losing control of the debate, and her racialized body became the most effective way to bring her down and stand judgment. Her "reckless" romance with an "undesirable" African American man and her arrest on gun possession further fixed her as an oversexed, vulgar femme fatale who was out of control and outside the law. López's first fall brings to mind A. B. Quintanilla's acute observation regarding the perils of subaltern success in "mainstream" culture: "You are allowed to cross the line. Whether you can stay there is another story."[37]

While López's specific answers to journalists who brought up the subject of her body continuously shifted from defiance and tantrums to boredom and resignation, López—like Selena—eventually became uncomfortable in her own mulatta skin: "while she loves her butt, she does not love the fact that her body has been touted as rounder and 'realer.'"[38] Since she is Bronx-tough and a kick-boxer, however, the fight was far from over. The opportunity to "kick ass" presented itself with the aptly titled release of *Out of Sight* (1998), a film budgeted at $50 million and an A-list crossover vehicle through which López achieved what generations of Hollywood Latino actors continue to dream about: ethnic "blind" casting.

In *Out of Sight,* López played the generically named Karen Frisco, a vaguely Latin-sounding last name that could come from either Italy or Argentina. In fact, Frisco's father was white, touting López's career objective. "The day I can make a movie and nobody is thinking of me as a Latina person—I'm thought of as just a person—that'll be a big thing."[39] If the movie *Selena* made her the top *Latina* actress in Hollywood, *Out of Sight* secured her place as top talent, period.

For this second trip, some excess baggage had to go to make the stay on top as long and pleasant as possible. "For her new movie *Out of Sight,*" read the *People* magazine copy, "López is pictured brandishing a shotgun with her back to the viewer—and observers are wondering, where's her bodacious body? Deflated? Exercised away? Brushed away by a Universal art department? . . . A Universal rep also said there was no such trimming; it's 'a drawing based upon a photograph and not a realistic photo.'"[40] Despite the brush's blotch, the tactic increasingly became clearer.

By the summer of 1998, López's comeback strategy showed its true colors: blond highlights, stepped-up body training, and a higher green fee. To aid her in this transformation, López announced that she was working out with the celebrity trainer Radu Teodorescu, who "helped perfect Cindy Crawford's heavenly body."[41] In acknowledging her hire, López must have swallowed hard, for Crawford was repeatedly quoted in the media dissing López's bodily proportions with drag queen meanness.

On the financial front, however, for the new López, no contract under $7 million was an option. In this context, her move to insure her body for a billion dollars has as much to do with personal finances as with the battle over the butt, the value of Latinas in America. For if the press and consumers put down her body and claimed that she was "low," López contended that her body, like a boxer's, was worth every pound—and at 120 pounds, that is $8.33 million each. In fact, regardless of what the world could say about the butt upon which López once said she could "serve coffee," the insurance policy effectively made her "the most valuable star on Earth."[42]

This time, she recovered the crown. After spending twenty-four hours in jail when her boyfriend Sean Combs's protégé Jamal Barrow fired a gun and wounded three people at a Manhattan disco, she gave in to her management's advice that "you can't be Hollywood's sweetheart if you're running from the cops."[43] López said goodbye to Puff Daddy and hello to a $9 million paycheck for her film, *The Wedding Planner* in which she (again) played an Italian.

Despite the backlash triggered by her association with Puff Daddy, López rebounded. She is now "J-Lo," internationally recognized star of screen, music, and television, preferred Christmas gift to be left under the tree for American males under 35,[44] "Sexiest Woman in the World" according to *Playboy*, Britain's *FHM Magazine*'s "sexiest woman alive" for two consecutive years,[45] Hanes Hosiery's "Sexiest Celebrity Legs,"[46] and the "best body among all world celebrities."[47] Remarkably, in granting López its "Best Body" award, *Entertainent Wire* announced that the prize is designed to honor "the woman whose physical presentation defines our popular [American] notion of beauty."[48] Touché.

But Jennifer López knows better. Never feeling secure, López understands that culture is a battle and that wins are never absolute: "I always feel like I'm at the bottom and crawling to the top," says López.[49] Yet the next battle she has promised to wage is not over money or the shame of racialization. With her Bronx twang still intact and her $14 million price tag showing, Jennifer assures us now that "It's not about being pretty. It's about being *real*."[50] And this, of course, is another beautiful fiction to behold.

10 Ricky's Hips

The Queerness of Puerto Rican "White" Culture

I watch my audiences and I listen to them and I know that we're all getting something out of our system but none of us know what it is.

—Elvis Presley

Hungrily pursued by marketing executives for his golden touch, appreciated by Latinos for giving "good" face, and hounded by the tabloids for his alleged homosexuality, the carefully crafted hologram named "Ricky Martin" put in considerable sweat equity in a cultural workout after his 1999 Grammy Awards appearance. If Jennifer López (chapter 9) afforded me—and so many others—a glimpse at our own "low" pleasure mediated by the globalized entertainment industry, Martin "raised" the bar by exposing a largely unseen *boricua* identity worldwide: white upper-class Islanders, or *blanquitos*.

An ambivalent slur, *blanquito* ("little white") may simultaneously refer to the subject's wealth, lineage, and contemptuous attitude toward less fortunate others. The entertainer is not a *blanquito* in the strict sense of the term—he is of middle-class origins, does not belong to an influential family of politicians, bankers, or intellectuals, and cultivates a gentle persona. Nevertheless, in making his spectacular upward mobility part of his star image, Martin became an honorary member.

By positively performing "white" *boricuaness,* Ricky confirmed not only that Puerto Rican culture is syncretic but also that a variety of cultural articulations coexist and are differently appreciated, consumed, and distributed in the marketplace. Rather than Americanized in the conventional sense, Martin represents the market potential of middle-class Island whites, for whom mainstream "Western" culture, fluency in Spanish and English, and economic ambitions are constitutive values. Like many *boricuas* of his background, Martin is simultaneously Paulo Coehlo and Deepak Chopra, Madonna and Celia Cruz, queer-as-folk haircuts and Armani suits. That is why, as José Quiroga eloquently put it, "Ricky is a difficult doll to play with."[1]

Ricky Martin, the writer Rosario Ferré (chapter 7), and Puerto Rican Barbie (chapter 8)—all Island "originals"—address and seduce American consumers in ways not available to darker-skinned *boricuas.* Before Ricky, Puerto Ricans were, to some extent, all the "same." After Martin, some are more Puerto Rican than others, to paraphrase George Orwell in *Animal Farm.* But if there is any off-white *blanquita* kid growing up in an Orlando or San Juan suburb who feels that being Puerto Rican itself limits the ability to register as value, she can now shop for a wide range of fragments of her own identity at the nearby Blockbuster, Spec's, and Plaza Theaters, leaving no doubt as to her mercantile potential, a moment that I was not expecting, but that queerly places me.

"Normal" Childhoods (Like Mine)

As children, little Ricky and I crossed paths on the suburban streets of Cupey. Our parents went to the same high school. My own school was the incubator of three of the original Menudos. I still vividly remember the excitement around the launching of the kiddie singing group, even attending a very early presentation as a way to support our classmate Oscar. Today, Martin and I even live in the same neighborhood—Miami Beach—along with another half dozen former inhabitants of our old block.

It is then impossible for me to ride Ricky's hips without conceding that it is not lust that makes me trip, but a binding familiarity with Martin's public biography as a commodity. In contrast to most of his critics worldwide, when Ricky's hips quiver I do not think about his limited vocal prowess, but of the difficulties of transfiguring shame from Puerto Rican national identity; when his frosted locks stay dutifully in place with foam gel, I recall the street that I still call home; and when the music plays, I marvel at why it took so long for *boricua* suburbia to take center stage.

Dozens of biographers hint that Martin's success is precisely the product of "a perfectly normal childhood in suburban Puerto Rico."[2] "Normal" in this context refers to middle-class whiteness, a categorization of a geographical spot that, up until Martin, was widely represented as antithetical to those values. Ironically, faced with "normal" suburban strife as a boy (his divorced parents often argued about custody access), little Ricky wanted nothing more than to be on television as part of Menudo, a world-famous, quasi-freakish singing package that lived nine out of twelve months on the road, touring. "While he bounced back and forth between his parents, he escaped from his real life into the magical world of television . . . and for the next few years, he found an escape from his bickering, proprietary parents."[3]

So appalled by normality was young Ricky that he saw television as the best line of escape. He was willing to give up his family and community for the seductive powers of illusion and the opportunities that objectification could afford him. "Did you want to become an artist or did you want to become a star?" asked Barbara Walters in a 2000 interview. "I wanted to be a star. I needed to be in the spotlight," quickly answered Martin.[4] Menudo, then, became the best vehicle, not to pursue a singing career—this has never been the ultimate goal—but to call attention to the fractured self and to become someone else.

The induction of Quiquito, or Kiki, as Martin was known to friends and family, into Menudo required more than a change of address. Born Enrique Martín Morales, Martin finally opted for the fully Anglicized and flamboyantly WASP version of his name as part of his flight to the stars. While not that long ago the unaccented "Ricky Martin" name would have been understood as a blatant effort by Enrique Martín, Jr., to hide the shame of his *boricua* heritage, each of the name's origin myths implicates globalization in the rejection not of the motherland itself but the paternal law, a protest against his father's request that he choose between his parents after their divorce. In this domestic drama, Enrique Sr. represents macho Puerto Rican culture; Ricky, a softer, more caring masculinity, sensitive to the mother's vulnerability as a woman.

Martin's star narrative in fact consistently represents commodified transculture as a source of greater agency for Puerto Rican whites, even if at a cost. Similar to the other famous Ricky—Ricardo, that is—being "Ricky" made each entertainer more palatable to the American and global markets by symbolically chopping the head off their (low) Latin masculinity. As Gustavo Pérez Firmat suggests referring to Desi Arnaz's famous alter ego, "Ricardo signifies that the subject is Hispanic; Ricky signifies that the Hispanic subject—the 'I' in *I Love Lucy*—has been acculturated, domesticated, maybe even emasculated. Ricardo is the Latin lover, Ricky is the American husband."[5] In Martin's case the name "Ricky," a leftover from his childhood fame, preserves him as eternally youthful and virginal, turning off adult questions about sexuality. Normal indeed.

The commodity named "Ricky Martin" has now obscured little Kiki, although Martin never fails to mention how the reversibility of his name acts as a reminder of a certain unexplained, if persistent, sense of duality, which is fitting for a man who is an only child but grew up as part of a musical "concept" in which individuality was anathema. This doubleness is apparent when Martin often publicly speaks of himself in the third person: "I have my days where I just have to say, "What's going to happen with Ricky in ten years?"[6] and when the star called "Ricky Martin" asks the boy Quiquito Martín if he likes the man he has become. Most of the time, Ricky says, Quiquito answers yes: the two are, so to speak, joined at the hip. And this is one of the two fundamental affinities that Martin has to another man—and myth—with whom he is often compared.

A myth so uncanny that its subject is remembered as two distinct people and embodied by hordes of imitators who labor long hours to prevent his social death. A man who, since birth, was also defined by duality, when a twin brother died and his mother claimed that "the one that lived got all the strength of both."[7] Like Ricky, Elvis Presley allegedly also spoke frequently to his double. "At age five, [he] began to hear Jesse Garon's voice and regularly spoke to his 'psychic soulmate' throughout his adult life."[8] In speaking of Elvis and Ricky, however, there is so much more than meets the hip.

Kings of the Hip: The Ricky-Elvis Counterpoint

In an attempt to account for Martin's success within the parameters of American pop music history, the U.S. press reached for the figure that seemed to resemble him the most in body and effect. "Ricky," says the journalist Cintra Wilson, "is a young multicultural Elvis for the new millennium."[9] "Martin," declares the *Miami Herald*, "has become the hottest hipshaker since Elvis."[10] Journalists used the Presley reference as a disposable shorthand to little gain, but the juxtaposition of the two kings actually helps to raise questions that have been ignored in both the American and the Puerto Rican public spheres, due to each sector's focus on Ricky Martin solely as a pop phenomenon or a national icon, respectively.

As has already been digested for mass consumption, the white rock and roller Elvis Presley is credited with "mainstreaming" African American music under the guise of a modern minstrel act. Yet Presley's relationship to African American music and the music's relationship to "white" culture in the United States are significantly more complex than this assertion implies. The difference between Elvis and the scores of lesser-known black artists he worked with or was influenced by had less to do with the musical elements the King fused to create his own style, and more with the possibilities that a white performer offered as a commodity in a sharply raced cultural marketplace.

Given the apartheid that prevailed in the South, racially privileged consumers made significant efforts to uphold clear demarcations between white and black music (under the rubric of "taste") even when practice had collapsed these boundaries among many musicians. The bottom line was not that whites disliked African American music but that they refused to accept that its creators were a valuable part of the United States and hence themselves. Sam Phillips, a white producer who courted "the wildest, blackest blues and R&B singers he could find,"[11] minced no words when he said, "If I could find a white man who had the Negro sound and the Negro feel, I could make a billion dollars."[12]

What whites ultimately needed to prepare their bodies for musical desegregation was a Trojan horse, and into Phillips's Sun Records offices walked Elvis Presley, a name so unreal to some that he had to be the chosen one. In Christian terms, Elvis's "sin" was that although he integrated music styles and in some cases public space, his stardom was predicated on the conditions imposed by segregation. Elvis's first hit, "That's All Right (Mama)," for instance, was written and recorded first by Arthur Cudrup, a sharecropper and bootlegger from Mississippi who made from $75 to $100 per recording session and never received any royalty payments, even when his publishing house was the same as Elvis's.[13] For many, Presley's body and voice became the closest thing to an (un)holy union between "white" commerce and the "black" soul, even when these two elements had been inseparable since slavery invented the dichotomy.

Elvis's soulful performance was indebted not only to black music and performance styles but also to his white Pentecostal upbringing—a foundational and fundamentalist matter. As Elvis once declared, "When music starts, I gotta move."[14] The Pentecostal church in fact resembled African American religious practices in their emphasis on emotion, release, and spontaneity. "During the singing," Presley recalls, "the preachers would cut all over the place, jumping on the piano, moving every which way. The audience liked them. And I guess I learned a lot from them."[15]

In embodying black performance styles and Pentecostalist histrionics, the "Pelvis" demonstrated that white people could enjoy African American culture without the shame attached to being black. On the contrary, through shamans like himself and for the minimum amount of cash needed to purchase a record or attend a performance, whites could get in touch with those repressed parts of themselves that only the racialized poor could unleash under the critical gaze of middle-class America. It is in this context that John Lennon's famous words make the most sense: "Before Elvis, there was nothing." Because what came after Elvis—through the youth revolution of rock and roll, postwar angst, prosperity, and the civil rights movement—was a significantly different cultural landscape.

"Elvis was a blessing," says Little Richard. "They wouldn't let black music through. He opened the door for black music."[16] The trope of the door has also been used in the current juncture by Latino singers such as Gloria Estefan to describe Martin's impact on breaking the glass ceiling. According to Estefan, her Latin-tinged pop, best exemplified by the hit song "Conga" (1985), brought Latino musicians to the door, but it was Ricky Martin who "tore the door down."[17] While Estefan is alluding to the corporate reluctance to back Latino musical product, within a broader cultural context, Martin had a Presley-like integrating aftereffect.

Only one year after Martin's 1999 Grammy presentation, the 2000 Grammy Awards focus was on Latin music and the search was on for the next singing sensation. The hunger pangs for Latino talent were so urgent that singers like Shakira and Carlos Ponce were lauded in mainstream publications for their crossover success, even before they had recorded or released English albums. This enthusiasm also spilled over to Latinos toiling in other sectors of the entertainment industry, who now experienced a previously unimagined increase in value. As the cover of *Latin Heat*, a Latino film and television trade publication, put it, "Thank you Ricky Martin!"[18]

Without trivializing the distances between the segregated America of the 1950s and the diverging cultural landscape of the 1990s, in less than a year, Martin managed to enter every home and radio in the United States, making the "Latin" presence felt every few minutes, in the midst of an invigorated anti-Latino backlash signified by Propositions 187, 209, and 227. "By the time Ricky released the all-English *Ricky Martin* on May 11, it was estimated that somewhere in the world a Ricky Martin song was playing every forty seconds."[19] In this context, Ricky's hips became a social lubricant, introducing seemingly foreign material into the (American) cultural bloodstream. With characteristic good New Age vibes, Martin assured millions that the new face of (Latino) America was his and no one should be afraid: "Hold my hand and you're halfway there" could have been the motto of the day.

Predictably, although Elvis and Ricky gave face to different cultural and racial articulations that were here to stay—white Negro and Latin white—music veterans and critics concurred that neither would enjoy long-lasting success. According to the singer Randy Wood, the mood backstage during Elvis's early presentations was far from laudatory: "We'd just stand in the wings and shake our heads. 'It can't be, it can't last, it's got to be a fad.'"[20] The skepticism was considerably less subtle in the New York press. "Mr. Presley has no discernible singing ability," wrote Jack Gould.[21] Ben Gross of the *Daily News* goes a step further: "Elvis, who rotates his pelvis, was appalling musically."[22]

Martin detractors often have been kinder and gentler, but particularly among Latinos, the criticism has been equally devastating: "*Ricky Martin,* el disco, alcanzará el tan deseado *crossover* porque la bobería es universal" (*Ricky Martin,* the record, will achieve the desired crossover because stupidity is universal).[23] But although critics panned the heartthrobs's singing, their hips never failed to agitate typewriters and word processors, albeit to tie up different social ends.

By the mid-fifties, Elvis's gyrations infuriated a growing portion of white adults who saw his bodily thrusts as a shameless challenge to "respectable" middle-class white society. Press reviews routinely compared Elvis's moves with "darkest Africa's fertility tom-tom displays."[24] In April 1956 "the North Alabama White Citizen's Council accused the NAACP of using rock 'n roll in a plot to corrupt white Southern teenagers."[25] Jacksonville's Juvenile Court Judge Marion Gooding threatened Presley with obscenity charges if he did not "clean" up his act. Elvis responded by "waving his little finger suggestively during drum rolls" while moving his body as little as possible.[26] This pleased both the judge and the fans, who shrieked with the same intensity as if he had shaken his hips.

"It's a beat that gets you," said Presley in his defense, a motion Gloria Estefan would second.[27] Still, for all the paranoia of middle-class America, they did understand that rock and roll launched an attack against their standards of respectability. "Elvis wiped out four thousand years of Judeo-Christian uptightness about sex in fifteen minutes of TV," commented the press.[28] Appropriately, Elvis's fans often seem possessed by a pagan fury to destroy, touch, and release all that pent-up energy constrained by the *Ozzie and Harriet* years, particularly upon inanimate objects belonging to the singer such as his Cadillacs, which often emerged from live concerts with "names and phone numbers scratched in the paint or painted in lipstick, broken windows, torn upholstery, and dented fenders."[29]

Considerably less threatening than Elvis, Ricky's hips elicit attention but no alarm. While Elvis was the devil incarnate for many, Martin is "definitely the kind of guy you'd want to bring home to mother!"[30] The difference in perception begs the question, if Martin is Elvis's successor, why are his moves not remotely menacing of the status quo? Or is it that Ricky's hips are doing God's work in a very different way?

The most obvious response is that Martin is, after all, *boricua,* and Latinos are, as far as most Americans are concerned, "inherently musical."[31] While it was disturbing to see a white man groove like a black dude in the 1950s, it causes absolutely no pandemonium to see a Latino move the way he is supposed to. At the same time, for some Latinos—as for African Americans watching Elvis decades ago—the constant allusion to Ricky's dancing hips is, to say the least, intriguing: "Ricky repeats two or three known steps, throws kicks in the air, smoothly moves his waist or makes forceful pelvic thrusts, but as far as dancing is concerned, *nothing.*"[32] Martin himself agrees that his shaking is not quite dancing, but instead embodies how he "feels": "My movements are not choreographed. It is what comes from my heart. . . . I had choreographed dances in Menudo for six years. . . . I don't want anymore [*sic*] choreographies."[33]

Martin's rejection of choreography provides the most obvious beat, so to speak, to race his hip in a certain way and locate Ricky's Latin white specificity. Contrary to mass-produced spectacles such as Menudo, which seek to homogenize, or classical dance, in which coordination of movement and tradition play a significant role in its enjoyment, Martin invokes a distinct "black" diaspora tradition of improvisational bodily expression that makes the dancing body a part of the "music" itself, a dialogue with instruments and onlookers.

Ricky's constrained feet movements and his circular gyrations also memorialize slavery and the musical forms it spurred most directly. Unlike the mambo and other contemporary dances, in the *bomba* and the *plena*—like the rumba—dancers take up as little space as possible. "The slaves who first danced this were usually chained up at night by the ankle, so they were forced to limit their movements: when they danced their rumbas, it was with much movement of the hips and little movement of the feet."[34] Accordingly, one of Ricky's major Spanish hits, "La Bomba," can be understood as a pop homage to the most African of Puerto Rican rhythms, and a key reference for all subsequent Island popular music—including his own, very distant, blend.

In the U.S. context, Ricky's hips are actively performing ethno-national desires for visibility and affirming Africa as a constitutive force in shaping Puerto Rican culture, even for dislocated Island whites. Yet in dancing from (another's) "memory," Martin gives hip service to a history in which he is both dominant and dominated. While on the white American stage it appears that *la sangre llama*, blood calls, as a white Puerto Rican of middle-class origins, Ricky incorporates black rhythms in a way that already exhibits a certain degree of restraint, symptomatic of the adoption of these styles by upwardly mobile social classes. As Jane C. Desmond has commented, movements that emerge from subaltern classes are "refined," "polished," and often "desexualized" on their way up the economic food chain.[35]

Ricky's hips simultaneously show off a process of whitening that has been a constant feature of transcultural commodification and serve as a site of *boricua* memory within pop music's drive toward homogenization. José Piedra observes that in rumba, the "hips, exaggerated, voyeuristic, exhibitionist, deified and prostituted as they might appear to be, might also be a signifier of both acceptance of our bodies and defiance of foreign impositions."[36] In this twist, Ricky's hips are an open acknowledgment that in the Caribbean, often regardless of your color, "when the *bomba* calls, he who does not wiggle an ear, shakes his butt,"[37] even if for the many *cocolos* lining up those open-air *cafetines* in Río Piedras, Martin's hyped hips only manage to convey that *el tipo es un blanquito con suerte;* that's one lucky white dude.

The singer's hip duality is also evident not only in the movements indebted to black Caribbean rhythms (which, as Celia Cruz never fails to remind us with her proverbial "azúcar," are joined to the experience of the sugarcane plantation), but also in a number of specific contexts that he is called upon to perform. By executing the hip for American and European audiences in exchange for money, Martin is part of a long history of Caribbean entertainers, often of African descent, vying for acceptance and upward mobility within asymmetrical power relationships. Similarly, Ruth Glasser has observed in relation to musicians in New York between the world wars that "Puerto Ricans on both the island and the mainland fought for respectability and power through music."[38]

Performing oneself for the pleasure of the other has often provided a way out of onerous economic conditions, and it is precisely in these junctures that Ricky's hips appear the most sexual, as they are separated from other signifying spaces. If Martin's movements often seem lively—"fun"—but not erotic to *boricuas,* it is partly because they are alluding to a broader social and cultural context, not to a strictly racialized erotic exchange. As Fernando Ortiz has suggested in a parallel context, African dance forms are "vital expressions" that link the dancer to an entire social milieu, "in the plenitude of its shared consciousness; which is sex, but it's also maternity, family, tribe, religion, work, war, happiness, and disgrace."[39]

But not everybody is convinced that it is *boricuaness* that makes up Ricky's hips. "There's something uncontrolled and vaguely queeny about Martin's pelvis gyrations that wasn't part of the Dionysian tribal humping of the early ecstatic Elvis Presley or the lascivious Tom Jones," pontificates Camille Paglia.[40] Under this microscope, Ricky's hips are the location not of his overtly signified Latinness or Afro-Caribbean heritage but of his unspoken sexual practices. The queering of Ricky's hips is in fact something of a pastime, particularly among gay men, Latino or not, and has been repeatedly noted by the general and alternative gay press.

The widely shared desire that Ricky's hips move primarily for gay men can be verified by conducting a modest survey, especially if you happen to live in a heavily gay community. Upon hearing that I was writing about Ricky's hips, a queer Puerto Rican journalist who has interviewed Martin several times immediately snapped at me, "You mean, Ricky's very *gay* hips." A dejected Anglo fan, who was fooled into going to a performance in a gay bar thinking Martin would be there, consoled himself with the idol's videos on the monitor: "I think he's a femme bottom." A successful Puerto Rican gay businessman insisted that Ricky had to be gay; he presented the following piece of irresistible evidence: "Only a Puerto Rican gay man would sing an anthem to 'living la vida loca,' accent on *la lo-ca*" (literally "crazy," a slang term for gays). The openly gay composer and cowriter of the aforementioned song, Desmond Child, gives some credence to this when he says, "I love putting a message in my music."[41]

Popularity with gay men or adopting queer styles is not, however, specific to Martin as a pop idol. Like Ricky, Elvis also had gay fans, including the prominent artist Andy Warhol and the flamboyant pianist Liberace, whose flashy wardrobe Elvis admired and even imitated. Contrary to Paglia's contemporary appreciation, Elvis's style and body movements were continuously criticized for their effeminacy. Elvis's mode of walking was said to belong to the repertoire of "blonde bombshells of the burlesque runway,"[42] while his long eyelashes were considered emblematic of the "Valentino-like mascaraed look."[43] Presley's biographer Albert Goldman explicitly commented that after Elvis's army stint (1960), he looked "outrageously gay."[44]

It is then both performers' racial ambiguity and equivocal masculinity as queer white Negro and Latin white queer that make their hips appear to be doing similar work. Not coincidentally, when Elvis first started playing on the radio, the race question posed by listeners was couched in familiar queer coordinates: "when the record came out, a lot of people liked it and you hear folks around town saying, 'Is he, is he?' and I'm going 'Am I, am I?'"[45] Similarly, Ricky's charm is that his spectators are not certain what exactly lies under his otherwise convincingly white skin and black leather pants.

Still, Martin's seduction has less to do with popularized sexual practices, and more with the "innocence" that he brings to the coordinates of race, sexuality, nationality, and ethnicity. In contrast to Elvis, whose queer redneck heterosexuality is widely documented (including the fact that he liked to watch lesbians making out and raised his bride Priscilla at Graceland from age fourteen and sent her to Catholic school), Ricky's sexual persona is produced by a concocted ethereal image ratified by a seemingly romanceless life. While Elvis always had a constant supply of women in his bed, Ricky claims that he is "married" to his career. The lack of enthusiasm for coupling is evident when Martin comments about his first presumably heterosexual experience, "It was not what I expected."[46]

Unlike Elvis, who could bring a crowd into frenzy by burping or wiggling a finger, Martin seems almost incapable of lewd or sexual acts. He was, after all, a Catholic altar boy who by his own admission "sang in the choir, but listened to David Bowie."[47] Yet as if some queer karmic force dictated these references, in Puerto Rico, *cantar en el coro* (to sing in the choir) is a euphemism for being gay, and David Bowie is, of course, a widely acknowledged gay icon. If Elvis's Pentecostal and mystical inclinations made him all the more lascivious, Martin's cross of Eastern mysticism and Catholic iconography is designed to neuter him sexually.

Indeed, his most ardent comment on marriage to date brings to mind the Blessed Mother herself: "I actually have more of a desire to be a dad than a husband."[48] Not in vain, Ricky's sole body tattoo is a rose around a heart trespassed by a spade with the letter *E* at the center. Whereas Elvis unleashed the projected hypersexuality and alleged dangerousness of blackness on white middle-class America, sexualizing white men in a colored way, Ricky pulled it back and tamed it as white Latinness. And it was this racial re-engendering that made Martin a primary candidate to take on another even more lucrative job that, however, reinscribed him as queerly white.

Popping the Bubble: Filling the Void with Ricky's Whiteness

If Elvis was as "funky as a white boy could be,"[49] Martin is "performing and embodying the Latino craze, while he was also in some way performing whiteness with that super cool funky cat look."[50] Sony CEO Tony Mottola, for instance, has been quoted as saying, "There hasn't been a white male star of this kind since George Michael. So there is a void, a space that needs to be filled. And Ricky Martin is more than happy to fill it."[51] The allusion to the "void" also recalls similar commentary about Elvis: "It wasn't socially acceptable for white kids to buy black records at the time," wrote Maureen Ort. "Elvis filled a void."[52] In both cases, it is the interplay of race and sexuality that qualifies each performer to introduce himself in the big white void of American pop culture.

The acceptance of Martin as an honorary white recalls how capital continuously resignifies ethnic groups without affecting how racism functions. As Immanuel Wallerstein comments, "The recurrent birth, restructuring and disappearance of ethnic groups is thereby an invaluable instrument of flexibility in the operation of the economic machinery."[53] Critically similar to the 1950s, Ricky's hip whiteness and seemingly "clean" existence come at the perfect moment for a music industry that has seen some of its prominent rappers embroiled in murder and crime, pop master Michael Jackson implicated in child molestation, and diva Whitney Houston fleeing airports with a little too much marihuana in her baggage. But Mottola could not have put it better, for in what ways is Martin like the reluctantly outed George Michael? Is the hole called "mainstream" culture inherently queer and/or off-color?

Whereas the actress Jennifer López's butt (chapter 9) can evoke an enormous amount of hostility from men and women, Ricky's hips seduce girls and grandmothers alike into movement, in part because he lacks the Latin/black signifier par excellence. Ironically (or maybe not), Martin's alleged favorite body part is "el trasero,"[54] even though he laments, "I have no butt. Everybody tells me that. It's tiny. . . . Not even rock climbing helps."[55] Martin's identification with his own cultural processing of Afro–Puerto Rican culture makes him perform the hip, but it is precisely the fact that he "hasn't got back" that allows him to have the non-Latin world at his hip bone. More so than Elvis, whose ambivalent racialization was riddled with more deeply felt anxieties than Ricky's, Martin communicates that you do not have to have a big booty to shake your bon bon, and you don't need to be Latino to take pleasure in Latin *joie de vivre*.

Perfect teeth, boundless "positive" energy, a 6'2" frame, and the ultimate sign of whiteness in Puerto Rican culture—good hair—further signify Ricky's whiteness. In fact, in 1999, thirteen thousand Fantastic Sams stylists gave him the "Best Hair, Male" award for that year.[56] Yet these markers would not be enough to valorize Ricky as white. Regardless of whether he is gay or not, I would argue that it is Martin's assumed queerness that facilitates his access to honorary whiteness and broad acceptability. His presumed homosexuality unmakes—and unmarks—him as an ordinarily racialized Latin Lover, thus feminizing Latino masculinity and Latinizing Anglo masculinity in an unexpectedly queer way, quite different from Warhol Superstar Holly Woodlawn's (chapter 4).

Even Martin's pop sound, movements, and lyrics are individualistic and "effeminate," when compared to the Latin macho genres such as rap and *salsa*, genres he does not cultivate. Classic *salsa*, for instance, speaks to and from "peoplehood" and community while espousing the alternative values of the criminalized market economy and the wealth of pleasurable activities that lie outside the state's control. As Mayra Santos would put it, *salsa* addresses "the space of the street, urbanism, the tradition of *guapería*."[57]

Although many may consider Martin *guapo* (good-looking), nobody sees him as *un guapo* (a tough, macho dude). Martin's idea of competition with other men can best be encapsulated in his conversation with Sting behind the Grammy stage in 1999: "Hey, Sting, you know what? [wiggling his hips] Check this out, bro'."[58] In "wiggling his hips" at another man, Martin is recasting Puerto Rican masculinity, made toxic by five decades of insistently violent portrayals in American media, and performing a feminized ritual of courtship, with ambivalent racial connotations.

Moreover, in Hispanic Caribbean culture, only women's hips are spoken of or eulogized, and more often than not, the women alluded to are "hot" mulattas: "The poetic emotions raised by a mulatta woman refer to her hips, and above all, her butt, more than her eyes, her breasts, or her waist."[59] Hence, in this liminal space, between the back and front of the stage, Ricky's hip parade seems to joyously camouflage what is, however, so openly displayed, his "show of love and love of show."[60] More radically for Martin, true power shoots from the hip, not the phallus, as the singer made clear when he suggested fighting European racism not with masculine weapons but with feminine wiles: "we can *seduce* them and win" (my emphasis).[61] In this, Ricky espouses a strategy that rejects direct confrontation and upholds symbolic play and cultural syncretism, although not everyone is dazzled, "Martin's cutesy, plastered-on, Ken doll smile—he seems to have only one facial expression—gets boring very quickly," adds Paglia.[62]

Ricky, of course, shares many qualities with Barbie and her boyfriend Ken, including rumors of homosexuality, a perpetual smile, and overt yet inaccessible sexuality, signified by a lack of penis or a "bump." But what Paglia fails to notice is that Ricky Martin's smile—like Elvis's—is also a stylized grin, "an indication of pleasure, amusement" and also a way to "show the teeth as a snarling dog or a person in pain."[63] Ricky grins when he dances and when Oprah compliments him. He grins holding the Grammy award and because the world is at his feet with a turn of the hip. Ricky also grins when Barbara Walters insists that if he only came out the world would be a better place, so the question washes out at sea and drowns. The grin is, again, double: seductive, reflective, and perhaps the most efficient talisman against dangerous queries—to a point.

The *guarachera de Oriente* Celia Cruz once commented that Ricky Martin has been great for Hispanics because "no tiene escándalo."[64] Still, it is the specter of "scandal" that is his most serious concern as he carries the burden of a country's ethno-national shame upon his slight white hips. "I'm not concerned about my reaction," says Martin of his reluctance to clarify his sexuality. "I'm concerned about *my people's* reactions. . . . I give it all when I'm on stage. I give it all in interviews, but you've got to keep something for yourself sometimes, and that's for me."[65] In warding off the glaring lights of Anglo identity obsessions, Martin has also claimed that speaking about his sexuality is against his upbringing as a Puerto Rican, invoking a precarious cultural defense: "I go back to my culture. It's something you don't talk about."[66] Significantly, the only two groups who must be discreet about their sexuality in sex-saturated Puerto Rico are women and gays.

Shame is, in fact, perhaps the most important common thread between Elvis and Ricky. At the height of their huge popularity, both performers lived with the fear of what others might think about core aspects of themselves. According to the biographer Peter Guralnick, Elvis's first producer, Sam Phillips, saw in his protégé's insecurity the "sense of inferiority—social, psychological, perceptual—that was projected by the great Negro talents he had sought out and recorded."[67] The son of a sharecropper (who served time in jail for forging figures on a check) and a seamstress and laundress who earned two dollars for every twelve-hour day, Elvis could never escape the stigma attached to his "white trash" origins. Despite his fame, Elvis seemed to be aware that he was still a "freak," and hence always expressed himself with the extreme deference expected of Negroes—yes'm, yes sir. Elvis's father, Vernon, also spent most of his public life rejecting a label that nevertheless stuck:

"Poor we were, I'll never deny that. But trash we weren't. . . . We never put anybody down."[68]

Ricky assumes the taunts with a similar degree of humility. "I really don't have a problem. I respect everybody and that's all I want. I want people to respect me the same way."[69] And Martin is also respectful in return: "I say that anyone can fantasize whatever they want. I have no problem, quite the contrary, I support them, and I see no difference between the gay and the straight communities."[70] Like Elvis's working-class white origins, Martin's presumed queerness is both what makes him who he is and what threatens to shame him.

The sway of Ricky's hips oscillates between undoing the shame of being *boricua* and the Puerto Rican national shame it would be if Martin confirmed that he is gay. While I agree with José Quiroga that Ricky's refusal to become a transparent piece of gay merchandising enacts a more progressive politics within the queer context, Martin's challenge to gay identity-based strategies does not prevent him from becoming a "Puerto Rican doll" that must remain publicly heterosexual to avoid lowering the value of *criollo* capitalism. I have personally experienced the implacable force of this thrust when I was censored at a Puerto Rico daily after asking a seemingly harmless question in my weekly column: What does it mean for the "nation" that the most famous Puerto Rican in history may not be heterosexual? The publisher chastised me because I was displaying an inexplicable lack of gratitude after all Ricky had done for *boricuas* and decided not to run the column.[71] Essentially, I was punished for not being patriotic and protective of the nation's hip assets.

In many ways, Ricky's San Juan and Elvis's South have much in common. For those who are born in these shamed places, with legacies of poverty and exclusion but a strong sense of place and belonging, the world beyond always elicits a reflection on home. What was once written about Elvis could also be said about Ricky:

> One way of understanding Presley's career is to see him as a man trying to transcend his roots, while affirming them, to weave together the com-

plex, conflicting and tortuous strands of identity that are a part of every Southerner—racial, regional, national and human—and perhaps of every American. . . . However they relate to reality, all Southerners must come to terms with two racial identities, if they are to come to terms with themselves.[72]

When Elvis returned to Memphis from New York in 1956, "the reception had a fire and enthusiasm never in memorable history granted a native son."[73] Upon receiving the keys to the city, Presley affirmed that "those people in New York are not gonna change me none."[74] Martin eventually returned to Puerto Rico to a royal welcome. Both singers' prodigal arrivals to their home cities enact a longing to either be fully accepted in their birthplace (Elvis) or to elevate the birthplace in the eyes of the world (Ricky). In Memphis, and for the rest of his life, all Elvis wanted was, to quote Bob Johnson, to be "thought well of at home."[75] All that Ricky seems to want is to elevate his homeland in the eyes of the world—even at the risk of shame. Call him Puerto Rick-o.

"'I' Am Puerto Rico": The Ambiguities of White Shame

After two years of crushing success everywhere he went, Martin returned to the Island for a series of concerts in February 2000. According to eyewitness Barbara Walters, "The reception he received is closer to that of a patriotic war hero than a rock star. The twenty-eight-year-old has conquered the world and returned home."[76] The local response to his visit was part of the *boricua* constant battle between the shame of national performance and the desire to outperform shame, a predicament that Martin is very aware of when he affirms that "I have to have some quality in my music. Not just shake my ass."[77]

In the capital city it was the high quality of Martin's spectacle that became the measure of self-esteem, not his music, always suspect due to its non-"native" elements. The public came to see the man who had elevated Puerto

Ricans from the low place of their origins—up from their bootstraps—to prove that "a boy from San Juan can rise to the level of a world-renowned superstar."[78] The massive and enthusiastic reception enjoyed by Martin, particularly among the middle classes, overtly demonstrated that they had watched how he "showed them" and were grateful. As the local journalist Javier Santiago put it, "the public, evidently proud, was willing to reward his work by making that [concert] night an unforgettable one for this world idol of Borinquen."[79]

Martin's performance was further aimed at reassuring himself and his community that they remain very much alive despite their transcultural tastes—still Puerto Rican—not the living dead decried by nationalist intellectuals (chapter 2). In fact, these are "euphoric" subjects, as headlines such as "Livin' la euforia boricua" repeatedly reinforced.[80] Appropriately, euphoria refers to a state of contentment or satisfaction, "the result of good health or induced by drugs."[81] And it is the drug-like sensation of feeling good about yourself that accounts for Ricky's high status among many Puerto Ricans and U.S. Latinos, for he gets the respect of all audiences, even when (or actually because) he acts like a (white) *boricua*.

Showing Puerto Ricans in arguably their best light, Martin became one of a few contemporary public figures who can hail the politically divided *blanquito* nation to shake their probably small "bon-bons" and enjoy themselves through the same medium. Among those who came to pay their respects to Martin's achievement were the sons of Carlos Ignacio Pesquera, the 2000 pro-statehood candidate for governor, as well as the children of the rival party resident commissioner, Aníbal Acevedo. There were fellow singers like Manny Manuel and Ednita Nazario and bank CEOs like Richard Carrión. They all came to see "el niño dorado," the golden boy.[82] In Patricia Vargas's terms, "How did Puerto Rico feel after Ricky Martin? Surely with more pride than ever, with a great deal of satisfaction at having found what we were looking for and more."[83]

Yet even if the single most repeated word in the San Juan concert reviews was "pride," what made backers smile was the fact that the most highly sponsored concert in the history of Puerto Rico produced $3 million in profits over three days and was attended by ninety-three thousand fans.[84] Ricky brings not only pride to the fans, but profit to countless sectors of the Puerto Rican economy. A ringing example of the commodification of Martin's image for domestic consumption was Cellular One's seductive campaign, featuring an ad with a headshot of Martin and prepaid cellular cards. The campaign's slogan simply read, "How much time do you want with him?"[85] Not in vain, Martin's former manager, Angelo Medina, once affirmed that "When I'm doing something for Ricky, I feel that I am doing something for Puerto Rico."[86]

Martin's value as a symbol of national pride cannot be separated from his rank as a commodity. The Puerto Rican press's pride does not entirely come from the heart. Ricky Martin definitely sells, including newspapers and magazines. The Latino and Puerto Rican press in fact showers as much attention on Martin's hips as on his even more attractive assets. Calling him a "jewel for export," *El Nuevo Herald* claims that "The sale of his records and shows is equivalent to the total exports of Puerto Rico to Mexico in 1996 ($106 million) and almost five times more than the proposed $17.9 million budget proposed for the Institute of Puerto Rican Culture in 1998."[87]

Like Selena, Ricky makes careers and gives journalists stories to write so they can keep—or in my case lose—their jobs and keep the symbolic and financial economy going. By marketing Ricky as a national "treasure," the Puerto Rican and Latino press of course deliberately overlooks the fact that Martin's success is not, by any stretch, made in or primarily serving Puerto Rico. The spectacle before Islanders was made possible by "American," Cuban American, Croatian, and/or Nuyorican "talent" and capital. In this sense, *boricua* attendees experienced a transnational spectacle financed by globalized capital while enjoying a nationalist party of pride.

If music often stands for the collectivity, serving "to unify the nation by providing an identity and to market the nation abroad,"[88] Puerto Rico is sounding quite different than it used to, and to greater gain. By singing American-style pop in Spanish and English, Martin locates himself (and his "people") in a much more advantageous position to show off and market "*nuestro* Puerto Rico"—modern, technologically advanced, white, and middle-class—to the world. As Martin argues in an often quoted statement, "the fact that people think Puerto Rico is *Scarface,* that we ride donkeys to school—that has to change."[89]

Yet the constant reference to Ricky Martin as a valorized Puerto Rican "star" also removes us to another, specifically political galaxy. The explicit politicization of the term "estrella" has accompanied Martin since at least the 1998 primary campaign in Puerto Rico, when governor Pedro Rosselló used "The Cup of Life" as part of his political campaign. The line that Ricky sings, "tienes que pelear por una estrella" (you have to fight for a star), "seemed an all-too perfect motto to punctuate the party's desire to become a state."[90] While Martin's former manager, the pro-statehooder Angelo Medina, sought distance from the episode, the dancing body demonstrated once again that it is never too far from politics.

In the conflation between pride and shame, the star performer and the flag's star, Martin embodies the widespread Puerto Rican ambivalence regarding full incorporation into the United States and a privileged insertion into capitalist structures that threaten to reconstitute *boricua* identity in different terms. One of the most frequently asked questions to Martin in the Puerto Rican press is in fact whether Islanders will "lose him" to the shaming metropolis; whether this shining star will one day defect to the *pecosa*—the multi-starred American flag. During a San Juan press conference, for instance, Martin was asked, "How come you didn't mention Puerto Rico at the Grammys?"[91] The implication was that once he became accepted as a star in the United States he would never look back and, like Judas, renounce his country of origin. To which Martin has responded, "I am Puerto Rico. The day that happens, I quit."[92]

Being Puerto Rico, of course, has its perils. Martin's participation in George W. Bush's inauguration in January 2001 stirred doubts among U.S. Latinos as to exactly how *boricua* Ricky really is. In a one-sided argument played out in the press, Martin's childhood friend and musical collaborator

Robi Draco Rosa warned Martin not to use his music during the event. "Singing 'The Cup of Life' at George Bush's inauguration is like playing the fiddle while Rome burns," said Rosa in a prepared statement. "This is a very partisan act. This is a betrayal of everything that every Puerto Rican should stand for."[93] In shaking his bon bon for conservative U.S. national politics, Martin was probably only trying to help the sagging sales of "She Bangs." But given his status as the greatest *boricua* star in pop culture history, for whom his light shines must be carefully monitored to avoid national shame and insure the reproduction of Puerto Rican ethno-national identity.

Martin's awareness that in becoming a globalized star he may have shamefully "sold out" is evident in his continuous and excessive performance as a "straight" national subject. Ricky repeatedly attempts to reassure his Puerto Rican fans at each concert that he is not abandoning them by singing "¡Qué bonita bandera!" even when he cannot help but seize every opportunity to sermonize them: "Let us improve our way of life. Let us start to grow and demand more from ourselves. If we are conformists, we will not keep up with the world."[94] Wrapped around a Puerto Rican flag with a world globe behind him, Martin grinningly affirms that although his hips are performed for everyone in exchange for money, he has left Puerto Rico only "to show the world who we are."[95] In a statement that would make the patriarch of Puerto Rican letters, Antonio S. Pedreira, proud, Martin adds, "because we are proud of who we are and what we have. . . . We are Latinos, gentlemen. We are from Puerto Rico."[96]

Martin's purely ethno-nationalist presentation engineered by global capital significantly highlights another aspect of *blanquito* identity. While *blanquitos* are among the most "patriotic" of Puerto Ricans, defending the motherland from linguistic impositions and insults, they are also among the closest to a wide range of "first world" values associated with the United States. Martin, for instance, upholds classic American Dream myths in their idealized form, even when these are questioned or derided by many Americans. Ricky's wholehearted pledge to capital as performative labor has in fact made him more "American" than most, to the extent that he became the best man to sell not only Pepsi but also that quintessential icon of U.S. capital and might, Ford cars: "A new Ford Focus will accompany Martin on stage for two months while he performs in 2 cities. Ford hopes to link Martin's popularity to the new Focus, which is geared to gringo buyers."[97]

Martin's music is fittingly concerned with loss and a straight-from-the-heart eulogy to hard work and the competitive spirit: "we are going to win. We will not stay behind."[98] Anthems like "La copa de la vida" and his appearance at a sports event further underline this "win" attitude—"Go, go, go, allez, allez, allez"—although Ricky admits that he's no good with balls: "The ball plays with me instead."[99] At a historical moment in which states, parties, labor unions, and organizations seem corrupt and inefficient, Martin's message of individual redemption through work strikes a modernist pose in the belief that the "system"—capitalism, democracy, American neocolonialism—can work for "us" too, if we know how to crank it. "It's something I got from my parents," says Martin, "not to be mediocre and just go for it, not to be one more guy along the way."[100]

In Martin's tribute to individuality and work, he is articulating a core middle-class value, different from the social narratives and desires present in other Puerto Rican musical forms and performances of identity, which are more indebted to black and urban working-class *boricua* culture. As Celeste Fraser Delgado and José Esteban Muñoz point out, "in the critical tradition of blacks in the West, social self creation through labor is not the core of emancipatory hopes. For the descendants of slaves, work signifies only servitude, misery and subordination."[101] For the triumphant commodity that is Ricky—"at this time he is valued at $350 thousand per appearance"—work is the road to redemption, providing a new face to Puerto Ricans, cast miles away from the stereotypes of the welfare recipient and underachiever.[102]

Unlike many *boricuas* who have no hope of ever obtaining a well-paying job or even a job at all, Martin embraces work as the only way to escape the shame that constitutes him as a "lazy" spic, regardless of his class or efforts. By mapping the economy of the hip and its impact on providing public venues for the exorcism of shameful identifications, I do not then claim that

Ricky's "dancing body enacts an opposition unassimilable to rational under-standing of resistance as productive work."[103] While dance may signify a number of things to both performer and audience, there is no doubt that Ricky is comfortable with putting his hips to work. In contrast to the en-slaved Africans in the Americas, for whom dance was a way of escaping the reduction of their bodies as instruments of labor (production of babies, pro-duction of commodities), Ricky's corpus, despite its improvisational quality and joy, participates and relishes in its own exploitation because it pays off. Martin is, then, production and performance, seductive image and selective memory.

At the same time, Ricky's commodification has diversified the parameters to offset shame that is not linked to strictly political, high culture, or legal discourse, the realm of nationalist public intellectuals and politicians. The pride of Ricky's star persona is based on the fact that a certain packaging of Puerto Rican performative talent can be competitive in the marketplace and able to integrate the internal colonies to metropolitan—and global—circuits of accumulation without the need to alter the current political status or as-similate to the United States as Americans. Stardom locates Martin outside colonial relations, low ethnic status, and economic need, into a realm where *boricuas* have the world "at their feet."[104]

In this staging of *boricua* identity, Martin is a showcase for the idea that Puerto Ricans not only can have the "best of both worlds"—Latin culture, American wealth—but can actually have the best of every corner of the world. As his close collaborator, the songwriter Desmond Child, comments, Ricky rules because "he isn't satisfied with being king of the Latin music world. He wants to rule the charts everywhere!"[105] At the same time, in order to maintain the precarious balance between national identity and global de-mands, Martin must compulsively assert his loyalty to the lone star of the Puerto Rican flag by repeating that "it's always in my mind and in my heart."[106] Ricky's risk is that in acquiring such great value as a commodity, he may succeed in displacing one set of shameful identifications (as low ethno-national other) but acquire a new set: the shame of selling out *boricuaness*.

271

Postscript

Words from the Grave

The second half of 2001 spectacularly demonstrated how fleeting spectacles of pride could be in offsetting the shame of national identity. Beauty queen Denise Quiñones's reign is over, Félix "Tito" Trinidad, the Island's boxing joy, lost his crown to Philly bad boy Bernard Hopkins, and 9/11 temporarily knocked the subject of Vieques off the front pages. The Island economy further deteriorated with a wave of plant closings and a downturn in tourism, and the pride fest was muffled under a shroud of silence, as political and economic uncertainty loomed large. Which brings me to a conclusion—or to a fresh start.

During the height of the left-inspired nationalist activism of the 1970s, a popular slogan, now no longer in use perhaps because it is omnipresent, was "Despierta *boricua*, defiende lo tuyo" (Wake up, *boricua*, defend what is yours). The ambiguity of this summons is striking, yet the trope of the dream to represent the slumber of Puerto Rican ethno-nationality was not new. In the nineteenth century the patriotic writer Lola Rodríguez de Tió, for instance, had rewritten "La Borinqueña," the *danza* that was to become the national anthem, by asking her listeners to wake up from the dream, pick up the machete, and rescue Puerto Rico's "honor," all in one breath: "Wake up from that dream / it's time to fight. / Long live a Free Cuba / Death to the Spaniards / Long Live Puerto Rico / Free and with honor."[1]

Three decades later, the intellectual Antonio S. Pedreira would seek relief in "the appearance of a book, . . . the celebration of the Fourth Centenary of the Christian Colonization of Puerto Rico (1908), a musician, a journalist, and a poet touched the roots of our traditional, innermost core, and we felt that, although we were sleepy, we were still alive."[2] Even during the radical 1970s, an Argentinean observer frustratingly diagnosed Island Puerto Ricans as the subjects of cultural genocide, "zombies" to be exact, who could only elicit the question of whether *boricuas* are "autonomous, or mere vocal instruments?"[3]

AmeRícans have not been immune to this trope, although it has been couched in different, perhaps more accurate, terms. For the Nuyorican poet Pedro Pietri, the delusion that keeps us sleeping as an ethno-national group is the American Dream of upward mobility, not colonialism as such. In "Puerto Rican Obituary" Pietri writes,

> *Juan*
> *Miguel*
> *Milagros*
> *Olga*
> *Manuel*
> *All died yesterday today*
> *And will die again tomorrow*
> *Dreaming*
> *Dreaming about queens*
> *Clean-cut lily-white neighborhood*
> *Puerto Ricanless scene . . .*
> *The first spics on the block.*
> *Proud to belong to a community*
> *of gringos who want them lynched . . .*
> *They were born dead*
> *and they died dead.*[4]

Evidently, the death certificates issued to the *boricua* nation—from the precise moment in which they imagined themselves as such—can indeed fill many vaults.

In the context of this book, the questions around the dream—whose dream, what happens when the dreamer awakens—are crucial to a theory of ethno-national identity, since in the Puerto Rican case, the dreamer (colonial subject) never does seem to wake up from imperial subjection. If, as Cathy Caruth suggests, the true trauma occurs in awakening, then it should not surprise us that the majority of *boricuas* wish to keep their eyes wide shut as the overtly political texts of Puerto Rican ethno-nationality still do not offer a "good" awakening.

The three plebiscites held during the twentieth century, for instance, did not solve Puerto Rico's "status" or seriously advance (formal) decolonizing negotiations. Rather, they magnified the conflicted interests, desires, scorn, and fears that constitute not only U.S.-Puerto Rico relations, but intra-*boricua* ones as well. At a textual level, the *Seva* happening (chapter 2) awakened the nationalist reader to the "reality" of Puerto Rican nonheroism and the enigma of our survival, bringing us back to the shame of nationalist identity—colonial enjoyment.

But could it be that *boricuas* have always been asleep? One of the few texts that narrate a historical juncture in which Puerto Ricans were, arguably, "awake" is Vicente Géigel Polanco's *Despertar de un pueblo*. An apologist for the Partido Popular Democrático's program of industrialization, nationalist co-optation, and modernization, Géigel Polanco claims that it was during Operation Bootstrap that the people's consciousness awakened itself to its "full" aspirations: "The cry of 'Bread, Land, and Liberty' encompassed the common aspirations. . . . The sleepy people of Hostos and Betances finally shook off its slumber and gave clear signs of being alert to its rights, its justice, its destiny."[5] And perhaps here beats a second reason why most Puerto Ricans prefer to sleep: to be awake, Géigel Polanco tells the reader, is to be subjected to the political project of one or another power bloc, even if it brings some benefits.

Despite excessive arguments to the contrary (virtually the entire corpus of Puerto Rican high culture and conservative "Latino" discourse in the United States), I would have to conclude that *boricua* bodies seem more alive and well on the limits of nationalism—metropolitan or colonial—than at their virile cores. Even in arguably more enlightened Puerto Rican nationalist narratives, far from the crude sexism and racism of the patriots, one is confronted with the fact that subjects squarely under "nations" are not only in a bad "dream" but arrive at a *dead end.* And there is perhaps no better way to feel what lies beneath than to read "Cráneo de una noche de verano" by the popular writer Ana Lydia Vega.[6]

In this brief tale, Vega tells the story of a young black drug addict named Güilson (his Spanglish name is of course not accidental) who almost dies of an overdose. When his body begins to come around from the bad "trip" he has just undertaken, Güilson becomes very hungry—suddenly alive—and takes to the streets searching for a bite to eat. Since Güilson's story of what he sees and feels is suspect to the extent that he is suffering from the aftereffects of intoxication, it serves as an unthreatening site from which to imagine the deadly shameful day when statehood is officially declared and celebrated in Puerto Rico.

For Vega, full political integration into the United States is the trip from which we will never recover, a journey of self-destruction through which Puerto Ricans will immediately cease to be socially representable and linguistically apprehensible (like African Americans? Catalonians? Mapuche Indians?). Hence, when Güilson arrives at the celebration, he sees a woman crying and asks, "Who died, ah?"[7] No one answers, for "Puerto Rico" does not exist any more; a mere technicality (a stroke of the "other's" pen?) has rendered the nation mute. In finally awakening, Güilson not only loses his primary source of identification as a subject—his "nationality"—he virtually disappears, as his face turns "all white and drawn and wrinkled."[8] The "American nation" and the Puerto Rican nationalist prose, like Jonah's whale, have swallowed him (w)hole.

Traumatically predictable, the story guides us into familiar territory as though by the hand of that other essential biblical aide, Lazarus. A *blanquito* (a white upper-class Puerto Rican man) standing nearby finally tells Güilson what is going on at the rally: "Today they're announcing the 51st State."[9] As Güilson appears to be the only *boricua* who has not been informed of his own passing away, people begin to laugh and make fun of him "as if he were a Martian or a *faggot*" (my emphasis).[10] Again, it is a (queered) black young man who allows the "foreigner" to usurp the nation, this time not by passively enjoying it, but by failing to awaken from his slumber, by letting "them" (Americans and their "native" allies) take it (the *patria*, the signifying phallus). Yet, in joining the chorus, Vega confirms what all Puerto Rican nationalist narratives seem to oddly enough agree on: the "nation" appears to be physically alive as *boricua* "bodies" walk everywhere around us—but it is, in truth, deceased.

Although this fact is not immediately evident to Güilson, once he recovers from the narcotics' effects, he finally sees that, like René Marqués's black annexationist (chapter 1), his only option is to make his body agree with his mind: commit suicide. According to Marqués, the integrationist Puerto Rican of African descent is, after all, "a living dead, a suicidal who can never be totally realized, one condemned to destroy himself more every day as a Puerto Rican, without ever achieving it, as he can never totally destroy his Puerto Rican essence while there is a breath left in him."[11] And to cover the shame of Güilson's treacherous black body, the narrative offers a huge American flag "exploding with stars . . . alone and big, huge like an eagle's wing in a horror movie. Or as one would see it if when tripping and without hope of touching land."[12]

The strategy to defeat the devaluation implicit in lowering oneself to the position of an ethnic, racialized, and/or queer subject is, as we know, to wake up—on time. "Because you have to open up your eyes, man," says the unidentified narrator.[13] "If not, an old toothless horse will have you for lunch."[14] The allusion to a "toothless horse" again remits us to statehood as death since it is well known that the former pro-annexation governor Carlos Romero Barceló was called a "horse" and is associated by many with the harassment of the pro-independence movement during the 1980s that resulted in the deaths of two young men at Cerro Maravilla. Güilson's suicide would then be but a confirmation of what has already taken place, for when he returned from his trip, he was already gone: a dead *boricua*. Since the young man cannot answer the question of how he survived his social death, from the seeming safety of his physical integrity, Güilson kills himself.

The trope of the "trip" also returns us to migration as a dissolving "national" force. For many nationalists, migration is also a crossing without return, a journey through which new identities different from hegemonic Puerto Rican ones are created, lived, and reproduced. But if as José Luis González argues in *El país de los cuatro pisos,* and I concur, the U.S. colonial regime has inadvertently enabled subaltern culture to flourish, and many of these practices have emerged from processes of transculturation in the metropolis, I wonder if there is a deadly confusion and Ana Lydia Vega missed the point.

Inevitably, *boricuas* everywhere will one day awaken to change in their economic, cultural, and political ties to the United States and no longer remember why. Each community will once again reconfigure Puerto Rican ethno-nationality in ways that are already circulating—*boricuas,* Latinos, Americans. Yet from the grave, what is freakishly alive and cannot help but comfort us in these uncharted trips is the obstinate fact that even from the deadliest of dreams others, however shaken, always awaken.

Notes

Notes to the Preface

1. Taki Theodoracopulos, "Why Should We Pay?" *Spectator,* June 14, 1997, 62–63, 62.

2. "Taki's Tacky Attack on Puerto Ricans," Institute for Puerto Rican Policy, June 16, 1997.

3. The only founding myth in which scholars, activists, and eyewitnesses in the United States largely agree that Puerto Ricans either threw the first stone or incited others to do so is Stonewall, the urban riot that was posthumously credited with sparking the modern gay and lesbian movement. This will be one of the subjects of my upcoming book, *Giving Face.*

4. For differing perspectives, see "A Political Drama: Hillary Clinton and Puerto Ricans in New York," *Factual Analysis* 3, no. 2 (1999), www.truthinstitute.org/Hillary-Clinton-FA-vol3-2htm,and José Fuentes, "Clinton's Puerto Rico Policy Bombs in More Ways Than One," *Puerto Rico Herald,* reprinted from *Wall Street Journal,* October 5, 1999, www.puertorico-herald.org/issues/vol3n41/Clinton/PolicyBombs-en .shtml, Martin Kettle, "Hillary's Crossing of Clinton Angers Puerto Ricans," *Guardian,* September 7, 1999, www.guardian.co.uk/Print/0,3858,3899270,00.html.

5. Kettle, "Hillary's Crossing of Clinton Angers Puerto Ricans."

6. Juan Angel Silén, *Hacia una visión positiva del puertorriqueño* (Río Piedras: Editorial Edil, 1972), 185.

7. Eve Kosofsky Sedgwick, "Queer Performativity: Warhol's Shyness/Warhol's Whiteness," in *Pop Out: Queering Warhol,* ed. Jennifer Doyle, Jonathan Flatley, and José Muñoz (Durham: Duke University Press, 1996), 134–42, 142.

8. Carl D. Schneider, *Shame, Exposure, and Privacy* (Boston: Beacon, 1977).

9. Ibid., 20.

10. Bernardo Vega, *Memorias de Bernardo Vega* (Río Piedras: Huracán, 1984), translated in Suzanne Oboler, *Ethnic Labels, Latino Lives* (Minneapolis: University of Minnesota Press, 1995), 46.

11. Sedgwick, "Queer Performativity: Warhol's Shyness/Warhol's Whiteness," 141.

12. Silvan Tomkins, *Shame and Its Sisters,* ed. Eve Kosofsky Sedgwick and Adam Frank (Durham: Duke University Press, 1995), 133.

13. Susan Miller, *The Shame Experience* (Hillsdale, NJ: Analytic Press, 1985), 15.

14. For the use of the term "biography" in anthropological methodology, see Igor Kopytoff, "The Cultural Biography of Things: Commoditization as Process," in *The Social Life of Things: Commodities in Cultural Perspective,* ed. Arjun Appadurai (Cambridge: Cambridge University Press, 1986), 64–91.

15. Fernando Ortiz, *Contrapunteo cubano del tabaco y el azúcar* (Caracas: Editorial Ayacucho, 1987).

16. Mary Louise Pratt, *Imperial Eyes: Travel Writing and Transculturation* (New York: Routledge, 1992), 6.

17. After I completed this manuscript, a number of books have appeared that coincide in different ways with some of the analysis offered here. Among these are Rubén Ríos Ávila, *La raza cómica* (Río Piedras: Ediciones Huracán, 2002); Carlos Pabón, *Nación postmortem* (Río Piedras: Ediciones Callejón, 2002); and Arlene Dávila, *Latinos, Inc.: The Marketing and Making of a People* (Berkeley: University of California Press, 2001).

Notes to Chapter 1

1. Frederick Turner, "Shame, Beauty, and the Tragic View of History," *American Behavioral Scientist* 38, no. 8 (1995): 1060–61.

2. Angel Ricardo Oquendo, "Puerto Rican National Identity and United States Pluralism," in *Foreign in a Domestic Sense: Puerto Rico, American Expansionism, and the*

Constitution, ed. Christina Duffy Burnett and Burke Marshall (Durham: Duke University Press, 2001), 315–48.

3. Ralph de la Cruz, "Rethinking Puerto Rico, from the Jets to Mars," *South Florida Sun-Sentinel,* August 19, 2002.

4. Quoted in Nancy Morris, *Puerto Rico: Culture, Politics, and Identity* (Westport: Praeger, 1995), 39.

5. Kai Erikson, "Notes on Trauma and Community," In *Trauma: Explorations in Memory,* ed. Cathy Caruth (Baltimore: Johns Hopkins University Press, 1995), 183–99, 186.

6. For a discussion on Friedrich Nietzsche's writings on shame, see Carl D. Schneider, *Shame, Exposure, and Privacy* (Boston: Beacon, 1977).

7. Quoted in Morris, *Puerto Rico: Culture, Politics, and Identity,* 36–37.

8. For further comment on this concept, please see Ramón Grosfoguel, Frances Negrón-Muntaner, and Chloé Georas, introduction to *Puerto Rican Jam,* ed. Frances Negrón-Muntaner and Ramón Grosfoguel (Minneapolis: University of Minnesota Press, 1997), 1–36, 17–19.

9. María Pérez y González, *Puerto Ricans in the United States* (Westport: Greenwood, 2000), 152.

10. María Milagros López, "Post-Work Selves and Entitlement 'Attitudes' in Peripheral Postindustrial Puerto Rico," *Social Text,* spring 1994, 111–33, 111.

11. Kelvin Santiago-Valles, *"Subject People" and Colonial Discourses: Economic Transformation and Social Disorder in Puerto Rico, 1898–1947* (Albany: State University of New York Press, 1994), 53.

12. Quoted in Morris, *Puerto Rico: Culture, Politics, and Identity,* 50.

13. Félix Jiménez, *Vieques y la prensa* (San Juan: Editorial Plaza Mayor, 2001), 106.

14. Benedict Anderson, *Imagined Communities* (London: Verso, 1983), 104.

15. Antonio S. Pedreira, *Insularismo* (Río Piedras: Edil, 1973), 103.

16. Silvan Tomkins, *Shame and Its Sisters,* ed. Eve Kosofsky Sedgwick and Adam Frank (Durham: Duke University Press, 1995), 138.

17. María de los Angeles Castro Arroyo, "El 98 en dos tiempos: Del diario a la Crónica de Angel Rivero Méndez" (unpublished manuscript), 20.

18. Quoted in Carmelo Rosario, *Puerto Rico y la crisis de la guerra hispanoamericana* (Río Piedras: Editorial Edil, 1989), 19.

19. *La Democracia,* January 15, 1896. Original Spanish: "No hay más que un detalle en nosotros que establezca diferencias entre las dos islas del archipiélago antillano, nuestra mansedumbre perpetua; nuestra fidelidad de cuatro siglos. Nosotros no tenemos la práctica ni queremos tenerla, dígase si se quiere en nuestro daño, pero dígase, porque es la verdad, de empuñar el machete e irnos al campo a combatir por el derecho."

20. Silvia Alvarez Curbelo, "Despedidas," *Revista de Indias* 57, no. 211 (1997): 786. Original Spanish: "los puertorriqueños daríamos por fin una lección a Cuba y salvaríamos a España de la vergüenza."

21. Excellent accounts on the 1898 U.S. military invasion of Puerto Rico and its aftermath include Angel Rivero, *Crónica de la guerra hispanoamericana en Puerto Rico* (New York: Plus Ultra, 1973); Fernando Picó, *1898: La guerra después de la guerra* (Río Piedras: Ediciones Huracán, 1987); Santiago-Valles, *"Subject People" and Colonial Discourses;* and Mariano Negrón-Portillo, *Las turbas republicanas, 1900–1904* (Río Piedras: Ediciones Huracán, 1990).

22. Quoted in Willard B. Gatewood, Jr., *Smoked Yankees and the Struggle for Empire* (Fayetteville: University of Arkansas Press, 1987), 55.

23. Julio Cervera Baviera, *La defensa militar de Puerto Rico* (San Juan: Imprenta de la Capitanía General, 1898), 79–80. Original Spanish: "País tan servil, tan ingrato, no se ha visto jamás. . . . En 24 horas, el pueblo de Puerto Rico pasó de ser ferviente español, a entusiasta americano. Sin más razón que el cobarde miedo. Se *humilló* entregándose servilmente al invasor *como se inclina el esclavo* ante el poderoso señor" (my emphasis).

24. Quoted in Carmen Dolores Hernández, "El 98 y sus contextos," *El Nuevo Día,* January 4, 1998, 9. Original Spanish: "el país sufrido, el pueblo golpeado en 1887, azotado en las cárceles, conducido con esposas por las carreteras, amontonado en las fétidas prisiones, fugitivo o expatriado, herido en el rostro de mil maneras distintas, vilipendiado en su honor, menospreciado en su indulgencia y generosidad."

25. Virginia E. Sánchez Korrol, *From Colonia to Community: The History of Puerto Ricans in New York, 1917–1948* (Westport: Greenwood, 1983), 12.

26. Ibid., 11.

27. "Interview de Luis Muñoz Rivera siendo secretario de Estado en octubre de 1898 con un representante del *New York Tribune,*" in *Boletín Histórico de Puerto Rico,* vol.

13, ed. Cayetano Coll y Toste (San Juan: Tipografía Cantera, Fernández y Cía., 1914–1927), 342–45. Original Spanish: "Opino que mi país puede gobernarse y administrarse así propio, y que eso aspira la totalidad de los criollos. Hay elementos directores competentísimos y hay pueblo dócil que le secunda."

28. From Negrón-Portillo, *Las turbas republicanas*, translated in Santiago-Valles, *"Subject People" and Colonial Discourses*, 104.

29. Henry Teller, quoted in Juan Angel Silén, *Hacia una visión positiva del puertorriqueño* (Río Piedras: Editorial Edil, 1972), 79. Translated from the English: "No me gusta el puertorriqueño; no son peleadores como los cubanos; estuvieron sometidos a la tiranía española durante centenares de años sin mostrarse hombres para hacerles oposición. Tal raza es indigna de la ciudadanía."

30. While a detailed comparison between Cuban and Puerto Rican strategies of living with empire is beyond the scope of this book, it is important to stress that the mythical heroic narrative of the Cuban pro-independence struggles obscures the complex ways Cubans imagined—and obtained—their independence from and with the United States. In persistently casting Puerto Ricans as "queer" Cubans, in the sense of peculiar and unmanly, the larger island's national discourse displaces its own shame—of American intervention, the imposition of the Platt Amendment, the failure to found a people's "revolution" despite heroes, bloodshed, and defiance, and the shame of being supported by exile dollars as well as foreign sexual tourism—onto Puerto Rico, which under consensual colonial rule has achieved a greater degree of political stability and freedom from hunger.

31. Quoted in Santiago-Valles, *"Subject People" and Colonial Discourses*, 63.

32. Quoted in F. E. Edwards, *The '98 Campaign of the 6th Massachusetts, U.S.V.* (Boston: Little, Brown, 1899), 93.

33. Susan Miller, *The Shame Experience* (Hillsdale, NJ: Analytic Press, 1985), 44.

34. Quoted in Schneider, *Shame, Exposure, and Privacy*.

35. Santiago-Valles, *"Subject People" and Colonial Discourses*, 63.

36. Antonio S. Pedreira, "La actualidad del jíbaro," in *El jíbaro de Puerto Rico: Símbolo y figura*, ed. Enrique Laguerre and Esther Melón (Sharon, CT: Troutman Press, 1968), 14.

37. Lillian Guerra, *Popular Expression and National Identity in Puerto Rico* (Gainesville: University Press of Florida, 1998), 76.

38. Pedreira, "La actualidad del jíbaro," 20.

39. Ibid., 23. Original Spanish: "del atropello de la zona urbana y de la negra competencia de la costa."

40. René Marqués, "El puertorriqueño dócil (literatura y realidad psicológica)," in *Ensayos* (Río Piedras: Editorial Antillana, 1972), 151–215.

41. Ibid., 175. Original Spanish: "el *machismo,* versión criolla de la fusión y adaptación de dos conceptos seculares, la *honra* española y el *pater familiae* romano."

42. Silén, *Hacia una visión positiva del puertorriqueño,* 224. Original Spanish: "Cuando nosotros llegamos a la universidad en 1955 encontramos un enorme vacío que tuvimos que llenar con nuestros cojones."

43. For different approaches to subaltern masculinities in Puerto Rico, see Santiago-Valles, *"Subject People" and Colonial Discourses;* and María del Carmen Baerga Santini, "¡A la organización, á unirnos como un solo hombre . . . !: La Federación Libre de Trabajadores y el mundo masculino del trabajo," *Op.Cit.,* 11 (1999): 219–51. Baerga Santini makes a compelling case that patriarchal discourses substantially informed the mostly male working class movement's leadership in Puerto Rico during the first half of the century and as a consequence inconsistently incorporated women's concerns in their political practice.

44. Pérez y González, *Puerto Ricans in the United States,* 64.

45. Clara Rodríguez, *Puerto Ricans: Born in the U.S.A.* (Boston: Unwin Hyman, 1989), 3.

46. Ibid., 11.

47. Santiago-Valles, *"Subject People" and Colonial Discourses.*

48. Sánchez Korrol, *From Colonia to Community,* 27.

49. Ramón Grosfoguel and Chloé Georas, "The Racialization of Latino Caribbean Migrants in the New York Metropolitan Area," *Centro* 8, nos. 1–2 (1996): 191–201.

50. Ibid., 194.

51. History Task Force, Centro de Estudios Puertorriqueños, *Labor Migration under Capitalism: The Puerto Rican Experience* (New York: Monthly Review Press, 1979), 128.

52. Ibid.

53. Ruth Glasser, *My Music Is My Flag* (Berkeley: University of California Press, 1995), 73.

54. Jack Lait and Lee Mortimer, *New York Confidential* (New York: Crown, 1948), 126.

55. Pérez y González, *Puerto Ricans in the United States,* 56.

56. Quoted in Richie Pérez, "From Assimilation to Annihilation: Puerto Rican Images in U.S. Films," *Centro* 2, no. 8 (spring 1990): 8–27, 12.

57. Lillian Jiménez, "From the Margin to the Center: Puerto Rican Cinema in the United States," *Centro* 2, no. 8 (spring 1990): 29–43, 30.

58. Turner, "Shame, Beauty, and the Tragic View of History," 1066.

59. History Task Force, *Labor Migration under Capitalism*, 150.

60. Roberto P. Rodríguez-Morazzani, "Beyond the Rainbow: Mapping the Discourse on Puerto Ricans and 'Race,'" *Centro* 8, nos. 1–2 (1996): 151–69, 153.

61. Oscar Lewis, *La vida: A Puerto Rican Family in the Culture of Poverty* (New York: Vintage, 1966), xii.

62. Susan S. Baker, *Understanding Mainland Puerto Rican Poverty* (Philadelphia: Temple University Press, 2002), 134.

63. Pérez y González, *Puerto Ricans in the United States*, 65.

64. Baker, *Understanding Mainland Puerto Rican Poverty*, 120.

65. Linda Chávez, *Out of the Barrio: Toward a New Politics of Hispanic Assimilation* (New York: Basic Books, 1991), 159.

66. López, "Post-Work Selves and Entitlement 'Attitudes,'" 112.

67. Pérez y González, *Puerto Ricans in the United States*, 68.

68. Baker, *Understanding Mainland Puerto Rican Poverty*, 135–36.

69. Quoted in ibid., 136.

70. Pérez y González, *Puerto Ricans in the United States*, 71.

71. Ibid., 70.

72. For recent statistics, see José R. Madera, "Federal Funds Keep Adding Up," *Caribbean Business*, July 11, 2002.

73. López, "Post-Work Selves and Entitlement 'Attitudes,'" 14.

74. Morris, *Puerto Rico: Culture, Politics, and Identity*, 124–25.

75. Efraín Barradas and Rafael Rodríguez, *Herejes y mitificadores* (Río Piedras: Ediciones Huracán, 1980), 14–15.

76. Marithelma Acosta, "Carta abierta a Rosario Ferré," *Diálogo*, May 1998, 40. Original Spanish: "no nos tenemos que avergonzar. Un país donde la frase 'soy boricua' no suscita un gesto de repugnancia en el interlocutor."

77. López, "Post-Work Selves and Entitlement 'Attitudes,'" 113.

78. Guerra, *Popular Expression and National Identity in Puerto Rico*, 209.

79. Pérez y González, *Puerto Ricans in the United States*, 54.

80. "Trasfondo e historia," National Puerto Rican Day Parade, Inc., www.nationalpuertoricandayparade.org/acercadenosotros.htm.

81. Ibid.

82. Tomkins, *Shame and Its Sisters,* 144.

83. Judith Butler, "Imitation and Gender Insubordination," in *Inside/Out: Lesbian Theories, Gay Theories,* ed. Diana Fuss (New York, Routledge, 1991), 13–31, 24.

84. Angel G. Quintero Rivera, *Salsa, sabor y control* (Mexico: Siglo XXI, 1998), 266–67.

85. Other, more amply documented, means are political activism, education, and community organizations.

86. Lewis, *La vida,* xiv.

87. Anna Indych, "Nuyorican Baroque: Pepón Osorio's Chucherias," Art Journal, *Puerto Rico Herald,* April 1, 2001, www.puertorico-herald.org/issues/2001/vol5n18/Nuyorican-en.shtml, 6.

88. Tim Edwards, *Contradictions of Consumption: Concepts, Practices and Politics in Consumer Society* (Philadelphia: Open University Press, 2000), 192.

89. Frank Griffiths, "Christmas Is Big Business in Puerto Rico," The State.com, December 25, 2002, www.thestate.com/mld/thestate/news/world/4810953.htm.

90. Pedreira, *Insularismo,* 96.

91. Fufi Santori, "Que bonita bandera!" *El Nuevo Día,* December 22, 1995, 78. Original Spanish: "un poquito menos que cubanos y dominicanos aunque comamos mejor."

92. Arlene M. Dávila, *Sponsored Identities: Cultural Politics in Puerto Rico* (Philadelphia: Temple University Press, 1997), 169–207.

93. Arlene M. Dávila, *Latinos, Inc: The Marketing and Making of a People* (Berkeley: University of California Press, 2001), 11, 12.

94. Arjun Appadurai, "Introduction: Commodities and the Politics of Value," in *The Social Life of Things: Commodities in Cultural Perspective,* ed. Arjun Appadurai (Cambridge: Cambridge University Press, 1986), 3.

95. Karl Marx discussed in Appadurai, "Introduction: Commodities and the Politics of Value," 8.

96. Appadurai, "Introduction: Commodities and the Politics of Value," 3.

97. Jonathan Flatley, "Warhol Gives Good Face: Publicity and the Politics of Prosopopoeia," in *Pop Out: Queering Warhol,* ed. Jennifer Doyle, Jonathan Flatley, and José Muñoz (Durham: Duke University Press, 1996), 101–30, 107.

98. Stuart Hall, "Notes on Deconstructing the Popular," in *People's History and Socialist Theory,* ed. Raphael Samuel (London: Routledge and Kegan Paul, 1981), 227–40.

99. Juan Flores, "Nueva York, Diaspora City," *David Rockefeller Latin American Center News,* spring 2000, www.fas.harvard.edu/~drclas/pages/tabages/publications/newsletters/spring00/flores.htm (August 9, 2001).

100. Jiménez, "From the Margin to the Center: Puerto Rican Cinema in the United States," 30.

101. Pérez, "From Assimilation to Annihilation: Puerto Rican Images in U.S. Films," 9.

102. Richard Dyer, *Heavenly Bodies: Film Stars and Society* (New York: St. Martin's, 1986), 18.

103. Miller, *The Shame Experience,* 33.

104. Jacques Lacan, *Ecrits* (New York: Norton, 1977), 1–7.

105. Gregory Rodríguez, "Latinos Finally Hit the U.S. Mainstream," *San Juan Star,* April 16, 2001, 17.

106. Rosario Ferré, "Puerto Rico, USA," *New York Times,* March 19, 1998.

107. Diana Fuss, introduction to *Inside/Out: Lesbian Theories, Gay Theories,* 1–10, 4.

108. Ortiz, *Contrapunteo cubano del tabaco y el azúcar.*

Notes to Chapter 2

1. Mimi Whitefield, "Survey Reveals Lack of Knowledge of Island," *Miami Herald,* August 13, 1998, 13.

2. Quoted in Ivonne García, "Three Players in 'The Splendid Little War,'" *San Juan Star,* December 31, 1997, 14.

3. Silvan Tomkins, *Shame and Its Sisters,* ed. Eve Kosofsky Sedgwick and Adam Frank (Durham: Duke University Press, 1995), 138.

4. Arcadio Díaz Quiñones, *Luis Lloréns Torres: Antología de verso y prosa* (Río Piedras: Ediciones Huracán, 1986), 62.

5. Francisco Manrique Cabrera, *Historia de la literatura puertorriqueña* (Río Piedras: Editorial Cultural, 1982), 160. Original Spanish: "Era sencillamente el trauma: el violento desgarre histórico consumado sin la intervención nuestra, y ante el deslumbramiento ingenuo, pueril, cuando no iluso y vacuo, de muchos liberales isleños que confundieron colorines y palabras con realidades."

6. Ramón Grosfoguel, Frances Negrón-Muntaner, and Chloé Georas, introduction to *Puerto Rican Jam: Rethinking Colonialism and Nationalism,* ed. Frances Negrón-Muntaner and Ramón Grosfoguel (Minneapolis: University of Minnesota Press, 1997), 1–36.

7. Helen Merrell Lynd, *On Shame and the Search for Identity* (New York: Science Editions, 1961), 32.

8. Laura S. Brown, "Not Outside the Range: One Feminist Perspective on Psychic Trauma," in *Trauma: Explorations in Memory,* ed. Cathy Caruth (Baltimore: John Hopkins University Press, 1995), 100–112, 102.

9. Kai Erikson, "Notes on Trauma and Community," in *Trauma: Explorations in Memory,* 183–99, 186.

10. Ibid., 185.

11. Gilles Deleuze and Felix Guattari, *Kafka: Toward a Minor Literature* (Minneapolis: University of Minnesota Press, 1986), 57.

12. Ramiro Guerra y Sánchez, *La guerra de los diez años* (Havana: Colección Histórica y Americana, 1986), 341–42.

13. Quoted in José González Ginorio, *Luis Muñoz Rivera: A la luz de sus obras y de su vida* (Boston: D. C. Heath, 1919), 30. Original Spanish: "un pueblo viril, de alma de fuego, con el valor tenaz del espartano y la altivez indómita del griego."

14. Benedict Anderson, *Imagined Communities* (London: Verso, 1983), 14.

15. Eve Kosofsky Sedgwick, "Queer Performativity: Warhol's Shyness/Warhol's Whiteness," in *Pop Out: Queering Warhol,* ed. Jennifer Doyle, Jonathan Flatley, and José Muñoz (Durham: Duke University Press, 1996), 134–42, 135.

16. Arcadio Díaz Quiñones, *Luis Lloréns Torres: Antología de verso y prosa,* 2d ed. (Río Piedras: Ediciones Huracán, 1996), 52.

17. Olga Nolla, *El castillo de la memoria* (Mexico: Alfaguara, 1998).

18. Olga Nolla, "La guerra hispanoamericana y el inconsciente colectivo puertorriqueño," *El Nuevo Día/Revista Domingo,* July 19, 1998, 5–7, 6.

19. Slavoj Zizek, *The Sublime Object of Ideology* (London: Verso, 1989), 47.

20. José Luis González, *Nueva visita al cuarto piso* (Madrid: Libros del Flamboyán, 1987), 122.

21. Juan Gelpí, *literatura y paternalismo en Puerto Rico* (Río Piedras: Universidad de Puerto Rico, 1993), 74–75. Original Spanish: "los maestros que le imparten lecciones al país son, por supuesto, los patriotas, y la educación que recibe consiste en ejemplos que necesita seguir para sobreponerne al letargo y a las carencias morales."

22. Fernando Picó, quoted in Josean Ramos, "Crónica: Un sueño que hizo historia," in *Seva: Historia de la primera invasión norteamericana de Puerto Rico ocurrida en mayo de 1898,* by Luis López Nieves (Río Piedras: Editorial Cordillera, 1987), 57–87, 72. Original Spanish: "Los lectores de *Claridad* probablemente estén entre los más sofisticados y más críticos de la isla; catedráticos y estudiantes, universitarios, cuadros de la izquierda, abogados, dirigentes obreros, profesionales."

23. *Claridad,* December 16–22, 1983.

24. Zizek, *The Sublime Object of Ideology,* 32–33.

25. Quoted in the opening pages of López Nieves, *Seva,* unpaginated. "*Seva* es la verdad de lo que somos; la verdadera historia del heroísmo puertorriqueño."

26. Ramos, "Crónica: Un sueño que hizo historia," 64.

27. Sigmund Freud, "Creative Writers and Day-Dreaming," in *The Freud Reader,* ed. Peter Gay (New York: Norton, 1989), 436–43, 440.

28. Quoted in Ramos, "Crónica: Un sueño que hizo historia," 84. Original Spanish: "Ahora sabemos que no somos dóciles e impotentes."

29. Ibid., 83. Original Spanish: "Llevaba varias semanas sumido en el estudio de 'la deslumbrante y maravillosa épica española' cuando de golpe comprendió cuál era la causa de la nostalgia: echaba de menos una epopeya puertorriqueña. Esta tristeza ya no lo abandonó y tal vez para deshacerse de ella, a los pocos meses tomó una seria determinación: ya que no existía (o conocía) una gloriosa y potente epopeya que 'me emocionara y llenara de orgullo, sólo quedaba una cosa por hacer: inventarla.'"

30. Angel Rivero, *Crónica de la guerra hispanoamericana en Puerto Rico* (New York: Plus Ultra, 1973), 229. Original Spanish: "hasta se dijo que una sección de *macheteros,* cargando al arma blanca contra los americanos los habían obligado a reembarcarse con grandes pérdidas. Un ayudante de campo del general Macías, al pedirle noticias, me dijo en secreto: 'Los hicimos reembarcar a bayonetazo limpio.'"

31. López Nieves, *Seva,* 30. Original Spanish: "Debo admitir que opusieron una resistencia feroz, organizada, heroica, digna de nuestra guerra de independencia contra los británicos y a la altura de un Cid o Wellington."

32. Ibid., 24.

33. Cathy Caruth, introduction to *Trauma: Explorations in Memory,* 3–11, 8.

34. Ramos, "Crónica: Un sueño que hizo historia," 83.

35. Deleuze and Guattari, *Kafka: Toward a Minor Literature,* 6.

36. López Nieves, *Seva,* 30, 33. Original Spanish: "Tomamos acción rápida pero el exterminio no fue fácil, a pesar de que éramos casi 4,000 contra 721. . . . Hemos tomado 650 durante el combate; habíamos apresado a los restantes 71 (40 mujeres, 8 hombres, 23 niños). Pero ya que es necesario borrar toda huella, al otro día ordené que los fusilaron a todos. Terminamos de quemar y demoler lo poco que quedaba del pueblo."

37. Ibid., 34. Original Spanish: "antes de la ejecución, uno de esos negritos ('niggers') se escapó."

38. Quoted in Jim Zwick, ed., *Anti-Imperialism in the United States, 1898–1935,* www.boondocksnet.com/ai/index.html (January 20, 1996).

39. Ibid.

40. Karen Hanson, "Reasons for Shame, Shame against Reason," in *The Widening Scope of Shame,* ed. Melvin R. Lansky and Andrew P. Morrison (Hillsdale, NJ: Analytic Press, 1997), 155–79, 174.

41. Myrna García Calderón, "*Seva* o la reinvención de la identidad nacional puertorriqueña," *Revista de Crítica Literaria Latinoamericana* 20, no. 39 (1994): 199–215, 201.

42. José de Olivares, *Our Islands and Their People as Seen with Camera and Pencil* (New York: N. P. Thompson, 1899).

43. Roland Barthes, *Mythologies* (New York: Hill and Wang, 1972), 143.

44. Ibid., 143.

45. Ramos, "Crónica: Un sueño que hizo historia," 63. Original Spanish: "En los sectores intelectuales, artísticos, independentistas y académicos del país no hubo otro tema durante esta semana."

46. Susan Sontag, *On Photography* (New York: Farrar, Straus and Giroux, 1984), 23.

47. López Nieves, *Seva,* 53. Original Spanish: "Don Ignacio Martínez, aún temiendo represalias de parte de las fuerzas invasoras norteamericanas, nos ha pedido que no publiquemos su foto. Sin embargo, hemos dejado este espacio en blanco, en espera del día en que sea posible mostrar el rostro del único sobreviviente de la MASACRE de SEVA."

48. Guillermo Baralt, *Esclavos rebeldes* (Río Piedras: Ediciones Huracán, 1982), 168. Original Spanish: "Los Beauchamp llevaron sus esclavos hasta Lares y estos saquearon las tiendas de españoles en el trayecto. Este fue uno de los episodios más violentos del levantamiento de Lares."

49. Barthes, *Mythologies*, 125.

50. Rubén Arrieta, "El desembarco," *El Nuevo Día/Revista Domingo*, July 19, 1998, 15.

51. Quoted in Martín Sagrera, *Racismo y política en Puerto Rico* (Río Piedras: Editorial Edil, 1973), 48–49.

52. Marco Rosado Conde, "¿Seva: Historia, engaño o concreción de un sueño?" in López Nieves, *Seva*, 109–12, 110. Original Spanish: "Por mi parte pienso que quienes han sido capaces de conmoverse ante la imagen de *Seva*—que no es sino la condensación dramática de nuestra lucha casi centenaria-demuestran que son legatarios de Aguila Blanca (¿el hombre o el mito?), de Hostos, de Betances, el artesano, el obrero, o el campesino que tuvieron que tragarse en silencio la ignominia de la invasión."

53. Juan Manuel Delgado, "Aguila Blanca y la ética de investigar," *Claridad*, July 3–15, 1993, unpaginated. Original Spanish: "'Aguila Blanca' no tiene reconocimiento público más allá del círculo de independentistas, la minoría del mundo académico y una docena de ancianos que aún lo recuerdan."

54. Luis Penchi, "Aseguran que Ponce luchó contra los invasores," *El Nuevo Día*, August 1, 1998, 43.

55. José Maldonado, "Personal," *El Correo de Puerto Rico*, December 26, 1898, 3.

56. Olivares, *Our Islands and Their People*, 361.

57. Lanny Thompson, *Nuestra isla y su gente: La construcción del "otro" puertorriqueño en* Our Islands and Their People (Río Piedras: Centro de Investigaciones Sociales y Departamento de Historia, 1995), 12.

58. Anderson, *Imagined Communities*, 14.

59. Vicente Rafael, "The Undead: Photography in the Philippines under United States Rule, 1898–1920s" (paper presented at Princeton University, March 27–29, 1998), 4–5.

60. Barthes, *Mythologies*, 133.

61. Tomás Blanco, *Prontuario histórico de Puerto Rico* (Río Piedras: Ediciones Huracán, 1981), 150. Original Spanish: "El dilema es, pues: o tomar en nuestras manos, con serenidad y firmeza, nuestro destino, o someternos, como retrasados mentales, a una lenta agonía, prolongada por paliativos y aparatos ortopédicos, hasta llegar al límite de la miseria física y la postración moral, hasta la total y completa transformación del pueblo isleño en peonaje de parias, en hato de coolíes. Entonces sólo se salvarían los muertos."

62. Gay, *The Freud Reader,* 594–626, 598.

63. Edgardo Sanabria Santaliz, "1898," in *El día que el hombre pisó la luna* (Río Piedras: Editorial Antillana, 1984).

64. For an overview of Sanabria Santaliz's works, see Frances Negrón-Muntaner, "Edgardo Sanabria Santaliz," in *Latin American Writers on Gay and Lesbian Themes,* ed. David William Foster (Westport: Greenwood, 1994), 396–400.

65. Sanabria Santaliz, "1898," 75.

66. Carl D. Schneider, *Shame, Exposure, and Privacy* (Boston: Beacon, 1977), 35.

67. Sanabria Santaliz, "1898," 83.

68. Ibid., "1898," 76. Original Spanish: "No le inspiraba confianza el remedio del tatuajista, quedaría la cicatriz, pero a quien más, a dónde iba a poder recurrir sin que se sintiera *más humillado* de lo que ya estaba."

69. Ibid., 83.

70. Ibid., 81–82. Original Spanish: "la picuda cabeza de un águila—debe de tener abiertas las alas bajo la camisa, piensas—. El hombre percibe tu fascinación. (¿Te gustan?)"

71. Ibid., 73. Original Spanish: "desajustado maniquí tendido en una mesa."

72. Ibid., 76. Original Spanish: "como si su imagen [Bebe] fuera un alfiler acercado con deleite."

73. Ibid., 77. Original Spanish: "desvístete, mandaron los labios."

74. Ibid., 74. Original Spanish: "el cosquilleo ingobernable y casi perverso que le recorría aun en el más recio de la golpiza de resquemor y disgusto que estaba recibiendo."

75. Ibid., 74. Original Spanish: "la mirada baja retemblándole gelatinosa en su rostro color subido."

76. Tomkins, *Shame and Its Sisters,* 137.

77. Sanabria Santaliz, "1898," 73.

78. Ibid., 76. Original Spanish: "una aplacadora sensación de limpieza y de alivio de una insorportable carga."

79. Edgardo Rodríguez Juliá, *Puertorriqueños* (Madrid: Plaza Mayor, 1992).

Notes to Chapter 3

1. For a review of the campaign, see Frances Negrón-Muntaner, *"West Side Story Strikes Again,"* www.soloella.com/topic/et/article.jhtml?article_id=10844&ac_id= 12853.

2. Mal Vincent, "Lopez Is Bursting into Hollywood Spotlight," *Virginian-Pilot,* March 22, 1997, E8.

3. Andrew Essex, "Not So Little Ricky," *Entertainment Weekly,* April 23, 1999, 31–35, 35.

4. Blanca Vázquez, "Puerto Ricans and the Media: A Personal Statement," *Centro* 3, no. 1 (winter 1990–1991): 5–15, 5.

5. Alberto Sandoval, *"West Side Story*: A Puerto Rican Reading of 'America,'" *Jump Cut* 39 (1994): 59–66.

6. Quoted in ibid., 65.

7. Quoted in Al Kasha and Joel Hirschorn, *Notes on Broadway: Conversations with the Great Songwriters* (Chicago: Contemporary, 1985), 15.

8. Joan Peyser, *Bernstein: A Biography* (New York: Beech Tree, 1987), 264–65.

9. *Variety Film Reviews, 1959–1963* (New York: Garland, 1983), September 27, 1961, unpaginated.

10. Stanley Kaufman, "The Asphalt Romeo and Juliet," *New Republic,* October 23, 1961, 28.

11. Francisco A. Scarano, "The *jíbaro* Masquerade and the Subaltern Politics of Creole Identity Formation in Puerto Rico, 1745–1823," *American Historical Review,* December 1996, 1398–1431, 1424.

12. Ella Shohat and Robert Stam, *Unthinking Eurocentrism* (New York: Routledge, 1994), 103.

13. Scarano, "The *Jíbaro* Masquerade," 1424.

14. Kelvin Santiago-Valles, *"Subject People" and Colonial Discourses: Economic Transformation and Social Disorder in Puerto Rico, 1898–1947* (Albany: State University of New York Press, 1994), 209.

15. Sandoval, *"West Side Story*: A Puerto Rican Reading of 'America,'" 60.

16. Meryle Secrest, *Leonard Bernstein: A Life* (New York: Knopf, 1994), 212.

17. Anne Nichols, *Abie's Irish Rose* (New York: Samuel French, 1927).

18. Peyser, *Bernstein: A Biography,* 257.

19. Leonard Bernstein, *Findings* (New York: Doubleday, 1993), 148. My emphasis.

20. Kasha and Hirschorn, *Notes on Broadway: Conversations with the Great Songwriters,* 15.

21. Toni Morrison, *Playing in the Dark: Whiteness and the Literary Imagination* (New York: Vintage, 1993), 17.

22. Michael Rogin, *Blackface, White Noise: Jewish Immigrants in the Hollywood Melting Pot* (Berkeley: University of California Press, 1996), 28.

23. Mason Wiley and Damien Bona, *Inside Oscar* (New York: Ballantine Books, 1987), 333.

24. George Hadley-García, *Hispanic Hollywood* (New York: Citadel Press, 1990), 174.

25. Esmeralda Santiago, *When I Was Puerto Rican* (New York: Vintage, 1994), 230.

26. Stuart Hall, "What Is This 'Black' in Black Popular Culture?" in *Representing Blackness: Issues in Film and Video,* ed. Valerie Smith (New Brunswick: Rutgers University Press, 1997), 1–11.

27. Nan Robertson, "Maria and Anita in *West Side Story,*" *New York Times,* February 22, 1980, C-4.

28. These include Daniel Torres, *Morirás si da una primavera* (Miami: Iberian Studies Institute, 1993), and Sandoval, "*West Side Story*: A Puerto Rican Reading of 'America.'"

29. Torres, *Morirás si da una primavera,* 26–27.

30. Richard Meyer, "Warhol's Clones," *Yale Journal of Criticism* 7, no. 1 (spring 1994): 79–109.

31. David Van Leer, "Visible Silence: Spectatorship in Black Gay and Lesbian Film," in Smith, *Representing Blackness: Issues in Film and Video,* 157–82, 178.

32. Greg Lawrence, *Dance with Demons: The Life of Jerome Robbins* (New York: Putnam's, 2001), xiv.

33. Ibid., 87.

34. Secrest, *Leonard Bernstein: A Life,* 179.

35. Ibid., 320.

36. Ibid., 319.

37. Peyser, *Bernstein: A Biography,* 190–91.

38. Shohat and Stam, *Unthinking Eurocentrism,* 223.

39. Richard Dyer, "Entertainment and Utopia," in *Movies and Methods,* ed. Bill Nichols (Berkeley: University of California Press, 1985), 220–32, 222.

40. George Chauncey, "Gay New York" (paper presented at the "Sin Vergüenza: Latino Sexualities" conference, University of Michigan, April 16, 2000).

41. David Bourdon, *Warhol* (New York: Abradale Press, 1989), 200.

42. Susan Suntree, *Rita Moreno: Hispanics of Achievement* (New York: Chelsea House, 1993), 41.

43. "Rita Moreno Herstory," www.cannylink.com/ritamoreno.htm.

44. Quoted in Luis Reyes and Peter Rubie, *Hispanics in Hollywood* (New York: Garland, 1994), xviii.

45. Suntree, *Rita Moreno: Hispanics of Achievement,* 37.

46. Quoted in Jane Ellen Wayne, *Lana: The Life and Loves of Lana Turner* (New York: St. Martin's, 1995), 166–67.

47. Quoted in ibid., 166.

48. Suntree, *Rita Moreno: Hispanics of Achievement,* 30.

49. Quoted in Ally Hacker, *Reel Women: Pioneers of the Cinema, 1896 to the Present* (New York: Continuum, 1991), 114.

50. Ibid., 114.

51. Quoted in Hadley-Garcia, *Hispanic Hollywood,* 16.

52. "Rita Moreno Herstory."

53. "Rita Moreno: An Actress's Catalog of Sex and Innocence," *Life,* March 1, 1954, 65–68, 65.

54. Ibid., 68.

55. Ibid.

56. Ibid., 65.

57. Sandoval, "*West Side Story:* A Puerto Rican Reading of 'America,'" 64.

58. Suntree, *Rita Moreno: Hispanics of Achievement,* 81.

59. Ibid.

60. Mikhail Bakhtin, *Rabelais and His World* (Bloomington: Indiana University Press, 1984), 376.

61. José Esteban Muñoz, *Disidentifications: Queers of Color and the Performance of Color* (Minneapolis: University of Minnesota Press, 1999), 193–94.

Notes to Chapter 4

1. Arnaldo Cruz Malavé, "'What a Tangled Web!': Masculinidad, abyección y la fundación de la literatura puertorriqueña en los Estados Unidos," *Revista de Crítica Literaria*, no. 45 (1997): 327–440, 332. Original Spanish: "son daddies, o son *stuff*, en una cadena jerárquica, unilateral de abyección."

2. Holly Woodlawn and Jeff Copeland, *A Low Life in High Heels* (New York: Harper, 1991), 43.

3. Ibid., 210.

4. Ibid., 42–43.

5. Holly Woodlawn, interview by author, February 7, 2003.

6. Woodlawn and Copeland, *A Low Life in High Heels,* 74.

7. Ibid., 218.

8. Ella Shohat and Robert Stam, *Unthinking Eurocentrism* (New York: Routledge, 1994), 302.

9. Carl D. Schneider, *Shame, Exposure, and Privacy* (Boston: Beacon, 1977), 26.

10. Jean Baudrillard, *Seduction* (New York: St. Martin's, 1990), 96.

11. Woodlawn and Copeland, *A Low Life in High Heels,* 31.

12. Ibid., 31–32.

13. Ibid., 112.

14. Woodlawn, interview.

15. Woodlawn and Copeland, *A Low Life in High Heels,* 73.

16. Ibid., 6–7.

17. Woodlawn, interview.

18. Lou Reed, quoted in Woodlawn and Copeland, *A Low Life in High Heels,* xiii.

19. Ibid., 16.

20. Ibid., 3–4.

21. Judith Butler, *Bodies That Matter* (New York: Routledge, 1993), 133.

22. Guy Flatley, "He Enjoys Being a Girl," *New York Times,* November 15, 1970, 15.

23. Woodlawn and Copeland, *A Low Life in High Heels,* 111.

24. Woodlawn, interview.

25. Ibid.

26. Butler, *Bodies That Matter,* 125.

27. Woodlawn and Copeland, *A Low Life in High Heels,* 212.

28. Woodlawn, interview.

29. Woodlawn and Copeland, *A Low Life in High Heels,* 11.

30. Paul Morrissey, preface to Woodlawn and Copeland, *A Low Life in High Heels,* ix.

31. Kelvin Santiago-Valles, *"Subject People" and Colonial Discourses: Economic Transformation and Social Disorder in Puerto Rico, 1898–1947* (Albany: State University of New York Press, 1994), 201.

32. Ultra Violet, *Famous for Fifteen Minutes* (San Diego: Harcourt Brace Jovanovich, 1988), 17.

33. David Bourdon, *Warhol* (New York: Abradale Press, 1989), 271.

34. Woodlawn, interview.

35. Woodlawn and Copeland, *A Low Life in High Heels,* 163.

36. Andy Warhol, *THE Philosophy of Andy Warhol* (San Diego: Harcourt, Brace, 1975), 92.

37. Ibid., 54.

38. Jon Gartenberg, "The Films of Andy Warhol: Preservation and Documentation," in *The Films of Andy Warhol* (New York: Whitney Museum of American Art, 1988), 12–18, 19.

39. Patrick Smith, *Andy Warhol's Art and Films* (Ann Arbor: UMI Research Press, 1986), 175.

40. Bourdon, *Warhol,* 249.

41. Smith, *Andy Warhol's Art and Films,* 529.

42. Andy Warhol, *The Andy Warhol Diaries,* ed. Pat Hackett (New York: Warner Books, 1989), xiv.

43. Ultra Violet, *Famous for Fifteen Minutes,* 235.

44. Andy Warhol and Pat Hackett, *POPism: The Warhol '60s* (New York: Harcourt Brace Jovanovich, 1980), 297.

45. Bourdon, *Warhol,* 13.

46. Warhol and Hackett, *POPism: The Warhol '60s,* 153.

47. Woodlawn and Copeland, *A Low Life in High Heels,* 163.

48. Warhol, *THE Philosophy of Andy Warhol,* 55.

49. Ultra Violet, *Famous for Fifteen Minutes,* 28.

50. Ibid., 134.

51. Woodlawn and Copeland, *A Low Life in High Heels,* 6.

52. Smith, *Andy Warhol's Art and Films,* 245.

53. Ultra Violet, *Famous for Fifteen Minutes,* 134.

54. Smith, *Andy Warhol's Art and Films,* 525.

55. Paul Morrissey, quoted in *Images in the Dark,* ed. Raymond Murray (Philadelphia: TLA, 1994), 114.

56. Flatley, "He Enjoys Being a Girl."

57. Woodlawn and Copeland, *A Low Life in High Heels,* 144.

58. Ibid., 25.

59. María Milagros López, "Post Work Selves and Entitlement Attitudes in Peripheral Post-Industrial Puerto Rico" (unpublished manuscript, 1993), 1–65, 23.

60. Schneider, *Shame, Exposure, and Privacy,* 20.

61. Woodlawn, interview.

62. Woodlawn and Copeland, *A Low Life in High Heels,* xi.

63. Rick Roemer, *Charles Ludlam and the Ridiculous Theatrical Company* (Jefferson, NC: McFarland, 1998), 54.

64. Woodlawn and Copeland, *A Low Life in High Heels,* 253.

65. Flatley, "He Enjoys Being a Girl."

66. Woodlawn and Copeland, *A Low Life in High Heels,* 145.

67. Ibid., 24.

68. Ibid., 10,12.

69. Woodlawn, interview.

70. Smith, *Andy Warhol's Art and Films,* 246.

71. Woodlawn and Copeland, *A Low Life in High Heels,* 268.

72. Peter Schieldahl, "Trash," *The New York Times Film Reviews* (1969–1970) (New York: New York Times and Arno Press, 1971), 232.

73. Ela Troyano, filmmaker, private conversation, 2001.

74. Charles Ludlam, "Mr. T. or El Pato in the Gilded Summer Palace of Carina-Tatlina," in *Ridiculous Theater: Scourge of Human Folly: The Essays and Opinions of Charles Ludlam,* ed. Steven Samuels (New York: Theater Communications Group, 1992), 150.

75. George Chauncey, "Work-in-Progress" (oral presentation, "Sin Verguenza/ Latino Sexualities," University of Michigan, April 15, 2000).

76. Ludlam, "Mr. T. or El Pato in the Gilded Summer Palace of Carina-Tatlina," 149.

77. Ibid., 150.

78. Bourdon, *Warhol,* 196.

79. Warhol and Hackett, *POPism: The Warhol '60s,* 267.

80. Ludlam, *Ridiculous Theater,* 153.

81. Warhol and Hackett, *POPism: The Warhol '60s,* 91.

82. Roemer, *Charles Ludlam and the Ridiculous Theatrical Company,* 59.

83. Woodlawn, interview.

84. Woodlawn, interview.

85. Woodlawn, interview.

86. Bourdon, *Warhol,* 198.

87. Jack Babuscio, quoted in Roemer, *Charles Ludlam and the Ridiculous Theatrical Company,* 57.

88. Woodlawn, interview.

89. Roemer, *Charles Ludlam and the Ridiculous Theatrical Company,* 57.

90. Flatley, "He Enjoys Being a Girl."

91. Tom Garretson, "I Survived Warhol," www.idotvads.com/hw/interviews.html.

92. Ludlam, *Ridiculous Theater,* 17.

93. Bourdon, *Warhol,* 350.

94. Warhol, *THE Philosophy of Andy Warhol,* 93.

95. Ludlam, *Ridiculous Theater,* 31.

96. Ibid., 22.

97. Warhol and Hackett, *POPism: The Warhol '60s,* 195.

98. Woodlawn and Copeland, *A Low Life in High Heels,* 2.

99. Quoted in Roemer, *Charles Ludlam and the Ridiculous Theatrical Company,* 68.

100. Flatley, "He Enjoys Being a Girl."

101. Anna Indych, "Nuyorican Baroque: Pepón Osorio's Chucherias," Art Journal, *Puerto Rico Herald,* April 1, 2001, www.puertorico-herald.org/issues/2001/vol5n18/Nuyorican-en.shtml, 3.

102. Pedro Pietri, *Puerto Rican Obituary* (New York: Monthly Review Press, 1973).

103. María E. Pérez y González, *Puerto Ricans in the United States* (Westport: Greenwood, 2000), 50.

104. Warhol, *The Andy Warhol Diaries,* 241.

105. Ibid., 320.

106. Ibid., 311.

107. Ludlam, *Ridiculous Theater,* 255.

108. Susan Sontag, *On Photography* (New York: Farrar, Straus and Giroux, 1984), 49.

109. Juan A. Suárez, *Bike Boys, Drag Queens, and Superstars* (Bloomington: Indiana University Press, 1996).

Notes to Chapter 5

1. Quoted in John Gruen, *Keith Haring: The Authorized Biography* (New York: Fireside, 1991), 86.

2. Greg Tate, "Nobody Loves a Genius Child: Jean Michel Basquiat, Flyboy in the Buttermilk," in *Flyboy in the Buttermilk* (New York: Fireside, Simon and Schuster, 1992): 231–44, 233.

3. Louis Armand, "Jean-Michel Basquiat: Identity and the Art of Dis(empowerment)," www.geocities.com/louis_armand/basquiat.html.

4. Robert Farris Thompson, "Royalty, Heroism, and the Streets," in *Jean-Michel Basquiat,* ed. Richard D. Marshall (New York: Whitney Museum of American Art, 1997), 28–42, 30.

5. There are, of course, notable exceptions, such as the work of Alberto Sandoval Sánchez, José Quiroga, and Arlene Dávila.

6. Rene Ricard, "The Radiant Child," *Artforum,* December 20, 1981, 35–45, 38.

7. Robert Knafo, "The Basquiat File," www.spikemagazine.com/0397basq.htm; Armand, "Jean-Michel Basquiat."

8. Tate, "Nobody Loves a Genius Child," 234.

9. Patricia Bosworth, "Hyped to Death," *New York Times Book Review,* August 9, 1998, 4.

10. Karl Marx, *Grundrisse: The Foundations of Political Economy* (New York: Vintage, 1973).

11. John Seed, "Recollections of JMB," www.johnseed.com/basquiat.html.

12. George Condo, quoted in Gruen, *Keith Haring: The Authorized Biography,* 126.

13. Keith Haring, *Journals* (New York: Penguin Books, 1996), 64–65.

14. George Lipsitz, "'We Know What Time It Is': Youth Culture in the 90's," *Centro,* summer 1993, 10–21, 17.

15. Phoebe Hoban, *Basquiat* (New York: Penguin Books, 1998), 56.

16. María Milagros López, "Post Work Selves and Entitlement Attitudes in Peripheral Post-Industrial Puerto Rico" (unpublished manuscript, 1993), 1–65, 48.

17. Gruen, *Keith Haring: The Authorized Biography,* 53.

18. Jean-Michel Basquiat, "Interview with Henry Geldhazhler," in *Basquiat* (Milan: Charta, 1999), LVII–LIX, LIX. Hereafter cited as *Basquiat* (Charta).

19. Quoted in Hoban, *Basquiat,* 83.

20. Andy Warhol, *The Andy Warhol Diaries,* ed. Pat Hackett (New York: Warner Books, 1989), 611.

21. Quoted in Cathleen McGuigan, "New Art, New Money," *New York Times Magazine,* February 10, 1985, 32.

22. Jean-Michel Basquiat, "Interview with Isabelle Graw," in *Basquiat* (Charta), LXVII.

23. Quoted in Hoban, *Basquiat,* 115.

24. Jennifer Clement, *Widow Basquiat* (Edinburgh: Payback Press, 2001), 80.

25. Hoban, *Basquiat,* 140.

26. Bosworth, "Hyped to Death."

27. Hoban, *Basquiat,* 131.

28. López, "Post-Work Selves and Entitlement 'Attitudes,'" 38.

29. Clement, *Widow Basquiat,* 32.

30. Hoban, *Basquiat,* 268.

31. Carl D. Schneider, *Shame, Exposure, and Privacy* (Boston: Beacon, 1977), 10.

32. Warhol, *The Andy Warhol Diaries,* 527.

33. Seed, "Recollections of JMB."

34. Clement, *Widow Basquiat,* 108.

35. Ibid., 44.

36. Warhol, *The Andy Warhol Diaries,* 605.

37. Keith Haring, "Painting the Mind," in *Basquiat* (Charta), XLVI–XLVII, XLVI.

38. Jean-Michel Basquiat, "Interview with Demosthenes Davvetas," in *Basquiat* (Charta), LXIII.

39. Hoban, *Basquiat,* 300.

40. *Basquiat* (Charta), 136.

41. Warhol, *The Andy Warhol Diaries,* 519.

42. Ricard, "The Radiant Child," 38.

43. Hoban, *Basquiat,* 59.

44. Warhol, *The Andy Warhol Diaries,* 594.

45. Hoban, *Basquiat,* 49.

46. Quoted in ibid., 95.

47. Clement, *Widow Basquiat,* 84.

48. Warhol, *The Andy Warhol Diaries,* 541.

49. Clement, *Widow Basquiat,* 49.

50. Frantz Fanon, *Black Skin, White Masks* (New York: Grove Weidenfeld, 1967), 170.

51. Ricard, "The Radiant Child," 40.

52. Ibid., 38.

53. Warhol, *The Andy Warhol Diaries,* 627.

54. Elisabeth Sussman, ed., *Keith Haring* (New York: Whitney Museum of American Art, 1997), 14.

55. Quoted in Gruen, *Keith Haring: The Authorized Biography,* 65.

56. Ibid., 70.

57. Clement, *Widow Basquiat,* 38.

58. Gruen, *Keith Haring: The Authorized Biography,* 84.

59. Clement, *Widow Basquiat,* 132.

60. Warhol, *The Andy Warhol Diaries,* 533.

61. Gruen, *Keith Haring: The Authorized Biography,* 88.

62. Quoted in ibid., 63.

63. "A Conversation with Fred Brathwaite, Fred Schneider, Jellybean Benitez, and Junior Vasquez," in Sussman, *Keith Haring,* 152–62, 156.

64. Robert Farris Thompson, introduction to Haring, *Journals,* xxxi.

65. Clement, *Widow Basquiat,* 136.

66. Quoted in Gruen, *Keith Haring: The Authorized Biography,* 96.

67. Hoban, *Basquiat,* 168.

68. Ibid., 265.

69. Quoted in ibid., 41.

70. Ibid., 34.

71. Gruen, *Keith Haring: The Authorized Biography,* 125.

72. David Frankel, "Keith Haring's American Beauty," in Sussman, *Keith Haring,* 58–62, 61.

73. Quoted in Gruen, *Keith Haring: The Authorized Biography,* 81.

74. Quoted in ibid., 95.

75. Ibid., 91.

76. Quoted in ibid., 115.

77. Haring, *Journals,* 189.

78. Blanca Vázquez, Juan Flores, Pablo Figueroa, Interview, "KMX Assault: The Puerto Rican Roots of Rap," *Centro* 5, no. 1 (1993): 38–51, 41.

79. Doze Green, "Interview," in *Urban Scribes* (San José: MACLA, 1999), 3–4, 3.

80. Richard D. Marshall, "Repelling Ghosts," in Marshall, *Jean-Michel Basquiat,* 15–27, 16.

81. Raquel Z. Rivera, "Boricuas from the Hip Hop Zone: Notes on Race and Ethnic Relations in New York City," *Centro* 8, nos. 1–2 (spring 1996): 203–17, 206.

82. Hoban, *Basquiat,* 279.

83. Thomas McEvilley, "Royal Slumming," *Artforum International,* November 1992, 93–97, 96.

84. Armand, "Jean-Michel Basquiat."

85. Tate, "Nobody Loves a Genius Child," 240.

86. bell hooks, "Altars of Sacrifice: Re-membering Basquiat," *Art in America,* June 1993, 68–74, 74.

87. Thompson, "Royalty, Heroism, and the Streets," 30.

88. Ibid.

89. Quoted in Hoban, *Basquiat,* 17.

90. *Basquiat* (Charta), 24.

91. Quoted in Hoban, *Basquiat,* 243.

92. Luca Marenzi, "Pay for Soup/Build a Fort/Set That on Fire," in *Basquiat* (Charta), XXXI–XLIII, XXXVI.

93. Marshall, "Repelling Ghosts," 16.

94. Ella Shohat and Robert Stam, *Unthinking Eurocentrism* (New York: Routledge, 1994), 306.

95. Clement, *Widow Basquiat,* 155.

96. Bruno Bischofberger, "Collaborations: Reflections on and Experiences with Basquiat, Clemente and Warhol," in *Basquiat* (Charta), 149–153, 150.

97. Schneider, *Shame, Exposure, and Privacy,* 7.

98. *Basquiat* (Charta), 186.

99. Fanon, *Black Skin, White Masks,* 154.

100. Jonathan Flatley, "Warhol Gives Good Face: Publicity and the Politics of Prosopopoeia," in *Pop Out: Queering Warhol,* ed. Jennifer Doyle, Jonathan Flatley, and José Muñoz (Durham: Duke University Press, 1996), 101–30, 106.

101. Dick Hebdige, "Welcome to the Terrordome: Jean-Michel Basquiat and the 'Dark' Side of Hybridity," in Marshall, *Jean-Michel Basquiat,* 60–70, 61.

102. Quoted in Hoban, *Basquiat,* 312.

103. Richard Polsky, "Jean-Michel Basquiat," www.auctionwatch.com/awdaily /collctors/bsh/basquiat/.

Notes to Chapter 6

1. Barbara O'Dair, introduction to *Madonna: The Rolling Stone Files* (New York: Hyperion, 1997), 1–22.

2. Ibid.

3. Camille Paglia, "Madonna II: Venus of the Radio Waves," in *Sex, Art, and American Culture* (New York: Vintage, 1992), 6–13, 6.

4. J. Randy Taraborrelli, *Madonna: An Intimate Biography* (New York: Simon and Schuster, 2001), 74.

5. Dora Pizzi Campos, "Su primer romance fue con un puertorriqueño," *Vea* 25, no. 1266 (November 14, 1993): 8–12, 12.

6. Taraborrelli, *Madonna: An Intimate Biography,* xiii.

7. Quoted in ibid., 32.

8. Sheryl Garratt, "¿Quién es la verdadera Madonna?" *El Nuevo Día,* November 13, 1994, 10. Original Spanish: "Yo tengo carne. Me puedes agarrar por donde quieras y encuentras carne, así es que eso es absurdo."

9. Madonna, "Madonna's Private Diaries," *Vanity Fair,* November 1996, 174–88, 223–32, 224.

10. Mikhail Bakhtin, *Rabelais and His World* (Bloomington: Indiana University Press, 1984), 317.

11. Laurie Schulze, Anne Barton White, and Jane D. Brown, "'A Sacred Monster in Her Prime': Audience Construction of Madonna as Low-Other," in *The Madonna Connection,* ed. Cathy Schwichtenberg (Boulder: Westview, 1993), 15–37, 27.

12. Bakhtin, *Rabelais and His World,* 303.

13. O'Dair, introduction to *Madonna: The Rolling Stone Files,* 4–5.

14. Schulze, White, and Brown, "'A Sacred Monster in Her Prime': Audience Construction of Madonna as Low-Other," 16.

15. Madonna, *Sex* (New York: Warner, 1992), 75.

16. Ibid., 5.

17. bell hooks, "Power to the Pussy: We Don't Wanna Be Dicks in Drag," in *Madonnarama,* ed. Lisa Frank and Paul Smith (Pittsburgh: Cleis Press, 1993), 65–80, 73.

18. Bill Zehme, "Madonna: The *Rolling Stone* Interview," in *Madonna: The Rolling Stone Files,* 99–114, 112.

19. Quoted in Taraborrelli, *Madonna: An Intimate Biography,* 7.

20. John Simon, "Immaterial Girl," in *Desperately Seeking Madonna,* ed. Adam Sexton (New York: Delta, 1993), 240–42, 241.

21. Madonna, *Sex,* 41.

22. Pat Califia, "Sex and Madonna, or, What Did You Expect of a Girl That Doesn't Put Out on the First Five Dates?" in Frank and Smith, *Madonnarama,* 169–84, 174.

23. Madonna, *Sex,* 6.

24. Carrie Fisher, "True Confessions: The *Rolling Stone* Interview with Madonna, Part One," in *Madonna: The Rolling Stone Files,* 170–85, 175.

25. Jeffrey Ressner, "The Madonna Machine," in *Madonna: The Rolling Stone Files,* 213–16, 216.

26. Quoted in Taraborrelli, *Madonna: An Intimate Biography,* 66.

27. Quoted in Evelyn McDonnell, "What Does Madonna Mean?" *Miami Herald,* August 12, 2001, 1M, 6M.

28. Quoted in Taraborrelli, *Madonna: An Intimate Biography,* 66.

29. Zehme, "Madonna: The *Rolling Stone* Interview," 106.

30. Taraborrelli, *Madonna: An Intimate Biography,* 67.

31. Frantz Fanon, *Black Skin, White Masks* (New York: Grove Weidenfeld, 1967), 14.

32. Fernando González, "Crossing Borders," *Miami Herald,* November 16, 1997, 1L–8L.

33. Madonna, *Sex,* 120.

34. Taraborrelli, *Madonna: An Intimate Biography,* 9.

35. *Cristina* 7, no. 8 (1997). Original Spanish: "Hasta para los nombres de sus mascotas, Madonna demuestra su fiebre latina: se llama [su perro] Chiquita."

36. Quoted in John Gruen, *Keith Haring: The Authorized Biography* (New York: Fireside, 1991), 92.

37. Doris Sommer, *Foundational Fictions: The National Romances of Latin America* (Berkeley: University of California Press, 1991).

38. Camille Paglia, "Animality and Artifice," in *Sex, Art, and American Culture*, 3–5, 4.

39. Juan A. Suárez, *Bike Boys, Drag Queens, and Superstars* (Bloomington: Indiana University Press, 1996), 131–32.

40. Toni Morrison, *Playing in the Dark: Whiteness and the Literary Imagination* (New York: Vintage, 1993), 17.

41. Eunice Castro, "Madonna, Chapter IV," *El Nuevo Herald*, September 4, 1997, 4C.

42. Quoted in Taraborrelli, *Madonna: An Intimate Biography*, 27.

43. Stated in "Girlie Show" concert, Sydney, Australia, 1993, as prelude to "In This Life" number.

44. bell hooks, "Is Paris Burning?" in *Black Looks: Race and Representation* (Boston: South End Press, 1992), 145–56, 155.

45. Jaime Baily, *La noche es virgen* (Barcelona: Anagrama, 1997), 34. Original Spanish: "mi adorada madonna, que sale al escenario con unas ganas increíbles de decirle al mundo yo soy así, una puta con mucha clase, una puta-riquísima-millonaria-cabrona-que cacharon-quien-chicha-le-da-la-gana, y que además tiene una debilidad por los maricones guapísimos, y yo también madonna, y por eso me caes divinamente, porque, como tú dices, eres un cuerpo de mujer con alma de hombre gay. te adoro, madonna, mandona, mamona, y no dejes que todos los gansos que te critican te bajen la moral."

46. Thomas K. Nakayama and Lisa N. Peñaloza, "Madonna T/Races: Music Videos through the Prism of Color," in Schwichtenberg, *The Madonna Connection*, 39–55, 47.

47. Quoted in Howard Cohen and Sam Eifling, "Madonna 'World' Tour a Hot Ticket, Show of Excess in South Florida," *Miami Herald*, August 15, 2001, 1–2A.

48. Quoted in Lisa Henderson, "Justify Our Love: Madonna and the Politics of Queer Sex," in Schwichtenberg, *The Madonna Connection*, 107–28, 122.

49. Taraborrelli, *Madonna: An Intimate Biography*, 69.

50. Madonna, "Madonna's Private Diaries," 180.

51. Pizzi Campos, "Su primer romance fue con un puertorriqueño," 9.

52. Ibid., 12.

53. Quoted in Ilene Rosenzweig, *I Hate Madonna Handbook* (New York: St. Martin's, 1994), 90–91.

54. Quoted in ibid., 91.

55. Sommer, *Foundational Fictions: The National Romances of Latin America,* 5.

56. Sandy M. Fernández, "Carlito's Way," *Latina,* November 1998, 56.

57. Jennifer Weiner, "In Los Angeles, Pop Star Madonna Gives Birth to a Girl," *Philadelphia Inquirer,* October 15, 1996, 1, 8.

58. Taraborrelli, *Madonna: An Intimate Biography,* 291.

59. Quoted in Fernández, "Carlito's Way," 58.

60. Ibid., 56.

61. Quoted in Taraborrelli, *Madonna: An Intimate Biography,* 85.

62. "Lourdes' Dad busted for Pot," *Miami Herald,* August 9, 2001, 4A.

63. Bakhtin, *Rabelais and His World,* 325.

64. "Censurada su acción," *Vea* 25, no. 1266 (November 14, 1993): 23.

65. Ibid.

66. Madeline Román, "El Girlie Show: Madonna, las polémicas nacionales y los pánicos morales," *Bordes,* no. 1 (1995): 14–21, 19.

67. Quoted in Frances Negrón-Muntaner, *Que Bonita Bandera* (video, work-in-progress).

68. "Esta imitación es una hazaña," *Vea* 25, no. 1266 (November 14, 1993): 98. Original Spanish: "me da coraje que alguien de afuera cobre tanto por su espectáculo y la gente no diga nada y lo pague. Sin embargo, si un artista de aquí cobrara lo mismo, pondrían el grito en el cielo."

69. Juan Carlos Pérez, "Madonna Fans Miffed by Concert Difficulties: Gate Slammed Shut on Many Irate Ticket-Holders," *San Juan Star,* October 28, 1993, 9.

70. Maite Vargas Baiges, "Díganle no al desorden sexual," *Vea* 25, no. 1266 (November 14, 1993): 6–18, 17. Orginal Spanish: "la pornografía, el sadomasoquismo, el lesbianismo y el erotismo fuera del matrimonio."

71. Dana Ramírez, "Madonna Sings, and Struts, Her Best Material," *San Juan Star,* October 28, 1993, F2.

72. Pizzi Campos, "Su primer romance fue con un puertorriqueño," 11.

73. Ramirez, "Madonna Sings, and Struts, Her Best Material."

74. "Censurada su acción," 23.

75. Carlos Pabón, "De Albizu a Madonna," *Bordes* 1 (1995): 22–40, 32.

76. Luis Muñoz Rivera, prólogo to *El Grito de Lares,* by Luis Lloréns Torres (San Juan: Editorial Cordillera, 1973), 29–32, 31–32. Original Spanish: "¡Bandera mía! . . . ondearás algún día en el tope de los castillos ciclópeos, erecta y resurrecta."

77. Maria Judith Luciano, "Total repudio cameral al indecoroso paso de baile," *El Nuevo Día,* October 29, 1993, 16. Original Spanish: "La medida expresa el repudio del Cuerpo a la señora Madonna Louise Veronica Ciccone."

78. Román, "El Girlie Show: Madonna, las polémicas nacionales y los pánicos morales," 15.

79. Pizzi Campos, "Su primer romance fue con un puertorriqueño," 12.

80. Gino Ponti, "Islanders Decry Madonna's Handling of the Flag," *San Juan Star,* October 28, 1993, 10.

81. Ibid.

82. Ivonne García, "Madonna: No Class Act," *San Juan Star,* October 28, 1993, 35.

83. Rob Palmer, "On Madonna's Flag Play," *Newsday,* October 29, 1993, 4.

84. Vargas Baiges, "Díganle no al desorden sexual," 18. Original Spanish: "Vivamos la moral que es lo que nos hace falta."

85. Quoted in ibid. Original Spanish: "hemos hecho un llamado . . . especialmente a los países hermanos que comparten nuestro idioma y nuestra cultura, para que también levanten su voz de protesta y le digan no al desorden sexual, no a la immoralidad, no a la pornografía, no a la obscenidad y no al espectáculo de Madonna."

86. Ponti, "Islanders Decry Madonna's Handling of the Flag," 10.

87. Ibid.

88. Ibid.

89. "Madonna: It's Only a Concert," *San Juan Star,* October 28, 1993, 36.

90. Lisa Frank and Paul Smith, "Introduction: How to Use Your New Madonna," in Frank and Smith, *Madonnarama,* 7–20, 12.

91. Madeline Román, "Madonna: La moral y lo nacional, un debate necesario," *Diálogo,* December 1993, 19.

92. Luis Dávila Colón, "En-madonnados," *El Nuevo Día,* October 29, 1993, 69. Original Spanish: "Mire míster, yo no sé por qué tanto barullo porque nunca antes la monoestrellada había ondulado tan bonito. Mejor entre las piernas de Madonna que en el fondillo del Macho Camacho."

93. Luciano, "Total repudio cameral al indecoroso paso de baile," 16.

94. "Reglamento para el uso de la bandera, el escudo y el himno, Los símbolos oficiales de Puerto Rico" (San Juan: Editorial Cordillera, 1991), 18. Original Spanish: "ninguna persona deberá mutilar, dañar, profanar, pisotear, insultar ni menospreciar con palabras u obras la Bandera del Estado Libre Asociado de Puerto Rico."

95. Ovidio Dávila, "El centenario de la adopción de la bandera de Puerto Rico," *Cultura* (Instituto de Cultura Puertorriqueña) 1, no. 12 (1997): 20–28, 21.

96. Ibid., 25.

97. Ibid., 21–22. "Un 11 de junio, a principios de los años 1890, mientras él se encontraba trabajando en su habitación sintió la necesidad de fijar su mirada, a modo de reposar la vista, en la bandera cubana que colgaba de la pared de su cuarto en Nueva York. Al cambiar la vista vio que, como consecuencia de un raro daltonismo, en su mente se invirtieron los colores de la bandera cubana: el rojo en azul y el azul en rojo."

98. Carmelo Rosario Natal, *La bandera puertorriqueña en su centenario* (San Juan: Comisión Nacional en Torno al Centenario de 1898, 1995), 60.

99. Juan Angel Silén, *Hacia una visión positiva del puertorriqueño* (Río Piedras: Editorial Edil, 1972), 117. Original Spanish: "La mera posesión de la bandera de Puerto Rico se llegó a considerar un delito."

100. Dávila, "El centenario de la adopción de la bandera de Puerto Rico," 28.

101. Tomás Blanco, *Prontuario histórico de Puerto Rico* (Río Piedras: Ediciones Huracán, 1981), 128.

102. Larry LaFountain, "Culture, Representation, and the Puerto Rican Queer Diaspora" (Ph.D. diss., Columbia University, 1999), 176.

103. Ruth Hernández, "NBC pide disculpas a boricuas," *El Nuevo Herald,* January 26, 1999, 5A.

104. Pizzi Campos, "Su primer romance fue con un puertorriqueño," 12. Original Spanish: "los fotoperiodistas tuvieron acceso al espectáculo cuando ya la primera canción casi terminaba y fueron sacados del Estadio Juan Ramón Loubriel tan pronto terminó la cuarta canción. De ahí que no haya evidencia gráfica de lo que realmente sucedió cuando Madonna tuvo en sus manos la bandera puertorriqueña."

105. Ibid. Original Spanish: "Lo que unos observaron fue que ella la abrió, se la enseñó al público, luego la tomó en su mano derecha e intentó introducírsela en un bolsillo para guardarla y al no encontrarlo se la devolvió al guardia."

106. "Madonna: It's Only a Concert."

107. McDonnell, "What Does Madonna Mean?" 6M.

108. Liz Smith, "Madonna Grows Up," *Good Housekeeping,* April 2000, 104.

109. "Oh Baby," *Miami Herald,* February 8, 1998, 2A.

110. Quoted in Taraborrelli, *Madonna: An Intimate Biography,* 304.

111. Smith, "Madonna Grows Up," 104.

112. Mimi Udovitch, "Madonna," in *Madonna: The Rolling Stone Files,* 247–52, 248.

113. Madonna, "Madonna's Private Diaries," 176.

114. Ibid., 180.

115. Ibid., 232.

116. O'Dair, introduction to *Madonna: The Rolling Stone Files,* 21.

117. McDonnell, "What Does Madonna Mean?" 6M.

118. Fernández, "Carlito's Way," 60.

119. Taraborrelli, *Madonna: An Intimate Biography,* 282.

120. Bakhtin, *Rabelais and His World,* 320.

121. Eve Kosofsky Sedgwick and Adam Frank, "Shame in the Cybernetic Fold: Reading Silvan Tomkins," in *Shame and Its Sisters,* by Silvan Tomkins, ed. Eve Kosofsky Sedwick and Adam Frank (Durham: Duke University Press, 1995), 22.

122. Ibid., 343.

123. Evelyn McDonnell, "Madonna's Concert Felt Like Work," *Miami Herald,* August 15, 2001, 2A.

124. Quoted in Smith, "Madonna Grows Up."

125. Morrison, *Playing in the Dark: Whiteness and the Literary Imagination,* 35.

126. CNN, August 17, 2001.

127. Bakhtin, *Rabelais and His World,* 416.

128. Quoted in Taraborrelli, *Madonna: An Intimate Biography,* 323.

129. Jo Tuckman, "That Frida Feeling," *Guardian,* August 30, 2001, www.film.guardian.co.uk/Print/0,3858,4247434,00 html.

Notes to Chapter 7

1. Quoted in Nilka Estrada, "De gala el idioma español," *El Nuevo Día,* April 6, 1991, 4. Original Spanish: "nos definimos ante nuestros ciudadanos de Estados Unidos y ante el mundo."

2. Severo Colberg, "En defensa del español," *El Mundo,* August 27, 1990, 24.

3. "'Sí' a los dos idiomas," *El Mundo,* September 24, 1990, 25. Jorge Luis Medina, "Spanish-Only Poll Results Get Happy Rosselló Reaction," *San Juan Star,* June 12, 1991, 10.

4. Doreen Hemlock, "Language Bill Ires Congress," *San Juan Star,* March 16, 1991, 1, 16.

5. Daniel Shoer Roth, "El español se vuelve una necesidad en Estados Unidos," *El Nuevo Herald,* May 10, 2001, 2A.

6. Frank Davies, "President to 'Reach Out' with Speech in Spanish," *Miami Herald,* May 4, 2001, 2A.

7. Max J. Castro, "The Future of Spanish in the United States," *Vista Magazine, Miami Herald,* September 1997, 8.

8. Fabiola Santiago, "Two Families Swept by Change," *Miami Herald,* March 1, 1998, 5L.

9. Gilles Deleuze and Felix Guattari, *Kafka: Toward a Minor Literature* (Minneapolis: University of Minnesota Press, 1986), 64.

10. Rosario Ferré, interview by author, Condado, Puerto Rico. January 3, 2002. Original Spanish: "La fama de independentista que me crearon cuando yo empecé a escribir . . . creo que fue hasta cierto punto una proyección. La gente me leyó y me interpretó de cierta manera, y creo que por eso mis libros de aquélla época alcanzaron tanto éxito."

11. Suzanne Hintz, *Rosario Ferré: A Search for Identity* (New York: Peter Lang, 1995), 14.

12. Frances Negrón-Muntaner, "English Only Jamás but Spanish Only Cuidado: Language and Nationalism in Contemporary Puerto Rico," in *Puerto Rican Jam: Rethinking Colonialism and Nationalism,* ed. Frances Negrón-Muntaner and Ramón Grosfoguel (Minneapolis: University of Minnesota Press, 1997), 257–85.

13. Ferré, interview. Original Spanish: "Se usa el español para definir no lo que es puertorriqueño, sino lo que es patriótico. Si no hablas ni escribes en español, eres un traidor."

14. Quoted in Eneid Routte-Gomez, "A 2nd Look at Language Law and Its Meaning," *San Juan Star,* April 21, 1992, 17.

15. Juan G. Gelpí, *Literatura y paternalismo en Puerto Rico* (Río Piedras: Universidad de Puerto Rico, 1993), 15.

16. Quoted in Fabiola Santiago, "Writer Paints Rich Portraits of Puerto Rico," *Miami Herald,* July 8, 2001, 2M.

17. Edna Acosta-Belén, "Rosario Ferré's Crossover Writing," *Latino Review of Books,* fall 1996, 30–31, 31.

18. Rosario Ferré, "Words from the Womb," *San Juan Star,* January 26, 1997, 8.

19. Quoted in Julio Ortega, *Reapropiaciones* (Río Piedras: Editorial de la Universidad de Puerto Rico, 1991), 211. Original Spanish: "yo siempre quise ser Virginia Woolf."

20. Ferré, interview. Original Spanish: "Yo no soy ninguna lengua."

21. Luis A. Ferré and Rosario Ferré, *Memorias de Ponce* (Río Piedras: Editorial Cultural, 1992).

22. Rosario Ferré, *The House on the Lagoon* (New York: Farrar, Straus and Giroux, 1995), 94–95.

23. Ferré, "Words from the Womb."

24. Gloribel Delgado Esquilín, "Sea lo que sea, en cualquier status," *El Nuevo Día,* July 23, 1998, 96–97.

25. Rosario Ferré, "Puerto Rico, USA," *New York Times,* March 19, 1998.

26. Ana Lydia Vega, "Carta abierta a Pandora," *El Nuevo Día,* March 31, 1998, 1B. Original Spanish: "Ojalá, querida Pandora, que aquélla que una vez abofeteara la cara hipócrita de la sociedad con la explosiva verdad de sus papeles, no se haya vendido ante la que hoy derrama estereotipos desmentidos por sus libros."

27. Ibid.

28. Liliana Cotto, "Carta abierta a una estadista híbrida," *El Nuevo Herald,* April 9, 1998, 13A.

29. Ibid. Original Spanish: "Lo escrito por Ferré denota sesgo e inexactitud en los datos y en las interpretaciones. La falta es grave porque desorienta al público lector de la prensa puertorriqueña, a los intelectuales y las clases políticas de Washington y a la elite culta latinomericana que leen el *New York Times.* Entre éstos, hay muchos y muchas que no conocen a nuestro país o a nuestra gente."

30. Pedro López-Adorno, "Papiros de Babel: Pesquisas sobre la polifonía poética puertorriqueña en Nueva York," in *Papiros de Papel: Antología de la poesía puertorriqueña en Nueva York* (Río Piedras: Editorial de la Universidad de Puerto Rico, 1991), 1–16, 11. Original Spanish: "Los poetas 'niuyorriqueños' . . . deben darse cuenta de la incompleta y, por lo tanto, peligrosa imagen que esa ideología puede proyectar alrededor del mundo de nuestra personalidad como pueblo y de nuestra cultura colectiva tanto en el ámbito isleño como en los Estados Unidos."

31. Bill Ashcroft, Gareth Griffiths, and Helen Tifflin, *The Empire Writes Back* (New York: Routledge, 1989).

32. René Marqués, "La ira del resucitado," in *En una ciudad llamada San Juan* (Río Piedras: Ediciones Cultura, 1983), 225–33, 232. Original Spanish: "Más le vale a este pequeñuelo ser mudo que tartamudear la manifestación de su espíritu."

33. Salvador Tió, *Lengua mayor* (Madrid: Plaza Mayor, 1991), 50. Original Spanish: "al tratar de incorporar otra lengua tropezamos con dos esollos que solamente pueden salvar a la perfección individuos excepcionales: el tartamudeo y la vacilación."

34. Ibid.

35. Negrón-Muntaner, "English Only Jamás but Spanish Only Cuidado," 257–85.

36. Tió, *Lengua Mayor,* 46. Original Spanish: "Al que habla mal lo que hay que hacer es enseñarle a hablar. Y si no quiere aprender que reviente."

37. Manuel Maldonado Denis, "Idioma y nacionalidad," *El Mundo,* August 28, 1990, 26; Obed Betancourt, "Revive el 'fantasma' del idioma," *El Mundo,* August 11, 1990), 12, among others.

38. Amílcar Barreto, *The Politics of Language in Puerto Rico* (Gainesville: University Press of Florida, 2001), 26.

39. "Poll: Too Much Attention Been Given to Vieques, English and Spanish Should Be Island's Official Languages," *Puerto Rico Herald,* September 11, 2001, www.puertorico-herald.org.

40. María E. Enchautegui, "Fluidez en el idioma inglés y el Mercado de empleo en Puerto Rico" (presentation to the Senate of Puerto Rico's Education, Science, and Culture Commission Public Hearings, May 22, 2002).

41. René Marqués, *Ensayos* (Río Piedras: Editorial Antillana, 1972), 147.

42. Carmen S. Rivera, "Rosario Ferré," in *Modern Latin American Fiction Writers,* ed. William Luis and Ann González (Detroit: Gale Research, 1994), 130–69, 135.

43. Hintz, *Rosario Ferré: A Search for Identity,* 176.

44. Rosario Ferré, *Maldito amor* (Mexico: Joaquín Mortiz, 1986), 11.

45. Silvan Tomkins, *Shame and Its Sisters,* ed. Eve Kosofsky Sedgwick and Adam Frank (Durham: Duke University Press, 1995), 137.

46. Rosario Ferré, *Sweet Diamond Dust* (New York: Available Press, 1988), 67.

47. Ferré, "Words from the Womb."

48. Rosario Ferré, "Latino Writers Turn to English to Reach New Readers," *San Juan Star,* October 24, 1993, 8.

49. Ferré, *The House on the Lagoon,* 10.

50. Ibid., 14.

51. Ibid., 10.

52. Lola Aponte Ramos, "Recetario para el novelar híbrido: Esmeralda Santiago y Rosario Ferré," *Nómada,* no. 3 (1997): 34. Original Spanish: "tanteo tembloroso . . . de quien redacta en una lengua que no le es dúctil."

53. Ferré, *The House on the Lagoon,* 245.

54. Ibid., 22.

55. Ibid., 28.

56. Ibid.

57. Ibid., 164.

58. Ibid., 98.

59. Ibid., 140.

60. Ibid., 158.

61. Ibid., 164.

62. Ibid., 108.

63. Ibid., 386.

64. Ferré, *Sweet Diamond Dust,* 76.

65. Ferré, "Latino Writers Turn to English to Reach New Readers."

66. Ferré, *The House on the Lagoon,* 51.

67. Rosario Ferré, "The Soul of a Kiss," *Latina,* July 1999, 52–53, 53.

68. Ferré, "Latino Writers Turn to English to Reach New Readers."

69. Ibid.

70. Originally printed as "Puerto Rico, USA," *New York Times,* March 19, 1998, reprinted in *Miami Herald* as "Why Puerto Rico Ought to Become the 51st State," March 20, 1998, 25A.

71. Ferré, *The House on the Lagoon,* 150.

72. Ibid., 59.

73. Ibid., 60.

74. Ibid.

75. Ibid., 184.

76. Puerto Rico Constitutional Convention, *Diario de Sesiones,* 1952, 31.

77. Quoted in Routte-Gomez, "A 2nd Look at Language Law and Its Meaning."

78. Castro, "The Future of Spanish in the United States," 6.

79. Ferré, "Words from the Womb."

80. Roberto Fernández Retamar, *Calibán* (Maracaibo: Universidad de Zulia, 1973), 40. Original Spanish: "sólo leemos con verdadero respeto a los autores anticolonialistas *difundidos desde las metrópolis."*

81. Ada Muntaner, "The Language Question in Puerto Rico: 1898–1998" (Ph.D. diss., State University of New York-Stony Brook, 1991), 200.

82. Juan Duchesne Winter, "Del bilingüismo y otros demonios" (mimeograph, September 14, 1997), 1–11, 9. Original Spanish: "Una activa población hispanoparlante bilingüe es mucho más capaz de posicionar favorablemente al español en distintos contextos. Esta realidad continuará desarrollándose en el futuro bajo cualquier arreglo de status."

83. Aponte Ramos, "Recetario para el novelar híbrido: Esmeralda Santiago y Rosario Ferré," 33–37.

84. *El Mundo,* February 19, 1999, E11.

85. Eliseo Cardona, "Escribo porque sí," *El Nuevo Herald,* March 1, 1998, 3F.

86. Frances Negrón-Muntaner, "Nota de autora," in *Anatomía de una sonrisa* (Río Piedras: Editorial Isla Negra, 2003).

87. Ferré, interview. Original Spanish: "los dos son originales, porque no me identifico con uno más que con otro. Con los dos últimos libros, por ejemplo, el escrito en inglés salió primero por razones prácticas, porque así podía entrar al mercado internacional. Si se publicaba como una traducción del (o al) inglés, entonces no le daban la misma crítica, no aparecía en los medios."

88. Arlene M. Dávila, *Sponsored Identities: Cultural Politics in Puerto Rico* (Philadelphia: Temple University Press, 1997), 218.

89. Deleuze and Guattari, *Kafka: Toward a Minor Literature,* 17.

90. Mary Louise Pratt, *Imperial Eyes: Travel Writing and Transculturation* (New York: Routledge, 1992), 6.

91. Fabiola Santiago, "Dancing to the Forces of Passion, Devotion," *Miami Herald,* July 1, 2001, 3L.

92. José Esteban Muñoz, *Disidentifications: Queers of Color and the Performance of Color* (Minneapolis: University of Minnesota Press, 1999), x.

93. Frances Aparicio, "On Sub-versive Signifiers: U.S. Latina/o Writers Tropicalize English," *American Literature* 66, no. 4 (December 1994): 795–801, 797.

94. Ashcroft, Griffiths, and Tifflin, *The Empire Writes Back,* 38.

95. Ferré, "The Soul of a Kiss," 53.

96. Rosario Ferré, "Blessing of Being Ambidextrous," *San Juan Star,* January 12, 1997, 9.

97. Ferré, "Words from the Womb."

98. Ferré, interview. Original Spanish: "en última instancia, yo he tratado de hacer una cosa fundamental: devolverle al puertorriqueño su respeto a sí mismo."

99. Ibid. Original Spanish: "La gente perdió la tierra . . . y entonces no tenían nada de que sentirse orgulloso. No poseían nada."

100. Rosario Ferré, "La cocina de la escritura," in *La sartén por el mango,* ed. Patricia Elena González and Eliana Ortega (Río Piedras: Ediciones Huracán, 1985), 137–54, 151.

Notes to Chapter 8

1. Mireya Navarro, "A New Barbie in Puerto Rico Divides Island and Mainland," *New York Times,* December 27, 1997, A9.

2. Louis Aguilar, "Barbie Stirs Debate in Puerto Rico," *Miami Herald,* November 14, 1997, 25A.

3. Quoted in ibid.

4. Frances Negrón-Muntaner, "Feeling Pretty: *West Side Story* and Puerto Rican–American Identity," *Social Text* no. 63 (2000): 83–106.

5. M. G. Lord, *Forever Barbie* (New York: William Morrow, 1994), 7.

6. Quoted in Navarro, "A New Barbie in Puerto Rico Divides Island and Mainland," A9.

7. Margaret Carlisle Duncan, Garry Chick, and Alan Aycock, eds., *Play and Culture Studies* 1 (Greenwich: Ablex, 1998), 4.

8. Quoted in Froma Harrop, "Ask Real Barbie Experts," *Miami Herald,* January 6, 1998, 7A.

9. Quoted in Navarro, "A New Barbie in Puerto Rico Divides Island and Mainland," A10.

10. Lord, *Forever Barbie,* 298.

11. Walter Benjamin, "Old Toys," in *Selected Writings,* vol. 2 (Cambridge: Harvard University Press, 1999), 98–102, 100.

12. José Quiroga, *Tropics of Desire* (New York: New York University Press, 2000).

13. Ibid., 179.

14. Jeannette Rivera-Lyles, "Boricuas divididos con la Barbie puertorriqueña," *El Nuevo Herald,* December 31, 1997, 1, 16A.

15. Erica Rand, *Barbie's Queer Accessories* (Durham: Duke University Press, 1995).

16. Quoted in Louis Aguilar, "Barbie Has Serious Implications for Puerto Ricans," *Miami Herald,* November 9, 1997, 127.

17. Adrian Febles, "Coming Soon: Political Activist Barbie," *San Juan Star,* November 14, 1997, 76.

18. Aguilar, "Barbie Stirs Debate in Puerto Rico."

19. Patrick Olivelle, "Hair and Society: Social Significance of Hair in South Asian Traditions," in *Hair: Its Power and Meaning in Asian Cultures,* ed. Alf Hiltebeitel and Barbara D. Miller (Albany: State University of New York Press, 1998), 40–41.

20. Tomás Blanco, *El prejuicio racial en Puerto Rico* (Río Piedras: Ediciones Huracán, 1985), 138. Original Spanish: "El color y las facciones, valen más que la sangre."

21. Institute for Puerto Rican Policy (IPR), "Puerto Rico: 2000 Population and Racial Breakdrown," no. 25, April 2001.

22. Sidney Mintz, "Cañamelar: The Subculture of a Rural Sugar Plantation Proletariat," in *The People of Puerto Rico,* ed. Julian H. Steward et al. (Urbana: University of Illinois Press, 1972), 314–417, 410.

23. Julia de Burgos, "Ay ay ay de la grifa negra," in *Poema en veinte surcos* (Río Piedras: Huracán, 1997), 52–53, 52.

24. Francisco Arriví, *Sirena* (Río Piedras: Cultural, 1971), 45.

25. Luis Palés Matos, *Tuntún de pasa y grifería* (San Juan: Biblioteca de Autores Puertorriqueños, 1974).

26. Noliwe M. Rooks, *Hair Raising: Beauty, Culture, and African-American Women* (New Brunswick: Rutgers University Press, 1996), 14.

27. Quoted in Isabelo Zenón, *Narciso descubre su trasero* (Humacao, PR: Editorial Furidi, 1975), vol. 1, 79. From Renzo Sereno, "Cryptomelanism," *Psychiatry* 10, no. 3 (August 1947): 253–69, 262. Original Spanish: "la contextura del pelo—bueno o malo—puede decidir el matrimonio mixto."

28. Zenón, *Narciso descubre su trasero,* 84. Original Spanish: "Si no se despeina, queda fuera del grupo de privilegiados."

29. Eduardo Seda Bonilla, *Los derechos civiles en la cultura puertorriqueña* (Río Piedras: Ediciones Bayoán, 1973), 155.

30. Willie Perdomo, "Nigger-Reecan Blues," in *Aloud: Voices from the Nuyorican Poets Café,* ed. Miguel Algarín and Bob Holman (New York: Henry Holt, 1994), 111–13.

31. Quoted in Aguilar, "Barbie Stirs Debate in Puerto Rico."

32. Walter Benjamin, "Toys and Play," in *Selected Writings,* vol. 2, 117–21, 118.

33. Sieber and Herreman, *Hair in African Art and Culture,* 11.

34. Rivera-Lyles, "Boricuas divididos con la Barbie puertorriqueña," 16A.

35. Luis O. Zayas Micheli, "La trascendencia como coyuntura del jíbaro," in *El Jíbaro,* by Manuel Alonso (Río Piedras: Edil, 1992), 16. Original Spanish: "El 'denso contenido espiritual' es legado del alma hispana."

36. Francisco A. Scarano, "The *Jíbaro* Masquerade and the Subaltern Politics of Creole Identity Formation in Puerto Rico, 1745–1823," *American Historical Review,* December 1996, 1398–1431.

37. Antonio S. Pedreira, "La actualidad del jíbaro," in *El jíbaro de Puerto Rico: Símbolo y figura,* ed. Enrique Laguerre and Esther Melón (Sharon, CT: Troutman Press, 1968), 14.

38. Ibid., 20.

39. Arlene M. Dávila, *Sponsored Identities: Cultural Politics in Puerto Rico* (Philadelphia: Temple University Press, 1997), 72.

40. Virgilio Dávila, "La jibarita," in Laguerre and Melón, *El jíbaro de Puerto Rico: Símbolo y figura,* 100–101. Original Spanish: "como una flor escuálida de malogrado abril. . . . Un harapo / que cubre a duras penas un cuerpo virginal."

41. Salvador Brau, "La campesina," in Laguerre and Melón, *El jíbaro de Puerto Rico: Símbolo y figura,* 27. Original Spanish: "pobre mujer indolente y sensual."

42. Abelardo Díaz Alfaro, "El boliche," in Laguerre and Melón, *El jíbaro de Puerto Rico: Símbolo y figura,* 206. Original Spanish: "Mujeres gastadas por la maternidad y el trabajo excesivo."

43. Lillian Guerra, *Popular Expression and National Identity in Puerto Rico* (Gainesville: University Press of Florida, 1998), 117.

44. Navarro, "A New Barbie in Puerto Rico Divides Island and Mainland," A1.

45. Rivera-Lyles, "Boricuas divididos con la Barbie puertorriqueña," 16A.

46. Quoted in Shelley Emling, "Barbie Creates Brouhaha, This Time among Puerto Ricans," *Charlotte Observer,* December 30, 1997, www.charlotte.com/barbie1.html.

47. The anthropologist Marvette Pérez called my attention to Vientós Gastón's article. Nilita Vientós Gastón, "El 'traje típico' puertorriqueño," in *Indice Cultural,* vol. 1 (Río Piedras: Ediciones de la Universidad de Puerto Rico, 1962), 203–4, 204. Original Spanish: "un alarde de la fantasía, una invención. . . . Imagino que su destino será convertirse en disfraz."

48. Pedreira, "La actualidad del jíbaro," 8. Original Spanish: "Por encima de su angustia económica pondremos su valor humano, su bella calidad representativa."

49. Blanco, *El prejuicio racial en Puerto Rico,* 130. Original Spanish: "parece tener valor estético o de selección erótica."

50. Seda Bonilla, *Los derechos civiles en la cultura puertorriqueña,* 189.

51. Guerra, *Popular Expression and National Identity in Puerto Rico,* 111.

52. Lord, *Forever Barbie,* 8.

53. Guerra, *Popular Expression and National Identity in Puerto Rico,* 102.

54. Quoted in Navarro, "A New Barbie in Puerto Rico Divides Island and Mainland."

55. Emling, "Barbie Creates Brouhaha, This Time among Puerto Ricans."

56. Lord, *Forever Barbie,* 108.

57. Ibid., 190.

58. Ibid., 198.

59. "Mattel popularizó a Barbie mediante productos con licencias," *El Universal,* December 13, 2000, http://noticias.eluniversal.com/1998/06/28502AA.shtml.

60. Navarro, "A New Barbie in Puerto Rico Divides Island and Mainland, A9."

61. Dávila, *Sponsored Identities: Cultural Politics in Puerto Rico.*

62. Quoted in Rivera-Lyles, "Boricuas divididos con la Barbie puertorriqueña," 16A. Original Spanish: "lo que hizo Mattel fue hacerle la nariz más grande y oscurecerle los ojos. Ahora nos quieren vender como boricua la misma muñeca de siempre."

63. Anna Indych, "Nuyorican Baroque: Pepón Osorio's Chucherias," Art Journal, *Puerto Rico Herald,* April 1, 2001, www.puertorico-herald.org/issues/2001/vol5n18/Nuyorican-en.shtml, 2.

64. "Boy Toy," *Latina,* July 1998, 20.

65. Ibid.

66. Patricia Vargas, "Por la felicidad de un niño," *El Nuevo Día,* December 23, 1997, 77. Original Spanish: "O sea, que con una Barbie hemos podido hacer felices a muchos niños."

Notes to Chapter 9

I would like to thank Steve Huang, Larry LaFountain, Yolanda Martínez-San Miguel, and Chon Noriega for their useful suggestions and support in writing this essay.

1. Quoted in Bob Strauss, "Putting an Icon on Film," *Daily News of Los Angeles,* March 16, 1997, L3.

2. Quoted in Leila Cobo-Hanlon, "Jennifer Becomes Selena," *Latina,* April–May 1997, 48–53, 52–53.

3. Pam Lambert and Betty Cortina, "Viva Selena," *People,* March 24, 1997, 160–61, 161. My emphasis.

4. Lynn Carey, "Selena's Posthumous Celebrity Is Taking a Life of Its Own," *Tampa Tribune,* March 25, 1997, 5.

5. Quoted in Barry Koltnow, "Jennifer Lopez Plays Selena with Joy and Sorrow," *Dayton Daily News,* March 23, 1997, 5C.

6. Luz Villareal, "New Film Has Selena Fans Singing Star's Praises," *Daily News of Los Angeles,* March 21, 1997, N3.

7. Quoted in Mal Vincent, "Lopez Is Bursting into Hollywood Spotlight," *Virginian-Pilot,* March 22, 1997, E8. My emphasis.

8. Barbara Renaud-González, "Santa Selena," *Latina,* April–May 1997, 83.

9. Quoted in Joe Leydon, "Keeping Dreams Alive," *Los Angeles Times,* December 8, 1996, 6.

10. Quoted in *Daily Dish,* December 9, 1998, www.jenlopeztan.net/news.htm.

11. Quoted in Vincent, "Lopez Is Bursting into Hollywood Spotlight."

12. Lambert and Cortina, "Viva Selena," 160.

13. Quoted in Vincent, "Lopez Is Bursting into Hollywood Spotlight."

14. Sigmund Freud, "Character and Anal Eroticism," in *The Freud Reader,* ed. Peter Gray (New York: Norton, 1989), 293–97, 296.

15. Mikhail Bakhtin, *Rabelais and His World* (Bloomington: Indiana University Press, 1984), 373.

16. Quoted in "50 Most Beautiful People in the World," *People,* May 12, 1997, 124.

17. María Celeste Arrarás, *Selena's Secret* (New York: Simon and Schuster, 1997), 59–60.

18. Ibid., 81.

19. Quoted in Leydon, "Keeping Dreams Alive."

20. Carl D. Schneider, *Shame, Exposure, and Privacy* (Boston: Beacon, 1977), 35.

21. "Want to Date Jennifer Lopez?" *Daily Dish,* December 9, 1998, www.jenlopeztan.net/news.htm.

22. Simone de Beauvoir, *The Second Sex* (New York: Vintage Books, 1989), 158.

23. Magali García Ramis, "La manteca que nos une," in *La ciudad que nos habita* (Río Piedras: Ediciones Huracán, 1993), 83. Original Spanish: "un tun tún de grasa y fritanguería recorre las venas borincanas, nos une, nos aúna, nos hermana por encima de la política y los políticos, los cultos y las religiones, la salsa y el rock, el matriarcado y el patriarcado."

24. "50 Most Beautiful People in the World."

25. Original Spanish: "gran simpatía por su esplendor / antipatía por la razón / de que su palanca fuera su cuerpo y no su valor."

26. Edgardo Rodríguez Juliá, *Una noche con Iris Chacón* (Río Piedras: Editorial Antillana, 1986). Luis Rafael Sánchez, *La guaracha del Macho Camacho* (Barcelona: Argos Vergara, 1982). Original Spanish: "La vida es una cosa fenomenal / lo mismo pal de alante que pal de atrás."

27. Richard Corliss, "¡Viva Selena!" *Time,* March 24, 1997, 86–87.

28. Judith Butler, *Bodies That Matter* (New York: Routledge, 1993).

29. Jonathan Flatley, "Warhol Gives Good Face: Publicity and the Politics of Prosopopoeia," in *Pop Out: Queering Warhol,* ed. Jennifer Doyle, Jonathan Flatley, and José Muñoz (Durham: Duke University Press, 1996), 101–30, 104.

30. Rodríguez Juliá, *Una noche con Iris Chacón,* 117.

31. Vincent, "Lopez Is Bursting into Hollywood Spotlight."

32. Ilan Stavans, "Santa Selena," *Transition* 70 (1997): 36–43.

33. Frances Negrón-Muntaner, "Jennifer's Butt," *Aztlán* 2, no. 2 (fall 1997): 181–94.

34. *El Nuevo Herald,* January 6, 1999, 13D. Original Spanish: "el trasero más popular del mundo."

35. Ned Zeman, "She Makes Every Move," *Vanity Fair,* June 2001, 166–72, 234–36.

36. Jennifer Lopez, "Body and Soul," *In Style,* May 10, 1999, 275–81, 281.

37. A. B. Quintanilla, phone interview by author, September 10, 1999.

38. Kim France, "Out of Sight," *Elle,* July 1999, 168–71, 180.

39. Quoted in René Rodríguez, "Lopez on the Rise," *Miami Herald,* June 25, 1998, 1F, 5F.

40. "People Column," *Miami Herald,* June 14, 1998, 2A.

41. Elysa Garden, "She's All That," *In Style,* June 1999, 277.

42. Bill Hoffman, "Jennifer Lopez Is the $1B Babe," December 6, 1999, www.jenlopeztan.net/news.htm.

43. "Puffy-Lopez Romance Scrutinized by Mags," *Newsweek,* January 3, 2000, www.jenlopeztan.net/news.htm.

44. "What Do You Want for Christmas?" December 15, 1999, www.jenlopeztan .net/news.htm.

45. "La más sexy del mundo," *El Nuevo Herald,* May 20, 2001, 11A.

46. "Jennifer Lopez and Brad Pitt Voted Sexiest Celebrity Legs," Hanes Hosiery Press Release, January 25, 2000, www.jenlopeztan.net/news.htm.

47. "El mejor de los mejores," *El Nuevo Herald,* October 31, 2001, 8A.

48. E! Hand Out Golden Hanger Award, December 12, 1998, www.jenlopeztan .net/news.htm.

49. Quoted in Zeman, "She Makes Every Move," 236.

50. Linda Friedman, "Feeling So Good," *Teen People,* May 2000, 87–92, 89.

Notes to Chapter 10

1. José Quiroga, "Latino Dolls," in *Tropics of Desire* (New York: New York University Press, 2000), 169–90, 185.

2. Kathie Bergquist, *Ricky Martin* (London: Virgin Books, 1999), 7.

3. Maggie Marron, *Ricky Martin* (New York: Barnes and Noble, 1999), 14.

4. Ricky Martin, interview by Barbara Walters, ABC, March 26, 2000.

5. Gustavo Pérez Firmat, "I Came, I Saw, I Conga'd," in *Everynight Life: Culture and Dance in Latin/o America,* ed. Celeste Fraser Delgado and José Muñoz (Durham: Duke University Press, 1997), 238–54, 249.

6. Martin, interview by Barbara Walters.

7. Peter Guralnick, *Last Train to Memphis* (New York: Little Brown, 1994), 13.

8. Jill Pearlman, *Elvis for Beginners* (London: A Writers and Readers Documentary Comic Book in Association with Unwin Paperbacks, 1986), 9.

9. Quoted in Juan Manuel Rotulo, "Ricky Martin: Bonbón para las fans, pan para las editoriales," *El Nuevo Herald,* August 26–September 1, 1999, 22–23, 23. Original Spanish: "es un joven Elvis multicultural para el nuevo milenio."

10. "The Ricky Martin Phenomenon Gets Hotter and Hotter," *Miami Herald,* July 27, 1999, 2A.

11. Peter Silverton, *Essential Elvis* (London: Chameleon Books, 1997) 7.

12. Quoted in ibid., 14.

13. Ibid., 8.

14. Quoted in Mick Farren and Pearce Marchbank, *Elvis: In His Own Words* (London: Omnibus Press, 1994), 114.

15. Quoted in ibid., 30.

16. Quoted in Silverton, *Essential Elvis,* 65.

17. Telemundo, December 19, 1999.

18. *Latin Heat,* January–February 2000, 14–15, 14.

19. Nancy Krulik, *Ricky Martin: Rockin' the House* (New York: Bantam, 1999), 9.

20. Quoted in Guralnick, *Last Train to Memphis,* 142.

21. Quoted in ibid., 285.

22. Quoted in ibid.

23. Eliseo Cardona, "Ricky Martin," *El Nuevo Herald,* May 20–26, 1999, 29D.

24. Jesse Fontana, *Wise Men Say* (New York: Avon Books, 1999), 61.

25. Pearlman, *Elvis for Beginners,* 99.

26. Fontana, *Wise Men Say,* 58.

27. Quoted in Farren and Marchbank, *Elvis: In His Own Words,* 27.

28. Mojo Nixon, preface to *The Elvis Reader,* ed. Kevin Quain (New York: St. Martin's, 1992), xiii–xv, xiv.

29. Fontana, *Wise Men Say,* 85.

30. Bergquist, *Ricky Martin,* 11.

31. Ana López, "Of Rhythms and Borders," in Delgado and Muñoz, *Everynight Life: Culture and Dance in Latin/o America,* 310–44, 316.

32. Norma Niurka, "Ricky Martin: Una fiesta a todo dar," *El Nuevo Herald,* October 22, 1999, 1C–2C, 2C. Original Spanish: "Es curioso que sin ser bailarín ni bailador, ni aprenderse coreografía alguna, este artista se destaque por 'su baile,' sobre todo, entre sus fanáticos. Ricky repite dos o tres pasos conocidos, da patadas en el aire, mueve suavamente la cintura o hace fuertes movimientos pélvicos, pero de bailar, *nada.*"

33. Quoted in Letisha Marrero, *Ricky Martin: Livin' La Vida Loca* (New York: Harper, 1999), 37.

34. Oscar Hijuelos, *Mambo Kings Play Songs of Love* (New York: Farrar, Straus and Giroux, 1989), 279.

35. Jane C. Desmond, "Embodying Difference: Issues in Dance and Cultural Studies," in Delgado and Muñoz, *Everynight Life: Culture and Dance in Latin/o America,* 33–64, 39.

36. José Piedra, "Hip Poetics," in Delgado and Muñoz, *Everynight Life: Culture and Dance in Latin/o America,* 93–140, 107.

37. Original Spanish: "Cuando la bomba ñama el que no menea oreja menea una nalga."

38. Ruth Glasser, *My Music Is My Flag* (Berkeley: University of California Press, 1995), 201.

39. Fernando Ortiz, *Los bailes y el teatro de los negros en el folklore de Cuba* (Madrid: Música Mundana, 1998), 92. Original Spanish: "en la plenitud de su solidaria conciencia; que es sexo, pero también es maternidad, familia, tribu, religión, trabajo, guerra, felicidad y desgracia."

40. Camille Paglia, "Ricky Martin—Superstud or Closet Case?" www.salon.com, June 17, 1999.

41. Quoted in John Griffins, "Ricky Martin: The Gay Connection," *Advocate,* July 6, 1999, 27–32, 41.

42. Fontana, *Wise Men Say,* 56.

43. Ibid.

44. Quoted in Silverton, *Essential Elvis,* 62.

45. Quoted in Greil Marcus, *Mystery Train* (New York: Dutton, 1990), 152–53.

46. Martin, interview by Barbara Walters.

47. Ibid.

48. Marron, *Ricky Martin,* 45.

49. Ken Tucker, "Elvis Presley," *Entertainment Weekly,* no. 510 (winter 1999): 21–22, 21.

50. Quiroga, "Latino Dolls."

51. Kristin Sparks, *Ricky Martin: Livin' the Crazy Life* (New York: Berkeley Boulevard Books, 1999), 115.

52. Maureen Ort, "All Shook Up," in Quain, *The Elvis Reader,* 63–67, 65.

53. Immanuel Wallerstein, "The Construction of Peoplehood: Racism, Nationalism, Ethnicity," in *Race, Nation, and Class: Ambiguous Identities* (London: Verso, 1992), 71–85, 84.

54. Olga G. Gonzalo, *Ricky Martin* (Valencia: Editorial La Máscara, 1998), 47.

55. Quoted in "The Ricky Martin Phenomenon Gets Hotter and Hotter."

56. Krulik, *Ricky Martin: Rockin' the House,* 5.

57. Mayra Santos, "Salsa as Translocation," in Delgado and Muñoz, *Everynight Life: Culture and Dance in Latin/o America,* 175–88, 181.

58. Quoted in Marrero, *Ricky Martin: Livin' La Vida Loca,* 56.

59. Tomás Blanco, quoted in Ortiz, *Los bailes y el teatro de los negros en el folklore de Cuba,* 97. Original Spanish: "Las emociones poéticas levantadas por la hembra mulata, más que a sus ojos, a sus senos y su talle, se refieren a sus caderas, y sobre todo, a sus nalgas."

60. Piedra, "Hip Poetics," 119.

61. Quoted in Marrero, *Ricky Martin: Livin' La Vida Loca,* 62.

62. Paglia, "Ricky Martin—Superstud or Closet Case?"

63. *Random House College Dictionary* (New York: Random House, 1980), 581.

64. Telemundo, December 19, 1999.

65. Martin, interview by Barbara Walters.

66. Quoted in Griffins, "Ricky Martin: The Gay Connection," 35.

67. Guralnick, *Last Train to Memphis,* 134.

68. Quoted in Fontana, *Wise Men Say,* 12.

69. Martin, interview by Barbara Walters.

70. Quoted in "Crossover," *Eres,* October 15, 1999, unpaginated.

71. This column will be published in an upcoming book, tentatively titled *Irreverencias,* that includes other material censored by magazines and the press in Puerto Rico.

72. Van K. Borck, "Images of Elvis, the South and America," in Quain, *The Elvis Reader,* 126–58, 131–32.

73. Guralnick, *Last Train to Memphis,* 279.

74. Quoted in ibid., 304.

75. Ibid.

76. Martin, interview by Barbara Walters.

77. Quoted in Quiroga, "Latino Dolls," 184.

78. Patricia J. Duncan, *Ricky Martin* (New York: Warner, 1999), 99.

79. Javier Santiago, "Livin' la euforia boricua," *El Nuevo Día,* February 12, 2000, 68. Original Spanish: "el público, evidentemente orgulloso, estaba dispuesto a premiar su labor covirtiendo la noche en una inolvidable para este ídolo mundial de Borinquen."

80. Ibid.

81. *Pequeño Larousse ilustrado* (Paris: Larousse, 1977), 446. Original Spanish: "el resultado de una buena salud o provocado por drogas."

82. Maite Ribas, "Locura a la medida de Ricky," *El Nuevo Día,* February 20, 2002, 2.

83. Patricia Vargas, "Puerto Rico pos Ricky," *El Nuevo Día,* February 15, 2000, 89. Original Spanish: "¿Cómo quedó Puerto Rico después de Ricky Martin? De seguro con más orgullo que antes, con una gran satisfacción de haber encontrado lo que se esperaba y más."

84. Ibid.

85. *El Nuevo Día,* February 15, 2000, 53. Original Spanish: "¿Cuánto tiempo quieres con él?"

86. Quoted in Lissy de la Rosa, "Angelo Medina," *TeveGuía Especial,* 1999, 18–19, 19. Original Spanish: "Cuando yo hago algo por Ricky siento que estoy haciendo algo por Puerto Rico."

87. "Ricky Martin: Joya de exportación puertorriqueña," *El Nuevo Herald,* July 18, 1999, 2A. Original Spanish: "La venta de sus discos y espectáculo es igual al total de exportaciones de Puerto Rico a México en 1996 ($106 millones), y es casi cinco veces más que el presupuesto de $17.9 millones recomendado para el Instituto de Cultura Puertorriqueña en 1998."

88. López, "Of Rhythms and Borders," 323.

89. Andrew Essex, "Not So Little Ricky," *Entertainment Weekly,* April 23, 1999, 35.

90. Marrero, *Ricky Martin: Livin' La Vida Loca,* 92–93.

91. Essex, "Not So Little Ricky," 35.

92. Ibid.

93. "Composer 'Loco' over Ricky Martin's Plans," *Miami Herald,* January 13, 2001, 4A.

94. Quoted in Edgar Torres, "Reflexiones de Artista," *TeveGuía Especial,* 1999, 78–80, 80. Original Spanish: "Mejoremos nuestro estilo de vida. Empecemos a crecer y a exigir más de nosotros mismos. Si somos conformistas no nos quedaremos con el mundo."

95. Quoted in Lissy de la Rosa, "Personalidades Opinan," *TeveGuía Especial,* 1999, 114.

96. Quoted in Helda Ribera-Chevremont, "¡Qué clase' show!" *Vea* Supplement, February 27–March 4, 2000, 1–8, 3.

97. Cynthia Corzo, "Livin' la Vida, an Easy Sell," *Miami Herald,* September 25, 1999, 1C, 11C, 11C.

98. Marrero, *Ricky Martin: Livin' La Vida Loca,* 63.

99. Quoted in ibid., 92.

100. Quoted in ibid., 56.

101. Celeste Fraser Delgado and José Muñoz, "Rebellions of Everynight Life," in Delgado and Muñoz, *Everynight Life: Culture and Dance in Latin/o America,* 9–32, 18–19.

102. Omar Matos, "Se bautiza como millonario," *TeveGuía Especial,* 1999, 76–77, 77. Original Spanish: "Ricky Martin es la primera mega estrella, y en este momento se cotiza en $350 mil por actuación. El boricua vale y hay que pagarle."

103. Delgado and Muñoz, "Rebellions of Everynight Life," 18.

104. Krulik, *Ricky Martin: Rockin' the House,* 7.

105. Quoted in ibid.

106. Quoted in Torres, "Reflexiones de Artista," 79. Original Spanish: "está siempre en mi mente y en mi corazón."

Notes to the Postscript

1. Quoted in Angel G. Quintero Rivera, *Salsa, sabor y control* (Mexico: Siglo XXI, 1998), 262.

2. Antonio S. Pedreira, "La actualidad del jíbaro," in *El jíbaro de Puerto Rico: Símbolo y figura,* Ed., Enrique Laguerre and Esther Melón (Sharon, CT: Troutman Press, 1968),

7–24, 11. Original Spanish: "la aparición de algún libro . . . la celebración del Cuarto Centenario de la Colonización Cristiana de Puerto Rico, (1908), un músico, un periodista o un poeta tocaban las raíces de nuestras entrañas tradicionales, y sentíamos que, aunque adormilados, estaban vivos."

3. Martín Sagrera, *Racismo y política en Puerto Rico* (Río Piedras: Editorial Edil, 1973), 95.

4. Pedro Pietri, *Puerto Rican Obituary* (New York: Monthly Review Press, 1973), 4.

5. Vicente Géigel Polanco, *El despertar de un pueblo* (San Juan: Biblioteca de autores puertorriqueños, 1942), 5–14, 12. Original Spanish: "El grito de 'Pan, Tierra, y Libertad' concretó las aspiraciones communes. . . . El pueblo dormido de Hostos y Betances sacudía, al fin, su letargo y daba claras señales de estar alerta a su derecho, a su justicia, a su destino."

6. Ana Lydia Vega, "Cráneo de una noche de verano," in *Encancaranublado* (Río Piedras: Ediciones Huracán, 1987), 81–86.

7. Ibid., 81. Original Spanish: "¿Quién se murió, ah?"

8. Ibid., 82. Original Spanish: "Y cuando le salió su propia careta toa blanca y flaca y arrugá—él que era tofe, prieto y todavía no había votado en unas elecciones."

9. Ibid., 86. Original Spanish: "Hoy se declara el Estado 51."

10. Ibid. Original Spanish: "como si fuera un marciano o un maricón."

11. René Marqués, "El puertorriqueño dócil (literatura y realidad psicológica)," in *Ensayos* (Río Piedras: Editorial Antillana, 1972), 165–66. Original Spanish: "un muerto en vida, un suicida nunca del todo realizado, un condenado a sí mismo a destruirse como puertorriqueño más y más cada día, sin lograrlo nunca, puesto que no puede destruir totalmente su esencialidad puertorriqueña mientras en él aliente vida."

12. Vega, "Cráneo de una noche de verano," 86. Original Spanish: "reventando de estrellas . . . sola y grande, grandota como ala de águila de película e miedo. O como una la vería si estuviera tripeando mano y sin esperanza de aterrizar."

13. Ibid., 81. Original Spanish: "Porque hay que abrir el ojo, men."

14. Ibid. Original Spanish: "Si no, se lo almuerza a uno el viejo caballo mellao."

Index

Abie's Irish Rose (Nichols), 63–64
Acosta, Marithelma, 25
African American culture, 65, 138, 214
African American music, 251–52
Agrón, Salvador, 75
Aguila Blanca (José Maldonado), 48–49
AIDS, 126, 156; shamefulness of, xvii–xviii
Ajzenberg, Joseph, 89
Albizu Campos, Pedro, 16–17, 168
Alverio, Rosita. *See* Moreno, Rita
"Americanization" campaign, 4
Americans (*see also* United States; *specific topics*): awareness of Puerto Rico, 33; contempt for Puerto Ricans, 13
AmeRícans, 24, 25, 274 (*see also specific topics*)
Appadurai, Arjun, 29
Armand, Louis, 137

Arrarás, María Celeste, 235–36
autonomistas, 7, 9
avant garde, 106–14

Baker, Susan, 23
Bakhtin, Mikhail, 234
Barbie(s), 206–10; dress of, 220–21; femininity and sexual desirability of, 222–24; hair of, and *boricua* identifications, 210–15; Puerto Rican identity and, 207; selling out Puerto Ricanness, 223–27; "Spanish Talker," 224; as wavy-haired mulatta *vs.* straight-haired and white, 209–11; why so many islanders loved, 215–23
Barbone, Camille, 153
Barthes, Roland, 45, 47
Basquiat, Jean-Michel, 29, 115–16; art, capital, and, 116–27; Haring,

Basquiat, Jean-Michel (*Continued*) hip hyped utopia, and, 127–36; as "primitive," 130; as SAMO, 116–18, 125; sexuality, 125–26; shame, *boricua* identity, and the transcultural paintings of, 136–44
Baudrillard, Jean, 91, 133
Baviera, Julio Cervera, 11
Bayly, Jaime, 156–57
Bernstein, Leonard, 60, 63, 64, 73–74
Beveridge, Albert J., 13
bicephalous political status, 199
bilingualism, 110, 181, 188, 202, 204 (*see also* English language)
black characters in literature, 47–48, 194
"black" subject, photography and the unrepresentable, 45–50
blacks (*see also* Barbie(s), hair of; race): in mass media, 68 (see also under *West Side Story*); in visual art, 120, 141
Blanco, Tomás, 52, 212
blanquitos, 247–48, 269, 277
blondness, 150–51
Boas, Franz, 213
Bona, Damien, 65–66
Bond, Justin, 153
boricua pride, 3, 5–6
boricuas, meaning and connotation of the term, xiii
Bosworth, Patricia, 118, 121
Bourdon, David, 110, 111
Brau, Salvador, 219
breakdancing, 134
Bright, Susie, 174
Brown, Laura S., 35
Bush, George W., 181; inauguration, 268–69
Butler, Judith, 26

buttocks, 54 (*see also* López, Jennifer); toward an epistemology of, 233–39

Cabañas, Victor, 38, 41, 43, 44, 46, 53
Calderón, Myrna García, 44
Califia, Pat, 151–52
Canino, Marcelino, 41
Carbia, Awilda, 161–62
Caruth, Cathy, 42
Catholicism, 64, 65, 107–8, 157–58
Cepeda, Don Martín, 57
Chacón, Iris, 238–39
Chakiris, George, 66
Chauncey, George, 107
Chavez, Linda, 22
Child, Desmond, 258, 271
childhoods, "normal," 248–51
Claridad, 38, 39; photographs in, 45, 46
Clement, Jennifer, 122, 123, 126, 129
Clinton, Bill, xii
Clinton, Hillary Rodham, xii
Colón, Willie, 153–54, 238–40
colonialism, 6–7, 9–15, 33, 36, 138–39, 201; Barbie and, 221
Cortez, Hernán, 138
Cotto, Liliana, 186
Cramer, Doug, 119
Crawford, Cheryl, 60
criollos/criollo elites, 9, 10, 12, 14, 17, 33, 34, 53, 194, 197 (*see also* elites)
Cruz-Malavé, Arnaldo, 87–88
Cuba, 9–11, 13, 167, 168
Cuban War of Independence, 10
Cubans, *boricuas* as "queer," 13
cultural marketplace, buying *boricuaness* in the, 26–32
cultural practices, 145; Puerto Ricans' role in creation of, xi

culture, as a mask, 5
Dallesandro, Joe, 101
Danhakl, Harold Santiago. *See* Wood-
    lawn, Holly
Dávila, Arlene, 28, 219
Dávila, Virgilio, 219
Dávila Colón, Luis, 165
de Burgos, Julia, 213
de Goénaga, Francisco R., 11
de Olivares, José, 44, 45, 49
death, 94
"defacing," 142
Deitch, Jeffrey, 115
DeLang, Gay, 147
Delgado, Juan Manuel, 48
Desmond, Jane C., 256
Diaz, Al, 125, 130
"discretion-shame," xiii–xiv
discrimination. *See* prejudice; racism
"disgrace-shame," xiii
"Docile Puerto Rican, The" (Marqués),
    17–18
dominance *vs.* submission, 88 (*see also*
    Madonna; power relations)
drag (queens), 92, 94, 98, 105, 107–12
    (*see also* Montez, Mario)
drug use, 101, 122, 127, 160
Duchesne Winter, Juan, 201
Dyer, Richard, 30

"1898" (Sanabria Santaliz), 53-57
elections, xii
elites, 15–16, 18, 34–36, 218, 219 (see
    also *criollos/criollo* elites)
emancipation, 47
emasculation, 17, 23
emptiness, 50
English language, 4, 180, 183–88,

199–201 (*see also* bilingualism; Ferré,
    Rosario; literature)
entertainers, xii–xiii (*see also* pride, pop;
    specific entertainers)
Estado Libre Asociado (ELA), 6–8
Estefan, Gloria, 253, 255
"ethnic defense" strategies, 6
ethno-nation, 5–8
ethno-national identity, 3, 5–6, 33–34,
    54, 185, 194, 198–99, 273, 275 (*see
    also* flag; nationalism; *Seva*; shame;
    West Side Story)
Evita (film), 147, 172, 173

families, 23
Fanon, Frantz, 142, 153
Fernández Retamar, Roberto, 200
Ferré, Rosario, 32, 181–84, 200–205;
    backlash against her Anglophilia,
    184–89; *The House on the Lagoon* and
    the cannibalized text, 189–99; novels
    of, as ethno-national products, 205
flag: Madonna's "incident" with the
    Puerto Rican, 160–67; queer history
    of the *boricua*, 167–71
Flatley, Guy, 101, 142
Florida, 209
Foraker Act of 1900, 12
Fox, Vanessa, 226
Fraser Delgado, Celeste, 270

Gagosian, Larry, 143
"garbage" aesthetic. *See* trash
García, Ivonne, 164
García Passalacqua, Juan Manuel,
    164–65, 209, 223
García Ramis, Magali, 183, 237–38
Gartenberg, Jon, 98

gay dolls, 210
gay men, 17–18, 107, 129 (*see also specific individuals*); Madonna and, 156, 158; Ricky Martin, Elvis, and, 258–59
gay subjectivity, Jewish, 72
Géigel Polanco, Vicente, 275
gendering of Puerto Ricans as women, 62
Georas, Chloé, 20
Glasser, Ruth, 257
González, José Luis, 37, 38
Grace, J. Peter, 23
graffiti, 127–31, 133–36, 140
Grammy Awards, 253
Grosfoguel, Ramón, 20
Guerra, Lillian, 16, 220, 223
Guerra y Sánchez, Ramiro, 36
Guzmán, Daniel, 164

Hackett, Pat, 99
hair. *See* Barbie(s)
Hall, Stuart, 29, 68
Haring, Keith, 118, 123–24; Basquiat, hip hyped utopia, and, 127–36
Hernández Colón, Rafael, 179–80, 217
heroism, 46 (*see also* literature)
Hintz, Suzanne, 189
hip hop culture, 134, 135 (*see also under* Basquiat, Jean-Michel)
Hoban, Phoebe, 119, 125
homoerotic literature, 53–57 (see also *West Side Story*, queerness of)
House on the Lagoon, The (Ferré): and the cannibalized text, 191–95
humor, 82

Imitation of Life (film), 77
imperialism, 7 (*see also* colonialism)

Indych, Anna, 27, 226–27
interracial romance, 66–67

Jewish experience, American, 64, 65, 67
Jewish gay subjectivity, 72
jibarismo, 217, 219, 223
jíbaro, 15–16, 217–23
job market. *See* labor force
jokes, 82
Jones, Bill T., 129–30

K (Basquiat), 139
Kaufman, Stanley, 61
KMX Assault, 134

"La Bomba" (Martin), 256
LA II, 131–33
La llegada (González), 37
La Malinche, 15
labor force, 12–13, 19–23, 27, 120–22
language, 82, 139, 140, 180 (*see also* bilingualism; Ferré, Rosario; literature; nationalism, linguistic); English, 4, 180, 183–88, 199–201; Spanish, 138, 179–81, 183
Lares revolt, 47
Laurents, Arthur, 63, 64, 73
Laviera, Tato, 24
León, Carlos, 159–60, 174
Levins Morales, Aurora, 208
Lewis, Oscar, 22
Lindbergh, Charles, 5
literature (*see also* Ferré, Rosario): de-insularizing Puerto Rican, 199–205; national, 182–84
Little Richard, 253
López, Jennifer, 175–76, 229, 239–41; cast as Selena, 230–33; identification with Selena, 232; kissing her (lashed)

butt, 241–46; on Selena, 230, 234; speaking about her buttocks, 234, 236–37; on *West Side Story*, 59

López, María Milagros, 23, 103, 119

López Nieves, Luis, 37, 38, 40–42, 44, 45

López-Adorno, Pedro, 186

Lourdes (Madonna's daughter), 159, 160, 171, 172, 174

Low Life in High Heels, A (Woodlawn), 88–96

Luciano, Maria Judith, 163

Ludlam, Charles, 106–10, 113

Lugardo, Luis, 164

machismo, 17

Madonna, 123, 145–47; born-again whitening, 171–76; food and queer Latin hunger of, 147–49; indulgence in Latino things, 154–55; Latin sex life, 158–59; Latino *vs.* U.S. media coverage of, 158–59; power, masculinity, and, 146; in Puerto Rico, 158, 161–67; (quasi)-foundational romance, 154–60; as "vampire," 153; as (very) white woman on top, 149–54

Maldito amor (Ferré), 189–94

Manrique Cabrera, Francisco, 34, 50

Margarita, Irma, 207

Marqués, René, 17–18, 56, 179, 187, 277

Marshall, Richard, 140

Martin, Ricky, 59, 133, 247–51; filling the void of whiteness, 260–65; gay men and, 258; hips of, 249, 255–58, 261–64; "I am Puerto Rico," 268; origin of his name, 249–50; pride of, 266–68; Ricky-Elvis counterpoint, 251–60; and southern roots, 264–65

Martínez, Ignacio, 46, 47, 52

masculinity, 17, 71 (*see also* "1898"; emasculation; queerness)

matriarchy, 17

Mattel, 217 (*see also* Barbie(s))

Maura Montaner, Antonio, 9

Mayer, Louis B., 76

McEvilley, Thomas, 136

Medina, Angelo, 268

Mejil, Simón, 47–48

Mexican Americans, 230

migration, 19–21, 87

Miles, Nelson, 14, 38, 43, 44, 46

Miller, Marc, 130

Mintz, Sidney, 212–13

Mirisch brothers, 65–66

Montez, María, 109, 204

Montez, Mario, 75, 106–12, 114

Moreno, Rita, 66–67, 76, 97; queer career of, 76–82, 84

Morrison, Toni, 65, 175

Morrissey, Paul, 96, 97, 104

Mottola, Tony, 260, 261

Muñoz, José Esteban, 83, 270

Muñoz Rivera, Luis, 12, 13, 36, 179

Musto, Michael, 157

National Puerto Rican Day Parade, 25–26

nationalism, 3–4, 16–18, 36, 182, 273, 276, 278 (*see also* ethno-national identity; flag); linguistic, 181–83, 187–89 (*see also* Ferré, Rosario; literature)

Natives Carrying Some Guns, Bible, Amorites on Safari (Basquiat), 138

Nava, Gregory, 232, 241

Negrón-Portillo, Mariano, 13

New York, 21–22; white queer art, 106–14

Nichols, Anne, 63–64

Nolla, Olga, 37
Noriega, David, 163, 166
Nosei, Annina, 119, 121

O'Dair, Barbara, 149
Official Spanish Law, 179–80
Olivelle, Patrick, 211
Ortiz, Fernando, 257–58
Ott, Maureen, 260
Our Islands and Their People (Olivares), 44–45
Out of Sight (film), 244–45

Paglia, Camille, 146, 155, 258, 262
Pedreira, Antonio S., 15, 269
Pérez, Lourdes, 211
Pérez y González, María, 23
Pero, Taylor, 77
Perón, Eva, 172, 173
Phillips, Sam, 252
photographs of the dead, 50–53
photography: and the unrepresentable "black" subject, 45–50; visualizing pain and other displaced matters, 50–53
Pietri, Pedro, 112, 274
Piñero, Miguel, 87–88
politics, xii
Polsky, Richard, 143–44
poverty, 23, 27 (*see also* welfare)
power relations, 62, 125 (*see also* dominance *vs.* submission; Madonna)
Pratt, Mary Louise, 202–3
prejudice (*see also* racism), pride and, 18–26
Presley, Elvis, 247, 258–60, 263–65; African American music and, 251–53; effeminacy and queerness, 258–59; Pentecostal church and, 252; Ricky-Elvis counterpoint, 251–55; and southern roots, 264–65
pride, 266–68; *boricua*, 3; pop, 26–32; and prejudice, 18–26
prosopopoeia, 142–43
public assistance. *See* welfare
Puerto Ricans (*see also specific topics*): history, 9–22, 217–18; making them over in the diaspora, 88–96; in the news, xii
Puerto Rico (*see also specific topics*), economics, 27–28
"Puerto Rico Obituary" (Pietri), 274
Puff Daddy, 246

queer art, New York's white, 106–14
queerness, 13, 87, 134 (*see also* drag; "1898"; flag; Madonna; Moreno, Rita; *Seva*; shame, queer; *West Side Story*); Holly Woodlawn and, 88–90, 92–96
Quiñones, Andrés, 225
Quintero, Angel, 26

race, 67, 108–14, 117, 125, 126, 141–43 (*see also* black characters in literature; *West Side Story*; whiteness); of Barbie, 209–15, 222; Basquiet, Haring, hip hyped utopia, and, 127–31; Elvis and, 251–53; interracial romance, 66–67; Rosario Ferré and, 194–97
racism, 212
Ramos, Josean, 39, 40, 45
Ramos Perea, Roberto, 33
Renaud-González, Barbara, 232
Ricard, Rene, 125, 126, 142
Ricky Martin (Martin), 254
Ritchie, Guy, 174
Robbins, Jerome, 63, 66, 73
Rodríguez, Victor, 207

Rodríguez de Tió, Lola, 273
Rodríguez Negrón, Enrique, 163
Rogin, Michael, 65
Rosselló, Pedro, 161, 180, 207, 208

salsa, 261–62
Sanabria Santaliz, Edgardo, 53–57
Sandoval, Alberto, 59
Santaliz, José Enrique, 48
Santiago, Esmeralda, 89
Santiago-Valles, Kelvin, 15, 62
Santori, Fufi, 27–28
Scarano, Francisco A., 61, 217
Schnabel, Julian, 136
Seda Bonilla, Eduardo, 213–14, 222
Sedgwick, Eve Kosofsky, 36
Seed, John, 118, 123
Selena (film), 228–45; casting of, 230–33;
    marketing, 233–34
Selena Remembered (video), 235
Seva (López Nieves), 37–57
Sex (Madonna), 149–52
shame, xiii, xvii–xviii, 3, 236 (*see also*
    pride); ambiguities of white, 265–71;
    and the body, xiv–xv (*see also*
    "1898"); of identity, 33–39; labor, mi-
    gration, and ethno-national, 18–26;
    nature of, xiv–xv; psychodynamics
    of, 8; and purely Puerto Rican "na-
    tional" identity, 9–18; queer, 73–74,
    89–90 (*see also* "1898"); Ricky Martin,
    Elvis, and, 263–71; social identity
    and, xiii; strategies to offset, xiv;
    types of, xiii–xiv; *West Side Story* and,
    59, 61–63
Shipman, David, 77
Shohat, Ella, 74, 140
Silén, Juan Angel, 18
Simon, John, 151

slavery, 47, 138, 256
Smith, Jack, 106, 107, 110
Sondheim, Stephen, 60
Sontag, Susan, 45
soul (music), 153–54
Spaniards, *boricuas* trying to "pass" as,
    xiv
Spanish language, 138, 179–81, 183 (*see
    also* English language)
Spanish rule (*see also* colonialism), revolt
    against, 47
Spanish-American War, 10, 34 (*see also*
    United States, invasion and occupa-
    tion of Puerto Rico)
Spanish-Cuban-Filipino-American wars,
    11
"specialness," sense of, 5
"spic," xiv, 20
Stam, Robert, 74, 140
statehood, 5, 8
Stavans, Ilán, 241
Stewart, Michael, 128
Sting, 262
sugarcane, 19
Suntree, Susan, 77
Superstars, 96–99
Sweet Diamond Dust (Ferré), 189–94

Tate, Greg, 117
tattoos. *See* "1898"
Television and Cruelty to Animals
    (Basquiat), 141
Teller, Henry, 13
Thompson, Robert Farris, 116, 137–38
Tió, Salvador, 187
Tomkins, Silvan, 56, 191
Torres, Daniel, 69
Torres Santiago, José Manuel, 40
transcultural erotics, 160

transculturation, 89, 146–47, 185, 187, 278
transvestites. *See* drag
trash, 112–13
Trash (film), 101–5
trauma, 34–35; of literature, 34–36, 51–53 (see also *Seva*)
Truth or Dare (film), 152–53
Turner, Frederick, 21
Turner, Lana, 77, 79, 81

United States (*see also* Americans; *specific topics*): exploitation of Puerto Ricans, 20, 24, 27 (*see also* labor force); invasion and occupation of Puerto Rico, 9, 12–17, 33–36, 50 (see also *Seva*); investment in Puerto Rico, 20; negative attitudes toward Puerto Ricans, xi, 24
Untitled (Defacement) (Basquiat), 142
utopia, 134 (*see also under* Basquiat, Jean-Michel)

Van Leer, David, 73
Vázquez, Blanca, 59, 62
Vega, Ana Lydia, 185–86, 198–99, 276–77
Vélez, Antonio, 168
Vélez, León, 78
Vientós Gastón, Nilita, 220–21
violence, 62

Wainwright, Rufus, 153
Wallerstein, Immanuel, 260

Warhol, Andy, 98–99, 113, 129; Basquiat and, 123, 124, 126, 127, 132–33, 142; on drag (queens), 98; as "Drella," 99; Holly Woodlawn and, 92, 98–100, 102, 104–5; Paul Morrissey and, 97; portfolios of, 111, 150
welfare, 23–24, 103–4
Wells, Henry, 4
West Side Story (film): blackness and, 65, 67, 68; history and production of, 63–66, 70; as musical, 74; the Puerto Rican "thing" and makeup of identity, 63–69; queerness of, 62, 69–75, 157; race, racism, and, 62, 66–75; Rita Moreno's queer career, 76–84; sexuality in, 73; and shame, 59, 61–63; and U.S. Puerto Rican identity, 58–63
white shame, ambiguities of, 265–71
whiteness, 194, 218, 277 (*see also under* Madonna; Martin, Ricky; Woodlawn, Holly)
Wiley, Mason, 65–66
Wood, Natalie, 59, 66
Woodlawn, Holly (Harold Santiago Danhaki): Factory days, 96–101; *A Low Life in High Heels*, 88–96; performing *boricuaness* from trash, 101–5; and the unbearable whiteness of being, 106–14

Zayas, Luis, 217
Zenón Cruz, Isabelo, 213, 233
Zizek, Slavoj, 38, 39

About the Author

FRANCES NEGRÓN-MUNTANER is an award-winning filmmaker, writer, journalist, and cultural critic. Her films include *Brincando el Charco: Portrait of a Puerto Rican*. She is also the author of several books, including *Anatomy of a Smile,* and the coeditor of *Puerto Rican Jam: Rethinking Colonialism and Nationalism.* She currently teaches Latino literature and culture at Columbia University.